Baptist Identity and the Ecumenical Future

Baptist Identity and the Ecumenical Future
Story, Tradition, and the Recovery of Community

Steven R. Harmon

BAYLOR UNIVERSITY PRESS

Unless otherwise stated, Scripture quotations are from the New Revised Standard Version Bible, copyright 1989, Division of Christian Education of the National Council of the Churches of Christ in the United States of America. Used by permission. All rights reserved.

Cover Design by Trudi Gershinov
Cover image: Third Ecumenical Council, held at Ephesus, 431 AD (wall painting), Axenti, Symeon (16th century) / Church of St Sozomenos, Galata, Cyprus / Sonia Halliday Photographs / Bridgeman Images

Library of Congress Cataloging in Publication Data

Names: Harmon, Steven R. (Steven Ray)
Title: Baptist identity and the ecumenical future : story, tradition, and the recovery of community / Steven R. Harmon.
Description: Waco : Baylor University Press, 2016. |
Includes bibliographical references and index.
Identifiers: LCCN 2015026598 | ISBN 9781602585706 (hardback : alk. paper)
Subjects: LCSH: Baptists—Relations. | Christian union.
Classification: LCC BX6329.A1 H37 2016 | DDC 286—dc23
LC record available at http://lccn.loc.gov/2015026598

Printed in the United States of America on acid-free paper with a minimum of 30% post-consumer waste recycled content.

For James Leo Garrett, Jr.

Contents

Preface

This book took shape during the period that marked the transformation of my vocational self-understanding from "Baptist professor of systematic theology and researcher in patristic theology" to "Baptist ecumenical theologian." I had already written a book that made a case for the relevance to contemporary Baptist ecclesial life of the pre-Reformation tradition that included the early church fathers and mothers, characterizing it as a living tradition that extends beyond the Reformation and includes Baptists along with the whole divided church.[1] In the midst of my work on that volume, I had my first experience of ecumenical dialogue as a member of the Baptist World Alliance delegation to the North American phase of the international bilateral dialogue between the BWA and the Anglican Communion. During my participation in those conversations in Wolfville, Nova Scotia, in September 2003, I realized that all other aspects of my theological work seemed oriented toward and fulfilled in this ecumenical task of theology in the service of the divided church. I recognized it as a calling within my vocation to a ministry of theological education; I later read that Catholic theologian Yves Congar had a similar experience long before the official entry of his church into the modern ecumenical movement.[2] Soon I had other opportunities to participate in bilateral

---

[1] Steven R. Harmon, *Towards Baptist Catholicity: Essays on Tradition and the Baptist Vision* (Studies in Baptist History and Thought, vol. 27; Milton Keynes, UK: Paternoster, 2006).

[2] In his words, Congar "recognized an ecumenical vocation which was, at the same time, an ecclesiological vocation" through the confluence of his choice of the unity of the church as the topic for his thesis at Le Saulchoir (then in Belgium, relocated to France after the Second World War) beginning in 1928 and his meditation on John 17 in preparation

and multilateral ecumenical dialogue that made significant contributions to this book: the second series of conversations between the BWA and the Catholic Church, 2006 through 2010, with meetings in Birmingham (Alabama, USA), twice in Rome (Italy), Durham (North Carolina, USA), and Oxford (UK); the World Council of Churches Faith and Order Plenary Commission meeting at the Orthodox Academy of Crete (Greece), October 7–13, 2009, representing the BWA; "pre-conversations" between the BWA and the Eastern Orthodox Ecumenical Patriarchate, Heraklion, Crete (Greece), October 30–November 2, 2011; and in an ecclesially non-representative capacity, a consultation convened by the Foundation for a Conference on Faith and Order in North America at the Graymoor Spiritual Life Center of the Franciscan Friars of the Atonement in Garrison, New York (USA), January 3–5, 2006.

Baptist Identity and the Ecumenical Future is rooted in these experiences of dialogue, and I must acknowledge the debt my thinking owes to conversations with the participants in these ecumenical gatherings, which, as this book will argue, possess "ecclesiality" to the extent that they function as what John Howard Yoder described in this connection as "ad hoc 'churches.'"[3] These dialogue partners include Paul S. Fiddes, Bruce Matthews, Gregory Cameron, Tony Cupit, Paul Avis, Alyson Mary Barnett-Cowan, Howard Loewen, Saundra Richardson, Ronald Stevenson, Douglas Theuner, David Wheeler, William Brackney, Curtis Freeman, Audrey Morikawa, Alan Stanford, Andrew MacRae, Malcolm B. Yarnell III, Arthur Serratelli, John Radano, Gregory Fairbanks, Peter Casarella, William Henn, Krysztof Mielcarek, Teresa Francesca Rossi, Jorge Scampini, Susan Wood, Dennis McManus, Sara Butler, Fausto Aguiar de Vasconcelos, Neville G. Callam, Fred Deegbe, Timothy George, Lillian Lim (†), Nora O. Lozano, Tomás Mackey, Anthony Peck, Rachael Tan, Tadeusz Zelinksi, Denton Lotz, Massimo Aprile, Nancy Elizabeth Bedford, Elizabeth Newman, Gennadios Limouris, Georges Tsetsis, William G. Rusch, Lorelei Fuchs, Joseph Small, Ann Riggs, Douglas Foster, Anthea Butler, Robert Jenson, Cheryl Bridges Johns, Kevin Mannoia, Jeffrey Gros (†), Mary Reath, and the approximately 120 members of the 2009 WCC Plenary Faith and Order Commission (some of whom were also among the dialogue and consultation participants mentioned here by name).

---

for his ordination to the priesthood in 1930 (Éric Mahieu, "Introduction," in Yves Congar, *My Journal of the Council*, trans. Mary John Ronayne and Mary Cecily Boulding, ed. Denis Minns [Collegeville, Minn.: Liturgical Press, 2012], vi).

[3]   John Howard Yoder, *The Royal Priesthood: Essays Ecclesiological and Ecumenical*, ed. Michael G. Cartwright (Grand Rapids: William B. Eerdmans, 1994), 236.

My perspectives have also been shaped by dialogue with the hosts and audiences of ecumenical-themed lectures I was invited to deliver in the midst of my work on this book: the Lourdes College Ecumenical Lecture in Sylvania, Ohio, March 21, 2010; the Durham University Theology and Ethics Seminar led by Paul Murray in Durham, UK, December 8, 2010; the Young Scholars in the Baptist Academy seminar at the International Baptist Theological Seminary in Prague, Czech Republic, July 24–30, 2011; the Robert K. Campbell Memorial Lectures on Christian Unity sponsored by the Lehigh County Conferences of Churches at DeSales University, Center Valley, Pennsylvania, March 12, 2013; and the Fall Ecumenical Lectures at Mount Aloysius College in Cresson, Pennsylvania, October 9, 2014. I also led workshops on ecumenical engagement for the Ecumenical Relations Committee of Eastern Area Community Ministries and the Kentucky Council of Churches in Louisville, Kentucky, January 22, 2012, and at General Assemblies of the Cooperative Baptist Fellowship (Houston, Texas, July 1–3, 2009) and the Cooperative Baptist Fellowship of North Carolina (Asheville, North Carolina, March 25, 2011, and Raleigh, North Carolina, March 23–24, 2012), as well as congregational studies on ecumenism for a number of Baptist and Episcopal churches. Preparing these lectures and presentations and pondering the questions and responses of those who heard them made it clearer to me what I wanted to say in this book, and I hope it will be correspondingly clearer to its readers as a result.

I am indebted as well to faculty colleagues and students at the institutions where I have lived out my vocation as a theological educator during this segment of my pilgrimage with the church toward its future: Campbell University Divinity School in Buies Creek, North Carolina; Samford University's Beeson Divinity School in Birmingham, Alabama; and now the School of Divinity at Gardner-Webb University in Boiling Springs, North Carolina. I should mention also Duke University Divinity School in Durham, North Carolina, and Lutheran Theological Southern Seminary in Columbia, South Carolina, where I taught in visiting/adjunctive roles during this period. My courses in Theology and the Quest for Christian Unity at Campbell University Divinity School and Ecumenical Theology at Lutheran Theological Southern Seminary were significant opportunities to envision out loud the ecumenical future in collaboration with the next generation of the ministers who will lead the church into it.

My own congregation's relation of the Baptist vision to the ecumenical future has sustained me ecclesially while writing. My introduction to St. John's Baptist Church in Charlotte, North Carolina, was an invitation to lead a three-week teaching series there on Baptists and ecumenism a few years ago, and I quickly discovered that its membership was way ahead of the Baptist curve on ecumenical openness. Our sessions were in Broach Hall, named for the church's longtime former pastor Claude U. Broach, who served as senior minister 1944–1974. Troubled that the Southern Baptist Convention with which St. John's was then affiliated had declined the invitation to send an official observer to the Second Vatican Council, Broach independently attended the council as a guest during its final session. While contrary to some tellings of the story he was not the only Baptist, or even the only Southern Baptist, to attend sessions of Vatican II as a guest, members of St. John's justifiably take great pride in the fact that their former pastor undertook this exceptional act of ecumenical engagement and upon his retirement became the first director of the Ecumenical Institute jointly sponsored by Benedictine-founded Belmont Abbey College and Baptist-founded Wake Forest University—launched under Broach's leadership at a worship service in Belmont Abbey Cathedral commemorating the tenth anniversary of the promulgation of *Unitatis Redintegratio*, the Vatican II Decree on Ecumenism. Current pastor Dennis Foust frequently refers to our congregation as "St. John's Ecumenical Baptist Church," and it lives up to that designation, embracing as its own many of the best gifts of the whole church while faithfully offering to the whole church the best gifts of the Baptist tradition.

I deeply appreciate Carey Newman's enthusiasm for this project, and his patience when its completion was not as swift as I originally projected. Under his leadership Baylor University Press has become a preeminent publisher of serious theological explorations of the Baptist vision, and I am honored for this contribution to have its place among them. The editorial staff at Baylor University Press, in particular associate editor Jordan Rowan Fannin, provided expert guidance along the way. The anonymous referees of the earliest draft of my manuscript offered important suggestions for its improvement that have been incorporated into the final product. I am grateful for their criticism, and of course for their recommendation that this book be published.

I am grateful beyond the adequacy of words for the life I share with my wife Kheresa and son Timothy, whose life with Kheresa and me has fully coincided with the various stages of my work on this book, 2006 through the present. Timothy arrived in our household when I was finishing a paper for presentation to the first meeting of the second series of conversations between the BWA and the Catholic Church, and my volumes of the documents of Vatican II and William Lumpkin's collection of Baptist confessions of faith have been familiar sights to him ever since. Kheresa and Timothy have graciously shared me with these endeavors, and I owe them much.

Baptist Identity and the Ecumenical Future is dedicated to James Leo Garrett, Jr., who supervised my doctoral dissertation in patristic theology[4] and served as a delegate to an earlier series of "pre-conversations" between the BWA and the Ecumenical Patriarchate during the years of my doctoral studies.[5] While preparing to write this preface, I remembered having seen during that period a 1970 feature story about Garrett in *The Tie*, a publication of The Southern Baptist Theological Seminary in Louisville, Kentucky, where Garrett served on the faculty 1959–1973. Titled "Garrett . . . Ecumenical Baptist," the article explains much about aspects of Garrett's theological work that have influenced my own in enduring ways:

> You could call him an ecumenical denominationalist—and not be dealing in contradictions.
>
> James Leo Garrett, professor of Christian Theology at Southern Seminary since 1959, is a deeply committed Baptist who keeps a warm hand extended to other Christians in search of creative cooperation. . . .
>
> It was 1948 [when Garrett began graduate studies at Princeton Theological Seminary], and Garrett had entered Princeton just a month after the first meeting of the World Council of Churches. He studied under John A. Mackay, one of the Council's founders, who introduced Leo to the issues first-hand. Coupled with his Th.M. thesis in Roman Catholic theology, it was a dramatic year of discovery for the young professor-to-be.
>
> Returning to Fort Worth, Leo began a trend-setting course to interpret Catholic theology accurately for Baptist missionaries and ministers in an era of strong Protestant attacks on the Roman church. . . .
>
> Then, in 1956, he began work on a Ph.D. at Harvard University, returning to his interest in ecumenics with a thesis on the Protestant-Roman Catholic confrontation. . . .
>
> The week after delivering his completed thesis in Boston, he was privileged to stand in St. Peter's [Basilica] in Rome as a guest of Vatican

---

[4]   Steven R. Harmon, "*Apokatastasis* and Exegesis: A Comparative Analysis of the Use of Scripture in the Eschatological Universalism of Clement of Alexandria, Origen, and Gregory of Nyssa" (Ph.D. diss., Southwestern Baptist Theological Seminary, 1997), published in revised form as *Every Knee Should Bow: Biblical Rationales for Universal Salvation in Early Christian Thought* (Lanham, Md.: Rowman & Littlefield, 2003).

[5]   Papers Garrett presented to meetings of these "pre-conversations" with representatives of the Orthodox Ecumenical Patriarchate were published as James Leo Garrett, Jr., "Major Emphases in Baptist Theology," *Southwestern Journal of Theology* 37, no. 3 (Summer 1995): 36–46; idem, "The Authority of the Bible for Baptists," *Southwestern Journal of Theology* 41, no. 2 (Spring 1999): 4–40.

II, and there to hear the Pope promulgate the declaration on religious liberty. . . .

His newest involvement in interdenominational affairs is as chairman of the Baptist World Alliance Study Commission on Cooperative Christianity, which made its first report in Tokyo.[6]

Garrett more recently helped lay the foundation for the second series of conversations between the BWA and the Catholic Church, presenting a paper at a theological consultation between representatives of the BWA and the Pontifical Council for Promoting Christian Unity in Rome, December 3–4, 2000, in which he identified the issues that would need to be addressed in the hoped-for second series of conversations: the Petrine ministry; Marian doctrine and devotion; perspectives on the sacraments as *ex opere operato*; and the interrelationships of authority, Scripture, tradition, and magisterium.[7] Those proved to be precisely the topics we addressed in the five-year dialogue and its report, which referenced Garrett's characterization of Baptist perspectives on the authority of Scripture in relation to other sources of authority in his Systematic Theology as an account that represented an opening for ecumenical convergence.[8] Those conversations and this book are indebted to Garrett's pioneering efforts during his own pilgrimage as an "Ecumenical Baptist" to relate the Baptist vision to the ecumenical future.[9]

Boiling Springs, North Carolina
Commemoration of Karl Barth and Thomas Merton (December 10)
Advent 2014

---

[6] The Southern Baptist Theological Seminary, "Garrett . . . Ecumenical Baptist," *The Tie* 39, no. 6 (September 1970): 5. The works written by Garrett during his graduate studies referenced in the article are James Leo Garrett, Jr., "Thomas Aquinas' Doctrine of Penance: A Critical Analysis" (Th.M. thesis, Princeton Theological Seminary, 1949); idem, "Protestant Writings on Roman Catholicism in the United States between Vatican Council I and Vatican Council II: An Analysis and Critique in View of the Contemporary Protestant–Roman Catholic Confrontation" (Ph.D. diss., Harvard University, 1966).

[7] John A. Radano, "Report on Dialogue with Baptist World Alliance," *L'Osservatore Romano: Weekly Edition in English* (March 20, 2002): 9.

[8] Baptist World Alliance and Catholic Church, "The Word of God in the Life of the Church: A Report of International Conversations between the Catholic Church and the Baptist World Alliance 2006–2010," §62, *American Baptist Quarterly* 31, no. 1 (Spring 2012): 58 and 117, n. 57 (28–122).

[9] For an autobiographical account of his ecumenical pilgrimage, see James Leo Garrett, Jr., "Baptist Identity and Christian Unity: Reflections on a Theological Pilgrimage," *American Baptist Quarterly* 24, no. 1 (March 2005): 53–66.

PART I

THE BAPTIST VISION AND THE ECUMENICAL MOMENT

1

A Radical Baptist Proposal

In December 2010 a joint international commission of the Baptist World Alliance and the Catholic Church met in Oxford, the "city of dreaming spires," to envision the ecumenical future and how their communions might take concrete steps toward inhabiting it together. It was not the first time representatives of these seemingly polar opposite Christian traditions had engaged in this sort of ecumenical encounter. The Oxford conversations were the fifth installment of a five-year series of talks between the two communions held from 2006 through 2010, which resumed the work of an earlier series of international Baptist–Catholic conversations that took place from 1984 through 1988.[1] Many Baptists have applauded these steps toward greater expressions of unity between Baptist churches and the Catholic Church, and the community of global Baptists as represented by the General Council of the Baptist World Alliance voted to receive the reports from both series of conversations at their gatherings in 1989 and 2013. Leaders of some Latin American Baptist unions affiliated with

[1] Baptist World Alliance and Catholic Church, "Summons to Witness to Christ in Today's World: A Report on Conversations 1984–1988," in *Growth in Agreement II: Reports and Agreed Statements of Ecumenical Conversations on a World Level, 1982–1998*, ed. Jeffrey Gros, Harding Meyer, and William G. Rusch, 373–85 (Faith and Order Paper no. 187; Geneva: WCC Publications/Grand Rapids: William B. Eerdmans, 2000); Baptist World Alliance and Catholic Church, "The Word of God in the Life of the Church: A Report of International Conversations between the Catholic Church and the Baptist World Alliance 2006–2010," *American Baptist Quarterly* 31, no. 1 (Spring 2012): 28–122. The report from the 2006–2010 conversations is also published in *Pontifical Council for Promoting Christian Unity Information Service* 142 (2013): 20–65 and on the Vatican web site: http://www.vatican.va/roman_curia/pontifical_councils/chrstuni/Bapstist%20alliance/rc_pc_chrstuni_doc_20101213_report-2006-2010_en.html (accessed November 14, 2014).

the Baptist World Alliance, however, had expressed grave concerns about the first series of conversations when they were proposed, and again in response to the presentation and adoption of the report from the dialogue.[2] Therefore, great pains were taken in the planning of the second series of

[2]   The "Minutes of the Commission on Doctrine and Interchurch Cooperation, Buenos Aires, Argentina, July 19, 1983" (Baptist World Alliance Records, folder ff, American Baptist Historical Society Archives Center, Atlanta) record this from the session in which the proposal for the 1984–1988 conversations was presented and adopted:

> Chairman [Noel] Vose presented the history to date of proposed conversations between the BWA and the Roman Catholic Church. He reviewed the origin of the proposal in Toronto [at the Fourteenth Congress of the BWA, July 8–13, 1980], the General Council's concerns in San Juan [June 27–July 3, 1981], and the Commission's consideration of the matter in Nairobi [at the 1982 General Council meeting that charged a sub-committee with developing a formal proposal for conversations]. . . . Glenn Ingleheart described the work of the sub-committee. He and Reinhold Kerstan met in April in Germany with representatives of the Roman Catholic Secretariat for the Promotion of Christian Unity to develop a proposal for conversations. . . . The purpose of the conversation would be to 'come to a mutual understanding of convergences and divergences in doctrinal, ecclesial, pastoral and mission concerns between the Baptist and Roman Catholic world confessional families.' . . . Vose then encouraged the Baptist brethren from Latin America who were present to share their responses to the proposals. John Ratliff translated while Martin Chiri (Bolivia), Tomás Mackey (Argentina), John Cerallos (Ecuador), and Ebenezer Ferreira (Brazil) spoke. There were concerns expressed about continuing persecution of Baptists by Roman Catholics, fear that Baptist principles might be compromised, questions about the parameters of the conversations, opposition to any contact with Roman Catholics, and encouragement for the conversations. Vose also expressed the Commission's appreciation for these guests who had shared their viewpoints, and assured them that they had been heard by the Commission.

In his account of the origin, process, and outcome of this first series of conversations, Ian Randall notes that in the ensuing 1983 BWA General Council session a motion opposing going forward with the proposed dialogue was defeated; at the 1989 General Council meeting at which the report from the conversations was presented, in response to the motion that the report be accepted "Brazilian Irland Pereira de Azevedo spoke in opposition heatedly and at great length," but "after much discussion the Council voted to receive both the report and Azevedo's response" (Ian Randall, "Pro-Existence not Co-Existence: The Baptist World Alliance in the 1980s," in *Baptists Together in Christ 1905–2005: A Hundred-Year History of the Baptist World Alliance*, ed. Richard V. Pierard [Falls Church, Va.: Baptist World Alliance and Birmingham, Ala.: Samford University Press, 2005], 227–28 [194–234], citing minutes from the 1983 and 1989 Baptist World Alliance General Council meetings). E. Glenn Hinson, a member of the Baptist delegation to the first series of conversations, also recounts the responses to the conversations by Latin American Baptists in *A Miracle of Grace: An Autobiography* (Macon, Ga.: Mercer University Press, 2012), 225–26.

conversations to assure the global Baptist community that these concerns had been heard and would be addressed in the upcoming dialogue.[3]

In Oxford the members of the Baptist and Catholic delegations devoted a week to drafting the final report of their conversations on the theme "The Word of God in the Life of the Church" in a setting suggestive of just how far ecumenical relations have progressed in some ecclesial locales. In the neighborhood of multiple markers commemorating the martyrdoms Protestants and Catholics inflicted on one another during the sixteenth century, the joint commission had lodging, meals, morning and evening prayer, and working sessions at Regent's Park College. Regent's Park is a Baptist-founded "Permanent Private Hall" of the University of Oxford that owes its beginnings to the fact that students who were not members of the Church of England were excluded from admission to the major British universities until the 1870s (an experience shared by Baptists and Catholics in England, it is worth noting). Nestled between the Catholic private halls St. Benet's Hall and Blackfriars Hall along St. Giles', Regent's Park enjoys

---

[3]   The introduction to the report from the second series of conversations in 2006–2010 took note of the concerns about the first series and its report before summarizing the changed circumstances that made possible the second series ("The Word of God in the Life of the Church," §4, citing "Minutes of the Decision Meeting, BWA General Council/Annual Gathering, Mexico City, July 7, 2006," in *Baptist World Alliance Annual Gathering, Accra, Ghana, July 2–7, 2007* [Falls Church, Va.: Baptist World Alliance, 2007], 52). In a response to the report of the 2006–2010 conversations published along with the report in a special issue of the *American Baptist Quarterly*, Chilean Baptist theological educator and pastor Josué Fonseca commented on developments in Latin American Baptist attitudes toward ecumenical engagement with the Catholic Church, attributing their initial caution to the perception that the initiative for the first series of Baptist–Catholic conversations "came from members of the global Baptist family in the First World where Roman Catholics are a minority presence" who "are accustomed to undertaking such ecumenical dialogues without wider consultation and inclusive criteria that explain precisely how these conversations are conducted"; furthermore, among the Latin American Baptists "there was not a consensus of understanding that the reception of any report is always subject to Baptist polity and practice which respects congregationalism" (Josué Fonseca, "A Response to the Report of International Conversations between the Catholic Church and the Baptist World Alliance," *American Baptist Quarterly* 31, no. 1 [Spring 2012]: 125–26 [123–37]). One ameliorating factor in the second series of conversations that helped foster a more positive response was the globally representative makeup of the eleven-member Baptist delegation, which included three Latin American representatives: Nora O. Lozano, a professor of theology at the Baptist University of the Américas in San Antonio, Texas, but originally from Mexico; Tomás Mackey, a professor of theology in Argentina who had been one of the "Baptist brethren from Latin America" who communicated concerns about the first series of conversations in the 1983 commission meeting in San Juan; and Fausto Aguiar de Vasconcelos, Director of Study and Research for the Baptist World Alliance and former pastor of the First Baptist Church in Rio de Janeiro, Brazil.

warm collegial relations with these Catholic neighbors. When Greyfriars Hall, another Catholic private hall at Oxford, was closed in 2007, Regent's Park accepted the remaining Greyfriars students and began hosting Mass in its chapel to provide for their spiritual needs. The faculty and student makeup of the college is ecumenical, and members of the teaching staff are full members of the thoroughly ecumenical University of Oxford faculty. In a place where Baptists, Catholics, Anglicans, and other Christians now comfortably enjoy such forms of academic and ecclesial mutual accep-tance, one might be tempted to think that while ecumenical dialogues are in principle a good thing, the divisions they address are no longer painful and therefore not pressing. The church is already catholic in the sense that its multiple communions belong to the whole church and, for the most part, recognize one another as such.

Catholicity beyond the (Invisible) Universal Church

My book *Towards Baptist Catholicity: Essays on Tradition and the Baptist Vision* appeared in print five months before the joint commission for the second series of Baptist–Catholic conversations convened at Samford University's Beeson Divinity School in December 2006.[4] Soon after the penultimate meeting of the joint commission in Rome in December 2009, the journal *Pro Ecclesia* sponsored by the Center for Catholic and Evangelical Theol-ogy published a book symposium on *Towards Baptist Catholicity* featuring four articles reviewing the book by Catholic theologians Nicholas Healy and Maureen O'Connell and Baptist theologians Richard Crane and Eliz-abeth Newman, along with an author's response.[5] The *Pro Ecclesia* review-ers accurately discerned my intentions in writing *Towards Baptist Catholicity* as well as the rhetorical strategies I employed in its writing, often grasping just what it was that I was attempting to do better than I did when I was trying to do it. Their insightful responses prodded me to address more

---

[4]   Steven R. Harmon, *Towards Baptist Catholicity: Essays on Tradition and the Baptist Vision* (Studies in Baptist History and Thought, vol. 27; Milton Keynes, UK: Paternos-ter, 2006).

[5]   Richard Crane, "Explosive Devices and Rhetorical Strategies: Appreciation for Steven R. Harmon's *Towards Baptist Catholicity*," *Pro Ecclesia* 18, no. 4 (Fall 2009): 367–70; Nicholas M. Healy, "Traditions, Authorities, and the Individual Christian," *Pro Ecclesia* 18, no. 4 (Fall 2009): 371–74; Elizabeth Newman, "Remembering How to Remember: Harmon's Subversive Orthodoxy," *Pro Ecclesia* 18, no. 4 (Fall 2009): 375–80; Maureen H. O'Connell, "Towards a Baptist (and Roman Catholic) Catholicity," *Pro Ecclesia* 18, no. 4 (Fall 2009): 381–85; Steven R. Harmon, "Why Baptist Catholicity, and by What Authority?" *Pro Ecclesia* 18, no. 4 (Fall 2009): 386–92.

fully two questions raised by the book's arguments: Precisely why should Baptists embrace catholicity as essential to their identity? And by what authority would they do so?

If the catholicity of the church merely refers to the wholeness of its inclusion of all who belong to Christ, the book's title might suggest that Baptists still had a long way to go before they could recognize many others who claimed the name of Christ as truly belonging to his church. Perhaps recognition of other communities as "church" is in fact an ecumenical step that remains future for many Baptists. *Towards Baptist Catholicity* instead defined the catholicity toward which Baptists should move in a way that includes and builds upon historic Baptist affirmations of the church as catholic yet envisions a thicker sense of catholicity than they had in mind. Though of course there are many exceptions whenever one generalizes about Baptists, most Baptists would have no quibble with a *quantitative* understanding of the catholicity of the church, according to which there is a universal church to which all believers belong and which transcends visible local congregations. It is explicitly affirmed in the two most significant Baptist confessions from the seventeenth century. According to the Particular Baptist *Second London Confession* published in 1689, "The Catholick or universal Church, which (with respect to internal work of the Spirit, and truth of grace) may be called invisible, consists of the whole number of the Elect, that have been, are, or shall be gathered into one, under Christ the head thereof."[6] Likewise, the 1678 General Baptist confession called the *Orthodox Creed* appropriated three of the four classic "marks of the church" from the Nicene Creed, confessing in article 29 that "there is one holy catholick church, consisting of, or made up of the whole number of the elect, that have been, are, or shall be gathered, in one body under Christ, the only head thereof," and in article 30, ". . . we believe the visible church of Christ on earth, is made up of several distinct congregations, which make up that one catholick church, or mystical body of Christ."[7] Thus Judge Willis, President of the Baptist Union of Great Britain and Ireland, was able to invoke both the language of the ancient creeds and the Baptist confessional heritage in his "Address of Welcome" to the first Baptist World Congress in London in 1905 when he insisted, "We believe, and

---

[6]   *Second London Confession,* §26.1, in *Baptist Confessions of Faith,* 2nd rev. ed., ed. William L. Lumpkin, rev. Bill J. Leonard (Valley Forge, Pa.: Judson Press, 2011), 283.

[7]   *Orthodox Creed,* §§29–30, in *Baptist Confessions of Faith,* ed. Lumpkin, rev. Leonard, 327–28.

our fathers have believed, in the Holy Catholic Church"—an affirmation of Baptist catholicity that he seems to have intended quantitatively.[8]

But beyond this quantitative recognition that Baptists belong to the whole church and the whole church belongs to Baptists, catholicity also entails a "pattern of faith and practice that distinguished early catholic Christianity from Gnosticism, Arianism, Donatism, and all manner of other heresies and schisms" and is therefore "a *qualitative* fullness of faith and order that is visibly expressed in one eucharistic fellowship."[9] Baptists need this sort of catholicity first and foremost because it will help their churches form more faithful disciples of Jesus Christ.[10] To the degree that Baptist communities identify themselves as other than catholic in this qualitative sense, they are forming their members in a quasi-Gnostic pattern of faith and practice that is perilously close to being sub-Christian.[11]

[8]   This is the larger context of the quotation from Judge Willis' "Address of Welcome": "Let us, in all our supplications, remember all the members of other Churches, and ask that the choicest blessings may rest upon them. We believe, and our fathers have believed, in the Holy Catholic Church. The Church of Rome is right in affirming that the Church of Christ is catholic. The catholicity of the Church of Christ is not, however, a doctrine of Rome: it is an essential consequence resulting from the principles on which Christ's Church is founded. It is clearly written: 'There is one body, and one Spirit, even as ye are called in one hope of your calling; one Lord, one faith, one baptism, one God and Father of all, who is above all, and through all, and in you all'" (Baptist World Alliance, *The Baptist World Congress, London, July 11–19, 1905: Authorised Record of Proceedings*, ed. J. H. Shakespeare [London: Baptist Union Publication Dept., 1905], 2–3).

[9]   Harmon, *Towards Baptist Catholicity*, 204.

[10]   Baptist theologian James Wm. McClendon, Jr., whose own theological program has been labeled "radical catholicity," defined the doctrinal task of the church in terms that lend themselves to the connection I have made between a fuller catholicity and the formation of disciples: it is "the church teaching as she must teach if she is to be the church here and now" (James Wm. McClendon, Jr., *Doctrine: Systematic Theology, Vol. 2* (Waco, Tex.: Baylor University Press, 2012), 28. For a "radical catholic" reading of McClendon's project, see Curtis W. Freeman, "A Theology for Brethren, Radical Believers, and Other Baptists: A Review Essay of James McClendon's *Systematic Theology*," *Brethren Life and Thought* 50, nos. 1–2 (Winter/Spring 2006), 106–115, revised and expanded as "Introduction: A Theology for Radical Believers and Other Baptists," in McClendon, *Ethics: Systematic Theology, Vol. 1* (Waco, Tex.: Baylor University Press, 2012), vii–xxxviii (also included in the frontal matter of the Baylor University Press edition of the *Doctrine* and *Witness* volumes, with the same pagination).

[11]   In *Towards Baptist Catholicity* I suggested that some expressions of Baptist faith and practice have affinities with certain features of ancient Christian Gnosticism in these terms: "It is no mere coincidence that the most severely truncated versions of the Christian narrative in Gnosticism also denied the material order as the sphere of God's redemptive work. . . . In the history of Christianity there exist two primary patterns of conceiving of God's relationship to the world and of ordering Christian faith and practice in light of this conception: sacramental Christianity and Christian Gnosticism. There are of course

Baptists need a more qualitative catholicity for the sake of their own spiritual health. Even among Baptists who gladly declare their ecumenical openness to other Christians and their churches and thus are quantitatively catholic in their ecclesial outlook, there is much room remaining for progress toward a more fully qualitative Baptist catholicity.[12]

Catholicity and the Ecumenical Future

Yet as Richard Crane correctly observed in his review of *Towards Baptist Catholicity*, an improved state of Baptist ecclesial existence would be a penultimate end of the book's proposals. Crane asked, "Is 'Baptist Catholicity' the ultimate goal of 'Baptist catholicity'?"[13] If Baptist Catholicity (uppercase "C") means an entry of Baptists into communion with the bishop of Rome, then in a qualified sense Baptist catholicity (lowercase "c") does indeed have Baptist Catholicity (uppercase "C") as its goal. By the time I had written the concluding chapter of the book, I had come to the realization that what I was proposing was not only a program for the renewal of the Baptist tradition through retrieval of the larger tradition from which Baptists have become largely disconnected (though it was certainly that). I now regarded the proposed catholic renewal of Baptist life as necessary to the movement of the whole church toward the ecumenical future, and therefore I concluded the book with the "hope that all involved in the conversation [about the relation of the Baptist vision to the ancient tradition that Baptists share, or ought to share, with the rest of the church] will love Christ's church deeply enough to regard our cherished

---

various places on a continuum between these two primary patterns. But the extent to which a particular Christian tradition is non-sacramental is the extent to which that tradition is ultimately Gnostic in the way it conceives of God's relationship to the world and orders its faith and practice accordingly" (Harmon, *Towards Baptist Catholicity*, 163).

[12] This manner of distinguishing between the interrelated "quantitative" and "qualitative" dimensions of the catholicity of the church here and elsewhere in this book, now commonplace in ecumenical theology, has origins in the early ecclesiological work of Yves Congar, *Chrétiens désunis: Principes d'un "oecuménisme" catholique* (Unum Sanctam, no. 1; Paris: Éditions du Cerf, 1937), 115–17; ET, *Divided Christendom: A Catholic Study of the Problem of Reunion*, trans. M. A. Bousfield (London: Geoffrey Bles/Centenary, 1939), 93–94: "The Catholicity of the Church has long been interpreted in an exclusively geographical or, at any rate, quantitative sense, as the temporal and especially the local extension of the Church among all men and throughout the whole world. . . . But in the Fathers, except perhaps St. Augustine, and in the early theologians, this quantitative aspect is never affirmed in isolation, it is enumerated among other elements. . . . On thinking it over one is very quickly led to see that there cannot be quantitative Catholicity without qualitative, this being the necessary cause of the former."

[13] Crane, "Explosive Devices and Rhetorical Strategies," 367.

constructions of Baptist identity as temporary way stations en route to the realization of the visible unity of the body of Christ in one eucharistic fellowship."[14] My participation in the Baptist–Catholic joint commission over the next five years only strengthened the conviction that "Baptist catholicity" ultimately has to do with the ecumenical goal of the visible unity of the church.

While Baptists can easily point to aspects of the current faith and practice of the Catholic Church and other Christian communions as grounds for rejecting such a goal, Baptists are not responsible for the reformation of Catholic magisterial teaching or the transformation of that which they find objectionable in other churches. But Baptists can address the insufficiently catholic character of their own communities. The earliest description of the church as "catholic" by Ignatius of Antioch, writing to the Smyrneans not long after the New Testament Christianity that Baptists have endeavored to restore,[15] points to four marks of a qualitative catholicity in contrast to the faith and practice of the Docetists: a robustly incarnational Christology, sacramental realism, visible unity, and the ministry of oversight.[16] Apart from christological and trinitarian orthodoxy (and there have been shortcomings even at that point),[17] the Baptist pattern of being church has not typified this ancient configuration of catholicity. These deficiencies in catholicity are chief among the multiple factors that in Catholic perspective would preclude the communion of Baptist communities with the bishop of Rome. Baptists cannot by themselves do everything that would be necessary for the realization of full communion between their churches and those now in communion with Rome, but they can patiently work for the catholicization of Baptist faith and practice. Progress in heeding the ecumenical imperative of visible Christian unity disclosed in Jesus' prayer in John 17 depends in part on a Baptist embrace of the radically catholic core of the Christian faith.

---

[14]   Harmon, *Towards Baptist Catholicity*, 212–13.

[15]   The quest to restore the faith and practice of the New Testament church has figured prominently in the development of the Baptist tradition and serves as the key interpretive motif in a recent Baptist history text: C. Douglas Weaver, *In Search of the New Testament Church: The Baptist Story* (Macon, Ga.: Mercer University Press, 2008).

[16]   Ignatius of Antioch, *Smyrneans* 6–8, in *The Apostolic Fathers*, ed. and trans. Bart D. Ehrman (Loeb Classical Library, vol. 24; Cambridge, Mass.: Harvard University Press, 2003), 1:302–5 (295–309). Chapter 5 of the present book will develop more fully these four marks of qualitative catholicity in Ignatius of Antioch in relationship to the New Testament and the larger Christian tradition.

[17]   See Curtis W. Freeman, "God in Three Persons: Baptist Unitarianism and the Trinity," *Perspectives in Religious Studies* 33, no. 3 (Fall 2006): 323–44; idem, *Contesting Catholicity: Theology for Other Baptists* (Waco, Tex.: Baylor University Press, 2014), 143–90.

How might this happen? *Towards Baptist Catholicity* emphasized the role of Baptist theological educators who might succeed in forming a more catholic vision of Baptist life in a new generation of ministers, who would then slowly lead their congregations toward more fully catholic patterns of faith and practice with much patience and pastoral sensitivity. But as Newman noted in her symposium review, this remains for now an academic exercise—at least as far as Baptists in the United States are concerned.[18] Many Baptist communities in Europe have maintained greater degrees of continuity with the more catholic ecclesial outlook that once prevailed among the earliest Baptists in the seventeenth century,[19] and the Baptist World Alliance is giving renewed attention to the connectional and ecumenical dimensions of ecclesiology in meetings of its Commission on Doctrine and Christian Unity and other conferences.[20] Part of the "how?"

[18]   Newman, "Remembering How to Remember," 378.

[19]   That the notion of Baptist catholicity is not as alien to present-day European Baptists is evident in some features of the book's reception in that context. In a review of *Towards Baptist Catholicity* published in the *Journal of European Baptist Studies* 7, no. 2 (January 2007): 51–52, Keith Jones, a British Baptist serving as rector of the International Baptist Theological Seminary in Prague, observed: "Harmon has a desire for regular celebration of the Eucharist, which we applaud, but appears not to be aware of the deep tradition in the last century advocating such an approach here in Europe . . . the call he makes for renewal seems to be addressing another continent and not what is actually happening in Europe today."

[20]   In conjunction with the German Union of Free Evangelical (Baptist) Churches, the Baptist World Alliance sponsored a Symposium on Baptist Identity and Ecclesiology in Elstal, Germany, March 21–24, 2007, that addressed the question "Are Baptist Churches Autonomous?" Among the five affirmations agreed upon by the sixty-plus conference participants were these two: "That for Baptists, the local church is wholly church but not the whole church," and "That our local churches and Conventions/Unions are participants in the one church that God has called into being as we anticipate the full revelation of the children of God." Cf. Jean-Jacques von Allmen, "L'Église locale parmi les autres Églises locales," *Irénikon* 43 (1970): 512 (512–37), who as a Reformed ecumenist insisted that the local church is "wholly the church, but not the whole church," language closely echoed in the Elstal affirmation. (The statement from the Elstal symposium and the press release reporting on its proceedings are no longer available online at the Baptist World Alliance web site, but the affirmation referenced here is quoted and engaged by Elizabeth Newman, "Are Local Baptist Churches Wholly Autonomous?" *Baptist News Global* [June 12, 2007], accessed November 23, 2014, http://baptistnews.com/archives/item/2582-opinion -are-local-baptist-churches-wholly-autonomous). Three recent meetings of the BWA Commission on Doctrine and Christian Unity have reflected on Baptist ecclesiology in relation to significant ecclesiological convergence proposals that have emerged from the work of the World Council of Churches Commission on Faith and Order, offering and discussing Baptist responses to *The Nature and Mission of the Church: A Stage on the Way to a Common Statement* (Faith and Order Paper no. 198; Geneva: World Council of Churches, 2005) and *The Church: Towards a Common Vision* (Faith and Order Paper no. 214; Geneva:

of Baptist catholicity may be bringing more Baptists in the United States into these global Baptist conversations that are open to a more catholic orientation to Baptist ecclesiology.

Catholicity and Authority

But the practical question of how Baptists might become more fully catholic merely hints at a much more crucial and infinitely more problematic question: what would authorize a catholic pattern of Baptist faith and practice? In other words, where is the magisterium that could reliably guide Baptists toward catholicity? *Towards Baptist Catholicity* dodged this question, partly because its rhetorical goal was to convince theologically educated Baptists that their communities need a fuller catholicity and that there are precedents within the Baptist tradition itself for a more catholic vision of Baptist identity than currently prevails, and partly because I was not yet satisfied with my own provisional answers to it. The book's MacIntyrean construal of the authority of tradition as the authority of the *communio sanctorum* in its contestation of the tradition could be read as an argument for a "magisterium of the whole."[21] In such a pan-ecclesial construct of the location of the church's teaching authority, the voices that arise from what Nicholas Healy in his *Pro Ecclesia* review appreciatively identified as "Baptist individualism" would be heard and weighed along with other ecclesial voices.[22] But without greater specificity in its location of ecclesial authority, the theory lacks adequate safeguards against the very thing it seeks to avoid: self-chosen patterns of faith and practice by independent individuals and autonomous congregations in the configuration of a "selective catholicity" that, as Paul Avis perceptively pointed out in the book's foreword, embraces certain ancient marks of catholicity but

---

World Council of Churches, 2013): Santiago, Chile, July 2–7, 2012; Ocho Rios, Jamaica, July 1–6, 2013; and Izmir, Turkey, July 6–12, 2014.

[21] Harmon, *Towards Baptist Catholicity*, 39–69. This chapter titled "The Authority of the Community (of All the Saints)" drew from Alasdair MacIntyre's characterization of "a living tradition" as "an historically extended, socially embodied argument, and an argument precisely in part about the goods which constitute that tradition" (Alasdair MacIntyre, *After Virtue: A Study in Moral Theory*, 2nd ed. [Notre Dame, Ind.: University of Notre Dame Press, 1984], 222) in order to suggest that Baptists' "traditioning in dissent can also help them appreciate the critical function of tradition as the argument of the community and may help them find their place within this argument" (Harmon, *Towards Baptist Catholicity*, 66).

[22] Healy, "Traditions, Authorities, and the Individual Christian," 374.

ignores the episcopal office and its historical role as the ecclesial location of teaching authority that authorizes the other marks of catholicity.[23]

I am told that some non-Baptists who have taken note of the small but growing number of publications by Baptist theologians who advocate a more catholic identity for Baptists[24] are concerned about the dangers of eclecticism inherent in such an enterprise. I share these concerns. Many Baptist readers of *Towards Baptist Catholicity* have told me that they especially appreciated chapter 8, which urges the Baptist retrieval of catholic practices of corporate worship that include celebration of the full Christian year, use of the common lectionary, more frequent eucharistic celebration, confession of the ancient creeds, the use of patristic forms of prayer such as collects, acts of confession and pardon, the passing of the peace, narration of the lives of the saints, and the singing of hymn texts

---

[23] Paul Avis, "Foreword," in Harmon, *Towards Baptist Catholicity*, xvii–xviii; Newman, "Remembering How to Remember," 379.

[24] E.g., Barry Harvey, *Can These Bones Live? A Catholic Baptist Engagement with Ecclesiology, Hermeneutics, and Social Theory* (Grand Rapids: Brazos Press, 2008); Elizabeth Newman, *Attending the Wounds on Christ's Body: Teresa's Scriptural Vision* (Eugene, Ore.: Cascade Books, 2012); Freeman, *Contesting Catholicity*. A 2008 doctoral dissertation offered a critical and constructive analysis of this trajectory in Baptist theology: Cameron H. Jorgenson, "Bapto-Catholicism: Recovering Tradition and Reconsidering the Baptist Identity" (Ph.D. diss., Baylor University, 2008). Jorgenson's dissertation has subsequently been joined by a noteworthy number of dissertations by Baptists and others in the Free Church tradition at Baptist-related Baylor University and the Catholic-connected University of Dayton that address the intersection of ecclesiology and ecumenical theology in a "bapto-catholic" or "catholic baptist" fashion: Scott W. Bullard, "A Re-membering Sign: The Eucharist and Ecclesial Unity in Baptist Ecclesiologies" (Ph.D. diss., Baylor University, 2009), published as *Re-membering the Body: The Lord's Supper and Ecclesial Unity in the Free Church Traditions* (Free Church, Catholic Tradition; Eugene, Ore.: Cascade Books, 2013); Jeffrey W. Cary, "Authority, Unity and Truthfulness: The Body of Christ in the Theologies of Robert Jenson and Rowan Williams with a View toward Implications for Free Church Ecclesiology" (Ph.D. diss., Baylor University, 2010), published as *Free Churches and the Body of Christ: Authority, Unity, and Truthfulness* (Free Church, Catholic Tradition; Eugene, Ore.: Cascade Books, 2012); Aaron James, "Analogous Uses of Language, Eucharistic Identity, and the Baptist Vision" (Ph.D. diss., University of Dayton, 2010); Derek C. Hatch, "E. Y. Mullins, George W. Truett, and a Baptist Theology of Nature and Grace" (Ph.D. diss., University of Dayton, 2011); Jonathan A. Malone, "Changed, Set Apart, and Equal: A Study of Ordination in the Baptist Context" (Ph.D. diss., University of Dayton, 2011); Andrew Donald Black, "A 'Vast Practical Embarrassment': John W. Nevin, the Mercersburg Theology, and the Church Question" (Ph.D. diss., University of Dayton, 2013). For another perspective that draws on the Puritan/Reformed trajectory in the Baptist tradition to critique some of these "bapto-catholic" or "catholic baptist" proposals, see Gordon Lansdowne Belyea, "Living Stones in a Spiritual House: The Priesthood of the Saint in the Baptist *Sanctorum Communio*" (Th.D. thesis, Wycliffe College/University of Toronto, 2012).

of patristic composition. But what is to keep a Baptist adaptation of such aspects of the catholic liturgical tradition from falling prey to an undisciplined eclecticism? What are the criteria for planning "catholic Baptist" liturgies, other than the preferences of the ministers and members of particular local congregations? This is merely illustrative of the larger question of how one determines which elements of catholicity Baptists can embrace without betraying their Baptist identity. To ask such questions is to inquire about the location of magisterial authority in Baptist life. Whether they acknowledge it or not, Baptists and other Free Church evangelicals do have something approaching a magisterium inasmuch as they routinely turn to resources beyond themselves for guidance in matters of biblical interpretation, theology, and ethics—revered pastors, teachers, and authors as well as confessions adopted by associations of churches.[25] Yet

---

[25] This turn to resources beyond the self may involve an intentional openness to the resources represented by the community that gathers with the goal of bringing its life together under the lordship of Christ through the leadership of the Spirit who speaks through the members of the community. Often this turn to resources beyond the self is much less intentional, but it nevertheless involves some awareness of the insufficiency of the solitary self in interpreting the Scriptures and configuring the faith. Therefore, pastors preparing sermons or Bible studies consult biblical commentaries written by other members of the community of faith, and laypersons think about their current understanding of what Christian faith and practice ought to be in light of what they hear from their ministers and popular Christian speakers or read from their favorite devotional writers. This less-conscious reach for the help of others in forming the faith and faithfulness of members of the church is what David Gushee addresses in the course of expressing his concern that the theologians and pastors of his Baptist communion, the Cooperative Baptist Fellowship, have "not produced a particularly robust body of theological writings" to which CBF-affiliated ministers and laypersons could turn (David Gushee, "Blurry Vision and How We Got Here: The Ex-SBC, Part II," *Baptist News Global*, March 4, 2014, accessed November 23, 2014, http://baptistnews.com/news/item/28413-blurry-vision-how-we-got-here-the-ex-sbc-part-ii#.UzV2OfldWSo):

> To the extent that "our" people get their ideas about what it means to be a Christian from what they read, they are borrowing from other traditions. So some are reading Richard Rohr and some Shane Claiborne and some Dietrich Bonhoeffer and some Augustine and some Parker Palmer and some Tom Oden and some Barbara Brown Taylor and some Stanley Hauerwas and some N. T. Wright and some Frederick Buechner and some Anne Lamott. And maybe some are reading liberationists and voices from previously marginalized communities. And some are reading bloggers like Rachel Held Evans. And a lot read whatever pops up on Facebook. And some aren't reading much at all. Lacking leadership in our own fold, we default to the voices of others.

Baptists at other places on the theological spectrum would have their own "voices of others" to which they turn that could be named in a parallel inventory. Gushee notes that in voicing this concern he is "not arguing for Baptist parochialism" but "arguing for much more intellectual firepower coming from our side." Chapter 7 of the present book will

they lack the formal instruments that would facilitate the kind of collegial contestation of Christian teaching that marked the deliberations of the Second Vatican Council,[26] a collaborative enterprise involving not only bishops but the theologians and laity of the church as the necessary precursor to the ecclesial voice heard in the documents of Vatican II or the *Catechism of the Catholic Church*.[27]

The Baptist ecclesial voice is much more elusive. A few weeks before the current series of conversations between the Baptist World Alliance and the Catholic Church began in 2006, a Catholic theologian not participating in the dialogue posed the question to me and another member of the Baptist delegation, "What might it mean for the Baptists to speak with one voice in these talks?" The present inability of Baptists to speak with an ecclesial voice stems partly from their failure to take up the nature and authority of the teaching office in the church as a matter of serious Baptist theological reflection. The thing many Baptists most fear about an ecumenical future that involves visible unity is that it might mean communion with Rome, and the thing they find most objectionable about the specter of communion with Rome is its magisterium (a term some Baptists utter as if they were referring to the villainous entity in Philip Pullman's fantasy novel trilogy *His Dark Materials* and its film adaptation *The Golden Compass*).[28]

Pilgrim Catholicity

My admission that my hope for Baptist catholicity includes communion with Rome is qualified by my conviction that Baptists have their own

---

contend that there can be a beneficial, more intentional turn by Baptists to "the voices of others" that can assist Baptists in their pilgrim quest to bring their life together ever more fully under the rule of Christ.

[26] Giuseppe Alberigo, *History of Vatican II*, trans. Joseph A. Komonchak, 5 vols. (Maryknoll, N.Y.: Orbis Books, 1995–2006).

[27] Cf. also the guidelines for such relationships of collaboration and contestation proposed in National Conference of Catholic Bishops, *Doctrinal Responsibilities: Approaches to Promoting Cooperation and Resolving Misunderstandings between Bishops and Theologians* (Washington, D.C.: United States Catholic Conference, 1989), a document that was itself the product of collaboration between the Catholic Theological Society of America, the Canon Law Society of America, and the National Conference of Catholic Bishops (now the United States Conference of Catholic Bishops).

[28] Philip Pullman, *Northern Lights: His Dark Materials, Book 1* (London: Scholastic, 1995); idem, *The Subtle Knife: His Dark Materials, Book 2* (London: Scholastic, 1997); idem, *The Amber Spyglass: His Dark Materials, Book 3* (London: Scholastic, 2000); *The Golden Compass*, directed by Chris Weitz (Los Angeles: New Line Cinema, 2007).

distinctive ecclesial gifts to offer the church catholic, without which even the churches currently in communion with the bishop of Rome are something less than fully catholic themselves.[29] These gifts include a zeal for guarding conscience from coercion by civil or ecclesiastical powers, an insistence that God's freedom to be God in the life of the church not be constrained, an ecclesiology that emphasizes the mutuality of covenant responsibilities among the members of the church as a corollary of the necessity that each embrace the faith personally, and the healthy aversion to overly realized eschatologies of the church that are reflected in the Baptist understanding of the church as a pilgrim community seeking to become a community living fully under the rule of Christ—though these gifts are by no means unique to Baptists. I imagine an ecumenical future that would include a mutual sharing of the gifts of catholicity and Baptistness, facilitated by a recognition by Baptists and Catholics alike that being Baptist is a distinctive way of being Catholic, in communion with the bishop of Rome, comparable to the manner in which being a Benedictine is currently a distinctive way of living together as an ecclesial community that is in communion with Rome. I also imagine that this would require the recognition by Rome that the catholic church subsists "where two or three are gathered in my name" (Matt 18:20)[30] as well as "wherever the

---

[29] Cf. Yves Congar, *My Journal of the Council*, trans. Mary John Ronayne and Mary Cecily Boulding, ed. Denis Minns (Collegeville, Minn.: Liturgical Press, 2012), who in an entry dated November 21, 1962, portrays Catholic catholicity as something toward which the Catholic Church must move rather than as something presently fully realized in the Catholic Church: "There can be no doubt that the Council will have had this effect of forcing Rome to discover catholicity" (201).

[30] The Baptist location of the church in the community that is gathered by Christ and that gathers in response to Christ's initiative in gathering its members, rooted in this Matthean text, has been explored by, e.g., Robert C. Walton, *The Gathered Community* (London: Carey Press, 1946), and Freeman, *Contesting Catholicity*, chapter 6, "Where Two or Three Are Gathered," 225–71. Paul S. Fiddes, *Tracks and Traces: Baptist Identity in Church and Theology* (Studies in Baptist History and Thought, vol. 13; Milton Keynes, UK: Paternoster, 2003), 21–47, develops the "gathered" movement in terms of the covenant God makes with the community of the church and the "gathering" movement in terms of the covenantal pledges made by the members of the church to God and to one another; cf. idem, "Communion and Covenant," chapter in Paul S. Fiddes, Brian Haymes, and Richard Kidd, *Baptists and the Communion of Saints: A Theology of Covenanted Disciples* (Waco, Tex.: Baylor University Press, 2014), 127–55. The location of the church in the community of believers gathered in Christ's name is exemplified elsewhere in the broader Free Church/Believers' Church tradition by *The Design of the Christian Church (Disciples of Christ)*, adopted in 1968 and revised in 2013 by the General Assembly of the Christian Church (Disciples of Christ), §1: "Within the whole family of God on earth, the church appears wherever believers in Jesus the Christ are gathered in His name. Transcending all barriers within the human family, the one church manifests itself in ordered

bishop is" (Ignatius of Antioch, *Smyrneans* 8)[31] and that the church that is made by and makes the Eucharist[32] includes the churches that exercise congregational oversight as they gather in the name of Christ as well as those that are overseen by the historic episcopate.[33] As a Baptist, I believe that our own congregations are fully church, that the catholic church subsists in them, and that our celebrations of the Lord's Supper are indeed valid Eucharists in which Christ is present when we gather in his name, recount the words of institution and the story of his passion, re-present his sacrificial work, and participate in that which the bread and wine signify. I hope that the journey to the ecumenical future includes Catholic recognition of the Baptist instances of the catholicity that exists outside the

---

communities bound together for worship, fellowship, and service; in varied structures for mission, witness, and mutual accountability; and for the nurture and renewal of its members" (accessed October 20, 2014, http://disciples.org/our-identity/the-design/).

[31] Ignatius of Antioch, *Smyrneans* 8, in *Apostolic Fathers*, ed. and trans. Ehrman, 1:305. It should be noted that while this text does locate the church episcopally, it also does so christologically and therefore is capable of being related to a gathering church ecclesiology as well as to an episcopal configuration of the church: "Let the congregation be wherever the bishop is; just as wherever Jesus Christ is, there also is the [catholic] church." However, because for Ignatius the bishop represents Christ, the gathering of the church in the name of Christ is defined in terms of its connection to the episcopal representative of Christ: it is to "follow the bishop as Jesus Christ follows the Father," it is not to "do anything involving the church without the bishop," its Eucharist is valid only in that it "occurs under the bishop or the one to whom he entrusts it," it is to gather "wherever the bishop is," it "is not permitted either to baptize or to hold a love feast without the bishop." Yet Ignatius' bishop is also a member of the community that gathers in the name of Christ, and what Ignatius says about the authority of the bishop can be understood as a word about the bishop's distinctive role as a fellow gatherer, seeking along with all who gather in the name of Christ to bring their life together ever more fully under the rule of Christ.

[32] Cf. John Paul II's encyclical letter *On the Eucharist in Its Relationship to the Church* (*Ecclesia de Eucharistia*, April 17, 2003), accessed October 18, 2014, http://www.vatican.va/holy_father/john_paul_ii/encyclicals/documents/hf_jp-ii_enc_20030417_eccl-de-euch_en.html, and earlier in Henri de Lubac, *Meditation sur l'Église*, 2nd ed. (Paris: Aubier, 1953); ET, *The Splendour of the Church*, trans. Michael Mason (Théologie, vol. 27; New York: Sheed & Ward, 1956); and idem, *Corpus Mysticum: L'Eucharistie et l'Église au Moyen-Âge*, 2nd ed. (Paris: Aubier, 1949); ET, *Corpus Mysticum: The Eucharist and the Church in the Middle Ages*, trans. Laurence Paul Hemming and Susan Frank Parsons (Notre Dame, Ind.: University of Notre Dame Press, 2006).

[33] Cf. Baptist World Alliance and Catholic Church, "The Word of God in the Life of the Church," §§162–204. This section of the dialogue report addressing "The Ministry of Oversight (*Episkope*) and Unity in the Life of the Church" identifies functional convergences in the respective configurations of *episkope* in both communions (§§162, 165, 168–69, 173, 176, 179, 182, 184, 186–87, 189–90, 193, 197, 200–204) while noting the significant structural differences that remain (§§163–64, 166–67, 170–72, 174–75, 177–78, 180–81, 183, 185, 188, 191–92, 194–96, 198–99).

Catholic Church[34] and even Catholic reception of the best Baptist ecclesial gifts. In the meantime, Baptists must see to it that there is catholicity existing among them to be recognized.

The present book tackles head-on these unresolved issues. *Baptist Identity and the Ecumenical Future* explores the relation of the Baptist vision of the church as a pilgrim community seeking to bring its life ever more fully under the lordship of Christ to the ecumenical quest for the full visible unity of the church, arguing that neither can be fulfilled apart from a mutually receptive ecumenical engagement between Baptist communities and the churches from which they are separated. It proposes that while chief among the gifts Baptists have to offer the rest of the church are their pilgrim aversion to overly realized eschatologies of the church and their radical commitment to discerning the rule of Christ by means of the Scriptures, Baptists must be willing to receive from other churches neglected aspects of the radical catholicity from which the Scriptures are inseparable if Baptists—and their dialogue partners—are to progress on their pilgrim journey toward the fullness of the rule of Christ in their midst.

Baptists and members of other communions who take up this book's challenge to journey together toward the ecumenical future will likely not enjoy such warm relationships with many from their own tradition, for some of the greatest obstacles in this journey are located within particular communions rather than between them. Each day of the 2010 Baptist–Catholic conversations in Oxford, delegates passed the Martyrs' Memorial as they walked along St. Giles' across from Regent's Park College. The inscription below the monument's Gothic spire reads, "To the Glory of God, and in grateful commemoration of His servants, Thomas Cranmer, Nicholas Ridley, Hugh Latimer, Prelates of the Church of England, who near this spot yielded their bodies to be burned, bearing witness to the sacred truths which they had affirmed and maintained against the errors of the Church of Rome, and rejoicing that to them it was given not only to believe in Christ, but also to suffer for His sake; this monument was erected by public subscription in the year of our Lord God, MDC-CCXLI." The date and the explanation of the monument's origins are not-so-subtle clues that the monument is not really about the Protestant martyrs named in its inscription. The year 1841 fell in the midst of the most vitriolic period of public debate in England over the proposals of the Oxford Movement. The final tract of the *Tracts for the Times* was published

---

[34] Cf. Ola Tjøhom, "Catholic Faith outside the Catholic Church: An Ecumenical Challenge," *Pro Ecclesia* 13, no. 3 (Summer 2004): 261–74.

that year. In Tract 90 John Henry Newman, then four years away from his reception into the Catholic Church, had argued that the Tridentine expression of Catholic doctrine could be reconciled with the teachings of the Anglican *Thirty-Nine Articles*.[35] The Tractarians' opponent Charles Golightly, an Anglican cleric in Oxford, succeeded in raising funds for the construction of the memorial through a national subscription campaign.[36] Its message, directed against this early form of receptive ecumenism in the Church of England, was clear: "Roman Catholics are the epitome of evil, for they murdered the founders of your national church. Don't even think of moving in their direction, liturgically or theologically."

Baptists whose vision includes an ecumenical future in full communion with Catholics and other Christians are already the occasional object of similar rhetoric from some members of their own communion.[37] Like the leaders of the Oxford Movement, the contributions of these catholic Baptists may bear the fruit of a more widespread Baptist reception of the gifts of Catholics and other Christians in a way that becomes evident only many decades after their lifetimes. I have written this book in the hope that the tribe of those who long for the visible unity of Christ's church might increase among Baptists, and that other Christians might recognize them, so that together we can make our pilgrim journey toward the ecumenical future.

---

[35] John Henry Newman, "Remarks on Certain Passages in the Thirty-Nine Articles," *Tracts for the Times* 90 (London: J. G. F. & J. Rivington, 1841).

[36] On the Martyrs' Memorial episode of the controversies over the Oxford Movement, see C. Brad Faught, *The Oxford Movement: A Thematic History of the Tractarians and Their Times* (University Park: Pennsylvania State University Press, 2003), 90–92; Andrew Atherstone, *Oxford's Protestant Spy: The Controversial Career of Charles Golightly* (Studies in Evangelical History and Thought; Milton Keynes, UK: Paternoster, 2007), 57–83.

[37] E.g., Bruce Gourley, "Editorial: Baptists and Theology—Broad, Deep, and Diverse," *Baptist History and Heritage* 47, no. 2 (Summer 2012): 3 (2–3): "Bapto-Catholics wish to dissolve Baptists into a cauldron of ancient Church creeds, repealing the Protestant Reformation on a pilgrimage to Rome."

2

Seizing the Ecumenical Moment

While the church-dividing issues that surface in Baptist–Catholic ecumenical dialogue might seem to be among the greatest ecumenical impasses, the broader ecumenical movement is beset by far more serious maladies. Despite enthusiastic responses to the seemingly significant breakthroughs represented by the Faith and Order convergence text *Baptism, Eucharist and Ministry* (*BEM*) in 1982 and the Catholic–Lutheran *Joint Declaration on the Doctrine of Justification* in 1999 (joined by the World Methodist Council in 2006),[1] it is commonly acknowledged that the ecumenical movement is experiencing a season of winter at the outset of the twenty-first century. Several factors have contributed to the current ecumenical malaise and retrenchment. The institutions of international ecumenism associated with the World Council of Churches have given less and less attention to their work on the issues of doctrine and church order that must be contested before visible unity can become a reality.[2]

---

[1] World Council of Churches, *Baptism, Eucharist and Ministry* (Faith and Order Paper no. 111; Geneva: World Council of Churches, 1982); Lutheran World Federation and Catholic Church, *Joint Declaration on the Doctrine of Justification* (Grand Rapids: William B. Eerdmans, 2000); Geoffrey Wainwright, "World Methodist Council and the Joint Declaration on the Doctrine of Justification," *Pro Ecclesia* 16, no. 1 (Winter 2007): 7–13.

[2] The de-prioritizing of the Faith and Order stream of the modern ecumenical movement within the World Council of Churches in favor of the Life and Work stream's emphasis on the church's engagement with sociopolitical issues was identified as a contributor to the current ecumenical malaise by the unofficial, independent ecumenical working group that published Carl E. Braaten and Robert W. Jenson, eds., *In One Body through the Cross: The Princeton Proposal for Christian Unity* (Grand Rapids: William B. Eerdmans, 2003). George A. Lindbeck, one of the sixteen members of the "Princeton Project" working group, elaborated this concern in his article "The Unity We Seek: Setting the Agenda for Ecumenism," *Christian Century* 122, no. 16 (August 9, 2005): 28–31.

Their increasing attention to the political and social challenges faced by the contemporary church—a proper locus of ecumenical engagement—has sometimes contributed to further divisions, often within the particular communions that support these institutions, owing to widespread Christian disagreement about the social and political implications of the gospel.[3] Interreligious dialogue—also a proper ecumenical concern that cannot be neglected in the world the church inhabits—has shifted some of the movement's attention and energy away from the seemingly less pressing work on intra-Christian division. The ecumenical leaders of the past few decades are retiring and passing away, and few younger leaders are ready to take up their mantle. The denominations that were once heavily invested in the quest for Christian unity have now turned their energies to their worsening internal divisions. Conflicts *within* denominations over biblical authority, gender, and sexuality have greatly complicated efforts to secure unity *between* the denominations. Statements issued by the Congregation for the Doctrine of the Faith on the relation of the Catholic Church to other Christian communities in the first decade of the twenty-first century appeared to threaten the progress made in Protestant–Catholic dialogue in the wake of the Second Vatican Council, though they were capable of being read in less exclusionary ways.[4] Convergences attained

[3]   It must be emphasized that the ecumenical movement cannot eschew social and political engagement as a strategy for minimizing division, for visible unity entails that such a united church "act and speak together as occasion requires" according to the "New Delhi Definition" adopted by the Third Assembly of the World Council of Churches in New Delhi, India, in 1961 and now regarded as the classic definition of the visible unity sought by the ecumenical movement. See "Report of the Section on Unity," in *The New Delhi Report: The Third Assembly of the World Council of Churches, 1961* (New York: Association Press, 1962), 116.

[4]   On July 10, 2007, the Vatican released a June 29 document from the Congregation for the Doctrine of the Faith offering "Responses to Some Questions regarding Certain Aspects of the Doctrine of the Church" (accessed October 21, 2014, http://www.vatican.va/roman_curia/congregations/cfaith/documents/rc_con_cfaith_doc_20070629_responsa-quaestiones_en.html). Even though this document clearly reiterated what the Vatican II *Decree on Ecumenism* (*Unitatis Redintegratio*), November 21, 1964, in *Vatican Council II: The Conciliar and Post Conciliar Documents*, rev. ed., ed. Austin Flannery (Vatican Collection, vol. 1; Northport, N.Y.: Costello, 1992), 452–70; and John Paul II's encyclical *On Commitment to Ecumenism* ([*Ut Unum Sint*, May 25, 1995], accessed October 21, 2014, http://www.vatican.va/holy_father/john_paul_ii/encyclicals/documents/hf_jp-ii_enc_25051995_ut-unum-sint_en.html) had generously affirmed regarding the presence of Christ and the work of the Spirit in other churches and ecclesial communities that are separated from the Catholic Church, many regarded "Responses to Some Questions regarding Certain Aspects of the Doctrine of the Church" as a major step away from Rome's post–Vatican II commitments to ecumenical engagement. Similar dynamics were at play in the responses to the CDF's "Declaration '*Dominus Iesus*' on the

in international dialogues between denominational communions often have not been well received at the local level, and frequently local church leaders remain unaware of these agreements.[5] Thus, for now, "the great divisions remain, and few see a way forward."[6]

A Future for Faith and Order?

The abandonment in 2006 of plans for a Second Conference on Faith and Order in North America, envisioned as a more broadly inclusive sequel to the landmark 1957 North American Conference on Faith and Order in Oberlin, Ohio, is symptomatic of the current ecumenical status quo.[7]

Unicity and Salvific Universality of Jesus Christ and the Church" issued seven years earlier, on August 6, 2000 (accessed October 21, 2014, http://www.vatican.va/roman_curia/congregations/cfaith/documents/rc_con_cfaith_doc_20000806_dominus-iesus_en.html). Curtis W. Freeman, "Baptists & Catholics Together? Making Up Is Hard to Do," *Commonweal* (January 16, 2009): 18–21, situates Baptist responses to the 2007 CDF document "Responses to Some Questions regarding Certain Aspects of the Doctrine of the Church" in the larger historical context of Baptist–Catholic relations and offers a more appreciative reading of it; Jared Wicks provides a conciliatory Catholic perspective in his articles "Not So Fully Church: The Pope's Message to Protestants—and Catholics," *Christian Century* 124, no. 17 (August 21, 2007): 9–11, "Questions and Answers on the New Responses of the Congregation for the Doctrine of the Faith," *Ecumenical Trends* 36 (July/August 2007): 1–8, and "The Significance of the 'Ecclesial Communities' of the Reformation," *Ecumenical Trends* 30, no. 11 (December 2001): 170–73.

[5] Seasoned theological leaders of the ecumenical movement have identified the aforementioned factors as contributors to the current ecumenical status quo. See William G. Rusch, "The State and Future of the Ecumenical Movement," *Pro Ecclesia* 9, no. 1 (Winter 2000): 8–18; Braaten and Jenson, eds., *In One Body through the Cross*, 6–7; George Lindbeck, "Ecumenisms in Conflict," in *God, Truth, and Witness: Engaging Stanley Hauerwas*, ed. L. Gregory Jones, Reinhard Hütter, and C. Rosalee Velloso da Silva (Grand Rapids: Brazos Press, 2005), 212–28; Robert W. Jenson, "God's Time, Our Time: An Interview with Robert W. Jenson," *Christian Century* 123, no. 9 (May 2, 2006): 31–35.

[6] Carl E. Braaten and Robert W. Jenson, "To the Churches of North America, Judicatories, Ecumenical Agencies, Ecumenical Officers, Laity and Clergy," in *In One Body through the Cross*, ed. Braaten and Jenson, 7 (5–7).

[7] The Faith and Order stream of the modern ecumenical movement was given its initial institutional expression in the form of the World Conference on Faith and Order in Lausanne, Switzerland, in 1927 and in 1948 joined with the Conference on Life and Work (which had held its inaugural conference in Stockholm, Sweden, in 1925) to form the World Council of Churches. Emphasizing candid theological dialogue about the issues of doctrine and church order that presently preclude full visible unity among the churches, the Faith and Order movement originated in the work of Bishop Charles Brent (1862–1929), an Episcopal missionary to the Philippines from the United States who was one of the speakers at the Edinburgh World Missionary Conference in 1910. Convinced that the nascent modern ecumenical movement could not be content with merely seeking greater cooperation in missions among the denominations but must move toward

In December 1999 seventy-five notable signatories spanning the North American ecclesiastical and theological spectrum issued "A Call to the Churches for a Second Conference on Faith and Order in North America."[8] When it became apparent that the evangelical and Pentecostal voices that were not represented at the 1957 conference would not join in a new conference more fully inclusive of the Christian traditions unless the effort were disconnected from the National Council of Churches of Christ in the USA, in 2001 William G. Rusch resigned his position as executive director of the Faith and Order Commission of the NCCCUSA and formed the Foundation for a Conference on Faith and Order in North America as a sponsoring entity independent of the NCCCUSA to address these objections. A "Planning Consultation for a Second Conference on Faith and Order in North America" with approximately 120 participants was held at the University of Notre Dame, October 7–9, 2001, and the launch of a series of publications intended to lay the groundwork for the envisioned conference followed.[9] By 2005, however, it had become clear that despite

---

full visible unity by addressing the church-dividing issues of doctrine and church order, Brent proposed to representatives of the Catholic Church, the Orthodox Churches, and various Protestant communions that an international ecumenical study commission be created to work on these matters (see Alexander C. Zabriskie, *Bishop Brent, Crusader for Christian Unity* [Philadelphia: Westminster Press, 1948]). While the Conference on Faith and Order was formed without the participation of the Catholic Church, after the Second Vatican Council the Catholic Church, though not a member church of the WCC, formed a Joint Working Group between the Catholic Church and the WCC and has appointed Catholic theologians as official representatives in the membership of the WCC Commission on Faith and Order. The Faith and Order movement includes not only the work of the WCC Commission on Faith and Order and the Faith and Order commissions of national councils of churches but also the instruments of bilateral and multilateral dialogue in their attention to church-dividing issues of faith and order. In this book the capitalized terms "Faith and Order" refer to the expression of the modern ecumenical movement that seeks visible unity through theological work on these matters of faith and order, including but not limited to the work of the WCC Commission on Faith and Order. When "faith and order" appears without capitalization, the reference is to the churches' doctrine and ecclesial order rather than to the Faith and Order movement.

[8]　"A Call to the Churches for a Second Conference on Faith and Order in North America," in *Faith and Order: Toward a North American Conference. Study Guide*, ed. Norman A. Hjelm (Grand Rapids: William B. Eerdmans, 2004), 3–11.

[9]　The report from the Notre Dame planning consultation is published in *Faith and Order*, ed. Hjelm, 12–20. That small *Study Guide* volume was issued with this note announcing a series of publications: "Eerdmans will be publishing other volumes connected with the Conference on Faith and Order in North America: the papers from an April 2004 consultation at Princeton, New Jersey, on 'What Makes the Church One?' a historical study of Faith and Witness in Canada and Faith and Order in the United States, a volume of substantive essays on the Conference theme by scholars from a variety of Christian traditions, and the report of the 2005 Conference itself" (*Faith and Order:*

these efforts there was not sufficient support for plans for the conference to proceed, and in February 2006 the board of directors for the Foundation for a Conference on Faith and Order in North America voted to dissolve the foundation.[10] It would not seem an auspicious time for proposing that Baptists or anyone else jump on the bandwagon of the Faith and Order stream of the modern ecumenical movement as a means of conveyance to the ecumenical future.

Such were the circumstances when I served as a member of a consultation convened by the Foundation for a Conference on Faith and Order in North America that met January 3–5, 2006, at the Graymoor Spiritual Life Center of the Franciscan Friars of the Atonement in Garrison, New York. Our charge was primarily to examine the factors behind the failure of the envisioned Second Conference on Faith and Order in North America, but secondarily to contemplate the possibilities for such a conference in the future.[11] My role on the program of the consultation was to offer an "evangelical" perspective on whether or not there ought to be a Second Conference on Faith and Order in North America or something like it, notwithstanding the then-recent failure to come to fruition of the plans made for it.[12] This invitation presented me with something of a dilemma, for I was not particularly invested in claiming the label "evangelical" for myself (or in shunning it, for that matter), and the moderate/progressive stream of the Baptist tradition in North America with which I identify tends to distance itself from a self-consciously "evangelical" identity. Yet I welcomed the opportunity to make this case for the kind of ecumenical engagement represented by the abandoned vision for the conference and to make connections between evangelical identity and Baptist identity,

---

Toward a North American Conference, ed. Hjelm, x). To date only the *Study Guide* has been published.

[10] Robert W. Jenson offered this candid assessment of the reasons for the failure of the proposed conference: "It was undone by mainline Protestantism's present indifference to and distraction from the whole matter, by evangelicalism's unconcern about separation at the Lord's table, and by deliberate obstruction from within the established ecumenical apparatus" (Jenson, "God's Time, Our Time," 33).

[11] A pair of articles recounted the plans for a Second Conference on Faith and Order in North America, the abandonment of those plans in 2005, and the proceedings of the Graymoor consultation in which I participated in 2006: William G. Rusch, "What Are the Factors Necessary for a Conference on Faith and Order in North America?—A Report on the Graymoor Consultation," *Ecumenical Trends* 35, no. 4 (April 2006): 5/53–6/54; Jeffrey Gros, "What Are the Factors Necessary for a Conference on Faith and Order in North America?" *Ecumenical Trends* 35, no. 4 (April 2006): 7/55–9/57.

[12] See the summary of the major points of my paper presentation in Gros, "What Are the Factors Necessary for a Conference on Faith and Order in North America?" 9/57.

since I was convinced that evangelicals in general and Baptists in particular should seize what I regard as an opportune moment for wholehearted embrace of the varied instruments of the modern ecumenical movement, for their own good and for the good of the whole church—the ecumenical status quo notwithstanding.

Before outlining an evangelical perspective on why a new Faith and Order conference might be advantageous, I needed to identify the sense in which my perspective was "evangelical" and clarify the relationship of my own Baptist denominational tradition to evangelical Christianity. Almost every theologian who writes as a self-identified evangelical feels compelled to define "evangelical" as a matter of prolegomena, for "evangelical" is as broad an ecclesial category as the German usage "*Evangelische Kirche*" to designate the Protestant *Landeskirche* and as narrow a category as its frequent use by American media as a synonym for "fundamentalist." For the purposes of the consultation, I utilized as a working definition one proposed by a Baptist historian and theologian: "evangelicalism is a renewal movement within historic Christian orthodoxy" that has been shaped by "the trinitarian and christological consensus of the early church" expressed in the early ecumenical councils, "the Protestant Reformation" of the sixteenth century, the "evangelical awakenings" of the eighteenth and nineteenth centuries, and the "fundamentalist–modernist controversy" of the early twentieth century.[13] Evangelicalism thus defined is not quite as broad as "Protestantism," though it may include the majority of Protestants in North America, with the exclusion only of the continuing North American instantiations of the sort of neo-Protestantism that Karl Barth denounced as "*Kulturprotestantismus.*"[14] It is not as narrow as "fundamentalism," which is one particular type of ongoing response to the issues contested in the fundamentalist–modernist controversy; but evangelicalism thus defined does include fundamentalism—even if some self-identified fundamentalists deny that they are evangelicals. Evangelicalism is therefore a transdenominational pattern of Christian faith and practice that is widely represented within North American Protestant denominations,

---

[13] Timothy George, "The Unity of Faith: Evangelicalism and 'Mere Christianity,'" *Touchstone* 16, no. 6 (July/August 2003): 58–66.

[14] Though many associate this term with Barth, it was employed earlier as a general designation of the liberal Protestant tradition in Germany. It acquired negative overtones in its usage by the early dialectical theologians, including Barth, in their criticism of the tendency of liberal Protestantism to accommodate itself to its cultural context. See Mark D. Chapman, *Ernst Troeltsch and Liberal Theology: Religion and Cultural Synthesis in Wilhelmine Germany* (Christian Theology in Context; Oxford: Oxford University Press, 2001), 1, n. 1 and the literature cited therein.

parachurch movements, and so-called nondenominational congregations. It is a category that includes many Baptists in North America, even though some Baptists have objected to the use of "evangelical" as a descriptor of Baptists.[15] Yet Baptists, to the degree that they can be broadly described as evangelical, belong to a distinctive subcategory of "evangelical" that also includes other "Free Church"[16] or "Believers' Church"[17] traditions with origins in the Radical Reformation[18]—the traditions that James Wm. McClendon, Jr., designated as "baptist" with a lowercase "b."[19] I therefore offered my reflections as a Baptist who identifies more broadly with the lowercase-"b" baptist stream of the evangelical tradition and who has an interest in the retrieval of catholicity as the overarching ecclesial identity not only of Roman Catholic, Eastern Orthodox, and Anglican Christians but also of evangelicals—whether they be "Baptists" proper, lowercase-"b" baptists, or other Protestants who have sought renewal within their own communions and the one church to which they belong.

I argued that another Conference on Faith and Order in North America would be advantageous for evangelicals for reasons related to my hope for an evangelical retrieval of catholicity, provided that such a conference would maintain its focus on the purpose and goals already articulated in the planning documents for a second conference.[20] If its principal goal was "to call the churches to the goal of visible unity in one faith and one eucharistic fellowship, expressed in worship and in common life in Christ,"[21] then another Conference on Faith and Order would have been a call to the churches to reevaluate the extent to which their ecclesial communities currently realize catholicity as a mark of the church. This equation

---

[15] E.g., E. Glenn Hinson's contributions to James Leo Garrett, Jr., E. Glenn Hinson, and James E. Tull, *Are Southern Baptists "Evangelicals"?* (Macon, Ga.: Mercer University Press, 1983), 129–94 and 209–14. Garrett, on the other hand, contended that Southern Baptists were best understood as "denominational evangelicals" (31–127 and 195–208).

[16] Designation employed, e.g., by Franklin H. Littell, *The Anabaptist View of the Church* (Boston: Starr King, 1952), and Gunnar Westin, *The Free Church through the Ages*, trans. Virgil Olson (Nashville: Broadman Press, 1954).

[17] Designation employed, e.g., by Donald F. Durnbaugh, *The Believers' Church: The History and Character of Radical Protestantism* (New York: Macmillan, 1968), and in contributions to James Leo Garrett, Jr., ed., *The Concept of the Believers' Church: Addresses from the 1967 Louisville Conference* (Scottdale, Pa.: Herald Press, 1969).

[18] Designation employed, e.g., by George Huntston Williams, *The Radical Reformation* (Philadelphia: Westminster Press, 1962).

[19] James Wm. McClendon, Jr., *Ethics: Systematic Theology, Vol. 1*, rev. ed. (Waco, Tex.: Baylor University Press, 2012), 17–20.

[20] See *Faith and Order*, ed. Hjelm.

[21] By-laws of the Faith and Order Commission of the World Council of Churches, quoted in *Faith and Order*, ed. Hjelm, vii.

of "visible unity in one faith and eucharistic fellowship" with a mutual fuller realization of catholicity depends upon a particular understanding of what catholicity is: neither as imprecise as a "diffuse inclusivism"[22] nor as restrictive as its application to the churches in full communion with the Roman See, but the qualitative catholicity defined in the previous chapter of this book and elaborated in chapter 5.[23] Catholicity in this sense is a fullness of faith and order that is visibly expressed in one eucharistic fellowship.

Embracing Faith and Order

A Second Conference on Faith and Order in North America may be a dream deferred,[24] but other forms of ecumenical engagement can realize its potential for summoning the churches to a reclaimed catholic identity that reorients them to the ecumenical future. Embracing the multifaceted ecumenical movement through participation in councils of churches, bilateral and multilateral dialogues and their reception, "receptive ecumenism"[25] in its varied expressions, cooperative mission endeavors, and practices of "spiritual ecumenism" such as praying for the unity of the church[26] can have the same effect, provided they are seen as means toward the end of moving beyond the church's current disunity in faith and order.[27] The

---

[22]   A sense critiqued by Daniel H. Williams, "The Disintegration of Catholicism into Diffuse Inclusivism," *Pro Ecclesia* 12, no. 4 (Fall 2003): 389–93.

[23]   On the distinction between "quantitative" and "qualitative" catholicity, see Yves Congar, *Chrétiens désunis: Principes d'un "oecuménisme" catholique* (Unum Sanctam, no. 1; Paris: Éditions du Cerf, 1937), 115–17; ET, *Divided Christendom: A Catholic Study of the Problem of Reunion*, trans. M. A. Bousfield (London: Geoffrey Bles/Centenary, 1939), 93–94.

[24]   It should be noted that a commemorative conference was in fact held at Oberlin College in July 2007, somewhat more limited in scope and under the direct sponsorship of the Faith and Order Commission of the National Council of the Churches of Christ in the USA, with approximately three hundred participants. The proceedings are summarized by Joseph A. Loya and Julia Sheetz-Willard, " 'On Being Christian Together': U.S. Faith and Order Commission Celebrates 50 Years—Oberlin College, July 19–23, 2007," *Journal of Ecumenical Studies* 42, no. 3 (Summer 2007): 463–68; selected plenary presentations from that conference were published in *Journal of Ecumenical Studies* 42, no. 4 (Fall 2007): 497–570.

[25]   See chapter 6 for a discussion of "receptive ecumenism" as a paradigm for ecumenical convergence and its potential for relating the Baptist vision to the ecumenical future.

[26]   See chapter 10.

[27]   Lindbeck, "Unity We Seek," 28–31, has called attention to a set of conflicting visions within the ecumenical movement in terms of how attention to issues of Faith and Order should relate to other expressions of ecumenism. As Lindbeck sees it, one faction, exemplified by Michael Kinnamon, *The Vision of the Ecumenical Movement and How It Has Been*

assertions I made at the Graymoor consultation regarding the necessity of Faith and Order ecumenical engagement for evangelicals in general apply also to Baptists in particular. They are doubtless applicable to other communions, *mutatis mutandis.*

Diagnosing Baptist Deficiencies in Catholicity

Embracing Faith and Order ecumenical engagement is imperative for Baptists first because the Faith and Order quest for a shared qualitative catholicity would reveal the extent to which Baptists are currently insufficiently catholic. This claim is not intended to suggest that Baptist communities lack catholicity in the sense according to which the heretical and schismatic groups of the patristic period were not catholic. Baptist churches do belong to the one, holy, catholic, and apostolic church, and they can be considered catholic without resorting to the reduction of catholicity to something primarily invisible and deferred in its visible realization until the eschaton. Their gathering church ecclesiology is consistent with Ignatius of Antioch's

---

Impoverished by Its Friends (St. Louis: Chalice Press, 2003), sees the Life and Work emphasis on cooperation in seeking God's justice for the world and the Faith and Order emphasis on convergence toward visible ecclesial unity as "co-equal ends in themselves." The other faction, exemplified by the Princeton Proposal for Christian Unity (Braaten and Jenson, eds., *In One Body through the Cross*), contends that although the Life and Work concern for cooperative justice is indispensable, it must be properly related to the primacy of Faith and Order—which, it is argued, has lately been marginalized in the ecumenical movement. Yet both paradigms agree that the unity of the church is an end in itself and that the theological basis of such unity is God's action in Christ for the world's salvation. Kinnamon, in response, has construed the split differently in his more recent book *Can a Renewal Movement Be Renewed? Questions for the Future of Ecumenism* (Grand Rapids: William B. Eerdmans, 2014), 150–51. Some prioritize justice and see visible unity as an impediment to achieving it, and some fear that the ecumenical pursuit of justice has "politicized" the ecumenical movement to the point that progress on Faith and Order is made much more difficult. But both parties weaken the ecumenical movement if they shun the integration of the impulses for justice and unity that Kinnamon commends. As he notes in a chapter on environmental protection as a proper locus of ecumenical cooperation (46–55), not everyone can be fully involved in all expressions of the multifaceted ecumenical movement (53). Yet all expressions of the quest for Christian unity should be viewed by everyone as inseparable. Kinnamon's call for the integration of unity and justice does not in my judgment so much make them co-equal ends as coinherent expressions of the singular end of the church's unity. The coinherence of Faith and Order with Life and Work (as well as mission and evangelism and other expressions of the quest for a visibly united church) is what must be maintained. But if a choice must be made as to which stream of the ecumenical movement must be given priority, I concur with the signatories of the Princeton Proposal that it must be Faith and Order. Otherwise, the church's endeavors to participate in God's mission in the world and seek God's justice in it will remain attenuated in proportion to its lack of visible unity in matters of faith and order.

insistence that "wherever Jesus Christ is, there is the catholic church."[28]
The Baptist churches are catholic inasmuch as they have one Lord Jesus
Christ and share in one Holy Spirit. Thus they do have a christological
and pneumatological participation in the quantitative catholicity of the
church. But just as life in Christ seeks "the measure of the full stature
of Christ" (Eph 4:13) and the gift of the Spirit is "the first fruits" (Rom
8:23), a "first installment" (2 Cor 1:22), and a "guarantee" (2 Cor 5:5)
pointing toward the fullness of things, so the catholicity of the church in
which Baptists already share is a beginning point in the journey toward the
ecumenical future of a fuller qualitative catholicity manifested in "visible
unity in one faith and one eucharistic fellowship, expressed in worship
and in common life in Christ." Nor is this claim intended to suggest that
all Baptist communities are insufficiently catholic to the same degree or
in the same ways. Some patterns of Baptist faith and practice are arguably
more qualitatively catholic than others. I nevertheless generalize in identifying five main dimensions of Baptist identity that full participation in the
ecumenical movement, especially its Faith and Order efforts, might draw
into creative tension with a qualitative catholicity: trinitarian faith, the
function of tradition in patterns of authority, the place of baptism in the
Christian life and the life of the church, eucharistic theology and practice,
and congregational *episkopē* (oversight) as a pattern of church order.

Trinity

The Trinity is the most obvious and most significant doctrinal locus of
direct Baptist continuity with the ancient catholic faith. It may therefore seem odd to suggest that trinitarian faith might be a point at which
Baptists might discover that they are insufficiently catholic through participation in Faith and Order ecumenism. Though Baptists in the main
have affirmed the Trinity as an essential doctrine of the faith, the simple
biblicism that some of them have inherited from more radicalized versions
of the *sola scriptura* hermeneutic of the Reformation has sometimes resulted
in the suspicion that the orthodox doctrine of the Trinity might be a doctrine of merely human origins rather than a truth disclosed by God's acts
of revelation to which Scripture bears witness. The road from biblical text

---

[28] Ignatius of Antioch, *Smyrneans* 8.2, in *The Apostolic Fathers*, ed. and trans. Bart D.
Ehrman (Loeb Classical Library, vol. 24; Cambridge, Mass.: Harvard University Press,
2003), 1:304–5. But as noted in the previous chapter of this book, in this text Ignatius
does qualify the christological location of the church's gathering in terms of the connection of the church to its bishop.

to theological explanation of the relationships of Father, Son, and Spirit to the oneness of God can lead to Arius, Eustathius of Sebaste, and Fausto Socinus as well as to Athanasius, Gregory of Nazianzus, and John Calvin, and this has in fact happened in Baptist history.

The biblicism of Baptists has sometimes joined forces with rationalism to make modern Baptists deeply suspicious of doctrines that seem to them to have received their formulation from a later ecclesiastical hierarchy rather than from the Bible itself. Samuel Mansell, an anti-trinitarian British Baptist pastor of the late eighteenth century, exemplified an extreme form of this tendency in his rejoinder to a trinitarian opponent: "your method is to call all who differ from you, graceless, empty fools; and men fallen into damnable errors—and declare all damned who live and die rejecting your Popish tenet of Three Co-Equal Gods in one Godhead—though you have not one line of truth in all the Bible, as your authority so saying."[29] Reflection on the history of Baptist engagement with the doctrine of the Trinity could raise the suspicion that for the most part, "Baptists are unitarians that simply have not yet gotten around to denying the Trinity."[30] There is a rich heritage of explicitly articulated formulations of trinitarian theology in confessions of faith adopted by Baptists, some of the earlier of which clearly echo Nicaeno-Constantinopolitan trinitarian and Chalcedonian christological language,[31] but this confessional inheritance has not always had an impact on the formation of Baptists in a robustly trinitarian faith. If Faith and Order ecumenism calls the churches to an explicit embrace of Nicaeno-Constantinopolitan trinitarian faith as the doctrinal core of "visible unity in one faith" and pushes the churches to re-examine the place of the Trinity in the faith and practice of their own communions and to rectify any trinitarian deficiencies they discover, then participation in it will be salutary for Baptists in particular. At no other time in the history of modern theology has so much attention been focused on trinitarian theology and its implications for ecclesial praxis as at the beginning

---

[29] Samuel Mansell, *A Second Address to Mr. Huntington* (London: J. Parsons, 1797), v–vi, cited by Curtis W. Freeman, *Contesting Catholicity: Theology for Other Baptists* (Waco, Tex.: Baylor University Press, 2014), 167–68, and idem, "God in Three Persons: Baptist Unitarianism and the Trinity," *Perspectives in Religious Studies* 33, no. 3 (Fall 2006): 335 (323–44).

[30] Freeman, *Contesting Catholicity*, 181.

[31] On this feature of Baptist confessions of faith, see Steven R. Harmon, *Towards Baptist Catholicity: Essays on Tradition and the Baptist Vision* (Studies in Baptist History and Thought, vol. 27; Milton Keynes, UK: Paternoster, 2006), 71–87; idem, "Baptist Confessions of Faith and the Patristic Tradition," *Perspectives in Religious Studies* 29, no. 4 (Winter 2002): 349–58.

of the twenty-first century,[32] and Baptist theologians have been making significant contributions to this ongoing trinitarian renascence.[33] This may be the opportune moment for reengaging the trinitarian faith at the center of a qualitative catholicity and relating it to the practices of all of our churches en route to visible unity.

[32] E.g., Sarah Coakley, *God, Sexuality, and the Self: An Essay "On the Trinity"* (Cambridge: Cambridge University Press, 2013); Colin E. Gunton, *Father, Son, and Holy Spirit: Essays toward a Truly Trinitarian Theology* (London: T&T Clark, 2003); James J. Buckley and David S. Yeago, eds., *Knowing the Triune God: The Work of the Spirit in the Practices of the Church* (Grand Rapids: William B. Eerdmans, 2001); Bruce Marshall, *Trinity and Truth* (Cambridge: Cambridge University Press, 2000); Reinhard Hütter, *Suffering Divine Things: Theology as Church Practice* (Grand Rapids: William B. Eerdmans, 2000). Notable constructive trinitarian theologies in the decade before the turn of the twenty-first century include Catherine Mowry LaCugna, *God for Us: The Trinity and Christian Life* (San Francisco: HarperSanFrancisco, 1991); Robert Jenson, *Systematic Theology*, vol. 1, *The Triune God* (New York: Oxford University Press, 1997); David S. Cunningham, *And These Three Are One: The Practice of Trinitarian Theology* (Cambridge: Cambridge University Press, 1998); Miroslav Volf, *After Our Likeness: The Church as the Image of the Trinity* (Sacra Doctrina: Christian Theology for a Postmodern Age; Grand Rapids: William B. Eerdmans, 1998). These more recent projects build on the influential trinitarian works of the 1980s, which in turn continued in diverse ways a trajectory rooted in the Western recoveries of the centrality of the doctrine of the Trinity to Christian theology by Karl Barth (*Church Dogmatics*, 4 vols./13 parts, trans. Geoffrey W. Bromiley et al. [Edinburgh: T&T Clark, 1956–1975]) and Karl Rahner (*The Trinity*, trans. Joseph Donceel [New York: Herder & Herder, 1970]): notably Jürgen Moltmann, *The Trinity and the Kingdom: The Doctrine of God*, trans. Margaret Kohl (San Francisco: Harper & Row, 1981); Yves Congar, *I Believe in the Holy Spirit*, 3 vols., trans. David Smith (New York: Seabury Press, 1983); Walter Kasper, *The God of Jesus Christ*, trans. Matthew J. O'Connell (New York: Crossroad, 1984); John D. Zizioulas, *Being as Communion: Studies in Personhood and Church* (Contemporary Greek Theologians, no. 4; Crestwood, N.Y.: St. Vladimir's Seminary Press, 1985); Leonardo Boff, *Trinity and Society*, trans. Paul Burns (Theology and Liberation Series; Maryknoll, N.Y.: Orbis Books, 1988). The treatment of the doctrine of the Trinity in the first volume of Wolfhart Pannenberg's *Systematic Theology*, published in 1988 in German and in 1991 in English translation, functions as a bridge between the groundbreaking trinitarian work of the 1980s and its consolidation and extension in the following decade (Wolfhart Pannenberg, *Systematic Theology*, vol. 1, trans. Geoffrey W. Bromiley [Grand Rapids: William B. Eerdmans, 1991]).

[33] E.g., Paul S. Fiddes, *Participating in God: A Pastoral Doctrine of the Trinity* (Louisville, Ky.: Westminster John Knox, 2000); Stanley J. Grenz, *The Social God and the Relational Self: A Trinitarian Theology of the Imago Dei* (Louisville, Ky.: Westminster John Knox, 2001); idem, *Rediscovering the Triune God: The Trinity in Contemporary Theology* (Minneapolis: Fortress Press, 2004); idem, *The Named God and the Question of Being: A Trinitarian Theo-ontology* (Louisville, Ky.: Westminster John Knox, 2005); Myk Habets, *The Anointed Son: A Trinitarian Spirit Christology* (Princeton Theological Monograph Series, vol. 129; Eugene, Ore.: Pickwick, 2010); Stephen R. Holmes, *The Holy Trinity: Understanding God's Life* (Milton Keynes, UK: Paternoster, 2011); idem, *The Quest for the Trinity: The Doctrine of God in Scripture, History and Modernity* (Downers Grove, Ill.: IVP Academic, 2012).

Tradition

At the root of occasional ambivalence regarding the doctrine of the Trinity among Baptists is the disparity between their profession of *sola scriptura* and the reality of their hermeneutical practice in which Scripture is indeed being interpreted through lenses supplied by sources of authority beyond the Bible alone, even if unconsciously so. This is evident in both major types of confessional families that emerged from the Reformation. The churches of the Magisterial Reformation proclaimed a *sola scriptura* theological hermeneutic, but their hermeneutical practice is more accurately described as *suprema scriptura*: Scripture is the preeminent source of authority, but the traditional doctrinal formulations of the first four ecumenical councils, for example, possess a certain authoritative status in that they are faithful interpretations of the teachings of Scripture that supply helpful clarifications of their significance.[34] For these Reformers, *sola scriptura* was not the answer to the unqualified question "What is the source of authority for the faith and practice of the church?" Rather, the term answered to the narrower question "What is the normative source of authority in the church that norms all other sources to which the church may turn for the authorizing of its faith and practice?" Scripture is thus *sola* not in the sense of being the sole norm, but the *norma normans non normata*—the norm that norms all other norms but is not itself normed by anything else.[35] The churches of the Radical Reformation came closer to exemplifying a pure *sola scriptura* hermeneutic, but even they found it necessary to

[34] James Leo Garrett, Jr., *Systematic Theology: Biblical, Historical, and Evangelical*, vol. 1 (Grand Rapids: William B. Eerdmans, 1990), 181, suggested the terminology *suprema scriptura* to describe a pattern of authority in which Scripture is the supreme source of authority but not the only source of authority to which the church turns for the authorization of its faith and practice. Garrett's application of this term to Baptist patterns of authority and the recognition of Garrett's contribution by the reports from international bilateral ecumenical dialogues between the Baptist World Alliance and the Anglican Communion (2000–2005) and the Catholic Church (2006–2010) are discussed more fully in a note in chapter 3.

[35] Within the Lutheran tradition of a *sola scriptura* theological hermeneutic, Robert Jenson helpfully explains its import in relation to other sources of authority: "*once a canon of Scripture is in place*, it has authority also over against any particular dogmatic proposal, magisterial *responsum,* or apparently mandatory liturgical order, if our perplexity becomes so extreme as to need such authority. That is, canonical Scripture is—in the language of the Reformation—the *norma normans non normata*, the norm with no norm over it, although other norms establish it in this position and, as we will see, are necessary to its function in it" (Jenson, *Systematic Theology*, 1:26).

adopt confessions of faith,[36] and the echoes of patristic doctrinal formulations in their confessions of faith demonstrate that they could not easily dispense with the traditional lenses through which the church in its catholicity read the Scriptures.[37] Yet as the doctrine of the Trinity illustrates, not all theological concepts indispensable for classical Christian theology are self-evidently scriptural.[38] Along the road from the Bible to doctrine, one encounters multiple "Y"-intersections, and without the road map provided by Nicaeno-Constantinopolitan tradition one can all too easily choose the lane that leads to Arianism rather than catholic trinitarian faith.

The Baptist tradition has had a "tradition of rejecting tradition"[39] that has tended both to distance Baptists from the qualitative dimensions of

---

[36] See Howard John Loewen, *One Lord, One Church, One Hope, and One God: Mennonite Confessions of Faith in North America. An Introduction* (Elkhart, Ind.: Institute of Mennonite Studies, 1985).

[37] A. James Reimer, "Trinitarian Orthodoxy, Constantinianism, and Theology from a Radical Protestant Perspective," in *Faith to Creed: Ecumenical Perspectives on the Affirmation of the Apostolic Faith in the Fourth Century. Papers of the Faith to Creed Consultation, Commission on Faith and Order, NCCCUSA, October 25–27, 1989, Waltham, Massachusetts*, ed. S. Mark Heim (Grand Rapids: William B. Eerdmans, 1991), 147 (129–61), notes, "The 1985 publication of Howard Loewen's *One Lord, One Church, One Hope, and One God* has contributed significantly to this renaissance of interest in the fourth- and fifth-century theological formulations. Loewen's study suddenly brought to the attention of Mennonite readers, who had presumed that Mennonites like other radical protestant groups were noncredal, that the various Mennonite groups have produced probably more confessions in their 465 years than any other Christian tradition. Many of these confessions, in their general structure (theology, Christology, ecclesiology, eschatology) bear some remarkable similarities in their organization to classical creeds."

[38] George A. Lindbeck, *The Nature of Doctrine: Religion and Theology in a Postliberal Age* (Louisville, Ky.: Westminster John Knox, 1984), 74, observes that "most biblicistic Protestants . . . adhere in practice to postbiblical trinitarianism: they do not deny what the Nicene Creed teaches, but they ignore the creed itself and act as if its teachings were self-evidently Scriptural." Elsewhere Lindbeck describes this tendency more positively as a phenomenon with ecumenical possibilities: "It is among Evangelicals, Pentecostals, Roman Catholics, and the Orthodox, polar opposites though they seem, that there is a measure of agreement on where and how the apostolic tradition is to be located and retrieved. They do not find it necessary to invent a special 'ecumenical hermeneutic' in order to legitimate their search for the tradition in Scripture, under the guidance of the affirmations regarding God the Father, Son, and Holy Spirit confessed, for example, in the Nicene Creed. Even professedly creedless Evangelicals and Pentecostals do not deny the Trinity nor that Jesus Christ is true God and true man. Without ever having heard of the catholic creeds in many cases, Evangelicals and Pentecostals seek to read their Bibles in accordance with them, which makes theological convergence possible" (Lindbeck, "Ecumenisms in Conflict," 227–28).

[39] Language employed by Philip E. Thompson, "Re-envisioning Baptist Identity: Historical, Theological, and Liturgical Analysis," *Perspectives in Religious Studies* 27, no. 3 (Fall 2000): 302 (287–302).

catholicity and to make them extremely susceptible to the internal denominational divisions that have greatly complicated the ecumenical quest for visible unity. For many contemporary Baptists in the United States, the slogan "no creed but the Bible"—which some Baptists have appropriated from the Stone–Campbell "Restoration" movement[40]—expresses what these Baptists hold as an essential principle of Baptist theology: the Bible is the only sufficient rule for faith and practice, and therefore any postbiblical theological development is superfluous, is theologically suspect, and possesses no authority for Christians today. As Baptists in North America came to grips with modernity, the consciously negative stance toward tradition represented by such slogans as "no creed but the Bible" served well the theological agenda of both fundamentalism and liberalism. By appealing to the text of a Bible they regarded as inerrant, Baptist fundamentalists could argue that the traditions of Rome on the one hand and the innovations of the unbelieving liberals on the other hand were corruptions of biblical faith. The use of historical-critical methods of interpretation made Baptists of more liberal inclinations better able to distinguish between what the biblical texts in their original contexts actually said and what had become traditional Baptist assumptions about how those texts should be interpreted. But without a place for postbiblical tradition in their hermeneutic, they were theoretically free to jettison any or all traditional

---

[40] The slogan "no creed but the Bible" is actually not indigenous to the Baptist movement proper but rather seems to have originated in the Restorationist movement led by Barton W. Stone, Walter Scott, and Thomas and Alexander Campbell—which, it should be noted, belongs to the lowercase "b" baptist tradition so designated by McClendon; a variant slogan, "no creed but Christ," emerged later in the movement. See M. Eugene Boring, *Disciples and the Bible: A History of Disciples Biblical Interpretation in North America* (St. Louis: Chalice Press, 1997), 18; William Tabbernee, "Unfencing the Table: Creeds, Councils, Communion, and the Campbells," *Mid-Stream* 35, no. 6 (1966): 417–32; and William Tabbernee, "Alexander Campbell and the Apostolic Tradition," in *The Free Church and the Early Church: Bridging the Historical and Theological Divide*, ed. Daniel H. Williams (Grand Rapids: William B. Eerdmans, 2002), 163–80. In the latter essay, Tabbernee points to evidence that Alexander Campbell's aversion was not to patristic creeds properly utilized, but rather to the inappropriate use of post-Reformation confessions to exclude people from the fellowship of the church, and Campbell in fact frequently referenced the ancient creeds in order to defend orthodox trinitarian and christological positions. By the time of the formation of the Southern Baptist Convention in 1845, the slogan "no creed but the Bible" had become such a common axiom in Baptist circles that founding president W. B. Johnson could declare, "We have constructed for our basis no new creed; acting in this manner upon a Baptist aversion to all creeds but the Bible" ("The Southern Baptist Convention, To the Brethren in the United States; To the Congregations Connected with the Respective Churches; and to All Candid Men," in *Proceedings of the Southern Baptist Convention in Augusta, Georgia, 8–12 May 1845* [Richmond: H. K. Ellyson, 1845], 17–20).

interpretations of Scripture while remaining true to their allegiance to "no creed but the Bible."[41]

As a call to "visible unity in one faith," attention to the Faith and Order stream of the ecumenical movement would remind the churches that the "one faith" has an identifiable traditional shape and thus would pose a challenge to a-traditional expressions of Baptist ecclesial life, perhaps leading Baptists to rethink the relationship between the larger Christian tradition and their own patterns of faith and practice. Inasmuch as such a reconsideration of tradition could play a role in addressing the intradenominational rifts that may be even more serious obstacles to visible unity than the divisions between the denominations, Baptists along with all Christian communions would profit from the attention that an engagement with the ecumenical movement's concern for unity in faith and order would focus on the proper place of tradition in patterns of Christian authority.[42] At the same time, within the larger Christian tradition Baptists have historically occupied a place of dissent, an ecclesial location that has shaped one of the distinctive gifts Baptists have to offer the rest of the church: the "pilgrim church" stance toward the traditional faith and order of the church that will be explored more fully in chapter 9 of this book.

Baptism

Though North American evangelicals differ among themselves in their theologies and practices of baptism, in the interest of evangelical unity they have tended to regard these differences as adiaphora (things neither specified nor prohibited by Scripture), as long as baptism is at some point joined with personal faith (prebaptismal faith in the case of the "Believers'

---

[41] Baptist ethicist David Gushee has argued that as a result of the lack of a place for the broad, stabilizing catholic tradition in the Southern Baptist episodes of the twentieth-century polarization of Protestant denominations in North America, "neither the conservatives nor the moderates were generally well-informed or deeply rooted in the broader tradition of the church, a tradition which might have shown us how to draw the right kinds of boundaries. Thus the conservatives (in the name of the Bible) sometimes attacked what did not deserve to be attacked, while the moderates (in the name of freedom) sometimes defended what did not deserve to be defended. How desperately we needed at that time the perspective that could have been offered by the wisdom of the Christian tradition in its broadest and richest formulations" (David P. Gushee, "Integrating Faith and Learning in an Ecumenical Context," in *The Future of Baptist Higher Education*, ed. Donald Schmeltekopf and Dianna Vitanza [Waco, Tex.: Baylor University Press, 2006], 47–48 [25–51]).

[42] Chapter 9 in part explores the attention given to the question of the authority of tradition in international bilateral dialogues with Baptist participation.

Church" evangelical communions, postbaptismal faith in the case of pedobaptist evangelical traditions—which may also point to the faith of the believing community that participates in the baptism of an infant and subsequently nurtures the baptized toward an eventual personal embrace of that faith). This refusal to make baptism a matter of evangelical contention is both promising and paralyzing for evangelical involvement in an ecumenical quest for unity in faith and church order. Evangelical flexibility on baptism is promising from the standpoint of Faith and Order ecumenism, in that evangelicals constitute the stream of the Christian tradition that in theory might be the most likely to receive the pattern of baptismal convergence commended by *BEM*, even if evangelicals have heretofore given insufficient attention to the reception of the Lima document. On the other hand, some evangelicals may not see the point of investing in Faith and Order deliberations over baptism, inasmuch as they have already relativized the importance of baptismal theology and practice. This relativizing of baptism is largely due to the evangelical emphasis on conversion[43]—as long as there has been a personal embrace of Christian faith, some evangelicals may consider baptism relatively unimportant. Sometimes this unfortunately gives the impression that baptism is an optional "extra" that contributes little or nothing to one's experience of conversion beyond what has already happened in the transaction of personal commitment.[44]

Both promise and peril for advances toward baptismal unity are likewise found in the relationship of baptism to church membership in contemporary Baptist churches. Some Baptist congregations have an "open membership" policy with reference to the order and mode of one's baptism in a non-Baptist communion. While such policies might initially seem to hold forth much ecumenical promise, inasmuch as they do not require a candidate for membership in a Baptist congregation who has already been baptized as an infant in another communion to be rebaptized as a condition for membership, they may actually create more serious ecumenical difficulties by implicitly disregarding the importance of baptism: these policies are usually worded so as to make a profession of personal

---

[43] See David W. Bebbington, *Evangelicalism in Modern Britain: A History from the 1730s to the 1980s* (London: Routledge, 1989), 5–10. Bebbington identifies "conversionism" as one of four defining marks of evangelicalism, along with activism, biblicism, and crucicentrism. This influential definition of evangelicalism is frequently referred to as the "Bebbington Quadrilateral."

[44] For a description and critique of this tendency in Free Church evangelicalism, see Melanie Ross, "Dunking Doughnuts? Rethinking Free Church Baptismal Theology," *Pro Ecclesia* 14, no. 4 (Fall 2005): 433–46.

faith the primary criterion for membership, with no explicit affirmation of the candidate's previous baptism. To accept a candidate for membership in a Baptist congregation who was baptized as an infant in another Christian communion on the basis of his or her profession of Christian faith alone while shrinking from affirming the validity of that baptism is to imply that baptism is not a condition for church membership at all.[45] On the other hand, many Baptist congregations would require the rebaptism of a candidate for membership who had been baptized as an infant (though such congregations might not consider it a rebaptism on the grounds that they regard infant baptism, or any baptism that preceded personal faith, as no baptism at all; these are sometimes called "closed membership" congregations). Both "open membership" and "closed membership" Baptist congregations need to rethink their theologies and practices of baptism and their relationship to church membership from an ecumenical perspective. Full engagement with the agenda of Faith and Order ecumenism might help these Baptist communities to reflect on the catholicity of these theologies and practices by calling them to consider, perhaps for the first time, the rationales and recommendations for mutual baptismal recognition that have emerged from the multilateral contestation of this aspect of church order.

The present ecumenical moment may be the most opportune time for Baptists to engage the church's historic and current disagreements over baptismal theology and practice, for it can be argued that the church as a whole has never been more appreciatively receptive than it is now to the distinctive gifts that Baptists (and baptists) have to offer the whole church in connection with the practice that gives their communities the name by which they are known. In December 2008 the delegations to the second series of international conversations between the Baptist World Alliance and the Catholic Church (2006–2010) were hosted by the Baptist House of Studies at Duke University Divinity School in Durham, North Carolina. There veteran Methodist ecumenist Geoffrey Wainwright, who taught theology at Duke from 1983 until 2012, shared with us his perspectives on the progress and challenges of the modern ecumenical movement in light of his significant involvement in it, which has included serving as a member of the Faith and Order Commission of the World Council of Churches (1976–1991) and as chair of the editorial committee that drafted the final

---

[45]   John E. Colwell, *Promise and Presence: An Exploration of Sacramental Theology* (Milton Keynes, UK: Paternoster, 2006), 109–34, provides a thorough treatment of these issues that addresses some problematic ecclesiological implications of "open membership" policies in churches of the Baptist Union of Great Britain.

version of the widely acclaimed convergence text *Baptism, Eucharist and Ministry* (1982), as well as co-chairing the joint commission for the ongoing dialogues between the World Methodist Council and the Catholic Church since 1986. Members of both the Baptist and Catholic delegations to our conversations were taken aback by his opening observation: "As far as the issue of baptism goes, the Baptists have won."

Wainwright was referring to the current ecumenical consensus that believer's baptism by immersion is the normative biblical practice from which the practice of infant baptism derives its significance. *BEM* insists that "baptism upon personal profession of faith is the most clearly attested pattern in the New Testament documents."[46] Many Baptists would be surprised to learn that the *Catechism of the Catholic Church* now regards immersion as the mode most theologically expressive of the significance of baptism and insists that those baptized as infants must go on to have personal experience of God's grace.[47] The wildest hopes of the seventeenth-century Baptists could not have imagined the degree to which much of the church today has converged toward important aspects of their historic dissent from the majority of the Christian tradition.

The recent WCC study text *One Baptism: Towards Mutual Recognition* stands in continuity with these encouraging ecumenical developments, and constructive engagement with it is an excellent way for Baptist communities to begin seizing the ecumenical moment.[48] Baptists will be able to recognize themselves in its pages. It recognizes the concerns that churches that baptize only believers have about the adequacy of infant baptism as a disciple-making practice, and it asks infant-baptizing churches to consider how their communities might more intentionally help those baptized as infants become committed disciples. *One Baptism* also cites the report from the dialogue between the Baptist World Alliance and the World Alliance of Reformed Churches (1974–1977) as a helpful exploration of the relationship between divine and human action in baptism.[49] Baptists will

---

[46] World Council of Churches, *Baptism, Eucharist and Ministry*, IV.A.11 (p. 4). *BEM* also states, "The necessity of faith for the reception of the salvation embodied and set forth in baptism is acknowledged by all churches. Personal commitment is necessary for responsible membership in the body of Christ" (III.8, p. 3).

[47] Catholic Church, *Catechism of the Catholic Church* (Liguori, Mo.: Liguori, 1994), §§1214, 1231, 1239 (pp. 312, 316–17).

[48] World Council of Churches, *One Baptism: Towards Mutual Recognition. A Study Text* (Faith and Order Paper no. 210; Geneva: World Council of Churches, 2011).

[49] World Council of Churches, *One Baptism*, IV.B.71 (p. 13, n. 35); Baptist World Alliance and World Alliance of Reformed Churches, "Report of Theological Conversations Sponsored by the World Alliance of Reformed Churches and the Baptist World

also appreciate the rich engagement of Scripture throughout the document. The fathers and mothers of the church from the formative centuries of Christian history after the New Testament era are also the common heritage of the whole church and could have been cited in this connection, but instead *One Baptism* is rigorously biblical in its appeal to authoritative texts.[50]

One Baptism also poses hard questions to Baptists regarding their recognition of the baptisms of other churches. Many Baptist churches have required candidates for church membership who were baptized as infants but now testify to personal faith in Christ to be rebaptized, inasmuch as personal faith precedes baptism in the New Testament pattern. By shifting the emphasis from chronological orderings of faith, baptism, and formation in faith to the whole journey of the Christian experience in the company of the church, *One Baptism* offers a way for Baptists to discern in other patterns of baptismal practice comparable journeys of Christian experience, even while Baptist churches continue the internal practice of baptizing only believers as a witness and gift to the rest of the church.[51] On the question of rebaptism, *One Baptism* calls churches that require those previously baptized as infants to be rebaptized as a condition of membership, and churches that require the same of those previously baptized as believing adults but in a church of differing faith and order, to reflect on the implications of those requirements.[52] The document fails, however, to address a variation of the latter scenario with which many Baptist congregations must deal: members of Baptist churches who were baptized as believers, but at rather young ages, who later in life question whether they really understood the commitment they were making and now wish to be baptized following their more mature embrace of faith. Baptists may nonetheless find help in *One Baptism* for addressing such cases pastorally, for both the steps toward faith taken by young children who are then baptized and the mature faith of adults can be related to the baptism near the beginning of their journeys, which need not be repeated.[53]

Alliance, 1977," in *Growth in Agreement: Reports and Agreed Statements of Ecumenical Conversations on a World Level*, ed. Harding Meyer and Lukas Vischer (Faith and Order Paper no. 108; New York: Paulist Press/Geneva: World Council of Churches, 1984), §§14 and 21 (pp. 141 and 145 [132–51]).

[50] See in particular Section II, "Baptism: Symbol and Pattern of the New Life in Christ" (World Council of Churches, *One Baptism*, §§16–55 [pp. 5–11]).

[51] World Council of Churches, *One Baptism*, §§41–55, 83 (pp. 9–11, 16–16).

[52] World Council of Churches, *One Baptism*, §§93–95 (p. 18).

[53] *One Baptism* does address something of a parallel situation in infant-baptizing communities: "In still another case persons baptized as infants, and wishing to remain in their

Like many documents produced by multilateral dialogue, *One Baptism* is a study text, and its reception in the churches accordingly begins with its study.[54] Some Baptist churches are struggling with debates over whether church membership policies should be revised so that candidates who were baptized as infants in other churches but now profess personal faith in Christ may be admitted to full membership without rebaptism. Careful study of *One Baptism* will help everyone involved in such deliberations think through the implications of their decisions about this matter for their stances on the legitimacy of non-Baptist churches and their members' faith. Whether all Baptists find agreement with it or not, the study of *One Baptism* by Baptist ministers, laypersons, and whole congregations will yield a greatly enriched Baptist theology of baptism and potentially a more powerful baptismal practice.[55]

Biblical and historical scholarship and ecumenical theological work have now made it possible for *BEM, One Baptism*, and the reports from various bilateral dialogues to conceive of a qualitative baptismal catholicity that encompasses both believer's baptism as a paradigm for Christian initiation appropriate to the ecclesial context reflected in the New Testament and appropriate to the experience of adult converts to Christian faith today, and infant baptism as a paradigm for Christian initiation appropriate to the more established ecclesial context reflected in later patristic Christianity and appropriate to the contemporary experience of children raised in the church by Christian parents, yet which does not call for churches in the Believers' Church tradition to begin baptizing infants.[56] The potential

---

present church, seek rebaptism in order to 'experience' the baptism they do not remember from their infancy. . . . Recognizing the unique and repeatable character of baptism, and for the sake of the unity of the church, pastors should not assent to requests for rebaptism. With this in mind, the following question is asked: How can your church help such persons to find ways in which they may experience a renewal of their baptismal faith?" (World Council of Churches, *One Baptism*, §95 [p. 18]).

[54] Ecumenical reception as an ecumenical practice is addressed in chapter 10 of this book. A section of that chapter proposes concrete ways in which Baptists may engage in reception of the proposals of both multilateral convergence documents and study texts and the reports from bilateral dialogues.

[55] See Steven R. Harmon, "'One Baptism': A Study Text for Baptists," *Baptist World: A Magazine of the Baptist World Alliance* 58, no. 1 (January/March 2011): 9–10.

[56] Most if not all pedobaptist communions, including the Roman Catholic Church, have a rite for the initiation of adult converts that corresponds to the practice of believer's baptism (e.g., Catholic Church, *Rite of Christian Initiation of Adults* [Washington, D.C.: United States Catholic Conference, 1988]), and many churches that reject infant baptism nevertheless have a rite that recognizes the beginning of an infant's life in the fellowship of the church such as an "infant dedication" service (the best examples of which also include acts of parental and congregational commitment).

for this sort of convergence in baptismal catholicity is already present in Baptist life, and Baptists have important contributions to make to the ecumenical recognition of "one baptism" by participating in various expressions of Faith and Order ecumenism.[57]

Eucharist

While the Baptist tradition has typically espoused a reductionistic version of Zwinglian symbolic memorialism in its theology of the Lord's Supper, the qualitative catholicity requisite for "visible unity . . . in one eucharistic fellowship" will entail an ecumenical retrieval of the patristic eucharistic theology of real presence. As chapter 5 of this book will demonstrate, this theology was not a later corruption of the New Testament's portrayal of the celebration of communion in the primitive church: real presence is already explicit in Ignatius of Antioch, and it is clearly implicit in the Gospel of John. Protestantism, including expressions of Protestantism that identify themselves as "evangelical," encompasses a broad spectrum of eucharistic theologies from the "merely symbolic" to affirmations of real presence that stop short of transubstantiation. Baptists, especially in the United States, usually represent the "merely symbolic" pole among Protestant perspectives on the Eucharist.[58] Yet there is a growing recognition on the part of Baptist historians and theologians that this truncated understanding of the Supper has not always been the perspective of all Baptists and that it is not contrary to Baptist identity to seek a more catholic theology of the Eucharist for Baptist communities. Prior to Baptist reactions against the Oxford Movement in the nineteenth century, Baptist confessions of faith

---

[57]　Two international bilateral dialogues with Baptist participation have given significant attention to the possibilities for mutual recognition of baptism when baptism is placed in the context of whole journeys of Christian initiation and life-long growth in Christ in which common essentials may be discerned: Anglican Consultative Council and Baptist World Alliance, *Conversations around the World 2000–2005: The Report of the International Conversations between the Anglican Communion and the Baptist World Alliance* (London: Anglican Communion Office, 2005), §§40–52 (pp. 44–51), and Baptist World Alliance and Catholic Church, "The Word of God in the Life of the Church: A Report of International Conversations between the Catholic Church and the Baptist World Alliance 2006–2010," §§101–6 (published in *American Baptist Quarterly* 31, no. 1 [Spring 2012]: 69–72 [28–122]).

[58]　This perspective among Southern Baptists is exemplified by Herschel H. Hobbs, *The Baptist Faith and Message* (Nashville: Convention Press, 1971), 88–90: "Baptists believe that the elements merely symbolize the body and blood of Jesus, with no saving effect in partaking of them. . . . So the elements are merely symbols of his body and blood."

routinely called the Supper a "sacrament,"[59] and in the twentieth century many British Baptists have recovered a more sacramental understanding not only of baptism[60] but also of the Eucharist.[61] Funded by the sacramental possibilities of earlier Baptist patterns of faith and practice and fueled by a more acute consciousness of the ecumenical imperative than has characterized Baptist thought heretofore, some among a younger generation of Baptist theologians are now urging Baptists to understand the Eucharist in terms of real presence.[62] These theologians face an uphill battle, but the challenge of Faith and Order ecumenism to the churches to take steps toward "one eucharistic fellowship" may lead other Baptists to give more serious consideration to the possibility of a more thoroughly sacramental account of Baptist faith and practice.

Baptists in North America came of age at a time when the reigning set of polarities within Christianity was "liberalism" and "fundamentalism." That set of polarities belonged to an era when Enlightenment epistemologies dominated the Western intellectual tradition, and their perpetuation in current intradenominational divisions has obscured the existence of a much more enduring set of polarities. The history of Christianity has known two primary patterns of conceiving of God's relationship to the world and of ordering Christian faith and practice in light of this conception: catholic sacramental Christianity and Christian expressions of Gnosticism. Within the Christian tradition are various places on a continuum

[59]   E.g., the 1678 General Baptist confession *The Orthodox Creed*, which refers to baptism and the Lord's Supper as "the two sacraments" in article 27 (*Baptist Confessions of Faith*, 2nd rev. ed., ed. William L. Lumpkin, rev. Bill J. Leonard [Valley Forge, Pa.: Judson Press, 2011], 325).

[60]   Stanley K. Fowler, *More Than a Symbol: The British Baptist Recovery of Baptismal Sacramentalism* (Studies in Baptist History and Thought, vol. 2; Carlisle, UK: Paternoster, 2002); Anthony R. Cross, *Recovering the Evangelical Sacrament: Baptisma Semper Reformandum* (Eugene, Ore.: Pickwick, 2013); idem, *Baptism and the Baptists: Theology and Practice in Twentieth-Century Britain* (Paternoster Biblical and Theological Monographs; Carlisle, UK: Paternoster, 2000).

[61]   Anthony R. Cross, "The Myth of English Baptist Anti-Sacramentalism," in *Recycling the Past or Researching History? Studies in Baptist Historiography and Myths*, ed. Philip E. Thompson and Anthony R. Cross (Studies in Baptist History and Thought, vol. 11; Milton Keynes, UK: Paternoster, 2005), 128–62, treats the recovery by British Baptists of a sacramental understanding of the Eucharist as well as baptism, along with sacramental precedents in the period of Baptist origins.

[62]   See especially the following two essays published in Anthony R. Cross and Philip E. Thompson, eds., *Baptist Sacramentalism* (Studies in Baptist History and Thought, vol. 5; Carlisle, UK: Paternoster, 2003): Curtis W. Freeman, " 'To Feed upon by Faith': Nourishment from the Lord's Table" (chap. 11, pp. 194–210) and Elizabeth Newman, "The Lord's Supper: Might Baptists Accept a Theory of Real Presence?" (chap. 12, pp. 211–27).

between these two primary patterns with varying degrees of proximity to one pole or another. But the extent to which a particular Christian tradition is nonsacramental is the extent to which that tradition tends toward aspects of Gnosticism in the way it conceives of God's relationship to the world and orders its faith and practice accordingly. Baptists have sometimes tended toward the Gnostic pole of that continuum. A deeper Baptist engagement with Faith and Order ecumenism might make that tendency clear to Baptists and thus help Baptists to become less Gnostic and more fully incarnational and sacramental in faith and practice.

Church Order

Owing to the transdenominational character of evangelicalism, ecclesiology has not been a major interest of many expressions of the evangelicalism I was charged with representing in my presentation to the Graymoor consultation. This is especially true of the aspect of ecclesiology that concerns the ordering of ministry within the church. A typical evangelical perspective on ecclesial order is something like the following: the New Testament does not prescribe a particular church order, but rather gives evidence of a variety of patterns of order that have been adapted to differing local needs; the differing denominational patterns of order today are rooted in different New Testament expressions of order and reflect differing adaptations of biblical patterns in various contexts; since there is no single biblical pattern of church order, and since the various patterns that characterize the churches today can all claim biblical precedent, there is no justification for making order a bone of evangelical contention. Indeed, evangelicalism already encompasses communions that adhere to forms of episcopal, presbyterial, and congregational polity. On the one hand, this evangelical ambivalence about order presents an ecumenical opportunity, for many evangelicals will be willing to recognize the legitimacy of various patterns of ordered ministry in other communions. On the other hand, this ambivalence can easily become indifference: if various models are valid, why invest in efforts to seek greater degrees of visible unity through negotiating the differences in order that currently obstruct full communion?

Many Baptists are much less inclined to regard patterns of order as adiaphora. Baptists have often been very insistent on defending congregational polity as the truly biblical pattern and have tended to view other patterns of order, especially episcopal structures, as corruptions of the pure ecclesiology of the New Testament. Yet sustained ecumenical reflection on patterns of ecclesial life will often bring to light ways in which equivalent

ministries of *episkopē* are already operative in congregational communions.[63] Movement toward catholicity in ecclesial order will involve non-
episcopal communions finding ways to recognize the legitimacy of the
historic episcopate, but it will also involve the churches of the historic
episcopate recognizing functions of the episcopal office in the order of the
non-episcopal churches. The possibility of an ecumenical convergence on
this aspect of church order is modeled by a number of Baptist congregations in northern India that have united with Anglican congregations in
a united Church of North India. These churches have been able to find
a place within an episcopal structure that allows for multiple theological
interpretations of the nature of *episkopē* and provides for the involvement
of church councils, with lay representation, in consensual governance.[64]

Baptists have distinctive contributions to make to the quest for a mutually recognized ministry, as well as much to learn from it. Embracing more
fully the Faith and Order expression of the modern ecumenical movement can facilitate such a potentially fruitful ecclesiological encounter—
provided Baptists are willing to relinquish ecclesial self-sufficiency and
make themselves vulnerable to being changed by this encounter.[65]

---

[63] Such patterns of a functional ministry of *episkopē* (which one might argue are
instances of the "locally adapted" historic episcopate specified as one of four minimal
conditions for full ecclesial communion by the Anglican "Chicago-Lambeth Quadrilateral" adopted by the Lambeth Conference in 1888) among Baptists worldwide, most
of whom formally recognize two rather than three orders of ministerial office, were
brought to light and explored during the Anglican–Baptist International Conversations
and reported in Anglican Consultative Council and Baptist World Alliance, *Conversations
around the World 2000–2005*, §§69–78 (pp. 60–64). The report from the second series of
conversations between the Baptist World Alliance and the Catholic Church also highlighted the existence of a functional ministry of oversight among Baptists in the section
"The Ministry of Oversight (*Episkope*) and Unity in the Life of the Church": Baptist
World Alliance and Catholic Church, "The Word of God in the Life of the Church,"
§§162–83 (pp. 90–98).

[64] See Anglican Consultative Council and Baptist World Alliance, *Conversations around
the World 2000–2005*, §§74–75 (pp. 63–64).

[65] Cf. Joseph D. Small, "The Travail of Faith and Order," *Pro Ecclesia* 18, no. 3 (Summer 2009): 246 (241–54): "In sum, the lack of urgent striving, or even mild enthusiasm,
for the renewal of Faith and Order in North America is due, in part, to the illusion
of ecclesial self-sufficiency, the unwillingness to acknowledge deficit, and the resulting
incapacity to repent. At its best, Faith and Order ecumenism has involved deep, honest,
mutual exploring of doctrine, liturgy, and mission; grappling with difference; experiencing challenge; and acknowledging the possibility and necessity of change. It is *this*
Faith and Order that is problematic for churches that see both themselves and others as

Baptist Openness to Catholic Retrieval

Embracing Faith and Order ecumenical engagement is imperative for Baptists sec-ond because members of Baptist communities are already increasingly manifesting a noteworthy interest in the retrieval of a qualitative catholicity. Even though many Baptist and other Free Church communities may currently be distant from a catholic fullness of faith and order in the aforementioned ways, and even though the degree to which they may be distant from catholic fullness will present challenges to the quest for visible unity in faith and order, recent movements of some Baptists toward a more consciously catholic identity suggest that this may be the opportune moment for deeper Baptist invest-ment in attention to Faith and Order endeavors.

In the past two decades, there has been an explosion of interest among evangelicals and Free Church Christians in the retrieval of various aspects of ancient catholic Christianity as an indispensable means to the renewal of their churches today, not unlike the emphasis of the *nouvelle théologie* on the *ressourcement* ("retrieval") of patristic and medieval Christianity as the prerequisite for *aggiornamento* ("updating") in the renewal of Cathol-icism in the decades leading to the Second Vatican Council.[66] Thomas Oden's anthologizing of patristic "paleo-orthodox" sources of consensual Christian perspectives on theology, pastoral care, and biblical exegesis was a significant and influential early example of this trajectory (though it should be noted that Oden's programmatic emphasis on "consensual paleo-orthodox Christianity" is an artificial construct that distorts the

---

essentially complete. It is not that churches resist anything called 'Faith and Order,' but rather that they are content with polite ecumenical relationships that privilege goodwill and cooperation over the hard work of pursuing the unity that can only come from fundamental change. Because self-sufficient churches have difficulty in acknowledging defect, deep need of the other, and the possibility of change, Faith and Order remains one possible activity among others rather than a compelling necessity."

[66] The key shapers of this trajectory in twentieth-century Catholic theology were Henri de Lubac (1896–1991), Jean Daniélou (1905–1974), Yves Congar (1904–1995), and Hans Urs von Balthasar (1905–1988). Apart from their influence—particularly that of Congar—the Second Vatican Council would likely not have taken the steps it took toward ecumenical openness, and the modern ecumenical movement might still be largely a Protestant and Orthodox project. For helpful introductions to the *nouvelle théologie* and its import, see Feargus Kerr, "French Theology: Yves Congar and Henri de Lubac," in *The Modern Theologians: An Introduction to Christian Theology in the Twentieth Century*, 2nd ed., ed. David F. Ford (Cambridge, Mass.: Blackwell, 1997), 105–17; Mare-cellino D'Ambrosio, "Ressourcement Theology, Aggiornamento, and the Hermeneutics of Tradition," *Communio* 18 (Winter 1991): 530–55; John F. Kobler, "On D'Ambrosio and Ressourcement Theology," *Communio* 19 (Summer 1992): 321–25.

heterogeneity of Christianity in late antiquity).[67] Beyond Oden's project, evangelical and Free Church theologians have been increasingly writing books calling for an evangelical recovery of the catholic tradition,[68] focusing on patristic Christianity in meetings of their professional societies,[69] advocating the incorporation into evangelical and Free Church worship of the tradition-bearing liturgical practices that form worshipers in qualitative catholicity,[70] commending Catholic magisterial teaching as a

[67] Oden, whose mid-career dissatisfaction with the adequacy of modern theology for the critical engagement of modern culture led him to turn to "classical Christian thinking" as a corrective (a development announced in Thomas C. Oden, *Agenda for Theology: Recovering Christian Roots* [San Francisco: Harper & Row, 1979] and recounted in Thomas C. Oden, "Then and Now: The Recovery of Patristic Wisdom," *Christian Century* 107 [December 12, 1990]: 1164–68), has attempted to gain a fresh hearing of "paleo-orthodox" perspectives on Christian faith and practice by summarizing and anthologizing the sources of the classical Christian tradition in such projects as his three-volume systematic theology (Thomas C. Oden, *The Living God: Systematic Theology, Volume One* [San Francisco: Harper & Row, 1987]; *The Word of Life: Systematic Theology, Volume Two* [San Francisco: Harper & Row, 1992]; *Life in the Spirit: Systematic Theology, Volume Three* [San Francisco: Harper & Row, 1994]), the volumes in the *Classical Pastoral Care* series (Thomas C. Oden, *Classical Pastoral Care*, 4 vols. [Grand Rapids: Baker Books, 1987–1994]), and *The Ancient Christian Commentary on Scripture* (Thomas C. Oden, ed., *The Ancient Christian Commentary on Scripture* [Downers Grove, Ill.: InterVarsity Press, 1998–2010]).

[68] E.g., Daniel H. Williams, *Retrieving the Tradition and Renewing Evangelicalism: A Primer for Suspicious Protestants* (Grand Rapids: William B. Eerdmans, 1999); idem, ed., *The Free Church and the Early Church: Bridging the Historical and Theological Divide* (Grand Rapids: William B. Eerdmans, 2002); idem, *Evangelicals and Tradition: The Formative Influence of the Early Church* (Evangelical Ressourcement: Ancient Sources for the Church's Future, vol. 1; Grand Rapids: Baker Academic, 2005). Williams, a Baptist specialist in patristics who taught at Loyola University of Chicago before joining the faculty of Baylor University, served as an evangelical participant in the International Evangelical–Roman Catholic Dialogue sponsored by the Pontifical Council for Promoting Christian Unity and the World Evangelical Association.

[69] E.g., the Evangelical Theological Society, which has included a Patristics Study Group as a regular program unit in its annual meetings in recent years.

[70] Robert Webber actively sought a convergence of catholic liturgical patterns and practices with evangelical worship; see Robert E. Webber, *Ancient-Future Faith: Rethinking Evangelicalism for a Postmodern World* (Grand Rapids: Baker Books, 1999), and *Worship Old and New: A Biblical, Historical, and Practical Introduction*, rev. ed. (Grand Rapids: Zondervan, 1994). In a review of Thomas C. Oden's book *The Rebirth of Orthodoxy: Signs of New Life in Christianity* (New York: HarperCollins, 2003), Baptist ethicist David P. Gushee expresses an increasingly common yearning among evangelicals for the fuller liturgical catholicity from which many evangelical traditions have long been disconnected: "There is another level at which Oden's account of orthodoxy speaks to what it means to be Baptist. . . . When Oden speaks of praying the historic prayers, singing the historic songs, participating in the historic liturgy, all I can think of is the impoverished worship experience so common in our 'three songs and a sermon' Sunday morning experience. . . . as one

source of doctrinal and ethical wisdom for evangelicals and Free Church Christians,[71] and encouraging their graduate students to pursue doctoral studies in patristics—not a common field of specialization for evangelical and Free Church scholars in previous generations. At the same time, an increasing number of aspiring evangelical and Free Church historians and theologians in various specializations have been earning their doctorates at Catholic-affiliated institutions.

Baptists too have been notable participants in this larger trajectory of renewal through the retrieval of the "Great Tradition" to which all particular traditions are heirs. A number of younger Baptist theologians have manifested such a strong interest in recovering a more catholic form of ecclesial life that they have been characterized as "catholic Baptists" or "Bapto-Catholics."[72] But such retrieval is not the exclusive project of

---

who knows how rich the rhythms of ancient worship, ancient hymnody, and the ancient Christian calendar can be, sometimes I am all too aware that in light of the riches of the tradition we are serving our people very thin gruel indeed" (*Christian Ethics Today* 9, no. 5 [December 2003]: 25). For specific suggestions for a Free Church retrieval of liturgical catholicity from a Baptist perspective, see Steven R. Harmon, *Towards Baptist Catholicity*, 151–77; idem, "Praying and Believing: Retrieving the Patristic Interdependence of Worship and Theology," *Review and Expositor* 101, no. 4 (Fall 2004): 667–95.

[71] E.g., Michael D. Beaty, Douglas V. Henry, and Scott H. Moore, "Protestant Free Church Christians and *Gaudium et Spes*: A Historical and Philosophical Perspective," *Logos: A Journal of Catholic Thought and Culture* 10, no. 1 (Winter 2007): 136–65. Beaty, Henry, and Moore write as representatives of a broader Free Church identity, but they do so as members of Baptist churches who are faculty members of the Department of Philosophy at Baptist-related Baylor University.

[72] Curtis W. Freeman, "A Confession for Catholic Baptists," in *Ties That Bind: Life Together in the Baptist Vision*, ed. Garry A. Furr and Curtis W. Freeman (Macon, Ga.: Smyth & Helwys, 1994), 85 (83–97), employed the terminology "catholic baptist" in this fashion: "I suggest that Baptists may more easily explore the vast resources of Christian spirituality and that other Christians may more readily receive the unique contributions of Baptist spirituality if we attempt to think of ourselves (at least experimentally) as (little c) catholic (little b) baptists" (cf. also Freeman, *Contesting Catholicity*, 8–20). Others have described this trajectory as "bapto-catholic," e.g., Cameron H. Jorgenson, "Bapto-Catholicism: Recovering Tradition and Reconsidering the Baptist Identity" (Ph.D. diss., Baylor University, 2008); cf. E. Glenn Hinson, "Bapto . . . Catholic," in *Tradition and the Baptist Academy*, ed. Roger A. Ward and Philip E. Thompson (Studies in Baptist History and Thought, vol. 11; Milton Keynes, UK: Paternoster, 2011), 31–45, who applies the terminology to his own sense of Baptist identity in expanded form: "Only half facetiously I often refer to myself as a Bapto-Quakero-Methodo-Presbytero-Luthero-Episcopo-Catholic" (31). In Harmon, *Towards Baptist Catholicity*, 1–21 and idem, "'Catholic Baptists' and the New Horizon of Tradition in Baptist Theology," in *New Horizons in Theology*, ed. Terrence W. Tilley (Maryknoll, N.Y.: Orbis Books, 2005), 117–43, I named the following as "identifying marks" of the work of "catholic Baptist" or "Bapto-Catholic" theologians: (1) the explicit recognition of tradition as a source of theological authority,

Baptist academic theologians. Chapter 6 will give attention to the many ways in which Baptist churches and their members have been receiving the gifts of the whole church, especially the liturgical gifts of the church in its catholicity. A Baptist embrace of Faith and Order ecumenical endeavors would bring these various forms of Baptist engagement with qualitative catholicity to the attention of the ecumenical dialogue partners of Baptists. At the same time, Baptist engagement with Faith and Order would provide additional impetus for intra-Baptist renewal through the retrieval of qualitative catholicity. The hope for the ecumenical future is not the Protestantization of Catholicism and Eastern Orthodoxy, but rather the re-catholicization of the Protestant traditions. The new "catholic Baptist" theologians, along with the members and ministers of Baptist congregations that have been embracing the gifts of liturgical catholicity, will have important roles to play in re-catholicizing their own communions while conserving and communicating the enduring gifts of Baptists to the rest of the church catholic.[73]

Baptist Dissent and the Contestation of Catholicity

Embracing Faith and Order ecumenical engagement is imperative for Baptists third because the whole church needs the contribution of the Baptist practice of dissent to the earnest contestation of the faith and order that would constitute a qualitative catholicity. Alasdair MacIntyre's definition of a "living tradition" is immensely helpful not only for explaining how tradition functions but also for helping Baptists, who have a traditional identity as dissenters, to identify with a specific place within—rather than apart from—the catholic tradition: "a living tradition is an historically extended, socially embodied argument, and an argument precisely in part about the goods which constitute that

---

(2) the seeking of a place for the ancient ecumenical creeds in the liturgy and catechesis of Baptist communities, (3) attention to liturgy as the primary context in which Christians are formed by tradition, (4) the location of the authority of tradition in the community and its formative practices, (5) a sacramental theology, (6) the engagement of tradition as a resource for contemporary theological construction, and (7) a "thick" ecumenism.

[73] The existence of Baptists and other Free Church Christians who run against the grain of their own denominational traditions in their personal adherence to qualitatively catholic expressions of faith and practice—which in some ways make them more catholic than some Catholic communicants, even though they are currently separated from that visible eucharistic fellowship—is a phenomenon with enormous ecumenical potential and merits serious attention by the various instruments of the worldwide ecumenical movement, as well as by the Catholic Church itself. See Ola Tjøhom, "Catholic Faith outside the Catholic Church: An Ecumenical Challenge," *Pro Ecclesia* 13, no. 3 (Summer 2004): 261–74.

tradition."[74] This appropriation of MacIntyre's definition is not a commendation of dissent as a good in itself, but rather as an ecclesial practice
necessitated by the current failures of the church to embody the unity that
is an essential mark of the church. Dissent can be a step toward unity only
if pursued as a conversation that requires contestation because of the present participation of the church in the fallen nature of humanity en route
to the eschatological realization of the unity of the church. Baptists and
other evangelicals who have been traditioned as dissenters may need to be
reminded from time to time of the eschatology of this temporal contestation, but their traditioning in dissent can also help them appreciate the
critical function of tradition as the argument of the community and may
help them find their place within this argument.

Even though the planned Second Conference on Faith and Order in
North America was not to be, there need to be institutional forums for
the ecumenical contestation of what it would mean to be visibly the one,
holy, catholic, and apostolic church. At present, this function is served
by the bilateral dialogues between communions at the national, regional,
and international levels and the multilateral conversations that take place
within the commissions on Faith and Order of national councils of
churches and the World Council of Churches. If they are to embrace Faith
and Order ecumenical engagement, Baptists must identify more fully with
these instruments and their sponsoring institutions (including their world
Christian communion, the Baptist World Alliance, as well as national
councils of churches and the WCC). Their congregational ecclesial polity
means that they must also creatively seek ways to foster local reception of
the results of Faith and Order dialogue.[75]

Such forums for contesting the nature of qualitative catholicity are
needed neither as an academic exercise in theological debate (though some
of the best academic theology is produced in connection with ecumenical
dialogue) nor to score debating points that win support for the pattern of
catholicity embodied in any of our existing ecclesial structures (though
through such debate we may well conclude that some communions come

---

[74] Alasdair MacIntyre, *After Virtue: A Study in Moral Theory*, 2nd ed. (Notre Dame,
Ind.: University of Notre Dame Press, 1984), 222. Cf. Harmon, *Towards Baptist Catholicity*, 53–54, 66–69, 184–85, which draws constructively on MacIntyre's account of a
contested living tradition to place Baptists within the larger catholic argument about the
goods that constitute the Christian tradition.

[75] Chapter 10 will identify ways in which Baptist communities have already been
participating in these manifestations of the quest for visible Christian unity in faith and
order and propose ways in which Baptists might more intentionally take up the task of
ecumenical reception of the results of Faith and Order dialogue.

nearer to the embodiment of various dimensions of catholicity than others), but rather because our divided traditions share a common good that includes the Faith and Order goal of visible unity—the socially embodied realization of the *notae ecclesiae*. Baptists and other Free Church Christians need to be involved in the contestation of faith and order not because they have uniquely preserved Christian truth and need a chance to convince others of the truth they possess, but because if they are earnestly contesting the common ecclesial good, they will be open not only to considering the perspectives of other parties but even to being persuaded by other positions in the argument. At the same time, there may be as yet unenvisioned ways in which even Catholicism and Eastern Orthodoxy may come to participate in a fuller catholicity beyond the very full qualitative catholicity that already characterizes these communions, and a robust contestation of the shared catholicity that visible unity in one eucharistic fellowship would entail may make contributions to those possibilities. There is room in a qualitative catholicity for diversity in faith and practice within certain parameters. But the extent to which our divided traditions disagree on many matters of faith and order indicates that we cannot simply proclaim that catholicity is inclusive of all current patterns of Christian faith and practice. Our significant disagreements must be contested so that we might mutually move toward the truth.

The most viable hope for a genuine movement toward "visible unity in one faith and one eucharistic fellowship, expressed in worship and in common life in Christ" lies neither in a conversion en masse of Protestants to Roman Catholicism or Eastern Orthodoxy or of Roman Catholics or Orthodox to Protestantism nor in a latitudinarian affirmation of all conceivable patterns of ordering Christian faith and practice as valid expressions of the catholic faith; the latter possibility we might call a "thin ecumenism" that seeks to overcome difference through a too facile identification of lowest-common-denominator agreements between traditions. It lies rather in a "thick ecumenism" that proceeds on the basis of a shared commitment to deep exploration of the ancient catholic tradition as well as to deep exploration of the particularities of the respective denominational traditions. This is what Baptist theologian Tarmo Toom calls a "diachronic ecumenism" that "takes a deep look into the shared past of Christianity and finds there the basis for mutual understanding and appreciation."[76] Such a thick ecumenism would regard our currently divided

---

[76] Tarmo Toom, "Baptists on Justification: Can We Join the Joint Declaration on the Doctrine of Justification?" *Pro Ecclesia* 13, no. 3 (Summer 2004): 291, n. 7 (289–306).

and sometimes conflicting patterns of faith and order not as inconvenient obstacles to unity that ought to be regarded as inconsequential for the sake of ecumenical progress, but rather as matters of such significance that they must be earnestly contested within and between our separated churches as we mutually seek to recover qualitative catholicity in faith and order.

If Baptists, baptists, and evangelicals stem from various historical efforts to renew the one church, then the internal renewal of their communities through a reengagement with qualitative catholicity facilitated by Faith and Order ecumenism is consistent with their historic identities and would enable them to serve as agents of the renewal of the quantitatively catholic church to which they and all other Christians belong.[77] The ecumenical moment is right for this sort of catholicizing renewal; the ecumenical future, humanly speaking, may depend on it.

---

[77] Cf. the place for evangelical and Pentecostal Christians in the future of ecumenism envisioned in Braaten and Jenson, eds., *In One Body through the Cross*, §§67–68 (pp. 55–57).

PART II

BAPTISTS, BIBLICISM, AND CATHOLICITY

3

One Sacred Story

Nearly a century before the institutional beginnings of the modern ecumenical movement, the most influential confessional statement adopted by Baptists in the United States began with an article on the Scriptures insisting that the Bible "is, and shall remain to the end of the world, the true centre of Christian union."[1] The biblicism reflected in that

---

[1] *New Hampshire Confession (1833)*, §1, in *Baptist Confessions of Faith*, 2nd rev. ed., ed. William L. Lumpkin, rev. Bill J. Leonard (Valley Forge, Pa.: Judson Press, 2011), 378. While the *New Hampshire Confession* was commissioned in 1830 and approved in 1833 by the New Hampshire Baptist Convention, it influenced other Baptist confessional statements in the United States in ways disproportionate to its origins. Two decades later one of its co-drafters, J. Newton Brown, took it upon himself to revise the confession and include it in a Baptist church manual published by the American Baptist Publication Society (J. Newton Brown, *The Baptist Church Manual: Containing the Declaration of Faith, Covenant, Rules of Order and Brief Forms of Church Letters* [Philadelphia: American Baptist Publication Society, 1853]). Subsequently it was included in numerous other church manuals published throughout the nineteenth century, by means of which "this Confession became the most widely disseminated creedal declaration of American Baptists" (William L. Lumpkin, *Baptist Confessions of Faith*, rev. ed. [Valley Forge, Pa.: Judson Press, 1969], 361). In 1925 the *New Hampshire Confession* became the template for the *Baptist Faith and Message* adopted that year by the Southern Baptist Convention and revised in 1963 and 2000. The first article on the Scriptures from the *New Hampshire Confession* was retained in the *Baptist Faith and Message*, with progressively more substantial insertions in its original wording made in each version of the *Baptist Faith and Message*. The affirmation of the Bible as "the true center of Christian union" has remained unaltered, however, apart from changing the spelling "centre" to "center." See *Baptist Faith and Message (1925)*, §1, in *A Baptist Source Book: With Particular Reference to Southern Baptists*, ed. Robert A. Baker (Nashville: Broadman Press, 1966), 201; *Baptist Faith and Message (1963)*, §1, in *Baptist Confessions of Faith*, ed. Lumpkin, rev. Leonard, 410; *Baptist Faith and Message (2000)*, §1, in *Baptist Confessions of Faith*, ed. Lumpkin, rev. Leonard, 512.

statement has sometimes supplied a reason for Baptists to resist ecumenical ventures, convinced that they would compromise what Baptists believe to be biblical patterns of faith and practice through cooperation or union with patterns of faith and practice they regard as unbiblical. Yet Baptists can also find in the Bible grounds for ecumenical convergence toward other Christian communions with which they share these Scriptures.[2] Baptist theologian Fisher Humphreys accordingly begins his account of Baptist theology by naming eleven convictions Baptists share with all Christian traditions, concluding with the ecumenically shared conviction that "the Bible tells us this wonderful story" that is the basis of the other ten beliefs Baptists hold in common with the church catholic.[3]

Humphreys had previously participated in a three-year series of dialogues between Southern Baptist and Catholic scholars jointly sponsored by the Bishops' Committee for Ecumenism and Interreligious Affairs of the United States Conference of Catholic Bishops and the Interfaith Witness Department of the Southern Baptist Convention's Home Mission Board (1978–1980).[4] Baptist biblicism and the Catholic regard for tradition are often regarded as polar opposites as configurations of religious authority. In the course of these dialogues, however, a pair of papers by Catholic theologian John Donahue and Baptist theologian William Hendricks highlighted the role of Scripture in the life of the church as a key locus of Catholic–Baptist convergence.[5] Hendricks identified "the centrality of the Scriptures . . . for belief and practice" as "a guideline . . . Baptists and Romans Catholics share,"[6] and Donahue contrasted the affirmation of the inspiration and trustworthiness of Scripture by both communions with

---

[2]   Cf. Vatican II, *Decree on Ecumenism (Unitatis Redintegratio)*, November 21, 1964, §21: "But Sacred Scriptures provide for the work of dialogue an instrument of the highest value in the mighty hand of God for the attainment of that unity which the Saviour holds out to all." Accessed March 18, 2015, http://www.vatican.va/archive/hist_councils/ii_vatican_council/documents/vat-ii_decree_19641121_unitatis-redintegratio_en.html.

[3]   Fisher Humphreys, *The Way We Were: How Southern Baptist Theology Has Changed and What It Means to Us All*, rev. ed. (Macon, Ga.: Smyth & Helwys, 2002), 25–27; cf. idem, *Baptist Theology: A Really Short Version* (Brentwood, Tenn.: Baptist History and Heritage Society, 2007), 9.

[4]   From April 1978 to November 1980 six two-and-a-half-day sessions (two sessions per year) were held in Cincinnati, Ohio, USA (1978), St. Louis, Missouri, USA and Cincinnati, Ohio, USA (1979), and Conyers, Georgia, USA and Leakey, Texas, USA (1980). See E. Glenn Hinson, "Editorial Introduction," *Review and Expositor* 79, no. 2 (Spring 1982): 195–97.

[5]   John R. Donahue, "Scripture: A Roman Catholic Perspective," *Review and Expositor* 79, no. 2 (Spring 1982): 231–44; William L. Hendricks, "Scripture: A Southern Baptist Perspective," *Review and Expositor* 79, no. 2 (Spring 1982): 245–57.

[6]   Hendricks, "Scripture," 245.

modern tendencies toward the relativizing of biblical authority in other Christian groups.[7] Both theologians also identified areas of divergence, notably the canon and the ecclesial structures by which its authority is mediated.[8] Together they drafted a joint "Epilogue" to the pair of papers that summarized the two communions' convergences and divergences, along with issues warranting future mutual exploration:

> Both Roman Catholics and Southern Baptists would agree that the ultimate authority and object of faith is the triune God and that the primary source of our knowledge of God is in the revelation of God found in scripture. We concur also that the self-disclosure and gift of God in scripture is designed to bring about a redemptive relationship between God and creation (both humanity and nature). The mystery of God within scripture is both within and beyond our grasp. As offering to us the way, the truth, and the life (Jn. 14:6), it is within our apprehension but still beyond it since, as those who see through a glass darkly (cf. 1 Cor. 13:12), we are aware that "God hath yet more light to break forth from his word."
>
> Each communion would value tradition and heritage as an interpretive and shaping source of its understanding of scripture. While recognizing the implicit authority of tradition, the Baptist tradition affirms that all tradition must be tested against the explicit authority of scripture. In consequence of this the Baptist affirms the right of individual interpretation of scripture. The Catholic community affirms the necessity of individual appropriation of scripture but affirms that any interpretation of scripture must be measured against the tradition and teaching of the Church.
>
> As growth in dialogue and mutual understanding between Southern Baptists and Roman Catholics progresses, some further issues to be explored are canonicity, especially as this pertains to the status of the Old Testament apocrypha (often called in Roman Catholicism the deutero-canonical books), the meaning of inspiration, and adequate principles of hermeneutics.
>
> While candidly admitting the historical manifestation of our diversity we, nonetheless, should place no limits on what God can do for and through those who are united in the study and mediation of his word.[9]

---

[7]   Donahue, "Scripture," 240.

[8]   Hendricks, "Scripture," 256–57; Donahue, "Scripture," 240–41.

[9]   John R. Donahue and William L. Hendricks, "Scripture: An Epilogue," *Review and Expositor* 79, no. 2 (Spring 1982): 258. The main areas of convergence and divergence

The attention to agreed affirmations and remaining differences in this interchange hints at a trajectory in ecumenical theology that has manifested itself in various expressions:[10] the recognition of a "hierarchy of truths" and the identification of theological formulations that are "mutually complementary rather than conflicting" in the Vatican II Decree on Ecumenism *Unitatis Redintegratio*;[11] the language of "unity in reconciled diversity" applied by Harding Meyer to the Lutheran–Reformed Leuenberg Agreement of 1973;[12] "fundamental consensus" and "convergence (though not uniformity)" as expressed in the United States Lutheran–Roman Catholic Dialogue VII in 1983;[13] the essential unity of "different ways of looking at the same reality" posited by Pope John Paul II in his 1995 encyclical *Ut Unum Sint*;[14] and the affirmation of a "consensus on basic truths" with "remaining differences" or "differing explications" in the 1999 *Joint Declaration on the Doctrine of Justification*, frequently expressed as a "differentiated consensus" in the subsequent reception of the *Joint*

---

regarding Scripture, the formation of the canon, and tradition that surfaced in this three-year dialogue between Southern Baptist and Roman Catholic scholars in the United States have parallels in the report of the first series of Baptist–Roman Catholic International Conversations held from 1984 to 1988: Baptist World Alliance and Catholic Church, "Summons to Witness to Christ in Today's World: A Report on Conversations 1984–1988," in *Growth in Agreement II: Reports and Agreed Statements of Ecumenical Conversations on a World Level, 1982–1998*, ed. Jeffrey Gros, Harding Meyer, and William G. Rusch (Faith and Order Paper no. 187; Geneva: WCC Publications/Grand Rapids: William B. Eerdmans, 2000), 373–85, especially §12 (p. 376) and §§45–47 (pp. 382–83).

[10] A similar trajectory in Catholic approaches to ecumenism is traced in Avery Cardinal Dulles, "Two Languages of Salvation: The Lutheran–Catholic Joint Declaration," *First Things* 98 (December 1999): 25–30.

[11] Vatican II, *Decree on Ecumenism (Unitatis Redintegratio)*, November 21, 1964, §§11 and 17, in *Decrees of the Ecumenical Councils*, ed. Norman P. Tanner, vol. 2, *Trent to Vatican II* (London: Sheed & Ward/Washington, D.C.: Georgetown University Press, 1990), 915 and 917. In context, the reference to "mutually complementary rather than conflicting" theological formulations has in mind ecumenical relations with the Eastern Orthodox churches.

[12] William G. Rusch and Daniel F. Martensen, eds., *The Leuenberg Agreement and Lutheran–Reformed Relationships: Evaluations by North American and European Theologians* (Minneapolis: Augsburg, 1989), 139–54; Harding Meyer, *That All May Be One: Perceptions and Models of Ecumenicity*, trans. William G. Rusch (Grand Rapids: William B. Eerdmans, 1999), 109–13 and 121–22.

[13] Lutheran World Ministries and Bishops' Committee for Ecumenical and Interreligious Affairs, *The Common Statement on Justification by Faith from U.S. Lutheran–Roman Catholic Dialogue VII: A Fundamental Consensus on the Gospel* (Philadelphia: Board of Publications, Lutheran Church in America, 1985), especially §§152 and 164 (pp. 26 and 29).

[14] John Paul II, *On Commitment to Ecumenism (Ut Unum Sint*, May 25, 1995), accessed October 21, 2014, http://www.vatican.va/holy_father/john_paul_ii/encyclicals/documents/hf_jp-ii_enc_25051995_ut-unum-sint_en.html.

Declaration.[15] These expressions are not precisely parallel, and their reception in ecumenical discourse has been far from uniform. Yet they do suggest the possibility of identifying the sort of essential agreement necessary for moving toward a common confession of the apostolic faith, even where divided ecclesial traditions have developed divergent patterns of faith and practice that are funded by the same apostolic faith.

When applied to differing accounts of the ecclesial function of Scripture, the paradigm of differentiated consensus yields results that are promising not only for Catholic–Baptist convergence but for discerning an ecumenically shared relationship to the one sacred story that norms the faith and practice of the whole church. This chapter expands the areas of convergence with remaining divergences identified by Donahue and Hendricks into an eight-point differentiated Catholic–Baptist consensus on Scripture in the life of the church. I frame this proposal in relation to my participant-observer thick description of the role of Scripture in the first-order liturgy of Baptist churches and reflection on the place of Scripture in the second-order efforts of Baptist communities to craft confessional expressions of their faith, in tandem with my non-Catholic reading of articulations of Catholic perspectives on Scripture that include the section on Sacred Scripture in the *Catechism of the Catholic Church,*[16] the papal encyclical *Divino Afflante Spiritu,*[17] the Dogmatic Constitution on Divine

[15] Lutheran World Federation and Catholic Church, *Joint Declaration on the Doctrine of Justification* (Grand Rapids: William B. Eerdmans, 2000), §§5, 14, and 40 (pp. 10–11, 15, 25–26). While the *Joint Declaration* itself does not use the precise expression "differentiated consensus" to describe the agreement reached between the Lutheran World Federation and the Roman Catholic Church, the concept is certainly present in the language "consensus on basic truths" with "remaining differences" or "differing explications," and in the reception of the *Joint Declaration* the language "differentiated consensus" has become identified with the *Joint Declaration.* See Harding Meyer, "Die Prägung einer Formel: Ursprung und Intention," in *Einheit—Aber Wie? Zur Tragfähigkeit der ökumenischen Formel vom "Differenzierten Konsens,"* ed. Harald Wagner (Quaestiones Disputatae, ed. Peter Hünermann and Thomas Söding, vol. 184; Freiburg: Herder, 2000), 36–58.

[16] Catholic Church, *Catechism of the Catholic Church* (Liguori, Mo.: Liguori, 1994), §§101–41 (pp. 30–38).

[17] Pius XII, *Divino Afflante Spiritu,* in *Acta Apostolicae Sedis* 35 (Rome, 1943): 297–326; ET in *Rome and the Study of Scripture: A Collection of Papal Enactments on the Study of Holy Scripture together with the Decisions of the Biblical Commission,* 5th ed., ed. Conrad J. Louis (St. Meinrad, Ind.: Grail, 1953), 79–107. On the influence of *Divino Afflante Spiritu* on Catholic biblical scholarship, see Robert Bruce Robinson, *Roman Catholic Exegesis since Divino Afflante Spiritu: Hermeneutical Implications* (Society of Biblical Literature Dissertation Series, vol. 111; Decatur, Ga.: Scholars Press, 1988).

Revelation *Dei Verbum* from the Second Vatican Council,[18] and the Pontifical Biblical Commission report *The Interpretation of the Bible in the Church.*[19]

Participating in the Story

In the liturgical life of Baptist churches, Scripture has functioned both as the criterion of authentic worship and as the sine qua non of worship itself. The early Baptist quest for ecclesial purity included a concern for "biblical worship," and like the Genevan reformers the early Baptists jettisoned liturgical practices that lacked biblical precedent and retained those that were appointed in Scripture by "divine ordinance."[20] Scripture has ordered Baptist worship, and it has also supplied its essential content. Even when the shapers of earliest Baptist worship in the first decade of the seventeenth century in Amsterdam called for those entering into the worship service to lay aside all books, including Bibles, lest they impede a direct encounter with the living God, the extempore exposition and application of the message of the Bible in this more "charismatic" approach to Baptist worship presupposed the reading of the biblical text in preparation for worship.[21] The proclamation of Scripture has functioned as the central act of regular Sunday worship in the subsequent four centuries of the Baptist tradition.

While the reading and proclamation of Scripture has been central to Baptist worship, the presence of Scripture therein is even more pervasive if one understands the essence of Christian worship as the participatory rehearsal of the biblical story of the Triune God.[22] This narrative descrip-

---

[18]   Vatican II, *Dogmatic Constitution on Divine Revelation (Dei Verbum)*, November 18, 1965, in *Decrees of the Ecumenical Councils*, ed. Tanner, vol. 2, *Trent to Vatican II*, 971–81.

[19]   Pontifical Biblical Commission, *The Interpretation of the Bible in the Church* (Washington, D.C.: United States Catholic Conference, 1993); also, Joseph A. Fitzmyer, *The Biblical Commission's Document "The Interpretation of the Bible in the Church": Text and Commentary* (Subsidia Biblica, vol. 18; Rome: Pontifical Biblical Institute, 1995).

[20]   Christopher J. Ellis, *Gathering: A Theology and Spirituality of Worship in Free Church Tradition* (London: SCM Press, 2004), 75–79.

[21]   In a letter dated September 20, 1608, Thomas Helwys wrote, "All bookes even the originalles themselves must be layed aside in the tyme of spirituall worshipp, yet still retayninge the readinge & interpretinge of the Scriptures in the Churche for the preparinge to worshipp, Iudinge of doctrine, decidinge of Controversies as the grounde of [our] faithe & of [our] whole profession" (cited in Ellis, *Gathering*, 47, from Champlin Burrage, *The Early Dissenters in the Light of Recent Research (1550–1641)*, 2 vols. [Cambridge: Cambridge University Press, 1912], 2:167; the description of this approach to worship as "charismatic" is that of Ellis).

[22]   A characterization of Christian worship I employed both descriptively and prescriptively in Steven R. Harmon, *Towards Baptist Catholicity: Essays on Tradition and the Baptist*

tion of worship places Baptist worship in continuity with the earliest complete description of Christian liturgy outside the New Testament in the *First Apology* of Justin Martyr (d. c. 165):

> And on the day called Sunday, all who live in cities or in the country gather together to one place, and the memoirs of the apostles or the writings of the prophets are read, as long as time permits; then, when the reader has ceased, the president verbally instructs, and exhorts to the imitation of these good things. Then we all rise together and pray, and, as we before said, when our prayer is ended, bread and wine and water are brought, and the president in like manner offers prayers and thanksgivings, according to his ability, and the people assent, saying Amen; and there is a distribution to each, and a participation of that over which thanks have been given, and to those who are absent a portion is sent by the deacons. And they who are well to do, and willing, give what each thinks fit; and what is collected is deposited with the president, who succours the orphans and widows, and those who, through sickness or any other cause, are in want, and those who are in bonds, and the strangers sojourning among us, and in a word takes care of all who are in need. But Sunday is the day on which we all hold our common assembly, because it is the first day on which God, having wrought a change in the darkness and matter, made the world; and Jesus Christ our Saviour on the same day rose from the dead. For He was crucified on the day before that of Saturn (Saturday); and on the day after that of Saturn, which is the day of the Sun, having appeared to His apostles and disciples, He taught them these things, which we have submitted to you also for your consideration.[23]

All the acts of worship described by Justin rehearse, enact, and invite participation in the biblical story of the Triune God. The overarching pattern of word and table underscores the essential narrative character of early Christian worship in which the biblical story is heard, touched, tasted, and embodied in various ways. The story of God's saving acts in Jesus Christ is made present through the reading of "the memoirs of the apostles"—the gospels and perhaps other books that now comprise the New Testament

---

Vision (Studies in Baptist History and Thought, vol. 27; Milton Keynes, UK: Paternoster, 2006), 155; idem, "Praying and Believing: Retrieving the Patristic Interdependence of Worship and Theology," *Review and Expositor* 101, no. 4 (Fall 2004): 671 (667–95).

[23] Justin Martyr, *1 Apology* 67; ET in *Ante-Nicene Fathers of the Christian Church*, ed. Alexander Roberts and James Donaldson (Buffalo, N.Y.: Christian Literature, 1885–1896; repr., Peabody, Mass.: Hendrickson, 1994), 1:185–86 (163–87).

Scriptures—and it is connected to the larger story of the people of God, "the writings of the prophets"—that is, the Scriptures of our Old Testament. The exhortation "to the imitation of these good things," a homily or sermon, invites worshipers to make the biblical story their own and embody it. Corporate prayer simultaneously narrates the biblical salvation history through thanksgiving and leads believers to enter the story through their assent of "Amen" to the president's voicing of their supplications. "Participation" in the Eucharist is a tangible embrace of the story of Scripture and an enactment of its communal dimensions; this communal story is also embodied in the diaconal extension of the Eucharist to those who are absent and in the collection for the care of those in need. The rationale for Sunday as the day of the common assembly links the story rehearsed in the assembly with the Hebrew creation narrative and with the new creation inaugurated by the resurrection of Jesus Christ. Sunday worship also places the biblical story within the calendar, reinterpreting the progression of time in light of the Christian story.

Second-century Christians performed acts of worship not mentioned in Justin's brief summary, and in subsequent centuries other liturgical practices such as additional forms of prayer, credal recitation, and the various seasons of the full Christian calendar enriched the church's developing liturgical tradition. These developments retained the basic framework of word and table along with the essential narrative character of this framework and served in many cases to make the substructure of biblical narrative even more explicit in the liturgy. As worshipers have the biblical story imprinted upon them and find their place within this story, they are formed in the faith and fitted for the practices that constitute the Christian life.[24] This is how Scripture has functioned in the life of the church in its liturgical catholicity. The place of Scripture in the life of Baptist churches at worship is best interpreted in light of this function of the biblical story in the worship of the church catholic.

The participatory rehearsal of the biblical story of the Triune God is not alien to the Baptist experience of worship. Even though much Baptist worship has long been disconnected from some of these traditional means

---

[24] Cf. the observation of Susan K. Wood that "the Christian repeatedly participates in the liturgy in order to imprint that economy [of salvation-history] in his or her very being," so that "worship provides the parameters for thinking about Scripture and theology by keeping these reflections oriented toward their proper object, God, and within their proper context, the Christian community" (Susan K. Wood, "Participatory Knowledge of God in the Liturgy," in *Knowing the Triune God: The Work of the Spirit in the Practices of the Church*, ed. James J. Buckley and David S. Yeago [Grand Rapids: William B. Eerdmans, 2001], 109–10 [95–118]).

of making the divine story present in worship, a typical Baptist worship service also has an essential narrative character and includes various acts of worship that narrate scriptural salvation-history and invite people to make that story their own. The following generalizations about Baptist worship reflect my own experience of Baptist life in the southern United States. Yet a survey of patterns and practices of worship in Baptist communities that have been influenced by other historical and cultural factors suggests that the phenomena observed in my own Baptist context have parallels elsewhere in the Baptist tradition.

The overarching structure of a typical Baptist worship service in the United States reflects the influence of two factors: a deeply entrenched antisacramentalism and revivalism. In England Baptist reactions against the emphases of the Anglo-Catholic Oxford Movement led to the loss of a more robust sacramental life that had once characterized British Baptist churches; the factors involved in a corresponding phenomenon in the United States during the nineteenth century are less clear, but it was not occasioned directly by the public controversy over the Oxford Movement that raged in British newspapers.[25] On both sides of the Atlantic Baptists consequently lost an earlier sacramental theology that emphasized the sacraments as effective signs inseparable from the things they signified, and an earlier terminology of "sacrament" was replaced by "ordinance."[26] One manifestation of this antisacramentalism has been an aversion to weekly communion. A common rationale offered for more infrequent celebrations of "the Lord's Supper" is the concern that more frequent observance

---

[25] On reactions to the Oxford Movement by Baptists in England, see John H. Y. Briggs, *The English Baptists of the Nineteenth Century* (A History of the English Baptists, vol. 3; Didcot: Baptist Historical Society, 1994), 224–27. The move by Baptists in America away from a previously more sacramental account of their faith and practice might be attributed to the influence of Reformed reactions against the "Mercersburg Theology" advocated by John Nevin and Philip Schaff. This is a conjectural suggestion; on this point I am influenced by conversations and correspondence with Philip Thompson, Professor of Systematic Theology and Christian Heritage at Sioux Falls Seminary in Sioux Falls, South Dakota. Thompson notes that Southern Baptist theologian James P. Boyce studied with Charles Hodge at Princeton Theological Seminary from 1849 to 1851 at the height of the Princeton–Mercersburg debate and hypothesizes that Boyce, influenced by the perspectives of his Princeton mentor, may have played a role in desacramentalizing Baptist theology in the southern United States that paralleled the British Baptist reaction to the Oxford Movement, though Thompson emphasizes that much further research is needed before these plausible connections can be offered as a formal historiographical proposal (Philip E. Thompson, e-mail message to Steven R. Harmon, December 4, 2006).

[26] The term "ordinance," it should be noted, does not necessarily exclude a sacramental account of an ordinance.

would render it a meaningless ritual.[27] As a result, the typical Baptist worship service is not a service of word and table but rather a service of the word in which the proclamation of Scripture is the central feature of worship.

Revivalism has also left its imprint upon Baptist worship in the United States, not only in the addition of an evangelistic invitation to a service of the word but also in a different sort of twofold division of the service: the "singing service" and the "preaching service." This division reflects the role of nineteenth-century revivalist musicians in leading crowds at evangelistic rallies in congregational singing as a preparation for hearing the evangelistic sermon, but it also draws upon the widespread adoption among Baptists in England in the eighteenth century first of the singing of the biblical psalter and then of the singing of Scripture-laden hymns.[28] The congregational and choral singing that continues to precede the reading and preaching of the word is in its own right a significant means by which Baptists engage in the participatory rehearsal of the biblical story of the Triune God.

While hymns and other forms of sacred song interspersed throughout a Baptist service of worship do play their own roles in drawing worshipers into the biblical story of the God they worship, the reading of Scripture and its proclamation has been the central feature of Baptist worship since its seventeenth-century origins. This primacy of Scripture and sermon, along with their relation to other acts of worship that rehearse the biblical story, is evident in the seven patterns of Baptist worship surveyed by British Baptist liturgical theologian Christopher Ellis and summarized in the table below.[29] The eighth additional pattern exemplifies the worship of a historic urban congregation in the southern United States.

---

[27]   Such rationales for infrequent observance fail to convince, as those who offer them would likely deny emphatically that such regular acts of Baptist worship as the singing of hymns or the preaching of sermons lose their significance through weekly repetition.

[28]   Ellis, *Gathering*, 153–64.

[29]   Ellis, *Gathering*, 46–62.

Eight Patterns of Baptist Worship

1. Baptist Worship in Amsterdam, 1609 (led by John Smyth and Thomas Helwys)	Prayer Reading one or two chapters of Scripture Give the sense and discuss (*lay aside books*) Solemne Prayer Exposition of a text and prophesying out of the same Prophesying from same text by second speaker Prophesying by subsequent speakers, as time allows Prayer by first speaker Exhortation to contribute to the poor Collection Prayer
2. A Baptist Congregation in London, 1695 (Paul's Abbey, Barbican Baptist Meeting)	(9:30 and 1:30) Psalm Prayer Scripture Reading Sermon Prayer Psalm
3. Particular Baptist and Independent Worship, 1723 (Bury Street Church, London)	Morning Service: Psalm Short prayer Exposition of Scripture [Psalm or hymn] Prayer Sermon Psalm or hymn Short prayer Benediction Afternoon Service: Psalm Long prayer Sermon Psalm or hymn Short prayer Benediction
4. Norfolk Baptist Association, 1845	Prayer for the Holy Spirit Song of Praise Scripture Reading Prayer; supplications and intercessions, with thanksgiving Song of Praise Exposition [Hymn?]

Eight Patterns of Baptist Worship (cont.)

5. Early Twentieth-Century Baptist Worship	Invitation to worship Hymn Bible reading Hymn Prayer Notices Offering Hymn Sermon Hymn Benediction
6. Mid- and Late Twentieth-Century Liturgical Baptist Worship	Approach to Worship Call to Worship Hymn of Praise Prayer: Confession Lord's Prayer The Word of God Scripture: Old Testament Psalm or Hymn Scripture: New Testament Sermon Hymn Prayer: Intercession Te Deum The Offertory Offering of Alms Offering of Elements Offering of Penitence Words of Invitation The Consecration Eucharistic Prayer Thanksgiving Anamnesis and Oblation Invocation The Communion Words of Institution Fraction Delivery and Reception Lord's Prayer Nunc Dimittis Gloria in Excelsis Hymn Dismissal and Blessing

Eight Patterns of Baptist Worship (cont.)

7. Charismatic Baptist Worship	Worship Time *Usually a sequence of songs, with prayers* Sermon *Usually, but not always, preceded by Scripture reading* Ministry Time *Prayers for healing and help (often for individuals who come forward), active response to sermon and the exercising of charismata*
8. First Baptist Church of Raleigh, North Carolina (4th Sunday of Advent, 2006)	Prelude Trinity Chimes Welcome to Worshipers Invocation Carol Old Testament Reading Moment for Mission Carol Lighting of the Advent Candles (with responsive litany) Morning Prayer Lord's Prayer Carol Medley Gospel Lesson Anthem Sermon Hymn of Response Offertory Prayer Offertory Confession of Our Faith (The Nicene Creed) Presentation of Our Tithes and Offerings Congregational Concerns Benediction Postlude

While focused on Baptist life in England, the patterns surveyed by Ellis are representative of Baptist worship in America (cf. the order of service from the First Baptist Church of Raleigh, North Carolina[30]) and elsewhere. In

[30] From the Order of Service, First Baptist Church of Raleigh, North Carolina, December 24, 2006 (Fourth Sunday of Advent). In connection with my characterization of worship as "the participatory rehearsal of the biblical story of the Triune God," the trinitarian congregational response to the reading of Scripture in the weekly Sunday worship of this church, written by the pastor at that time, J. Daniel Day, is of interest:

LEADER: These are the Scriptures of God for the people of Christ.
PEOPLE: May the Spirit grant us understanding.

each case the reading and proclamation of Scripture constitute the core of the service, and in each case the broader anamnetic features of the service may also include the celebration of the Lord's Supper. The pattern given for "Liturgical Baptist Worship" was crafted by Neville Clark, a leader in the Baptist Union of Great Britain who recommended a weekly celebration of the Eucharist.

Within the overarching framework of a service of the word with its twofold division of the sung word and the preached word, Baptists typically perform numerous acts of worship that have the function of narrating the biblical story. These include parallels to the acts of worship described by Justin Martyr: the act of gathering on Sunday; the reading of Scripture, with the selection of texts influenced by the use of a fixed lectionary,[31] by expository preaching through biblical books in the tradition of the ancient practice of *lectio continua*, or by the pastor's discernment of the spiritual needs of congregation and community; a sermon; prayers; corporate responses such as Justin's "Amen," responsive litanies, and more informal responses invited by worship leaders; the Supper, when celebrated; and an offering. These acts evidence a basic continuity between mid-second-century early Christian worship as described by Justin and typical Baptist worship two millennia later. In addition to these, typical Baptist worship services often include other liturgical acts that narrate the biblical salvation-history and invite worshipers to become a part of it. Many Baptist congregations will sing the Doxology each Sunday in connection with the offering, underscoring the trinitarian shape of the Christian story and making the offering a response to the work of the Triune God in creation and redemption. Baptist worship frequently includes an opportunity to extend a greeting to fellow worshipers through handshakes, hugs, and informal conversation or through a more formal greeting such as the exchange of the peace. These interactions with fellow worshipers reinforce the communal nature of the biblical story and help to keep participation in the divine story from degenerating into a merely individual encounter with God. An invitation to respond to the challenges of the sermon and to the beckoning of God in other aspects of the service reflects the Baptist emphasis upon personal commitment and makes explicit the need for active appropriation of the Christian story in one's own life. The typical Baptist worship service thus

---

[31] Baptist ministers in the United States who have chosen to utilize a lectionary in worship tend to use the common three-year lectionary published by the Consultation on Common Texts under the title *The Revised Common Lectionary* (Nashville: Abingdon Press, 1992).

emphasizes the first-order telling of the biblical story of the Triune God via a variety of acts of worship that communicate this story.

In recent decades some Baptists have discovered that the narration of the biblical story in a typical Baptist service of worship may be enhanced through the retrieval of additional patterns and practices from the ancient catholic liturgical tradition that are capable of bearing even thicker narrations of the biblical story. These include observance of the full Christian year; adoption of a common lectionary for the reading and proclamation of Scripture; movement toward more frequent services of word *and* table; corporate recitation of the ancient creeds that summarize the biblical story; patristic forms of prayer, such as the collect, that narrate biblical salvation history and express the congregation's desire to participate in it more fully; confessions of sin and declarations of pardon, in which worshipers enact and experience the forgiveness that is central to the story of Scripture; the passing of the peace, which embodies the social dimensions of the biblical story; the telling of the stories of exemplary saints;[32] and the occasional singing of hymns with texts of patristic composition that enable contemporary worshipers to participate in the ancient church's participation in the biblical story of the Triune God.[33] Both the typical Baptist worship service and the enrichment of this service with the resources of the catholic liturgical tradition exemplify the hermeneutic of Scripture articulated by Baptist theologian James Wm. McClendon, Jr.: "this is that," and "then is

[32] Baptist theologian James Wm. McClendon, Jr., advocated a retrieval of the veneration of the saints in the worship and educational programs of congregations in an appendix to *Biography as Theology: How Life Stories Can Remake Today's Theology*, rev. ed. (Philadelphia: Trinity Press International, 1990), appendix, "Christian Worship and the Saints," 172–84. McClendon found the explanations of these practices and their theological presuppositions by Karl Rahner and Herbert Vorgrimler helpful for putting the best face on these Catholic practices and concepts for "baptist" and other non-Catholic readers (McClendon, *Biography as Theology*, 181–82, citing Karl Rahner and Herbert Vorgrimler, *Theological Dictionary*, ed. Cornelius Ernst, trans. Richard Strachan [New York: Herder & Herder, 1965], s.v. "Veneration of Saints").

[33] *The Baptist Hymnal* published under the auspices of the Southern Baptist Convention (Wesley L. Forbis, ed., *The Baptist Hymnal* [Nashville: Convention Press, 1991]) includes seven hymns with hymn texts written through the eighth century, all of which except *Glory Be to the Father* and *O Christ, Our Hope, Our Heart's Desire* were translated into English by John Mason Neale (1818–1866), an Anglican divine whose translations of Greek and Latin patristic and medieval hymns greatly enriched the hymnody of the Church of England. *Baptist Praise and Worship* (Oxford: Oxford University Press, 1991), a hymnal produced for the Baptist Union of Great Britain, includes ten hymns with texts of patristic origin, only four of which parallel the patristic contents of *The Baptist Hymnal* (1991).

now."[34] In other words, in their gathering for worship, Baptists approach Scripture as a living story in which the Spirit of the living God—whose historic actions and promised future are narrated in Scripture—encounters them now, draws them to participate in the divine life disclosed in the Bible, makes of them a people identified with the biblical people of God and the eschatological community envisioned in Scripture, and sends them to participate in this story in their life in the world.

Confessing the Story

Baptists have emphasized the primacy and sufficiency of the Scriptures as their authority for faith and practice, but their confessions of faith make it clear that they ascribe ultimate authority to the Triune God. While Baptist confessions have sometimes preferred the biblical terminology of Father, Son, and Spirit to explicitly trinitarian language that moves beyond the wording of Scripture, in the main Baptists are Nicaeno-Constantinopolitan trinitarians, even when they may not be conscious of the historical origins of their trinitarian faith.[35] With few exceptions, early Baptist confessions issued in the Netherlands and England begin not with statements about the authority of the Bible (and frequently lacked such statements), but rather with articles on the nature and attributes of the one God who is Father, Son, and Holy Spirit. It is not making too much of this ordering of confessional statements to discern in it the conviction that the God whose story Scripture tells is the ultimate authority for Christian faith and practice.[36] Confessions issued in North America during the nineteenth and twentieth centuries, however, have normally begun with an

---

[34] This restatement of the biblicism that has marked the "baptist" tradition (the lowercase "b" usage is intended by McClendon to be inclusive of other churches in the Free Church tradition that emphasize "believer's baptism" and congregational polity) is developed in James Wm. McClendon, Jr., *Ethics: Systematic Theology, Vol. 1*, rev. ed. (Waco, Tex.: Baylor University Press, 2012), 26–34; see especially 30: "Scripture in this vision effects a link between the church of the apostles and our own. So the vision can be expressed as a hermeneutical principle: *shared awareness of the present Christian community as the primitive community and the eschatological community*. In a motto, **the church now is the primitive church and the church on judgment day. . . .**" (italics and boldface as employed by McClendon).

[35] On the echoes of Nicaeno-Constantinopolitan trinitarianism in early Baptist confessions of faith, see Harmon, *Towards Baptist Catholicity*, 71–87; idem, "Baptist Confessions of Faith and the Patristic Tradition," *Perspectives in Religious Studies* 29, no. 4 (Winter 2002): 349–58.

[36] Cf. Jeff B. Pool, "Christ, Conscience, Canon, Community: Web of Authority in the Baptist Vision," *Perspectives in Religious Studies* 24, no. 4 (Winter 1997): 417–45.

article on the inspiration and authority of the Scriptures. This shift does not indicate a reversal of ultimate authorities in North American Baptist thought. Rather, the initial placement of articles on the Scriptures in these more recent confessions may be attributed to two factors. First, the *Philadelphia Confession* of 1742, the earliest Baptist associational confession adopted in the American colonies, inherited this placement of the article on the Scriptures from the *Second London Confession* of 1677, which in turn was derived from the ordering of the *Westminster Confession* of 1647.[37] The widespread adoption of the *Philadelphia Confession* by local churches and associations throughout the colonies no doubt influenced the ordering of later American confessions. Second, during the nineteenth and twentieth centuries American Baptists began to respond to the challenges of "modernism" in the form of historical-critical biblical studies and evolutionary theory, with some Baptist groups giving increased attention to the inspiration and authority of the Scriptures in their confessions. Even if these documents emphasize Scripture as the means by which God is known, the Baptists who have adopted and affirmed these confessions would agree that any legitimate source of religious authority derives from the God who is revealed in the person of Jesus Christ to whom the Spirit bears witness.

While Baptists ascribe ultimate authority to the Triune God, they identify Scripture as the supreme earthly source of authority that derives its authority from the Triune God who is the authorizing subject, the principal actor, and the living presence of the biblical story. Many early Baptist confessions lacked articles on the Scriptures,[38] but they evidenced a radical biblicism in their copious prooftexting of confessional statements with parenthetical and marginal biblical references.[39] Most Baptist con-

---

[37] For the *Second London Confession* and *Philadelphia Confession*, see *Baptist Confessions of Faith*, ed. Lumpkin, rev. Leonard, 222–97 and 366–67; for the text of the *Westminster Confession*, see *The Creeds of Christendom with a History and Critical Notes*, 6th ed., ed. Philip Schaff, rev. David S. Schaff, vol. 3, *The Evangelical Protestant Creeds* (New York: Harper & Row, 1931; repr., Grand Rapids: Baker Book House, 1990), 598–673 (page references are to reprint edition); *Creeds and Confessions of Faith in the Christian Tradition*, ed. Jaroslav Pelikan and Valerie Hotchkiss, vol. 2, *Reformation Era* (New Haven, Conn.: Yale University Press, 2003), 604–49.

[38] James Leo Garrett, Jr., "Sources of Authority in Baptist Thought," *Baptist History and Heritage* 13 (1978): 42 (41–49).

[39] Cf. E. Frank Tupper, "Biblicism, Exclusivism, Triumphalism: The Travail of Baptist Identity," *Perspectives in Religious Studies* 29, no. 4 (Winter 2002): 411–12 (411–26). Mikeal C. Parsons, "Luke among Baptists," *Perspectives in Religious Studies* 33, no. 2 (Summer 2006): 137–54, includes tables providing statistical data for references not only to passages from Luke but from all the Scriptures in twenty-five Baptist confessional documents from the *Declaration of English People Remaining at Amsterdam* (1611) to a brief declaration of

fessions adopted in North America have contained an article specifically addressing the inspiration and authority of the Scriptures. The *Philadelphia Confession* of 1742 contains a lengthy article (§1.6) on the Scriptures influenced by the *Westminster Confession* via the *Second London Confession*. The perspective of the *Philadelphia Confession* on the sufficiency of the Bible, illumined by the Spirit, as the authority for Christian faith and practice hints at a rejection of other possible sources of authority but allows for the adaptability of such things as the polity and worship of the church in light of reasoned reflection on social context:

> The whole Councel of God concerning all things necessary for his own Glory, Mans Salvation, Faith and Life, is either expressely set down or necessarily contained in the *Holy Scripture*; unto which nothing at any time is to be added, whether by new Revelation of the Spirit, or traditions of men. Nevertheless we acknowledge the inward illumination of the Spirit of God, to be necessary for the saving understanding of such things as are revealed in the Word, and that there are some circumstances concerning the worship of God, and the government of the Church common to humane actions and societies; which are to be ordered by the light of nature, and Christian prudence according to the general rules of the Word, which are always to be observed.[40]

The most widely influential article on the Scriptures in Baptist confessions issued in the United States is the article with which the *New Hampshire Confession* of 1833 begins:

> We believe [that] the Holy Bible was written by men divinely inspired, and is a perfect treasure of heavenly instruction; that it has God for its author, salvation for its end, and truth, without any mixture of error, for its matter; that it reveals the principles by which God will judge us; and therefore is, and shall remain to the end of the world, the true centre of Christian union, and the supreme standard by which all human conduct, creeds, and opinions should be tried.[41]

---

faith issued by the Baptist World Alliance at its Centennial World Congress in July 2005 (see table 1, p. 147, and table 2, p. 148).

[40] *Baptist Confessions of Faith*, ed. Lumpkin, rev. Leonard, 233 (this page reference is actually to Lumpkin's printing of the text of the *Second London Confession*, as Lumpkin only printed the two new articles of the *Philadelphia Confession* that were added to the *Second London Confession* in the section on the *Philadelphia Confession*).

[41] *Baptist Confessions of Faith*, ed. Lumpkin, rev. Leonard, 378.

This article was incorporated in or adapted by confessions printed in numerous Baptist church manuals and issued by such Baptist bodies as the American Baptist Association, the General Association of Regular Baptists, and notably the Southern Baptist Convention, which made the *New Hampshire Confession* the basis of the statement of the *Baptist Faith and Message* that the SBC adopted in 1925, revised in 1963, amended in 1998, and revised yet again in 2000. The successive modifications of the article on the Scriptures in the *Baptist Faith and Message* illustrate well the diversity that has characterized recent understandings of biblical authority in Baptist life in North America.

From the formation of the SBC in 1845 until 1925, Southern Baptists did not have an officially adopted confession of faith. In 1924 allegations that Baptist educational institutions were teaching evolutionary theory motivated Convention messengers to charge a committee with drafting a confession of faith. Chaired by SBC president E. Y. Mullins (who was also the president of The Southern Baptist Theological Seminary in Louisville, Kentucky), the committee added only one word to the article on the Scriptures in the *New Hampshire Confession*. Whereas the *New Hampshire Confession* called the Bible "the supreme standard by which all human conduct, creeds, and opinions should be tried," the 1925 *Baptist Faith and Message* qualified the "opinions" as "*religious* opinions."[42] This modification subtly limited the scope of biblical authority to matters of faith and practice—in other words, not scientific matters—and enabled both those who allowed for the possibility that evolution was the means by which God created human beings and those who opposed all forms of evolutionary theory to affirm the same statement on the authority of the Bible. It is significant that the convention declined to adopt a proposed anti-evolution amendment to the article on "Man."[43]

In 1961 Ralph Elliott, professor of Old Testament at Midwestern Baptist Theological Seminary (Kansas City, Missouri), published a book titled *The Message of Genesis* with Broadman Press, the Convention's publishing arm.[44] Controversy over the book's application of historical–critical

---

[42] *Baptist Faith and Message (1925)*, §1, in *A Baptist Source Book*, ed. Baker, 201.

[43] The proposed amendment read: "We believe man came into the world by direct creation of God, and not by evolution. This creative act was separate and distinct from any other work of God and was not conditioned upon antecedent changes in previously created forms of life." *Baptist Confessions of Faith*, ed. Lumpkin, rev. Leonard, 408.

[44] Ralph H. Elliott, *The Message of Genesis* (Nashville: Broadman Press, 1961). For an autobiographical perspective on the controversy engendered by this book, see idem, *The 'Genesis Controversy' and Continuity in Southern Baptist Chaos: A Eulogy for a Great Tradition* (Macon, Ga.: Mercer University Press, 1992).

methodologies to the interpretation of Genesis, as well as some of Elliott's specific interpretive conclusions, led messengers to the 1962 annual convention of the SBC in San Francisco to recommend that a committee chaired by SBC president Herschel Hobbs draft a new statement of faith that would provide guidelines for the agencies of the Convention. The resulting revision of the *Baptist Faith and Message*, approved by messengers to the 1963 Convention in Kansas City, Missouri, added a phrase and a sentence to the article on the Scriptures in the 1925 statement. The first addition asserted that the Bible "is the record of God's revelation of Himself to man."[45] This addition distinguished between the Bible and the revelation that preceded and resulted in the writing of Scripture, subtly allowing for interpretive approaches that reckoned seriously with the human dimensions of the biblical text. Such a distinction had been made decades earlier by Southern Baptist theologian W. T. Conner, who wrote in 1936, "Revelation preceded the Bible. . . . The Bible is the product of revelation."[46] The second addition, "The criterion by which the Bible is to be interpreted is Jesus Christ,"[47] was perceived by some as permitting those who saw some moral and theological progression in God's revelation from the earliest layers of the Old Testament to God's definitive revelation in Jesus Christ[48] to affirm the statement in good conscience. This revision seems to combine an affirmation of the trustworthiness of the Bible with openness to the contributions of contemporary biblical and theological scholarship to its interpretation.

Following decades of theological controversy from which more conservative Southern Baptists emerged in control of denominational agencies, a revision of the article on the Scriptures in 2000 moved in a different direction from its predecessors in 1925 and 1963. The article alters the statement that the Bible "is the *record* of God's revelation of Himself to man" to read that the Bible "*is* God's revelation of Himself to man" (emphasis added), thus seeming to equate the Bible, in its entirety, with revelation proper—though, it should be noted, this language does not

---

[45]   *Baptist Faith and Message (1963)*, §1, in *Baptist Confessions of Faith*, ed. Lumpkin, rev. Leonard, 410–11.

[46]   W. T. Conner, *Revelation and God: An Introduction to Christian Doctrine* (Nashville: Broadman Press, 1936), 78–79.

[47]   *Baptist Faith and Message (1963)*, §1, in *Baptist Confessions of Faith*, ed. Lumpkin, rev. Leonard, 411.

[48]   E.g., a progression from the divine sanctioning of "holy war" in the Old Testament to the peacemaking ethic of the reign of God taught by Jesus Christ in the New Testament.

require such an equation.[49] The final sentence added in the 1963 revision, "The criterion by which the Bible is to be interpreted is Jesus Christ," is deleted and replaced with "All Scripture is a testimony to Christ, who is Himself the focus of divine revelation."[50] These most recent modifications reflect a shift in North America's largest Baptist group toward an understanding of biblical authority defined in terms of a theory of biblical inerrancy along the lines of the 1978 Chicago Statement on Biblical Inerrancy drafted by a group of North American evangelical theologians.[51] In the larger Baptist context, many Baptists would affirm this understanding of the inspiration and authority of the Bible;[52] many Baptists would affirm standard historical-critical conclusions about the formation of the Bible and their usefulness for biblical interpretation;[53] and many other Baptists would view these battles as vestiges of a dying modernity and would prefer to move beyond them by focusing instead on the manner in which Scripture functions authoritatively for the Baptist communities that are gathered by its proclamation and study.[54] A focus on the authoritative function of Scripture in the life of the community implies a relationship between Scripture and other possible sources of authority to which members of the community may turn, consciously and unconsciously, when they interpret the Scriptures together.

[49] *Baptist Faith and Message (2000)*, §1, in *Baptist Confessions of Faith*, ed. Lumpkin, rev. Leonard, 512.

[50] *Baptist Faith and Message (2000)*, §1, in *Baptist Confessions of Faith*, ed. Lumpkin, rev. Leonard, 512

[51] International Council on Biblical Inerrancy, "Chicago Statement on Biblical Inerrancy," *Journal of the Evangelical Theological Society* 21 (December 1978): 289–96. For various Southern Baptist perspectives on the appropriateness of this conceptualization of the nature of biblical inspiration and authority, alongside representative non-Baptist evangelical perspectives, see Conference on Biblical Inerrancy, *The Proceedings of the Conference on Biblical Inerrancy, 1987* (Nashville: Broadman Press, 1987).

[52] E.g., L. Russ Bush and Thomas J. Nettles, *Baptists and the Bible*, rev. ed. (Nashville: Broadman & Holman, 1999).

[53] E.g., many of the essays in Robison B. James, ed., *The Unfettered Word: Southern Baptists Confront the Authority-Inerrancy Question* (Waco, Tex.: Word Books, 1987).

[54] E.g., Mikael Broadway, Curtis W. Freeman, Barry Harvey, James Wm. McClendon, Jr., Elizabeth Newman, and Philip E. Thompson, "Re-envisioning Baptist Identity: A Manifesto for Baptist Communities in North America," published initially in *Baptists Today* (June 1997): 8–10, and *Perspectives in Religious Studies* 24, no. 3 (Fall 1997): 303–10. This statement of "Re-envisioning Baptist Identity," popularly referenced as the "Baptist Manifesto," is also reprinted as appendix 1 in Harmon, *Towards Baptist Catholicity*, 215–23, and is available online (accessed November 28, 2014, http://divinity.duke.edu/sites/divinity.duke.edu/files/documents/faculty-freeman/reenvisioning-baptist-identity.pdf). The online version includes the names of several initial signees beyond the six authors.

Confessions adopted by Baptists have tended toward a *sola scriptura* understanding of authority in that they specify Scripture as the supreme authority but do not explicitly identify other subordinate sources of authority.[55] Yet like the Magisterial Reformers, the actual hermeneutical practice of Baptists might be better described as *suprema scriptura*.[56] Baptist confessions, especially those adopted during the seventeenth

---

[55]   Garrett, "Sources of Authority in Baptist Thought," 43.

[56]   James Leo Garrett, Jr., *Systematic Theology: Biblical, Historical, and Evangelical*, vol. 1 (Grand Rapids: William B. Eerdmans, 1990), 181, suggested that "Baptists who emphasize the use of Baptist confessions of faith and who insist on a clearly articulated doctrine of the Trinity, often using terms easily traceable to the patristic age, would do well to affirm *suprema Scriptura*." Garrett's suggestion of *suprema scriptura* as a more accurate descriptor of this functional pattern of authority among Baptists has influenced the text of the reports from the conversations between the Baptist World Alliance and the Anglican Consultative Council and from the second series of conversations between the Baptist World Alliance and the Catholic Church, an influence mediated by papers I presented on Scripture and authority to meetings of both series of conversations in which I called attention to Garrett's Baptist qualification of *sola scriptura* by *suprema scriptura*. See Anglican Consultative Council and Baptist World Alliance, *Conversations around the World 2000–2005: The Report of the International Conversations between the Anglican Communion and the Baptist World Alliance* (London: Anglican Communion Office, 2005), §26 (pp. 37 and 108, n. 46): "In particular, the debt to the doctrinal concepts of the Church Fathers with regard to Trinity and Christology, as evidenced in Baptist confessions, means that it would be more accurate to regard the Baptist view of Scripture as *suprema scriptura* rather than *sola scriptura*." Similarly, Baptist World Alliance and Catholic Church, "The Word of God in the Life of the Church: A Report of International Conversations between the Catholic Church and the Baptist World Alliance 2006–2010," §62, *American Baptist Quarterly* 31, no. 1 (Spring 2012): 28–122, invokes Garrett to show how a Baptist pattern of sources of authority in which tradition has a proper function in relation to the authority of Scripture is comparable to that described by the Vatican II Dogmatic Constitution on Divine Revelation *Dei Verbum*: "The phrase that certainty in faith comes 'not . . . from the holy Scriptures alone' (*non . . . per solam sacram scripturam*) is intended to acknowledge the way that tradition can contribute to our certainty about the meaning of the gospel. In confessing a trinitarian faith, for example, Baptists are dependent on post-biblical development of doctrine, i.e. tradition, for their 'certainty' about the triune nature of God. One Baptist theologian urges that 'Baptists who . . . insist on a clearly articulated doctrine of the Trinity, often using terms easily traceable to the patristic age, would do well to affirm *suprema Scriptura*' ['scripture as supreme'] rather than an unqualified *sola Scriptura* ['scripture alone']." Garrett is credited for this language in note 57 of the report. Cf. Steven R. Harmon, "Baptist Understandings of Authority, with Special Reference to Baptists in North America," paper presented to the Anglican–Baptist International Commission—North American Phase, Acadia University, Wolfville, Nova Scotia, September 12, 2003; idem, "Scripture in the Life of the Baptist Churches: Opportunities for a Differentiated Catholic–Baptist Consensus on Sacred Scripture," paper presented to the first round of the 2006–2010 bilateral conversations between the Baptist World Alliance Doctrine and the Catholic Church, Beeson Divinity School, Samford University, Birmingham, Alabama, December 10–15, 2006.

century, contain numerous echoes of the doctrinal formulations of Nicaeno-Constantinopolitan trinitarianism and Chalcedonian Christology, employing theological terminology with origins in the fourth century and later.[57] When Baptists affirm doctrinal formulations with patristic origins or embrace the authority of a biblical canon, they are at least unconsciously granting some degree of authority to tradition in the interpretation of Scripture.

Explicit Baptist recognition of tradition or other sources of theological authority in addition to Scripture thus far exists almost exclusively in the context of academic theological discourse;[58] extrabiblical sources of authority are seldom referenced by Baptist confessions of faith. A major exception to this generalization is the 1678 confession issued by General (i.e., non-Calvinistic) Baptists in England under the title *An Orthodox Creed*. Article 38 of the *Orthodox Creed* commends the reception and belief of the Nicene, (pseudo-)Athanasian, and Apostles' Creeds by Baptists, subordinating their authority to that of Scripture but regarding them as reliable summaries of biblical teaching:

> The three creeds, viz. Nicene creed, Athanasius' creed, and the Apostles creed, as they are commonly called, ought thoroughly to be received, and believed. For we believe, they may be proved, by most undoubted authority of holy scripture, and are necessary to be understood of all christians; and to be instructed in the knowledge of them, by the ministers of Christ, according to the analogy of faith, recorded in sacred scriptures, upon which these creeds are grounded, and catechistically opened, and expounded in all christian families, for the edification of young and old, which might be a means to prevent heresy in doctrine, and practice, these creeds containing all things in a brief manner, that are necessary to be known, fundamentally, in order to our salvation; to which end they may be considered, and better understood of all men, we have here printed them under their several titles as followeth. . . .[59]

---

[57] See Harmon, *Towards Baptist Catholicity*, 71–87; idem, "Baptist Confessions of Faith and the Patristic Tradition," 349–58.

[58] See Harmon, *Towards Baptist Catholicity*, 1–21; idem, " 'Catholic Baptists' and the New Horizon of Tradition in Baptist Theology," in *New Horizons in Theology*, ed. Terrence W. Tilley (Maryknoll, N.Y.: Orbis Books, 2005), 117–43; and the literature by "catholic Baptist" theologians cited therein.

[59] *An Orthodox Creed (1678)*, §38, in *Baptist Confessions of Faith*, ed. Lumpkin, rev. Leonard, 337–38. While the Lumpkin editions omitted the text of the "three creeds," they are printed in full as they were printed in the originally published edition of *An Orthodox Creed* in a recent transcription: Thomas Monck et al., "An Orthodox Creed,"

The first two sentences of this article are taken from article 8 of the *Thirty-Nine Articles* of the Church of England.[60] In addition, at least two recent European Baptist confessions of faith likewise make positive reference to the Apostles' Creed. The first paragraph of the confession adopted in 1977 by German-speaking Baptist unions in Germany, Austria, and Switzerland "presupposes the Apostles' Creed as a common confession of Christendom,"[61] and the initial paragraph of the confession approved by the Swedish-Speaking Baptist Union of Finland in 1979 "accepts the Apostolic Creed as the comprehensive creed for the union."[62] While these affirmations of a traditional rule of faith that summarizes the Bible and provides broad guidance for its proper interpretation suggest openings for a Catholic–Baptist convergence on the relation of Scripture to tradition, most Baptists will profess adherence to a *sola scriptura* theological hermeneutic. Yet Baptist laypeople and Baptist clergy alike are in fact reading the Bible through the lenses of all sorts of tradition and forming opinions about numerous issues of faith and practice on the basis of what seems reasonable to them and what best accords with Christian experience. The actual hermeneutical practice of Baptists is therefore *suprema scriptura*, with Scripture functioning as the supreme source of authority in a larger pattern of authority. But if one asks typical Baptists why they believe their conviction on a particular matter of faith or practice is the right one, they will likely respond that this is what they understand to be the teaching of the Bible.

Sharing the Story

In light of the foregoing account of the function of Scripture in the first-order liturgy and second-order confessions of Baptist communities and Catholic documents that give attention to the role of Scripture in the Catholic Church, I propose the following eight potential loci of a

---

transcribed by W. Madison Grace II, *Southwestern Journal of Theology* 48, no. 2 (Spring 2006): 168–70 (133–82).

[60] For the text of the *Thirty-Nine Articles* of the Church of England, see *The Creeds of Christendom*, 6th ed., ed. P. Schaff, rev. D. Schaff, vol. 3, *The Evangelical Protestant Creeds*, 487–516; *Creeds and Confessions of Faith in the Christian Tradition*, ed. Pelikan and Hotchkiss, vol. 2, *Reformation Era*, 528–40.

[61] G. Keith Parker, *Baptists in Europe: History & Confessions of Faith* (Nashville: Broadman Press, 1982), 57.

[62] Parker, *Baptists in Europe*, 111.

Catholic–Baptist differentiated consensus on the function of Sacred Scripture in the life of the church.[63]

First, Baptists and Catholics together regard the Bible as a book that is fundamentally liturgical in its overarching genre and proper first-order function.[64] It is the divinely authorized norm for faith and practice, but this normativity of Scripture is principally located in the liturgy of the church. The Bible was canonized by and for the worshiping community, and it comprises those writings that are suitable for public reading and preaching and for supplying the narrative content of other anamnetic acts of worship. Both the Roman *ordo missae* and Baptist services of song, prayer, Scripture reading,

---

[63] The careful reader of this chapter and of Baptist World Alliance and Catholic Church, "The Word of God in the Life of the Church," 28–122, will note significant parallels between my proposal of a Catholic–Baptist differentiated consensus on the function of Sacred Scripture in the life of the church and aspects of Section III on "The Authority of Christ in Scripture and Tradition" in "The Word of God in the Life of the Church." In the first meeting of this second series of conversations at Samford University's Beeson Divinity School in Birmingham, Alabama, December 10–15, 2006, I presented the paper "Scripture in the Life of the Baptist Churches: Opportunities for a Differentiated Catholic–Baptist Consensus on Sacred Scripture," which proposed an earlier version of these eight loci; that paper was paired with a paper by a member of the Catholic delegation, Dennis D. McManus, "The Use of Sacred Scripture in the Catholic Church," and both papers served as the basis for general discussion by the joint commission and by smaller working groups later that week before a final session in which the joint commission agreed on wording for a provisional expression of our convergences and remaining differences on the role of Scripture in the life of the church and the relationship of Scripture and tradition. I subsequently served along with Catholic theologian William Henn as co-drafter of an early version of the section on Scripture and Tradition in the report. The text of the final report, however, is the work of the whole joint commission and reflects modifications of the earlier draft agreed upon by the joint commission in its fifth and final annual meeting at Regent's Park College, University of Oxford, December 12–18, 2010. Where there are such parallels between the eight loci in this chapter and the section on "The Authority of Christ in Scripture and Tradition" in "The Word of God in the Life of the Church," these will be noted in subsequent notes.

[64] Cf. Baptist World Alliance and Catholic Church, "The Word of God in the Life of the Church," §37: "The Bible is the divinely-authorized written norm for faith and practice, but this normativity of Scripture is principally located in the worship of the church, from which its life and mission grows. The Bible was canonized by and for the worshipping community, and it comprises those writings that are suitable for reading, preaching, and supplying the narrative content of other acts of worship that recall and represent (in *anamnesis*) the mighty acts of God in the past. Both Catholic and Baptist patterns of worship presuppose that sacred Scripture is the source of the story of the Triune God in which worshippers participate." This paragraph is one of the "bold-type" paragraphs that set forth a fundamental Catholic–Baptist consensus, with the consensus enriched and/or differentiated in subsequent "regular-type" paragraphs. In this case, §§38–40 enrich the convergence on the liturgical nature and function of Scripture by describing this role of Scripture in the worship of both communions.

and preaching presuppose that Sacred Scripture is the source of the story of the Triune God in which worshipers participate.[65]

Second, Baptists and Catholics together are convinced that the liturgy of the word is sacrament-like in its effect on the lives of the faithful.[66] Scripture is the sine qua non of worship in both traditions, for while a weekly Eucharist is the norm in Roman Catholic parishes, there are services such as the hours of the divine office in which the liturgy of the word is the primary "place" where the divine reality narrated in the biblical story of the Triune God is made present. Furthermore, "[t]he church has always held the divine scriptures in reverence no less than it accords to the Lord's body itself, never ceasing—especially in the sacred liturgy—to receive the bread of life from the one table of God's word and Christ's body, and to offer it to the faithful," for "[i]n the sacred books the Father who is in heaven comes lovingly to meet his children and talks with them."[67] Likewise among Baptists, the Bible has a liturgical function that can best be expressed as the "sacramentality" of the word, even if most of the Baptist faithful might find such an expression foreign to the Baptist grammar of faith. Modern Baptists may have tendencies toward a reductionistic Zwinglian "mere symbolism" in their theology of baptism and the Supper, but no Baptist would claim that a sermon is "merely symbolic." Baptists believe that God is present in the preached word and that the faithful are transformed by their encounter with this presence. Some of them, such as British Baptist theologian John Colwell, have even explicitly named the ground of this expectation as the "sacramentality of the word."[68]

---

[65] Cf. my functional definition of Christian worship as "the participatory rehearsal of the biblical story of the Triune God" earlier in this chapter, which is reflected in the final sentence of Baptist World Alliance and Catholic Church, "The Word of God in the Life of the Church," §37: "Both Catholic and Baptist patterns of worship presuppose that sacred Scripture is the source of the story of the Triune God in which worshippers participate."

[66] Cf. Baptist World Alliance and Catholic Church, "The Word of God in the Life of the Church," §40: "For both Baptists and Catholics the liturgical function of Scripture might be expressed as the 'sacramentality' of the word." The remainder of §40 notes that while Baptists may not tend to use the language of sacramentality to describe this function, it may nevertheless be discerned in the Baptist regard for the Scriptures in worship that has parallels in Catholic worship.

[67] Vatican II, *Dei Verbum*, §21, in *Decrees of the Ecumenical Councils*, ed. Tanner, vol. 2, *Trent to Vatican II*, 979; cf. Catholic Church, *Catechism of the Catholic Church*, §§1.1.2.3.1.103–104 (pp. 30–31).

[68] John E. Colwell, *Promise and Presence: An Exploration of Sacramental Theology* (Milton Keynes, UK: Paternoster, 2005), chap. 4, "The Sacramentality of the Word," 88–105. *Promise and Presence* is Colwell's attempt to retrieve for his own Baptist (and more broadly Free Church/Protestant) tradition all seven sacraments identified as such in the medieval

Third, Baptists and Catholics together affirm that "God is the author of Sacred Scripture."[69] In the words of the Vatican II Dogmatic Constitution on Divine Revelation *Dei Verbum*, the Catholic Church "accepts as sacred and canonical all the books of both the old Testament and the new, in their entirety and with all their parts, in the conviction that they were written under the inspiration of the holy Spirit . . . and therefore have God as their originator: on this basis they were handed on to the church."[70] A series of Baptist confessional statements also declare that the Bible "has God for its author."[71] This locus is the fundamental consensus on which all other loci of a Catholic–Baptist convergence on Scripture depend.

Fourth, Baptists and Catholics together recognize that God has given the Scriptures to the church through human instrumentality.[72] According to a christological analogy, they believe that the Scriptures are both divine and human in authorship, and therefore that in their interpretation insufficient attention to the historical factors involved in their human composition can result in a "Docetic" view of Scripture, just as a failure to appreciate their divine authorship results in an "Ebionite" approach to the Bible.[73] The

---

tradition, prefaced by chapter-length treatments of the sacramentality of creation, the sacramentality of the church, and the sacramentality of the word. See also Steven R. Harmon, "The Sacramentality of the Word in Gregory of Nyssa's *Catechetical Oration*: Implications for a Baptist Sacramental Theology," in *Baptist Sacramentalism 2*, ed. Anthony R. Cross and Philip E. Thompson (Studies in Baptist History and Thought, vol. 25; Milton Keynes, UK: Paternoster, 2008), 239–53.

[69] Cf. Baptist World Alliance and Catholic Church, "The Word of God in the Life of the Church," §41; quotation is from Catholic Church, *Catechism of the Catholic Church*, §1.1.2.3.2.105 (p. 31).

[70] Vatican II, *Dei Verbum*, §11, in *Decrees of the Ecumenical Councils*, ed. Tanner, vol. 2, *Trent to Vatican II*, 975.

[71] *New Hampshire Confession (1833)*, §1, in *Baptist Confessions of Faith*, ed. Lumpkin, rev. Leonard, 378; this language is retained in the corresponding articles of the 1925, 1963, and 2000 versions of the *Baptist Faith and Message*, the confessional statement of the Southern Baptist Convention that utilized the *New Hampshire Confession* as a template: *Baptist Faith and Message (1925)*, §1, in *A Baptist Source Book*, ed. Baker, 201; *Baptist Faith and Message (1963)*, §1, in *Baptist Confessions of Faith*, ed. Lumpkin, rev. Leonard, 410; *Baptist Faith and Message (2000)*, §1, in *Baptist Confessions of Faith*, ed. Lumpkin, rev. Leonard, 512

[72] Cf. Baptist World Alliance and Catholic Church, "The Word of God in the Life of the Church," §42.

[73] This analogy is commonly employed in Protestant attempts to reconcile the divine inspiration of Scripture with the insights of historical-critical biblical scholarship and is exemplified by Baptist New Testament scholar Charles H. Talbert's essay "The Bible's Truth Is Relational," in *The Unfettered Word*, ed. James, 39–46. A slightly different analogy with the same force is offered by the Lutheran theologian Carl Braaten, who contrasted a proper "Chalcedonian hermeneutic" with two inadequate perspectives: an

papal encyclical *Divino Afflante Spiritu*, the dogmatic constitution *Dei Verbum*, and the Pontifical Biblical Commission report *The Interpretation of the Bible in the Church* all develop at length what is stated briefly in the section on Sacred Scripture in the *Catechism of the Catholic Church*: "the reader [of Sacred Scripture] must take into account the conditions of their time and culture, the literary genres in use at that time, and the modes of feeling, speaking, and narrating then current."[74] Just as these Catholic documents affirm the believing application of various methodologies of modern critical biblical scholarship in helping the reader "to take into account" these matters, so those Baptists who have valued formal theological education for their ministers have to varying degrees incorporated modern critical methodologies into their approach to the ecclesial interpretation of the Bible, and the article on "God's Word—the Bible" in the confession of faith adopted by the German Baptist Bund Evangelisch-Freikirchlicher Gemeinden in 1977 even explicitly affirms the humanity of the Scriptures and the compatibility of historical investigation with an affirmation of their divine inspiration.[75] Both Catholics and Baptists have experienced turmoil over the proper role of historical investigation in the interpretation of Scripture as each communion has labored to develop adequate ecclesial

---

unqualified theory of verbal inspiration fails to appreciate the humanity of the Bible and is guilty of interpretive Monophysitism, while historical exegesis apart from the community of believers in which the Spirit is active results in a kind of interpretive Adoptionism (Carl E. Braaten, *Mother Church: Ecclesiology and Ecumenism* [Minneapolis: Fortress Press, 1998], 131).

[74] Catholic Church, *Catechism of the Catholic Church*, §1.1.2.3.3.110 (p. 32); cf. Pius XII, *Divino Afflante Spiritu*, in *Rome and the Study of Scripture*, 79–107; Vatican II, *Dei Verbum*, §12; Pontifical Biblical Commission, *Interpretation of the Bible in the Church*.

[75] Bund Evangelisch-Freikirchlicher Gemeinden in Deutschland, *Die Rechenschaft vom Glauben*; ET, "Confession of Faith," trans. John Steely, in Parker, *Baptists in Europe*, 57–76; see §I.6, "God's Word—The Bible," par. 4: "The Bible is God's word in human language. Therefore its books bear the signs of the times in which they originated. Their language, their patterns of thought, and their literary forms are bound to the times and places whence they come. Therefore the historical understanding of Holy Scripture is an obligation of the Christian church and its theology, in their listening to the word of God. The historical interpretation of Scripture takes into account the working of the Holy Spirit, both in originating and expounding the Holy Scriptures of the Old and New Testaments. The Bible lives, because God speaks through it" (63–64). This confession is also noteworthy for its prefacing of the articles outlining distinctive Baptist beliefs with the full text of the Apostles' Creed as an expression of the faith Baptists share in common with other Christians (p. 57) as well as for its article on "God's Old and New Covenants" (I.5, p. 62), which explicitly repudiates a supersessionist understanding of the relationship between Israel and the church.

responses to the challenges of modernity,[76] but in the main, both Catholics and Baptists seek to practice a "Chalcedonian hermeneutic" that has a proper place for human instrumentality in the gift of the Scriptures to the church yet recognizes the limitations of historical-critical interpretation when exercised apart from the ecclesial reading of Sacred Scripture.[77]

Fifth, Baptists and Catholics together believe that the activity of the Holy Spirit among the people of Israel and the church of Christ that inspired the writing of the Old and New Testament Scriptures has also led these communities to discern these Scriptures as having canonical authority for faith and practice.[78] While the *Catechism of the Catholic Church* specifies that "it was by the apostolic Tradition that the Church discerned which writings are to be included in the list of the sacred books,"[79] Baptists are not given to explicitly extending the activity of the Spirit in inspiring the Scriptures to the continued activity of the Spirit in the ecclesial tradition that issues in the canon of Scripture. Yet this reticence does not mean that Baptists do not assume something very much like the providential guidance of the Spirit in the canonizing church. If they do not, their only alternative is to regard the canon as merely a historical accident or an arbitrary exercise of ecclesiastical power rather than as the divinely authorized norm for faith and practice recognized by the church through the guidance of the Spirit.

---

[76] Donahue, "Scripture: A Roman Catholic Perspective," 232, notes that "[t]he early decrees issued by the Biblical Commission (1905–1915)—which were only rescinded in 1955—mandated the most traditional position for Catholic scholars on virtually every issue raised by critical scholarship." In the recent controversies over biblical inerrancy and other theological issues in the Southern Baptist Convention, adherence to various standard critical positions on the authorship and dating of biblical books was often seen as a red flag for the presence of theological liberalism, even when some Baptist scholars accepting these critical conclusions also adhered to doctrinal orthodoxy.

[77] The ecumenical recognition of the limitations (and enduring contributions) of historical-critical interpretive methodologies and of the need for the renewal of the ecclesial/theological reading of Scripture is exemplified by Richard B. Hays and Ellen F. Davis, "Beyond Criticism: Learning to Read the Bible Again," *Christian Century* 121, no. 8 (April 20, 2004): 23–27, and the essays in Richard B. Hays and Ellen F. Davis, eds., *The Art of Reading Scripture* (Grand Rapids: William B. Eerdmans, 2003); cf. Robert W. Jenson, *Canon and Creed* (Interpretation: Resources for the Use of Scripture in the Church; Louisville, Ky.: Westminster John Knox, 2010).

[78] Cf. Baptist World Alliance and Catholic Church, "The Word of God in the Life of the Church," §43. This "bold-type" consensus section of the report and the "regular-type" elaboration and differentiation of the consensus in §§44–45 are derived from a parallel portion of my paper presentation "Scripture in the Life of the Baptist Churches: Opportunities for a Differentiated Catholic–Baptist Consensus on Sacred Scripture," the substance of which is the basis for this paragraph and the one that follows it here in this chapter.

[79] Catholic Church, *Catechism of the Catholic Church*, §1.1.2.3.4.120 (p. 34).

Nevertheless, the Baptist affirmation of the canon of Scripture is differentiated from the Catholic identification of the canon by its exclusion from the canon of the Old Testament of the deuterocanonical books included in the Septuagint and Vulgate versions and listed by the fourth session of the Council of Trent.[80] When Baptists have declared that "the books commonly called Apocrypha, not being of divine inspiration, are no part of the canon (or rule) of the Scripture, and therefore are of no authority in the Church of God,"[81] they have vested authority in the truncated canon they received from streams of the Protestant Reformation that preceded the Baptists. Yet it should be noted that Baptists have not completely neglected the deuterocanonical books. Even if early English Baptist Thomas Grantham was not persuasive in his contention that Baptists should accept the deuterocanonical books as Scripture and employ them as such in the church,[82] more recent Baptist New Testament scholars have recognized that in light of the echoes of the Wisdom of Solomon, the Wisdom of ben Sirach (Ecclesiasticus), and other deuterocanonical literature in the Pauline letters, any reading of the New Testament as part of a coherent canonical story must include an appreciation of the place of these texts in the life of the early church.[83] In addition, students in Baptist seminaries and divinity schools are routinely required to read 1 and 2 Maccabees in connection with historical introduction to the world of early Christianity in introductory New Testament courses. The canonical status of the Apocrypha is not a matter of fundamental consensus between Baptists and Roman Catholics, but Baptists do recognize its indispensability for an understanding of primitive Christianity, and some appreciate its value as devotional literature read alongside the Protestant Bible.[84] One

[80]   Council of Trent, Session 4, 8 April 1546, decree 1, in *Decrees of the Ecumenical Councils*, ed. Tanner, vol. 2, *Trent to Vatican II*, 663.

[81]   *Second London Confession* (1677), §1.3, in *Baptist Confessions of Faith*, ed. Lumpkin, rev. Leonard, 232.

[82]   Thomas Grantham, *Christianismus Primitivus: Or the Ancient Christian Religion, in Its Nature, Certainty, and Excellency, above Any Other Religion in the World* (London: Francis Smith, 1678), "Introduction." (The character of deranged Southern Baptist missionary Nathan Price in Barbara Kingsolver's novel *The Poisonwood Bible* [New York: Harper-Collins, 1998] is thus not as far-fetched as one might suppose at the point of his cherished soapbox contention that Baptists ought to accept the Apocrypha.)

[83]   E.g., Richard N. Longenecker, *Galatians* (Word Biblical Commentary, vol. 41; Dallas, Tex.: Word Books, 1990), *passim* (Longenecker is a Canadian Baptist originally from the United States).

[84]   As a professor at the Baptist seminary I attended in the early 1990s remarked one day in class, "If the early church fathers may be read as devotional literature, then so may the Apocrypha."

major Baptist theologian has even ventured to suggest that Free Church Christians might revisit the question of the canonicity of the deutero-canonical books in light of early precedents within their tradition and a rethought understanding of the role of the canon in the life of the church.[85]

Sixth, Baptists and Catholics together recognize that the canon of Scripture has some relationship to traditioning processes in the life of the patristic church.[86] This is not always an explicit recognition. Baptists know that the canon did not suddenly descend from heaven to the church with the completion of the last book of the New Testament, and to the degree that they have an awareness of the processes by which the canon received its formation and yet grant this canon an authoritative status, they have at least unconsciously granted some degree of authority to the church's tradition from which the canon cannot easily be separated. Some Baptists have openly acknowledged this relationship and have stated forthrightly its hermeneutical implications. Baptist patristics scholar Daniel Williams, for example, contends that there is a sense in which the patristic tradition, especially in its fourth-century development, must be understood as a canonical rule apart from which the Bible cannot be rightly interpreted.[87] The final shape of the canon Baptists regard as authoritative was configured by a rule of faith that had already ruled out Docetism, Marcionitism, and a wide variety of Christian Gnosticisms as interpretive possibilities for the church.[88] This is a point at which McClendon's articulation of the [B]aptist vision must be qualified: the "that" and the "then" of the biblical story are mediated to the present church by the ecclesial tradition that has configured and delivered the story in its present form.[89] But these new Baptist appreciations of the place

---

[85] James Wm. McClendon, Jr., *Doctrine: Systematic Theology, Vol. 2* (Waco, Tex.: Baylor University Press, 2012), 477: "[I]t is worth noting that the baptists of the sixteenth century [here McClendon has in mind the Anabaptists] generally preferred using the Catholic rather than the (shorter) Protestant canon, and in light of the understanding of Scripture advanced here, it is at least worth asking whether they were not on the whole right to do so. It is a topic on which the churches, once freed from the artificial constrictions of criticism, tradition, and inerrancy listed above, can helpfully converse."

[86] Cf. Baptist World Alliance and Catholic Church, "The Word of God in the Life of the Church," §§56–57.

[87] Daniel H. Williams, "The Patristic Tradition as Canon," *Perspectives in Religious Studies* 32, no. 4 (Winter 2005): 357–79; cf. the Lutheran perspective of Jenson, *Canon and Creed*.

[88] Chapter 5 will develop this point further.

[89] McClendon, however, developed this hermeneutical principle in a direction counter to what I have suggested here, in the context of "contrasting the present sense of 'the church now is the apostolic church' with a possible Catholic sense of those very words. . . . The baptist 'is' in 'this is that' is therefore neither developmental nor successionist, but mystical and immediate" (McClendon, *Ethics*, 32).

of tradition in the life of the church remain differentiated from what the Catholic insistence that "both Scripture and Tradition are to be accepted and honored with equal sentiments of devotion and reverence"[90] seems to affirm—a differentiation that the next chapter will revisit.

Seventh, Baptists and Catholics together insist that the Old Testament and New Testament together form a coherent story that requires a Christocentric interpretation.[91] In the words of the *Catechism of the Catholic Church*, "Christians . . . read the Old Testament in the light of Christ crucified and risen."[92] And as the *Catechism* quotes from Hugh of St. Victor, "'All Sacred Scripture is but one book, and that one book is Christ, because all divine Scripture speaks of Christ, and all divine Scripture is fulfilled in Christ.'"[93] The best of Baptist biblical interpretation also reads the Bible in this Christocentric fashion. Baptists too "read the Old Testament in the light of Christ crucified and risen": as the 1963 revision of the article on the Scriptures in the *Baptist Faith and Message* puts it, "The criterion by which the Bible is to be interpreted is Jesus Christ."[94] While some Baptists with historical or current connections to the Southern Baptist Convention have been concerned that the removal of that sentence in the 2000 revision of the *Baptist Faith and Message* eviscerates this Christocentric pattern of biblical interpretation, it must be noted that the sentence that replaces the 1963 language in the 2000 statement—"All Scripture is a testimony to Christ, who is Himself the focus of divine revelation"[95]—is compatible with the language of Hugh of St. Victor affirmed by the *Catechism*: "all divine

---

[90]   Catholic Church, *Catechism of the Catholic Church*, §1.1.2.2.2.82 (p. 26), quoting *Dei Verbum* §9. Cf. Timothy George, "An Evangelical Reflection on Scripture and Tradition," *Pro Ecclesia* 9, no. 2 (Spring 2000): 184–207.

[91]   Cf. Baptist World Alliance and Catholic Church, "The Word of God in the Life of the Church," §§46–47.

[92]   Catholic Church, *Catechism of the Catholic Church*, §1.1.2.3.4.129 (p. 36).

[93]   Catholic Church, *Catechism of the Catholic Church*, §1.1.2.3.5.134 (p. 37), quoting Hugh of St. Victor, *De Arca Noe* 2.8 (*Patrologiae Cursus Completus: Series Latina*, ed. J.-P. Migne [Paris: Garnier, 1844–1864], 176:642).

[94]   *Baptist Faith and Message (1963)*, §1, in *Baptist Confessions of Faith*, ed. Lumpkin, rev. Leonard, 410–11.

[95]   *Baptist Faith and Message (2000)*, §1, in *Baptist Confessions of Faith*, ed. Lumpkin, rev. Leonard, 512. On the other hand, it must also be pointed out that there are ways of applying the affirmation "all Scripture is a testimony to Christ, who is Himself the focus of divine revelation" that ignore another important statement of the *Catechism of the Catholic Church* on the Christocentric unity of the Old and New Testaments: "Such typological reading discloses the inexhaustible content of the Old Testament; *but it must not make us forget that the Old Testament retains its own intrinsic value as Revelation affirmed by our Lord himself*" (Catholic Church, *Catechism of the Catholic Church*, §1.1.2.3.4.129 [p. 36], emphasis added).

Scripture speaks of Christ." Taken together, the 1963 emphasis on the Christocentric "criterion" and the 2000 emphasis on the testimony of the whole of Scripture to Christ are parallel to the Catholic commitment to reading the whole Bible as a coherent, Christocentric story. This too is a matter of fundamental consensus.

Eighth, Baptists and Catholics together locate responsibility for the interpretation of Scripture in the community of the church, even while both communions affirm and encourage the individual reading of Scripture.[96] Catholics and Baptists together, but in distinctive ways, insist that the community indwelt by the Spirit who inspired the Scriptures is a more trustworthy interpreter of Scripture than the individual who attempts to read the Scriptures apart from this community. Catholics have located the communal interpretation of Scripture in the historically extended ecclesial community that is identified with its episcopal leadership: "The task of interpreting the Word of God authentically has been entrusted solely to the Magisterium of the Church, that is, to the Pope and to the bishops in communion with him."[97] Baptists also locate the communal interpretation of Scripture in the ecclesial community, but primarily in the form of the gathered local congregation.[98]

---

[96]   Cf. Baptist World Alliance and Catholic Church, "The Word of God in the Life of the Church," §§48–50.

[97]   Catholic Church, *Catechism of the Catholic Church*, §1.1.2.2.43.100 (p. 30); cf. Vatican II, *Dei Verbum*, §10.

[98]   The following characterization of early-seventeenth-century Baptist worship illustrates this perspective: "It was . . . primarily in the community that Baptists believed that Scripture bore the Word of God. In earliest Baptist worship, after the Scripture was read, the whole congregation conferred upon the sense of the passage prior to any of the day's four or five expositions. Interpretation of Scripture which was private and dissociated from the community was frowned upon by the Baptists. [Thomas] Helwys excoriated the Church of England for limiting the acceptable interpreters of Holy Writ to the bishops, for such private interpretation kept the Spirit in bondage and made the Word to no effect" (Philip E. Thompson, "Toward Baptist Ecclesiology in Pneumatological Perspective" [Ph.D. diss., Emory University, 1995], 65–66). Thompson cites in this connection Thomas Helwys, *A Short Declaration of the Mistery of Iniquity* (London: Thomas Helwys, 1611), 55, and *The Orthodox Creed* (1678), §37, "Of the Sacred Scripture" (*Baptist Confessions of Faith*, ed. Lumpkin, rev. Leonard, 335–37). See also Broadway, Freeman, Harvey, McClendon, Newman, and Thompson, "Re-envisioning Baptist Identity," §1: "*We affirm Bible Study in reading communities* rather than relying on private interpretation or supposed 'scientific' objectivity. . . . We thus affirm an open and orderly process whereby faithful communities deliberate together over the Scriptures with sisters and brothers of the faith, excluding no light from any source. When all exercise their gifts and callings, when every voice is heard and weighed, when no one is silenced or privileged, the Spirit leads communities to read wisely and to practice faithfully the direction of the gospel."

Baptists have sometimes emphasized freedom in the interpretation of Scripture, and some expressions of Baptist life since the nineteenth century, especially in the United States, have applied this freedom anthropocentrically—that is, they have stressed the freedom of individuals to interpret the Bible for themselves. This interpretive individualism is reflected in Hendricks' characterization of Baptist divergence from Catholic perspectives in his contributions to the joint "Epilogue" with Donahue quoted earlier in this chapter: "the Baptist affirms the right of individual interpretation of scripture."[99] The interpretive freedom prized by Helwys and the earliest Baptists, however, was a theocentric and specifically pneumatocentric freedom. From their perspective, the practice of "private interpretation" by individual bishops limited the freedom of the Spirit of God to speak through the Scriptures in the community rather than the freedom of individuals to read the Bible according to their inclinations. To the degree that contemporary Baptists recover this earlier concern to make room for the freedom of the Spirit of God to speak to and through the community gathered around the reading and proclamation of the Word, they move toward opportunities for convergence with the Catholic insistence that biblical interpretation is fundamentally ecclesial rather than individual. But this convergence remains sharply differentiated: for Catholics, adherence to magisterial teaching guards against the dangers of individual interpretation, while for Baptists, it is the gathered congregation that does so.[100]

Convergences between Catholic and Baptist perspectives on Sacred Scripture are by no means limited to the eight areas of differentiated consensus identified here. There are perhaps few Baptists who would not enthusiastically applaud the chapter on "Holy Scripture in the Life of the Church" that concludes the Vatican II Dogmatic Constitution on Divine Revelation *Dei Verbum*, for example.[101] Baptists and Catholics alike are indebted to the church in its pre-Reformation catholicity for mediating to them, and to all Christians, the shared story of the church that authorizes its faith and practice. If such seemingly polar opposite communities in terms of their configurations of authority as Catholics and Baptists are able to converge toward a consensus on the role of the sacred story that norms

---

[99]   Donahue and Hendricks, "Scripture," 258.

[100]   For a proposal extending to the larger *communio sanctorum* the interpretive authority traditionally located by Baptists in the congregation gathered under the lordship of Christ, see Harmon, *Towards Baptist Catholicity*, 39–69.

[101]   Vatican II, *Dei Verbum*, §§21–26, in *Decrees of the Ecumenical Councils*, ed. Tanner, vol. 2, *Trent to Vatican II*, 979–81.

ecclesial life, it is a convergence that potentially applies to the whole quantitatively catholic church in all its diversity. Baptists and other Free Church heirs of the Radical Reformation have had a historic vocation within the church catholic of calling the church to renewal through reengagement with its roots in this shared story. As Baptists and all other Christians find a meeting place in this shared story, they may discover in it the resources they need for growing more fully catholic in their faith and order as their churches progress in their pilgrim journey toward "visible unity in one faith and one eucharistic fellowship, expressed in worship and in common life in Christ."[102]

---

[102] By-laws of the Faith and Order Commission of the World Council of Churches, quoted in *Faith and Order: Toward a North American Conference. Study Guide*, ed. Norman A. Hjelm (Grand Rapids: William B. Eerdmans, 2004), vii.

4

One Contested Tradition

The place of the biblical story in the economy of divine revelation has great potential for highlighting convergences between Baptists and Catholics (and other members of the divided church), but their respective understandings of the relation of Scripture and tradition in this economy remain a primary source of many of their most intractable differences. The Vatican II Dogmatic Constitution on Divine Revelation *Dei Verbum* is replete with affirmations about the nature of revelation and the authority of Scripture that Baptists can enthusiastically applaud, but the seeming equation of the authority of Scripture and tradition in article 9 makes it a hard test case for the degree to which it is possible for biblicistic Baptists to converge ecumenically toward other communions' configurations of the relationship of Scripture and tradition in patterns of Christian authority.

Convergence on Revelation

Apart from a precious few sentences, *Dei Verbum* remains over four decades after its approval a cause for rejoicing among Baptists who cherish the Bible and long for deeper expressions of unity with other Christians who likewise give devotion and reverence to Sacred Scripture. There is not a sentence of chapter 1, "Revelation in Itself" (articles 2–6), that could not be affirmed by virtually all Baptists, with the possible exception of the reaffirmation in article 6 of the teaching of the First Vatican Council that "God . . . can be known with certainty from the created order by the natural light of human reason."[1] This might be regarded as anathema by those

---

[1] Vatican II, *Dogmatic Constitution on Divine Revelation (Dei Verbum)*, §6, November 18, 1965, trans. Robert Murray, in *Decrees of the Ecumenical Councils*, ed. Norman P.

Baptists who are convinced by Karl Barth's rejection of natural theology, but the next sentence regarding the radical dependence of humanity upon revelation even in those matters discernible by human reason, also reaffirmed from Vatican I, ought to satisfy such objections.[2] The characterization of revelation throughout this chapter as the self-disclosure of the Triune God is a matter of fundamental consensus. Baptists can embrace the concomitant emphases on the dynamic coinherence of divine works and words in God's relational communication with humanity (article 2), the evangelistic ends of this divine self-disclosure (articles 2–6), the "fullness of all revelation"[3] in Christ and the finality of this revelation (articles 2–4), the sheer gratuity not only of revelation itself but especially of God's enablement of all acts of free human response to God's revelation (article 5), and the Holy Spirit as the inward assistance for these acts of response and the illuminator of human understanding of revelation (article 5).

While Baptists may have concerns about the treatment of the authority of tradition and teaching office of the church in the section on "The Transmission of Divine Revelation" (articles 7–10), to which this chapter will next turn, the dominant emphasis of *Dei Verbum* is on the centrality of Scripture to the church-renewing encounter with divine revelation. Joseph Ratzinger, whose work as a *peritus* (theological expert) at the Second Vatican Council was closely intertwined with the evolution of *Dei Verbum*,[4] characterized its significance in that fashion both as a young theologian and as Pope Benedict XVI.[5] The stress on Scripture as the word

---

Tanner, vol. 2, *Trent to Vatican II* (London: Sheed & Ward/Washington, D.C.: Georgetown University Press, 1990), 973.

[2] Vatican II, *Dei Verbum*, §6, in *Decrees of the Ecumenical Councils*, ed. Tanner, vol. 2, *Trent to Vatican II*, 973: "Further, this teaching is to be held about revelation: 'in the present condition of the human race, even those truths about God which are not beyond the reach of human reason, require revelation for them to be known by all without great effort, with firm certainty and without error entering in.'" Cf. Vatican I, *Dogmatic Constitution on the Catholic Faith*, April 24, 1870, trans. Ian Brayley, in *Decrees of the Ecumenical Councils*, ed. Tanner, vol. 2, *Trent to Vatican II*, 806.

[3] Vatican II, *Dei Verbum*, §2, in *Decrees of the Ecumenical Councils*, ed. Tanner, vol. 2, *Trent to Vatican II*, 972: "Intima autem per hanc revelationem tam de Deo quam de hominis salute veritas nobis in Christo illucescit, qui mediator simul et *plenitudo totius revelationis* exsistit" (emphasis added).

[4] For documentation of Ratzinger's relationship to *Dei Verbum*, see Jared Wicks, trans. and ed., "Six Texts by Prof. Joseph Ratzinger as *Peritus* before and during Vatican Council II," *Gregorianum* 89, no. 2 (2008): 233–311. See also Joseph Cong Quy Lam, "Joseph Ratzinger's Contribution to the Preparatory Debate of the Dogmatic Constitution *Dei Verbum*," *Gregorianum* 94, no. 1 (2013): 35–54.

[5] This perspective on the main thrust of *Dei Verbum* is expressed in Ratzinger's postcouncil commentary on that dogmatic constitution: "K. Barth has rightly pointed out

of God in the final text of *Dei Verbum* was anticipated by the contributions of Hermann Volk, Bishop of Mainz, to a debate over a preliminary schema on divine revelation considered in a general congregation on October 6, 1964. In making the case for his suggested emendations to chapter 6 of the schema then under consideration, Volk argued:

> [A] special importance attaches to sacred scripture because it is in itself the word of God and does not simply contain it. In the sacred liturgy we incense sacred scripture and not tradition, and in this hall we are solemnly exalting sacred scripture and not tradition.[6]

that as against one chapter on tradition, in which in any case tradition is considered entirely in relation to Scripture, there are four chapters which are concerned more or less exclusively with Scripture. Thus even the external structure shows what importance the text accords to Scripture in the life of the Church and the building-up of its faith. Scripture is factually presented as a yardstick, and that is even stated in a well-known passage in article 21, which says that all the preaching of the Church and the whole Christian religion must be nourished and ruled by Scripture (*'nutriatur et regatur oportet'*). There is a similar statement in article 10, which declares that the Church's teaching office does not stand above the word of God, but serves it" (Joseph Ratzinger, "Dogmatic Constitution on Divine Revelation: Chapter II, The Transmission of Divine Revelation," trans. William Glen-Doepel, in *Commentary on the Documents of Vatican II*, ed. Herbert Vorgrimler, vol. 3 [New York: Herder & Herder, 1967–1969], 194 [181–98]). Cf. the address delivered by Benedict XVI to the Congress on Sacred Scripture in the Life of the Church that commemorated the fortieth anniversary of the publication of *Dei Verbum*: "We are grateful to God that in recent times, and thanks to the impact made by the Dogmatic Constitution *Dei Verbum*, the fundamental importance of the Word of God has been deeply re-evaluated. From this has derived a renewal of the Church's life, especially in her preaching, catechesis, theology and spirituality, and even in the ecumenical process. The Church must be constantly renewed and rejuvenated and the Word of God, which never ages and is never depleted, is a privileged means to achieve this goal. Indeed, it is the Word of God, through the Holy Spirit, which always guides us to the whole truth (cf. John 16:13). In this context, I would like in particular to recall and recommend the ancient tradition of *Lectio divina*: the diligent reading of Sacred Scripture accompanied by prayer brings about that intimate dialogue in which the person reading hears God who is speaking, and in praying, responds to him with trusting openness of heart. If it is effectively promoted, this practice will bring to the Church—I am convinced of it—a new spiritual springtime" (Benedict XVI, "Address of His Holiness Benedict XVI to the Participants in the International Congress Organized to Commemorate the 40th Anniversary of the Dogmatic Constitution on Divine Revelation *Dei Verbum*," September 16, 2005 [accessed November 13, 2014, http://www.vatican.va/holy_father/benedict_xvi/speeches/2005/september/documents/hf_ben-xvi_spe_20050916_40-dei-verbum_en.html]).

[6] Hermann Volk, quoted in *History of Vatican II*, ed. Giuseppe Alberigo, trans. Joseph A. Komonchack, vol. 4, *Church as Communion: Third Period and Intersession September 1964–September 1965*, trans. Matthew O'Connell (Maryknoll, N.Y.: Orbis Books, 2003), 227, citing Vatican Council II, *Acta Synodalia Sacrosancti Concilii Vaticani II* (Vatican City: Typis Polyglottis Vaticanis, 1970–1983), vol. 3, pt. 3, 344. The schema then under consideration was Form F that with the addition of a supplement proposed by the Theological

Consistent with this dominant emphasis, the majority of the constitution deals in chapters 3 through 6 (articles 11–26) with the inspiration, interpretation, canonical contents, Christocentric unity, historical trustworthiness, and function in the life of the church of Sacred Scripture. These articles take great pains to present Catholic teaching on the authority and function of Scripture in a manner most conducive to ecumenical convergence. Chapter 4 on "The Old Testament," for example, does not reiterate the Tridentine listing of the sacred books and thus makes no mention of the deuterocanonical books, and chapter 6 on "Holy Scripture in the Life of the Church" invites "collaboration with Christians of other denominations" in biblical scholarship, especially in the production of translations, so that "all Christians will then be able to use them."[7] Even if many Baptists do not embrace the sacramental realism expressed in the insistence at the beginning of article 21 that "the church has always held the divine scriptures in reverence no less than it accords to the Lord's body itself, never ceasing . . . to receive the bread of life from the one table of God's word and Christ's body," the devotion and reverence given to the Scriptures by Baptists mirrors the sacramentality of the word implicit in the following sentence later in the same article: "In the sacred books the Father who is in heaven comes lovingly to meet his children and talks with them."[8] To these features of *Dei Verbum* that are eminently consistent with

---

Commission became Form G approved as the final text of the constitution on November 18, 1965, according to the textual history of *Dei Verbum* detailed by Alois Grillmeier, "Die Wahrheit der Heilegen Schrift und ihre Erschließung: Zum dritten Kapitel der Dogmatischen Konstitution 'Dei Verbum' des Vaticanum II," *Theologie und Philosophie* 41 (1966): 161–81, and summarized by Ratzinger, "Dogmatic Constitution on Divine Revelation: Origin and Background," in *Commentary on the Documents of Vatican II*, ed. Vorgrimler, vol. 3, 165–66.

[7] Vatican II, *Dei Verbum*, §22, in *Decrees of the Ecumenical Councils*, ed. Tanner, vol. 2, *Trent to Vatican II*, 979.

[8] Vatican II, *Dei Verbum*, §21, in *Decrees of the Ecumenical Councils*, ed. Tanner, vol. 2, *Trent to Vatican II*, 979. The connection between real presence in the Eucharist and the sacramentality of the word has patristic roots, as exemplified by Caesarius of Arles *Sermo* 78.2: "I ask you, brothers and sisters—tell me: What seems greater to you, the word of God or the Body of Christ? If you will give a true reply, you surely must say that the former is no less than the latter. Therefore, with as great anxiety as we show when Christ's Body is ministered to us, lest nothing fall out of our hands onto the ground, with as great anxiety we should see to it that God's word which is dispensed to us may not perish from our hearts because we are thinking or talking about something else. The person who hears the word of God with inattention is surely no less guilty than one who allows Christ's body to fall on the ground through his carelessness" (*Saint Caesarius of Arles: Sermons, Volume I*, trans. Mary Magdeleine Mueller [Fathers of the Church, vol. 31; Washington, D.C.: The Catholic University of America Press, 1956], 361). On the possibility of a Baptist theology of the sacramentality of the word, see John E. Colwell, *Promise*

the Scripture principle of the Reformation and the place of the Bible in the life of Baptist churches, Baptists can easily register their *placet*.[9]

The Transmission of Revelation

Non placet will remain the Baptist response to the plain sense of a few key assertions in chapter 2, "The Transmission of Divine Revelation" (articles 7–10), however, pending broader Baptist reception of explanations of their background and significance (in which case *placet iuxta modum* might well represent Baptist perspectives). The difficulties encountered in articles 7, 8, and 10 are not insuperable if read with certain Baptist qualifications in mind. When article 7 echoes Irenaeus of Lyons in stating that "the apostles left as their successors the bishops, 'handing on their own teaching function to them,'"[10] Baptists can concur that local church pastors, whom they equate with *episkopoi* in their reading of New Testament ecclesiology, are charged with carrying on the apostolic task of safeguarding right teaching in the church.[11] The characterization of the church's magisterium in article 10 presents greater difficulties for Baptists: "The task of authentically

---

and Presence: An Exploration of Sacramental Theology (Milton Keynes, UK.: Paternoster, 2005), chap. 4, "The Sacramentality of the Word," 88–105; Steven R. Harmon, "The Sacramentality of the Word in Gregory of Nyssa's *Catechetical Oration*: Implications for a Baptist Sacramental Theology," in *Baptist Sacramentalism 2*, ed. Anthony R. Cross and Philip E. Thompson (Studies in Baptist History and Thought, vol. 25; Milton Keynes, UK: Paternoster, 2008), 239–53.

[9] When voting on documents, the bishops in council had three options: *placet* (yes; lit., "it pleases"), *non placet* (no; lit., "it does not please"), and *placet iuxta modum* (yes, with reservations; lit., "it pleases with amendment").

[10] Vatican II, *Dei Verbum*, §7, in *Decrees of the Ecumenical Councils*, ed. Tanner, vol. 2, *Trent to Vatican II*, 974; the apparatus cites Irenaeus of Lyons *Adversus Haereses* III.3.1 (*Patrologiae Cursus Completus: Series Graecae*, ed. J.-P. Migne [Paris: Garnier, 1857–1866], 7:848).

[11] While exceptions to this generalization abound, Baptists have tended to insist on a twofold ministry of pastors and deacons on the basis of what they interpret as an equivocation in the use of the terms "pastor," "elder," and "bishop" and their functions of "shepherding" and "overseeing" in Acts 20:17–28 and 1 Pet 5:1–2, coupled with the lists of qualifications for the two offices of overseer and deacon in the Pastoral Epistles. This Baptist account of a twofold ministry in which the pastoral function of oversight includes responsibility for the safeguarding and promotion of true doctrine is given expression in paragraphs of the report from the second series of international Baptist–Catholic conversations that differentiate the Baptist perspective on *episkopē* from that of the Catholic Church: Baptist World Alliance and Catholic Church, "The Word of God in the Life of the Church: A Report of International Conversations between the Catholic Church and the Baptist World Alliance 2006–2010," §§171, 174, and 192, in *American Baptist Quarterly* 31, no. 1 (Spring 2012): 93–95, 101.

interpreting the word of God, whether in its written form or in that of tradition, has been entrusted only (*soli*) to those charged with the church's ongoing teaching function, whose authority is exercised in the name of Jesus Christ."[12] Inasmuch as Baptists do conceive of the church as having a legitimate and necessary teaching function,[13] it is primarily the qualifier *soli* that remains problematic.

The most significant objections from the perspective of Baptists, and indeed of Protestants in general, are to the teaching of article 9 on the relationship of Scripture and tradition. A close reading of the four sentences in the Latin text of article 9 sustains these objections from the standpoint of Baptist theology even while revealing some openings for a Baptist appreciation of the trajectory in the development of Catholic teaching on tradition evident in this text. The Latin text printed in Norman Tanner's edition of the *Decrees of the Ecumenical Councils* appears here along with three of the English translations.[14]

---

[12] Vatican II, *Dei Verbum*, §10, in *Decrees of the Ecumenical Councils*, ed. Tanner, vol. 2, *Trent to Vatican II*, 975.

[13] Baptist theologian James Wm. McClendon, Jr., defined doctrine in terms of the church's necessary teaching function: "Doctrine *is* teaching . . . and by *Christian* doctrine I will here mean *a church teaching as she must teach if she is to be the church here and now*" (James Wm. McClendon, Jr., *Doctrine: Systematic Theology, Vol. 2* [Waco, Tex.: Baylor University Press, 2012], 23–24). Cf. Timothy George, "Scripture and Tradition: An Evangelical Baptist Perspective," paper presented to the first session of the 2006–2010 bilateral conversations between the Baptist World Alliance Doctrine and Interchurch Cooperation Commission and the Vatican Council for Promoting Christian Unity, Beeson Divinity School, Samford University, Birmingham, Alabama, USA, December 10–15, 2006: "Baptists and Catholics differ on the scope and locus of the *magisterium* but not on whether it exists as a necessary component in the ongoing life of the Church." Cf. idem, "An Evangelical Reflection on Scripture and Tradition," *Pro Ecclesia* 9, no. 2 (Spring 2000): 206 (184–207).

[14] "Dogmatic Constitution on Divine Revelation," trans. Murray, in *Decrees of the Ecumenical Councils*, ed. Tanner, vol. 2, *Trent to Vatican II*, 974–75; "Dogmatic Constitution on Divine Revelation," trans. Liam Walsh and Wilfred Harrington, in *Vatican Council II: The Conciliar and Post Conciliar Documents*, rev. ed., ed. Austin Flannery (Vatican Collection, vol. 1; Northport, N.Y.: Costello, 1992), 755 (the Prologue and chapters 1, 2, and 6 were translated by Walsh, while chapters 3, 4, and 5 were translated by Harrington; Walsh thus translated article 9); "Dogmatic Constitution on Divine Revelation *Dei Verbum*," accessed November 14, 2014, http://www.vatican.va/archive/hist_councils/ii_vatican_council/documents/vat-ii_const_19651118_dei-verbum_en.html.

Latin (ed. Tanner)	English (ed. Tanner)	English (ed. Flannery)	English (vatican.va)
Sacra traditio ergo et sacra scriptura arcte inter se connectuntur atque communicant. Nam ambae, ex eadem divina scaturigine promanantes, in unum quodammodo coalescunt et in eundem finem tendunt. Etenim sacra scriptura est locutio Dei quatenus divino afflante Spiritu scripto consignatur; sacra autem traditio verbum Dei, a Christo domino et a Spiritu sancto apostolis concreditum, successoribus eorum integre transmittit, ut illud, praelucente Spiritu veritatis, praeconio suo fideliter servent, exponant atque diffundant; quo fit ut ecclesia certitudinem suam de omnibus revelatis non per solam sacram scripturam hauriat. Quapropter utraque pari pietatis affectu ac reverentia suscipienda et veneranda est.	Hence sacred tradition and scripture are bound together in a close and reciprocal relationship. They both flow from the same divine wellspring, merge together to some extent, and are on course towards the same end. Scripture is the utterance of God as it is set down in writing under the guidance of God's Spirit; tradition preserves the word of God as it was entrusted to the apostles by Christ our lord and the holy Spirit, and transmits it to their successors, so that these in turn, enlightened by the Spirit of truth, may faithfully preserve, expound, and disseminate the word by their preaching. Consequently, the church's certainty about all that is revealed is not drawn from holy scripture alone; both scripture and tradition are to be accepted and honoured with like devotion and reverence.	Sacred Tradition and sacred Scripture, then, are bound closely together, and communicate with one another. For both of them, flowing out of the same divine well-spring, come together in some fashion to form one thing, and move towards the same goal. Sacred Scripture is the speech of God as it is put down in writing under the breath of the Holy Spirit. And Tradition transmits in its entirety the Word of God which has been entrusted to the apostles by Christ the Lord and the Holy Spirit. It transmits it to the successors of the apostles so that, enlightened by the Spirit of truth, they may faithfully preserve, expound and spread it abroad by their preaching. Thus it comes about that the Church does not draw her certainty about all revealed truths from the holy Scriptures alone. Hence, both Scripture and Tradition must be accepted and honored with equal feelings of devotion and reverence.	Hence there exists a close connection and communication between sacred tradition and Sacred Scripture. For both of them, flowing from the same divine wellspring, in a certain way merge into a unity and tend toward the same end. For Sacred Scripture is the word of God inasmuch as it is consigned to writing under the inspiration of the divine Spirit, while sacred tradition takes the word of God entrusted by Christ the Lord and the Holy Spirit to the Apostles, and hands it on to their successors in its full purity, so that led by the light of the Spirit of truth, they may in proclaiming it preserve this word of God faithfully, explain it, and make it more widely known. Consequently it is not from Sacred Scripture alone that the Church draws her certainty about everything which has been revealed. Therefore both sacred tradition and Sacred Scripture are to be accepted and venerated with the same sense of loyalty and reverence.

(1) *Sacra traditio ergo et sacra scriptura arcte inter se connectuntur atque communicant.* The affirmation of a bond that exists between Scripture and tradition (*connectuntur*) and the dynamic interchange between them that manifests this connectedness (*communicant*) is not by itself problematic for Baptists. The new appreciation for tradition in recent Baptist academic theology has been noted in the first three chapters of this book.[15] Within this trajectory, Baptist theologian James Wm. McClendon, Jr., clearly affirmed the coinherence of Scripture and tradition in his *Systematic Theology* in a passage that develops at length and concurs with the conception of the interrelationship of Scripture and tradition expressed concisely in this first sentence of *Dei Verbum* article 9.[16] The inferential *ergo* near the beginning of this sentence makes the preceding paragraph at the end of article 8 the logical ground for asserting the coinherence of Scripture and tradition. If this is what is meant by their being "bound together in a close and reciprocal relationship," Baptists can concur. Tradition is there portrayed as the servant of the Scriptures. According to the penultimate paragraph of article 8, tradition reflects the ongoing work in the church of the same Spirit that inspired the Scriptures (*traditio sub assistentia Spiritus*

---

[15]   See also these Baptist affirmations of the place of tradition in the life of the church: Daniel H. Williams, *Retrieving the Tradition and Renewing Evangelicalism: A Primer for Suspicious Protestants* (Grand Rapids: William B. Eerdmans, 1999); idem, *Evangelicals and Tradition: The Formative Influence of the Early Church* (Evangelical Ressourcement: Ancient Sources for the Church's Future, vol. 1; Grand Rapids: Baker Academic, 2005); Mark S. Medley, "Catholics, Baptists, and the Normativity of Tradition," *Perspectives in Religious Studies* 28, no. 2 (Summer 2001): 119–29; Stephen R. Holmes, *Listening to the Past: The Place of Tradition in Theology* (Carlisle, UK: Paternoster/Grand Rapids: Baker Academic, 2002); Steven R. Harmon, "'Catholic Baptists' and the New Horizon of Tradition in Baptist Theology," in *New Horizons in Theology*, ed. Terrence W. Tilley (Maryknoll, N.Y.: Orbis Books, 2005), 117–43; idem, *Towards Baptist Catholicity: Essays on Tradition and the Baptist Vision* (Studies in Baptist History and Thought, vol. 27; Milton Keynes, UK: Paternoster, 2006); Curtis W. Freeman, *Contesting Catholicity: Theology for Other Baptists* (Waco, Tex.: Baylor University Press, 2014).

[16]   McClendon, *Doctrine*, 469–70: "In the original Christian sense, 'tradition' (Greek, *paradosis*) is what is delivered or handed on of Christian teaching. Thus Paul writes to the Corinthians, 'First and foremost, I handed on to you the tradition (*paredōka*) I had received: that Christ died for our sins, in accordance with the scriptures' (1 Cor. 15:3). In that sense tradition is not only transmitted to today's believers by the written Scripture (in this case, Paul's first Corinthian letter); it also necessarily preceded it. . . . Such tradition undergirds and does not rival the Bible. . . . If, as Catholic and baptist Christians may now agree, Scripture and tradition (now in the sense of 1 Corinthians 15) are not two sources of authority but properly only one, both communities have a key to the role of creeds and confessions of faith as well. These can have no status as *additional* or supplemental authorities. Creeds and confessions cannot be invoked as witness to a truth that Scripture omits. But they may briefly witness to the truth that is more fully witnessed in Scripture."

sancti in ecclesia proficit).[17] The final paragraph of that article then links this work of the Spirit in the tradition of the church to the assistance of the Spirit in the church's recognition of the contents of the canon of Scripture, the church's understanding of the Scriptures, the church's hearing in the Scriptures of the voice of the God who spoke then and still speaks through the Scriptures today, and the church's evangelistic mission of proclaiming the living voice of the gospel (*viva vox evangelii*) from the Scriptures. *Ergo*, "Scripture and tradition are bound together in a close and reciprocal relationship." With this rationale for the coinherence of Scripture and tradition Baptists can agree.

(2) *Nam ambae, ex eadem divina scaturigine promanantes, in unum quodammodo coalescunt et in eundem finem tendunt.* Baptists can likewise concur with this manner of expressing a coinherence of Scripture and tradition (*coalescunt*) that owes to their common derivation from the self-revealing God (*ex eadem divina scaturigine*) and that participates in the evangelistic end of revelation (*in eundem finem tendunt*) emphasized throughout articles 2–6 and recapitulated in the final sentence of article 10, where Scripture and tradition, in association also with the church's *magisterium*, are directed "toward the salvation of souls" (*ad animarum salutem efficaciter conferant*)— "each in its own way" (*singula suo modo*) and "subject to the action of the one holy Spirit" (*sub actione unius Spiritus sancti*).[18] However, in that this image can seem to grant a status to tradition that approaches that of Scripture by virtue of a parallel relationship to divine revelation, they may not so easily embrace the tracing of the streams of Scripture and tradition to "the same divine wellspring" (*ex eadem divina scaturigine promanantes*). The intention of this language, however, was apparently to avoid any suggestion that Scripture and tradition are independent sources of revelation.[19] The "two-source" theory has been avoided here: rather than a revelation for which we depend upon the two sources of Scripture and tradition, here Scripture and tradition have their source in revelation.[20] If the flowing

---

[17]   Vatican II, *Dei Verbum*, §8, in *Decrees of the Ecumenical Councils*, ed. Tanner, vol. 2, *Trent to Vatican II*, 974.

[18]   Vatican II, *Dei Verbum*, §10, in *Decrees of the Ecumenical Councils*, ed. Tanner, vol. 2, *Trent to Vatican II*, 975.

[19]   So Ratzinger, "Dogmatic Constitution on Divine Revelation: Chapter II, The Transmission of Divine Revelation," in *Commentary on the Documents of Vatican II*, ed. Vorgrimler, vol. 3, 190: "The text shows clear signs of the firm position taken during the discussion against the idea of 'two sources' of revelation."

[20]   For a careful analysis of the usage of the language "source" and "sources" and associated concepts in Catholic theology from the Council of Trent through the deliberations at Vatican II that preceded the approval of *Dei Verbum*, see George H. Tavard,

forth of Scripture and tradition "from the same divine wellspring" represents something other than a two-source account of divine revelation,[21] and if "each in its own way" (article 10) suggests that Scripture and tradition may have qualitatively different sorts of relations to this one divine wellspring even while they are linked in a dynamic coinherence, then Baptist objections to the relation of Scripture and tradition in article 9 are not necessarily occasioned by this proposition therein.

(3) *Etenim sacra scriptura est locutio Dei quatenus divino afflante Spiritu scripto consignatur; sacra autem traditio verbum Dei, a Christo domino et a Spiritu sancto apostolis concreditum, successoribus eorum integre transmittit, ut illud, praelucente Spiritu veritatis, praeconio suo fideliter servent, exponant atque diffundant; quo fit ut ecclesia certitudinem suam de omnibus revelatis non per solam sacram scripturam hauriat.* Taken by itself, the first portion of this compound sentence (through the first semicolon) seems to affirm the material completeness of Scripture (some Baptists and other Protestants refer to the "sufficiency" of Scripture in this connection). If Scripture is "the utterance of God as it is set down in writing under the guidance of God's Spirit," it is not materially incomplete, needing to be supplemented by something that is disclosed only in some subsequent tradition, whether written or unwritten. This affirmation poses no difficulty for Baptists who hold that it is only Scripture that is "the supreme standard by which all human conduct, creeds, and religious opinions should be tried," in the language of a confession employed by many Baptists with connections to the Southern Baptist Convention in the United States and elsewhere.[22]

"Scripture and Tradition: Sources or Source?" *Journal of Ecumenical Studies* 1, no. 3 (Autumn 1964): 445–59.

[21] This intention seems to be confirmed by the intense debate during the week of November 14–21, 1962, over the preparatory schema on the sources of divine revelation, *De Fontibus Revalationis*, and its consequent withdrawal for rewriting. See Giuseppe Ruggieri, "The First Doctrinal Clash," chapter in *History of Vatican II*, ed. Alberigo, vol. 2, 233–66.

[22] Southern Baptist Convention, *Baptist Faith and Message (1963)*, §1, "The Scriptures," in *Baptist Confessions of Faith*, ed. Lumpkin, rev. Leonard, 410–11. Many churches now affiliated with the Cooperative Baptist Fellowship in the United States no longer identify themselves with the Southern Baptist Convention but continue to utilize the 1963 version of the *Baptist Faith and Message*, and several Baptist communions in other countries with origins in Southern Baptist missionary work have adopted the 1963 version of the confession as their own, making it perhaps the most widely embraced Baptist confession of faith today. The Southern Baptist Convention adopted a significant revision of the *Baptist Faith and Message* in 2000 (*Baptist Confessions of Faith*, ed. Lumpkin, rev. Leonard, 512–20).

To regard Scripture as the *"supreme* standard" does not deny the existence of other sources of authority, such as tradition, that derive their authority from the material completeness of the Scriptures that they interpret and therefore are normative only in relationship to their being normed by Scripture.[23] To say that "tradition preserves the word of God as it was entrusted to the apostles by Christ our Lord and the holy Spirit, and transmits it to their successors," however, may initially appear to be contrary to an affirmation of the material completeness of Scripture. Yet when compared with the first clause of the sentence to which this proposition is joined by a semicolon, it becomes evident that a proper distinction is being maintained between Scripture and tradition in their respective relations to the word of God.[24] If this is the relationship of tradition to the Scriptures that *Dei Verbum* has in mind, Baptists who have an appreciation for the authority of a tradition that is normed by the un-normed norm of Scripture can also appreciate the manner in which tradition is defined by its relationship to Scripture here.

The final clause of this third sentence of article 9 (following the second semicolon) seems to be directed against at least some expressions of the Reformation hermeneutical principle *sola scriptura*, inasmuch as it insists that the church draws its certainty regarding the full content of revelation *non per solam sacram scripturam*. Yet this clause does not state that the church depends upon something beyond the Scriptures as a supplementary source of the content of revelation. If that were the import of this language, it would communicate what the second sentence of article 9 has taken great pains to avoid. Rather, it is in the noetic dimension of the church's encounter with the content of revelation that the Bible does not stand

[23] For Baptist acknowledgments of such patterns of authority for Baptist faith and practice, see James Leo Garrett, Jr., "Sources of Authority in Baptist Thought," *Baptist History and Heritage* 13 (1978): 41–49; Steven R. Harmon, "Baptist Understandings of Theological Authority: A North American Perspective," *International Journal for the Study of the Christian Church* 4, no. 1 (2004): 50–63; idem, *Towards Baptist Catholicity*, 23–38.

[24] Cf. Ratzinger, "Dogmatic Constitution on Divine Revelation: Chapter II, The Transmission of Divine Revelation," in *Commentary on the Documents of Vatican II*, ed. Vorgrimler, vol. 3, 194: "If we return to our text, we shall see that, following the stress on the unity of Scripture and tradition, an attempt is made to give a definition of the two entities. It is important to note that only Scripture is defined in terms of what it *is*: it is stated that Scripture *is* the word of God consigned to writing. Tradition, however, is described only functionally, in terms of what it *does*: it hands on the word of God, but *is* not the word of God. If this makes clear the nature of Scripture, we can see from the more detailed characterization of tradition, whose task it is to 'preserve (it), explain it, and make it more widely known,' that it is not productive, but 'conservative,' ordained to serve as part of something already given."

alone. As Ratzinger explained, "The function of tradition is seen here as a making certain of the truth, i.e., it belongs to the formal and gnoseological sphere—and, in fact, this is the sphere in which the significance of tradition is to be sought."[25] The church does not learn anything belonging to the content of revelation from tradition that is other than or in addition to the truth conveyed by Scripture, but tradition in its various forms does contribute to the church's confidence in the doctrine that emerges from the ecclesial interpretation of the Scriptures in the company of the communion of saints. Karl Barth cautioned Protestants against quick objections to the phrase *non per solam sacram scripturam* in the course of a response to *Dei Verbum* solicited from Barth by Yves Congar:

> We do not live, think, and teach on the basis of a Scripture that is suspended all alone in the air, and thus not "*sola*" (=*solitaria*) *Scriptura*. We live, think, and teach . . . in the communion of the saints, as we listen with filial reverence and brotherly love to the voice of the pastors and teachers of God's people, those of the past as well as those of the present. But first and last we do so as we adhere to the revelation of God to which the Holy Scriptures bear witness, which is inspired by the Holy Spirit, and which gives inspiration; that is, we do so in obeying in faith the living voice of Jesus Christ.[26]

Baptists among the Protestants addressed by Barth can appreciate the priority given to Scripture in this qualification of *non per solam sacram scripturam.*

The trinitarian faith of Baptists illustrates their own dependence on the postbiblical development of doctrine for their certainty regarding the triune nature of God. Baptists affirm trinitarian doctrine in their confessions of faith,[27] but in a manner that is informed, however indirectly, by

---

[25]   Ratzinger, "Dogmatic Constitution on Divine Revelation: Chapter II, The Transmission of Divine Revelation," in *Commentary on the Documents of Vatican II*, ed. Vorgrimler, vol. 3, 195.

[26]   Karl Barth, "'Conciliorum Tridentini et Vaticani I Inhaerens Vestigiis,'" in *Ad Limina Apostolorum: An Appraisal of Vatican II*, trans. Keith R. Crim (Richmond, Va.: John Knox Press, 1968), 49–50.

[27]   E.g., *Second London Confession (1677)*, §2.1, in *Baptist Confessions of Faith*, ed. Lumpkin, rev. Leonard, 235–36: "In this divine and infinite Being there are three subsistences, the Father the Word (or Son) and Holy Spirit, of one substance, power, and Eternity, each having the whole Divine Essence, yet the Essence undivided, the Father is of none neither begotten nor proceeding, the Son is Eternally begotten of the Father, the Holy Spirit proceeding from the Father and the Son, all infinite, without beginning, therefore but one God, who is not to be divided in nature and Being; but distinguished by several peculiar, relative properties, and personal relations; which doctrine of the Trinity is the foundation of all our Communion with God, and comfortable dependence on him."

the formulations of Nicaea and Constantinople and their elucidation by Augustine of Hippo, the Cappadocian Fathers, Hilary of Poitiers, John of Damascus, and a host of other contributors to the church's reflections on the triadic narrative of the Bible that shaped the church's narration of the story of the Triune God. Baptist theologian James Leo Garrett, Jr., therefore recommends that "Baptists who emphasize the use of Baptist confessions of faith and who insist on a clearly articulated doctrine of the Trinity, often using terms easily traceable to the patristic age, would do well to affirm *suprema scriptura*" rather than an unqualified *sola scriptura*.[28] To the degree that Baptist faith and practice really reflect this *suprema scriptura* theological hermeneutic, the seeming repudiation of *sola scriptura* in article 9 does not stand against Baptist patterns of theological authority.

(4) *Quapropter utraque pari pietatis affectu ac reverentia suscipienda et veneranda est.* The recognition by Baptists that they do not depend upon the Bible alone in their efforts to understand the divine revelation transmitted by it does not, however, lead them to the logical conclusion (*quapropter*) that the dynamic interrelationship of Scripture and tradition requires that they receive and respond to tradition with expressions of devotion and reverence on a par with their responses to Scripture. The plain sense of the language *pari pietatis affectu ac reverentia* goes beyond an account of the dynamic interrelationship of Scripture and tradition, and it is difficult to conceive of it as meaning anything other than the equality of Scripture and tradition as sources of authority for the church. As long as Baptists understand this language to mean what it seems to communicate, they will continue to regard Baptist and Catholic perspectives on the relation of Scripture and tradition as incompatible.[29]

Yet it is possible that there are nuanced understandings of this final proposition in article 9 that may elicit from Baptists greater degrees of appreciation of this primary location of their objections to *Dei Verbum*. From the standpoint of Baptist theology, such appreciation might be fostered by answers to three questions about the synchronic import of *pari pietatis affectu ac reverentia*, quite apart from the much analyzed diachronic

---

[28] James Leo Garrett, Jr., *Systematic Theology: Biblical, Historical, and Evangelical*, vol. 1 (Grand Rapids: William B. Eerdmans, 1990), 181.

[29] So George, "Scripture and Tradition: An Evangelical Baptist Perspective": "Baptists can affirm the coinherence of sacred Scripture and sacred Tradition, but not their coequality. If I understand it correctly, no Baptist or Evangelical can say that both Scripture and Tradition 'are to be accepted and venerated with the same sense of loyalty and reverence' without becoming either Orthodox or Roman Catholic." Cf. idem, "An Evangelical Reflection on Scripture and Tradition," 207.

associations of this language to which this chapter will next turn. First, what exactly does it mean to give devotion and reverence to tradition? In other words, what are the specific attitudes and concrete actions on the part of the faithful in their response to tradition that ought to be parallel to the piety they manifest in relationship to Holy Scripture? The words of Herman Volk quoted earlier in this chapter distinguished between the proper liturgical response to Scripture and whatever may be the appropriate response to tradition.[30] If "like devotion and reverence" permits other proper distinctions to be made in the respective responses of the faithful to Scripture and tradition, perhaps Baptists might find this language less objectionable. Second, does an understanding of *pari* as indicating an exact equivalence in degree read into this word a precision that its use here does not require? Both the portion of the English translation prepared by Liam Walsh for the collection of conciliar and post-conciliar documents edited by Austin Flannery, which renders the phrase in question "equal feelings of devotion and reverence," and the English translation available on the official Vatican web site, which translates it as "the same sense of loyalty and reverence," suggest a stronger implication of equivalence in degree.[31] Robert Murray's translation of *Dei Verbum* in Tanner's edition of the *Decrees of the Ecumenical Councils*, on the other hand, reads "like reverence and devotion," which could conceivably admit an understanding of *pari* according to which the reverence and devotion given to Scripture and tradition are closely comparable in degree but not necessarily precisely identical—in other words, a connotation approaching the meaning of *simili*.[32] Third, given Ratzinger's judgment that the concern of article 9 is to define tradition in terms of its function of handing on the word of God that has been consigned to writing in the Scriptures, is it possible that

[30]   Volk, quoted in *History of Vatican II*, ed. Alberigo, vol. 4, 227.

[31]   Vatican II, "Divine Constitution on Divine Revelation," trans. Walsh and Harrington, in *Vatican Council II*, ed. Flannery, 55.

[32]   Vatican II, "Divine Constitution on Divine Revelation," trans. Murray, in *Decrees of the Ecumenical Councils*, ed. Tanner, vol. 2, *Trent to Vatican II*, 975. The collective force of the range of meanings associated with *par* in standard Latin lexica (e.g., Charlton T. Lewis and Charles Short, eds., *A Latin Dictionary*, rev. ed. [Oxford: Clarendon Press, 1955], s.v. "par, paris"; P. G. W. Glare, ed., *Oxford Latin Dictionary* [New York: Oxford University Press, 1982], s.v. "par, paris") does not argue strongly for the possibility that *pari* in the sense of "like" might mean "closely comparable in degree but not necessarily precisely equal," but neither does it exclude such a connotation. In the *Oxford Latin Dictionary* entry, the translations "equal" and "same" are supported by def. 1, "matching in magnitude . . . equal," and def. 7.b, "equal in degree," while the translation "like" in the sense here under consideration is supported by def. 5, "similar, like," and def. 10.a, "(of unlike qualities, attributes, etc.) corresponding in degree, proportional, commensurate."

the exhortation that reverence and devotion be given also to tradition is applicable only to the extent that tradition faithfully executes its proper function of handing on the word of God encountered in the Scriptures?[33] If this is the case, then there are additional questions to be asked about the means by which the church may distinguish between expressions of tradition that execute this function faithfully and those that do not, questions that may well be answered by the coinherence of Scripture, tradition, and *magisterium* in article 10.

At the end of this final sentence of article 9 appears an annotation that also belongs to the official text of *Dei Verbum*, noting that the source of this proposition is the decree "On the Canonical Scriptures" from Session 4 of the Council of Trent (April 8, 1546):[34]

Latin (ed. Tanner)	English (ed. Tanner)
[P]erspiciensque, hanc veritatem et disciplinam contineri in libris scriptis et sine scripto traditionibus, quae ab ipsius Christi ore ab apostolis acceptae, au tab ipsis apostolis Spiritu sancto dicante quasi per manus traditae ad nos usque pervenerunt, orthodoxorum partum exempla secuta, mones libros tam veteris quam novi testamenti, cum utriusque unus Deus sit auctor, nec non traditiones ipsas, tum ad fidem, tum ad mores pertinentes, tamquam vel oretenus a Christo, vel a Spiritu sancto dicatas et continua successione in ecclesia catholica conservatas, pari pietatis affectu ac reverentia suscipit et veneratur.	The council clearly perceives that this truth and rule are contained in written books and in unwritten traditions which were received by the apostles from the mouth of Christ himself, or else have come down to us, handed on as it were from the apostles themselves at the inspiration of the Holy Spirit. Following the example of the orthodox fathers, the council accepts and venerates with a like feeling of piety and reverence all the books of both the old and the new Testament, since the one God is the author of both, as well as the traditions concerning both faith and conduct, as either directly spoken by Christ or dictated by the Holy Spirit, which have been preserved in unbroken sequence in the catholic church.

We thus must interpret the phrase *pari pietatis affectu ac reverentia* not only in light of its Tridentine source but also in association with the statement in the introduction of *Dei Verbum* regarding the relationship of the constitution to the teaching of previous councils: "This council aims, then, following in the steps of the councils of Trent and Vatican I (*conciliorum Tridentini et Vaticani I inhaerens vestigiis*), to set forth authentic teaching on God's

---

[33] Ratzinger, "Dogmatic Constitution on Divine Revelation: Chapter II, The Transmission of Divine Revelation," in *Commentary on the Documents of Vatican II*, ed. Vorgrimler, vol. 3, 194.

[34] Council of Trent, Session 4, April 8, 1546, "First Decree: Acceptance of the Sacred Books and Apostolic Traditions," trans. Peter McIlhenny, in *Decrees of the Ecumenical Councils*, ed. Tanner, vol. 2, *Trent to Vatican II*, 663.

revelation and how it is communicated."[35] What does *inhaerens vestigiis* mean in this connection? Barth's rather positive assessment of *Dei Verbum* was rooted in his aversion to one possible translation, "in the succession of the Councils of Trent and First Vatican," which suggested to Barth that "following in their tracks, it intended to say the same thing they said," and his preference for understanding the expression instead in the sense of "moving forward from the footsteps of those councils."[36] Ratzinger concurred that "we can entirely agree with Karl Barth's suggested translation of this formula," which meant for Ratzinger that between these previous councils and Vatican II there is "a continuity that is not a rigid external identification with what has gone before, but a preservation of the old, established in the midst of progress," so "that we might perhaps see the relation of this text to its predecessors as a perfect example of doctrinal development."[37]

Is *pari pietatis affectu ac reverentia* then a reiteration of the Tridentine teaching on proper regard for Scripture and tradition, or does the reappearance of the phrase in *Dei Verbum* represent a nuanced development beyond Trent? If the latter is the case, then there may be clues to the nature of this development in the redaction of the language from Trent in the final text of article 9. In the decree of 1546, it is traditions in the plural that are to be accepted and venerated along with the Old and New Testament Scriptures with "a like feeling of piety and reverence." Though the Tridentine fathers refrained from identifying particular traditions, the plural evokes a concrete specificity in contrast to the singular employed in *Dei Verbum*. Does tradition in the singular according to its use in article 9 then refer to the dynamic process by which tradition hands on the word of God rather than to the particular traditions produced by this process? Baptist theologians who have given attention to tradition as a possible source of theological authority have tended to reject the authority of tradition when it is conceived as *traditia*, a body of particular traditions, but those who have come to appreciate tradition as a source of authority have tended to conceive of this tradition as *traditio*, the dynamic process of traditioning.[38] If *Dei Verbum* has here shifted the emphasis from the particular

---

[35]   Vatican II, *Dei Verbum*, proem., in *Decrees of the Ecumenical Councils*, ed. Tanner, vol. 2, *Trent to Vatican II*, 971–72.

[36]   Barth, "'Conciliorum Tridentini et Vaticani I Inhaerens Vestigiis'?" in *Ad Limina Apostolorum*, trans. Crim, 43–45.

[37]   Ratzinger, "Dogmatic Constitution on Divine Revelation: Preface," in *Commentary on the Documents of Vatican II*, ed. Vorgrimler, vol. 3, 168–69.

[38]   So observes Medley, "Catholics, Baptists, and the Normativity of Tradition," 126, in applying to Baptist perspectives on tradition evident in Baptist systematic theologies

content of tradition to its general function in relation to Scripture, there may be more of an opening for Baptist convergence toward its account of tradition than the language of "equal devotion and reverence" would otherwise indicate. Furthermore, Trent posited the existence and authority of "unwritten traditions" (*sine scripto traditionibus*), which include traditions Jesus entrusted to the apostles beyond what the canonical gospels recorded as well as traditions subsequently spoken by the Spirit and "which have been preserved in unbroken sequence in the catholic church." This sort of unwritten tradition would help account for what might otherwise appear to be the later emergence of elements of faith and practice that are unprecedented by the Scriptures,[39] but to Baptists (and not a few Catholics), this

---

Yves Congar's categories of *traditio* and *traditia* (Yves Congar, *Tradition and Traditions: An Historical and a Theological Essay*, trans. Michael Naseby and Thomas Rainborough [London: Burns & Oates, 1966]) as utilized in Terrence W. Tilley, *Inventing Catholic Tradition* (Maryknoll, N.Y.: Orbis Books, 2000).

[39] Ratzinger, "Dogmatic Constitution on Divine Revelation: Chapter II, The Transmission of Divine Revelation," in *Commentary on the Documents of Vatican II*, ed. Vorgrimler, vol. 3, 195, noted that this aspect of the Tridentine formulation was influenced by an echo of Basil of Caesarea mediated by the twelfth-century *Decree of Gratian*. The text in Basil is *De Spiritu Sancto* 27.66 (*Patrologiae Gracae*, ed. Migne, 32:188; ET, *St. Basil the Great: On the Holy Spirit*, trans. David Anderson [Crestwood, N.Y.: St. Vladimir's Seminary Press, 1980], 98–100):

> Concerning the teachings of the Church, whether publicly proclaimed (*kerygma*) or reserved to members of the household of faith (*dogmata*), we have received some from written sources, while others have been given to us secretly, through apostolic tradition. Both sources have equal force in true religion. No one would deny either source—no one, at any rate, who is even slightly familiar with the ordinances of the Church. If we attacked unwritten customs, claiming them to be of little importance, we would fatally mutilate the Gospel, no matter what our intentions—or rather, we would reduce the Gospel teachings to bare words. For instance (to take the first and most common example), where is the written teaching that we should sign with the sign of the Cross those who, trusting in the Name of Our Lord Jesus Christ, are to be enrolled as catechumens? Which book teaches us to pray facing the East? Have any saints left for us in writing the words to be used in the invocation over the Eucharistic bread and the cup of blessing? As everyone knows, we are not content in the liturgy simply to recite the words recorded by St. Paul or the Gospels, but we add other words both before and after, words of great importance for this mystery. We have received these words from unwritten teaching. We bless baptismal water and the oil for chrismation as well as the candidate approaching the font. By what written authority do we do this, if not from secret and mystical tradition? Even beyond blessing the oil, what written command do we have to anoint them with it? What about baptizing a man with three immersions, or other baptismal rites, such as the renunciation of Satan and his angels? Are not all these things found in unpublished and unwritten traditions, which our fathers guarded in silence, safe from meddling and petty curiosity? They had learned their lesson well: reverence for the mysteries is best encouraged by silence. The

would make of tradition a second and separate source of revelation that in effect renders Scripture materially insufficient. *Dei Verbum*, on the other hand, completely avoids the appeal to unwritten traditions. Even if it does not repudiate what Trent teaches at this point, this development beyond Trent moves in a direction Baptists can appreciate.

Contestation and Dissent

Thus far this chapter has engaged *Dei Verbum* primarily as a text, a focus in keeping with the tendency of much postconciliar analysis to treat Vatican II "in the abstract, as if it were merely an abundant, even excessive, collection of documents."[40] But Vatican II was first and foremost a living process of ecclesial theological deliberation that stood in relation to previous such processes. In this regard *Dei Verbum* offers a window into the communal formulation of magisterial teaching that points to additional possibilities for Catholic–Baptist convergence on the nature of tradition.

The retention of *pari pietatis affectu ac reverentia* from Trent obscures the extent to which the final language of the decree "On the Canonical Scriptures" was preceded by a robust contestation of its wording and its theological implications. Between February 8 and April 8, 1546, intense debates over the drafting of the decree made it clear that the Tridentine fathers were far from having the same mind about the most appropriate Catholic response to the challenge of the Lutheran version of *sola scriptura*.[41] When the general congregation of April 1 ended debate on the relationship of Scripture and tradition in the proposed wording of the decree, there were thirty-three votes for a statement of the parity of Scripture and tradition, but there were eleven votes in favor of replacing *pari*, "equal," with *simili*, "similar," plus an additional three votes in favor of a statement that traditions should be regarded with respect but without language declaring their parity with Scripture.[42] When a revised draft was

---

uninitiated were not even allowed to be present at the mysteries; how could you expect these teachings to be paraded about in public documents? . . . [W]hen the apostles and Fathers established ordinances for the Church, they protected the dignity of the mysteries with silence and secrecy from the beginning, since what is noised abroad to anyone at random is no mystery at all. We have unwritten tradition so that the knowledge of dogma might not become neglected and scorned through familiarity. Dogma is one thing, kerygma another; the first is observed in silence, while the latter is proclaimed to the world.

[40]   Alberigo, *Brief History of Vatican II*, xiii.

[41]   Hubert Jedin, *A History of the Council of Trent*, trans. Ernest Graf (St. Louis: B. Herder, 1961), vol. 2, 52–98.

[42]   Jedin, *History of the Council of Trent*, vol. 2, 82.

put forward for debate in a general congregation on April 5, four bishops once again proposed replacing *pari* with *simili*, and Giacomo Nacchianti, Bishop of Chioggia, defended the renewed proposal by contending, "To put Scripture and Tradition on the same level is ungodly." In response to the interjection by another bishop, "Are we ungodly people?" Nacchianti replied, "Yes, I repeat it! How can I accept the practice of praying eastward with the same reverence as St. John's gospel?"[43] That afternoon a working committee replaced *pari* with *simili* despite the vote of April 1, and on April 6 meetings of particular congregations revisited the issue and changed the wording back to *pari*. A general congregation on April 7 approved the final text of the decree with *pari*, but with a significant alteration elsewhere in the text: language declaring the truth of salvation to be found "partly" in Scripture and "partly" in tradition, *partim . . . partim*, was dropped in favor of *et*—that is, truth is revealed in Scripture and in tradition, but without a parceling out of some truths to Scripture and others to tradition.[44] In retrospect Baptists would readily identify with those bishops

---

[43] Jedin, *History of the Council of Trent*, vol. 2, 86–87.

[44] In the years just before the opening of the Second Vatican Council, there was a sharp debate among Catholic theologians over the significance of Trent's option for *et* rather than *partim . . . partim* that set the stage for the disagreements during the council over how the text that became *Dei Verbum* ought to characterize the relationship of Scripture and tradition. The controversy originated in a published interchange between German Catholic theologians. One party represented by Josef Rupert Geiselmann contended that the choice not to adopt the *partim . . . partim* language intentionally allowed for a single source reading in which Scripture is the sufficiently full source of revelation, and tradition, which is coinherent with Scripture, hands on the fullness of truth found in Scripture. The opposition to Geiselmann's position was represented by Heinrich Lennerz, who insisted that even though Trent did not finally include the *partim . . . partim* language, the intention and import of its teaching was the two-source account of the relation of Scripture and tradition to revelation that predominated after that council. See Josef Rupert Geiselmann, "Das Missverständnis über das Verhältnis von Schrift und Tradition und seine Überwindung in der katholischen Theologie," *Una Sancta* 2 (1956): 131–50 (English condensation published as "Scripture and Tradition in Catholic Theology," *Theology Digest* 6 [1958]: 73–78); idem, "Schrift—Tradition—Kirche: Ein ökumenisches Problem," in *Begegnung der Christen: Studien evangelischer und katholischer Theologen*, ed. Maximilian Roesle and Oscar Cullmann (Stuttgart: Evangelisches Verlagswerk, 1959), 131–59; ET, "Scripture, Tradition, and the Church: An Ecumenical Problem," in *Christianity Divided: Protestant and Roman Catholic Theological Issues*, ed. Daniel J. Callahan, Heiko A. Oberman, and Daniel J. O'Hanlon (New York: Sheed & Ward, 1961), 39–72; idem, *Die Heilige Schrift und die Tradition: Zu den neueren Kontroversen über das verhältnis der Heiligen Schrift zu den nichtgeschriebenen Traditionen* (Quaestiones Disputatae, vol. 18; Freiburg: Herder, 1962); partial ET, *The Meaning of Tradition*, trans. W. J. O'Hara (Quaestiones Disputatae, vol. 15; New York: Herder & Herder, 1966); Heinrich Lennerz, "Scriptura sola?" *Gregorianum* 40, no. 1 (1959): 38–53; idem, "Sine scripto traditions," *Gregorianum* 40, no. 4 (1959): 624–35; idem, "Scriptura et tradition in decreto 4. sessionis Concilii

who contended for *simili* over *pari* at Trent, and they would find the nod to the minority in the wording of the final version of the text more amenable than the *partim . . . partim* language it replaced.

A comparable difference of opinion over the proper relation of Scripture and tradition emerged in the long and tumultuous process leading from the initial presentation of the preparatory schema *De Fontibus Revelationis* on October 27, 1960, to the approval of *Dei Verbum* on November 18, 1965. Counting the preparatory schema, the text that became *Dei Verbum* had nine incarnations. Ratzinger's commentary captures well the relationship between this process and the end result:

> The text . . . naturally reveals traces of its difficult history; it is the result of many compromises. But the fundamental compromise which pervades it is more than a compromise, it is a synthesis of great importance. It combines fidelity to Church tradition with an affirmation of critical scholarship, thus opening up anew the path that faith may follow into the world of today. It does not entirely abandon the position of Trent and Vatican I, but neither does it mummify what was held to be true at those councils, because it recognizes that fidelity in the sphere of the Spirit can be realized only through a constantly renewed appropriation. With regard to its total achievement, one can say unhesitatingly that the labour of the four-year long controversy was not in vain.[45]

These "compromises" addressed the concerns of proponents of neo-Scholastic theology at one pole of the debate, advocates of a Catholic version of *sola scriptura* at the other pole, and a wide array of opinions in between them. As with Trent, the magisterial teaching that emerged from the contentious process of conciliar theological deliberation had taken into account a range of positions that included some with basic similarities to Baptist perspectives.[46] Even if such positions did not triumph over

---

Tridentini," *Gregorianum* 42, no. 3 (1961): 517–22. Yves Congar's posthumously published journal of his behind-the-scenes participation in the Second Vatican Council notes the role of these publications in conversations among theological contributors to the work of the council: Yves Congar, *My Journal of the Council*, trans. Mary John Ronayne and Mary Cecily Boulding, ed. Denis Minns (Collegeville, Minn.: Liturgical Press, 2012), 181, 201, 249, 262, 276, 283–84, 519.

[45] Ratzinger, "Dogmatic Constitution on Divine Revelation: Origin and Background," in *Commentary on the Documents of Vatican II*, ed. Vorgrimler, vol. 3, 164–65.

[46] Cf. Baptist World Alliance and Catholic Church, "The Word of God in the Life of the Church," §65: "In further exploring this theme [of the connection between Scripture and tradition in *Dei Verbum* §9], nevertheless we found that both the Council of Trent and Vatican II included Catholic bishops who voiced the same concern that Baptists would

the others in the final formulation of the dogmatic constitution, they did influence it and to some degree were incorporated into the "compromise" document that is *Dei Verbum*.

These processes of Catholic conciliarity[47] illustrate Alasdair Mac-Intyre's definition of a "living tradition" as "an historically extended, socially embodied argument, and an argument precisely in part about the goods which constitute that tradition."[48] The living Catholic theological tradition depends on the sort of contestation manifested in the debates over the relation of Scripture and tradition at Trent and Vatican II, constructive disagreement that contributes to the clarification of doctrine.[49] This intra-Catholic contestation of doctrine raises questions about the

---

have about attributing 'like devotion' to Scripture and tradition, that is, the potential danger of obscuring the unique authority of Scripture as the inspired Word of God. We noted that it was never the intention of the bishops at either council to call into question the inspiration and primacy of Scripture. In both councils, moreover, the bishops embraced the crucial distinction between apostolic tradition and merely ecclesiastical traditions. Normative tradition stems from the apostolic church of the time of the apostles, the primitive community which received the fullness of revelation in Christ. Such views, expressed in the debates and sometimes echoed in the final texts of Trent and Vatican II, are more congenial to the Baptist understanding of the relation of Scripture and tradition."

[47] "Conciliarity" here refers not to the understanding of magisterial structures that privileges the authority of general councils over papal authority, but rather to the communal nature of doctrinal deliberation that characterizes the work of these general councils. On the former sense of conciliarity, see Paul Avis, *Beyond the Reformation? Authority, Primacy and Unity in the Conciliar Tradition* (London: T&T Clark, 2006).

[48] Alasdair MacIntyre, *After Virtue. A Study in Moral Theory*, 2nd ed. (Notre Dame, Ind.: University of Notre Dame Press, 1984), 222.

[49] In a presentation I made to a meeting of the joint commission for the second series of conversations between the Baptist World Alliance and the Catholic Church in Rome in December 2007, I termed this phenomenon "constructive Catholic dissent" (Steven R. Harmon, "*Dei Verbum* §9 in Baptist Perspective," paper presented to the bilateral conversations between the Baptist World Alliance and the Catholic Church, Rome/Vatican City, December 2–8, 2007). Responses from members of the Catholic delegation helped me to recognize that my use of the language of "dissent" within the Catholic tradition was problematic from the perspective of Catholic theology. Although I did not employ "dissent" in the sense of the public opposition to magisterial teaching proscribed in the Congregation for the Doctrine of the Faith document "Instruction *Donum Veritatis* on the Ecclesial Vocation of the Theologian," issued May 24, 1990 (accessed November 14, 2014, http://www.vatican.va/roman_curia/congregations/cfaith/documents/rc_con_cfaith _doc_19900524_theologian-vocation_en.html), it is now clear to me that "contestation" is a more appropriate descriptor of the Catholic theological disagreement that precedes an agreed articulation of Catholic teaching. In Baptist perspective, however, dissent is commonly regarded as a positive good—not as an end in itself, but as a protest that must on occasion be communicated to other segments of the church so that all parties together might seek to be brought under the rule of Christ.

relation of legitimate Catholic theological disagreement to the dissent of non-Catholic churches and ecclesial communities from certain aspects of Catholic magisterial teaching. If Bishop Volk of Mainz, for example, had expanded the Catholic biblicism voiced in the debates over the wording of *Dei Verbum* into a theological monograph, would it have been published with the *Nihil obstat* and *Imprimatur*?[50] If so, there exists the possibility of substantial overlap between some expressions of Catholic theology that do not have the status of Catholic magisterial teaching, yet are not objectionable from the standpoint of the *magisterium*, and some expressions of Baptist theology for which the category of "catholic faith outside the Catholic Church" is appropriate.[51]

Baptists are dissenting catholic Christians. They are quantitatively catholic in the sense of acknowledging that they belong to the whole church, even if points of their dissent preclude for the time being their full visible unity with large segments of the whole church. They are qualitatively catholic to the degree that they share the incarnational and sacramental pattern of faith and practice that distinguished ancient catholic Christianity from various forms of heresy and schism. While Baptists cannot offer an unqualified endorsement of *Dei Verbum* article 9, they can find a place within the pattern of intra-Catholic theological debate that produced it. This text with which Baptists cannot unequivocally agree thus points to a larger opening for convergence between Catholics in their practice of conciliar contestation and Baptists in their identity as dissenting catholics—an opening large enough to include the whole church. The church catholic shares one contested tradition, coinherent with its Scriptures, and its ongoing life as "an historically extended, socially embodied argument" depends upon Baptist dissent, Catholic contestation, and the participation of all the church's divisions in this argument. In this connection Baptist dissent can serve as a gift to the whole church in its contentious journey to the full sharing of "one faith" (Eph 4:5).

---

[50] *History of Vatican II*, ed. Alberigo, vol. 4, 227.

[51] This language is suggested by Ola Tjøhom, "Catholic Faith outside the Catholic Church: An Ecumenical Challenge," *Pro Ecclesia* 13, no. 3 (Summer 2004): 261–74.

5

Radically Biblical, Radically Catholic

As dissenting catholic Christians, Baptists may find themselves contesting within the larger tradition convictions and practices they view as unwarranted developments beyond the teaching of the Bible, but which other Christians see as the natural flowering of the plant that is wholly contained in prospect within the seed of Scripture.[1] The commitment of other communions to affirming the real presence of Christ in the Eucharist is one such occasion for many Baptists. In my work as a Baptist theological educator, I have taught multiple versions of a master-of-divinity-level spiritual formation course based on or substantially involving the devotional study of the *Sayings of the Desert Fathers*.[2] Early in their reading of

---

[1]   The biological analogy in which the relation of the primitive Christianity to later developments in the Christian tradition is comparable to the continuity between the beginning form of an organism and its mature state, despite their outward differences at these respective stages of life, was invoked influentially in both ancient and modern Christianity by Vincent of Lérins (d. prior to 450) and John Henry Newman (1801–1890): Vincent of Lérins, *Commonitorium* 23 (*Patrologiae Cursus Completus: Series Latina*, ed. J.-P. Migne [Paris: Garnier, 1844–1864], 50:667–69 [hereinafter PL]; ET, "A Commonitory for the Antiquity and Universality of the Catholic Faith against the Profane Novelties of All Heresies," trans. C. A. Heurtley, in *Nicene and Post-Nicene Fathers: Second Series*, ed. Philip Schaff and Henry Wace [A Select Library of the Christian Church; New York: Christian Literature, 1887–1894; repr., Peabody, Mass.: Hendrickson, 1994], 11: 147–49); John Henry Newman, *An Essay on the Development of Christian Doctrine*, 5th ed. ([London: Longmans, Green, 1887], especially 195–99).

[2]   I have taught versions of this course under the titles "Devotional Study of a Christian Classic: *Sayings of the Desert Fathers*" at Campbell University Divinity School, Buies Creek, North Carolina (Fall 2002, Spring 2004, Spring 2005, Fall 2006, Fall 2007); "Early Christian Spirituality" at Beeson Divinity School, Samford University, Birmingham, Alabama (Spring 2009); and "Readings in Spiritual Classics" in the School of Divinity at Gardner-Webb University, Boiling Springs, North Carolina (Summer 2012).

the alphabetical collection of the *Sayings*, my mostly Baptist students have usually found themselves unsettled by their encounter with this saying attributed to Abba Daniel the Pharanite:

> Our Father Abba Arsenius told us of an inhabitant of Scetis, of notable life and of simple faith; through his naïveté he was deceived and said, "The bread which we receive is not really the body of Christ, but a symbol." Two . . . men having learned that he had uttered this saying, knowing that he was outstanding in his way of life, knew that he had not spoken through malice, but through simplicity. So they came to find him and said, "Father, we have heard a proposition contrary to the faith on the part of someone who says that the bread which we receive is not really the body of Christ, but a symbol." The old man said, "It is I who have said that." Then [they] exhorted him saying, "Do not hold this position, Father, but hold one in conformity with that which the catholic Church has given us. We believe, for our part, that the bread itself is the body of Christ and that the cup itself is his blood and this in all truth and not a symbol."[3]

Abba Daniel went on to tell how this patristic-era exponent of a seemingly Baptist theology of the Lord's Supper came to renounce his heresy and embrace the catholic affirmation of real presence: the old man and his two interlocutors went to church, where they saw an angel serving them a gory Eucharist of a child's blood and flesh. When the flesh became bread in the old man's hand, he saw the error of his ways.[4] Graphic and grotesque though the vision may be, the main thing that troubles my students about this saying is its insistence that a symbolic theology of the Eucharist is heresy and sacramental realism is orthodoxy.

Yet while this understanding of divine presence in the Eucharist is at odds with their Baptist traditioning, this same formation has fitted them with reading spectacles that quickly alleviate their eyestrain. They are heirs to a faith with a restorationist impulse at its core: New Testament Christianity is pure and true; the subsequent history of the pre-Reformation church has yielded more corruption and regression than development and clarification of the faith, so radical reform requires cutting the tradition down to the root of New Testament faith and practice. Read through restorationist lenses, Abba Daniel's saying offers no insuperable challenge to

---

[3]   Benedicta Ward, trans. and ed., *The Sayings of the Desert Fathers: The Alphabetical Collection* (Kalamazoo, Mich.: Cistercian, 1975), 53.

[4]   Ward, trans. and ed., *Sayings of the Desert Fathers*, 53–54.

Baptist presuppositions about eucharistic theology. The New Testament, it is supposed, does not teach the real presence of Christ in the Eucharist; the desert fathers and mothers are centuries removed from the New Testament and also lived after the "Constantinian fall of the church";[5] therefore, when they contend that "the bread itself is the body of Christ and that the cup itself is his blood and this in all truth and not a symbol," this is the real error, the unbiblical falsehood.

Simple biblicism is the most common sort of restorationist hermeneutic, but it has more sophisticated kinfolk. Embedded in Adolf von Harnack's Hellenization thesis is an agenda for the restoration of a more Hebraic, more ethical pre-Hellenistic Christianity.[6] More recently, the Foucauldian suspicion of power[7] discernible in the historiography of Elaine Pagels[8] and Bart Ehrman,[9] as well as the less respectable historiography narrated in *The Da Vinci Code*,[10] point in a similar direction: it would be well for the world if the state of affairs that preceded the hegemony of orthodoxy were restored. The restorationist impulse of biblicist piety and the popularized repackaging of Walter Bauer's proposals[11] may seem antithetical, yet they have surprisingly much in common. It is now not unthinkable that traces of the simple and sophisticated varieties of

---

[5]   See Daniel H. Williams, *Retrieving the Tradition and Renewing Evangelicalism: A Primer for Suspicious Protestants* (Grand Rapids: William B. Eerdmans, 1999), who surveys and critiques this paradigm for reading the history of the church in a chapter titled "The Corruption of the Church and Its Tradition" (101–31).

[6]   Adolf von Harnack, *Lehrbuch der Dogmengeschichte*, 4th ed. (Tübingen: J. C. B. Mohr, 1909–1910), 3 vols.; ET, *History of Dogma*, trans. Neil Buchanan (Gloucester, Mass.: Peter Smith, 1961), 3 vols.; idem, *Das Wesen des Christentums: Sechzehn Vorlesungen vor Studierenden aller Facultäten im Wintersemester 1899/1900 an der Universität Berlin gehalten* (Leipzig: Hinrichs, 1900); ET, *What Is Christianity?* (New York: Harper, 1957).

[7]   Cf. Michel Foucault, *Power/Knowledge: Selected Interviews and Other Writings, 1972–1977*, trans. Colin Gordon, Leo Marshall, John Mepham, and Kate Soper (New York: Pantheon Books, 1980), probably the most accessible entrée to Foucault's influential perspectives on the relationship between power and the assertion of knowledge.

[8]   E.g., Elaine H. Pagels, *The Gnostic Gospels* (New York: Random House, 1979); idem, *Adam, Eve, and the Serpent* (New York: Random House, 1988); idem, *Beyond Belief: The Secret Gospel of Thomas* (New York: Random House, 2003).

[9]   E.g., Bart D. Ehrman, *Lost Christianities: The Battle for Scripture and the Faiths We Never Knew* (New York: Oxford University Press, 2003); idem, *Misquoting Jesus: The Story behind Who Changed the Bible and Why* (New York: HarperSanFrancisco, 2005).

[10]   Dan Brown, *The Da Vinci Code: A Novel* (New York: Doubleday, 2003).

[11]   Walter Bauer, *Rechtgläubigkeit und Ketzerei im ältesten Chrisentum* (Beiträge zur historischen Theologie, no. 10; Tübingen: Mohr, 1934); ET, *Orthodoxy and Heresy in Earliest Christianity*, trans. Philadelphia Seminar on Christian Origins, ed. Robert A. Kraft and Gerhard Krodel (Philadelphia: Fortress Press, 1979).

restorationism should coexist in the mind of the same Sunday school–attending, History Channel–watching Christian.

My primary concern in this chapter, however, is with the New Testament restorationism that has driven the Baptist tradition since its beginnings.[12] One point of departure for rethinking the restorationist impulse is the tension between the antitraditional assumptions of a restorationist hermeneutic and the inseparability of the New Testament canon from the post-first-century rule of faith and other patristic traditions that configured this canon. Another window into these issues is the ancient concept of the catholicity of the church, for such odd ideological bedfellows as "Landmark" Baptists and Tübingen School New Testament scholars have supposed that the lowercase "c" catholic faith was radically discontinuous with primitive Christianity. After examining the earliest patristic usage of καθολικός as a descriptor of the church in Ignatius of Antioch in the first decade of the second century,[13] we will explore the relationship of this early-second-century configuration of catholicity to New Testament patterns of faith and practice, concluding with reflections on the implications of these connections for a rethinking of restorationist hermeneutics in ecumenical perspective.

Paleo-Catholicity: Ignatius of Antioch

"Catholicity" is notoriously difficult to define. Understandings of "catholic" as a mark of the church range from the (invisible) oneness of the (invisible) universal church all the way to an ecclesial status of communion with Rome.[14] In his book *The Catholicity of the Church*, Avery Dulles

---

[12] Cf. C. Douglas Weaver, *In Search of the New Testament Church: The Baptist Story* (Macon, Ga.: Mercer University Press, 2008).

[13] Ignatius of Antioch, *Smyrneans* 8.2, in *The Apostolic Fathers*, ed. and trans. Bart D. Ehrman (Loeb Classical Library, no. 24; Cambridge, Mass.: Harvard University Press, 2003), 1:305.

[14] So *Catechism of the Catholic Church* (Liguori, Mo.: Liguori, 1994), §834 (p. 221): "'Particular Churches are fully catholic through their communion with one of them, the Church of Rome 'which presides in charity' [quotation from Ignatius of Antioch *Romans* 1.1]. 'For with this church, by reason of its pre-eminence, the whole Church, that is the faithful everywhere, must necessarily be in accord' [quotation from Irenaeus *Against Heresies* 3.3.2]. Indeed, 'from the incarnate Word's descent to us, all Christian churches everywhere have held and hold the great Church that is here [at Rome] to be their only basis and foundation since, according to the Savior's promise, the gates of hell have never prevailed against her'" [quotation from Maximus the Confessor *Opuscula theologica et polemica*]. While the *Catechism* reserves the fullest sense of catholicity for churches in communion with Rome, in §838 (p. 222) it also grants that there are other senses in which non–Roman Catholic churches and Christians participate in the catholicity of the

identified five major usages of the term "catholic": (1) the opposite of "sectarian," (2) "universal" as opposed to local or particular, (3) "true or authentic as contrasted with false or heretical," (4) the kind of Christianity that values "visible mediation through social and institutional structures," and (5) "the title of the church which . . . is governed by the bishop of Rome."[15] Dulles noted the earliest Christian use of καθολικός in Ignatius of Antioch's letter to the Smyrneans, "wherever Jesus Christ is, there is the catholic church," but then Dulles dismisses the possibility that this text provides substantial clues to the early Christian meaning of catholicity.

I contend that in light of the larger anti-Docetic polemic in *Smyrneans* and the rest of the Ignatian correspondence, we may speak of a much more fully orbed notion of what it meant for Ignatius and his contemporaries to say that the church is catholic than Dulles allows. While Kirsopp Lake's translation in the original Loeb Classical Library edition of the Apostolic Fathers of ἡ καθολικὴ ἐκκλησία in *Smyrneans* 8.2 as "the catholic church" is transliterative,[16] other translators have rendered καθολικὴ in light of its etymological sense "according to the whole." Thus William Schoedel's *Hermeneia* commentary offers the translation "wherever Jesus Christ is, there is the whole church,"[17] and Bart Ehrman's translation in the recently revised Loeb Classical Library edition of the Apostolic Fathers reads "wherever Jesus Christ is, there also is the universal church."[18] This is what ecumenists have called a *quantitative* catholicity—one that encompasses the wholeness or totality or universality of the church.[19]

---

church, though to a lesser extent: "'The Church knows that she is joined in many ways to the baptized who are honored by the name of Christian, but do not profess the Catholic faith in its entirety or have not preserved unity or communion under the successor of Peter' [quotation from *Lumen Gentium* 15]. Those 'who believe in Christ and have been properly baptized are put in a certain, though imperfect, communion with the Catholic Church' [quotation from *Unitatis Redintegratio*]. *With the Orthodox Churches*, this communion is so profound 'that it lacks little to attain the fullness that would permit a common celebration of the Lord's Eucharist'" [quotation from Paul VI, Discourse, December 14, 1975; emphasis is that of the Catechism].

[15]　Avery Dulles, *The Catholicity of the Church* (Oxford: Clarendon Press, 1985), 185.

[16]　Ignatius of Antioch, *Smyrneans* 8.2, in *The Apostolic Fathers*, ed. and trans. Kirsopp Lake (Loeb Classical Library, vol. 24; Cambridge, Mass.: Harvard University Press, 1912), 1:261.

[17]　William R. Schoedel, *Ignatius of Antioch* (Hermeneia; Philadelphia: Fortress Press, 1985), 238.

[18]　Ignatius of Antioch, *Smyrneans* 8.2, in *Apostolic Fathers*, ed. and trans. Ehrman, 1:305.

[19]　On the distinction between quantitative and qualitative catholicity, see Yves Congar, *Chrétiens désunis: Principes d'un "oecuménisme" catholique* (Unam Sanctam, no. 1; Paris: Éditions du Cerf, 1937), 115–17; ET, *Divided Christendom: A Catholic Study of the Problem of Reunion*, trans. M. A. Bousfield (London: Geoffrey Bles/Centenary, 1939), 93–94.

A quantitative catholicity is one dimension of what Ignatius means by "catholic," and his emphasis on the christological basis of the church's universality is what seventeenth-century Baptist confessions that affirmed the catholicity of the church had in mind.[20] Yet the quantitative catholicity communicated in this text does not exclude from Ignatius' usage a much more narrow meaning that increasingly became associated with the later patristic use of the Greek καθολικός and the Latin *catholicus* with reference to the pattern of faith and practice that distinguished early catholic Christianity from Docetism and eventually from Gnosticism, Marcionitism, Arianism, Donatism, and all manner of other heresies and schisms.[21] Catholicity in this sense has to do with a *qualitative* fullness of faith and order that is visibly expressed in one eucharistic fellowship.[22]

---

[20]   According to the Particular Baptist *Second London Confession* (1677/89), §26.1, "The Catholick or universal Church, which (with respect to internal work of the Spirit, and truth of grace) may be called invisible, consists of the whole number of the Elect, that have been, are, or shall be gathered into one, under Christ the head thereof" (*Baptist Confessions of Faith*, 2nd rev. ed., ed. William L. Lumpkin, rev. Bill J. Leonard [Valley Forge, Pa.: Judson, 2011], 283). Likewise, the General Baptist *Orthodox Creed* (1678/79) appropriated three of the four Nicaeno-Constantinopolitan *notae ecclesiae* in confessing in article 29, "there is one holy catholick church, consisting of, or made up of the whole number of the elect, that have been, are, or shall be gathered, in one body under Christ, the only head thereof" and in article 30, "we believe the visible church of Christ on earth, is made up of several distinct congregations, which make up that one catholick church, or mystical body of Christ" (*Baptist Confessions of Faith*, ed. Lumpkin, rev. Leonard, 327–28).

[21]   G. W. H. Lampe, ed., *A Patristic Greek Lexicon* (Oxford: Clarendon Press, 1961), s.v. "καθολικός," A.2.b–c and A.3; Charlton T. Lewis and Charles Short, eds., *A Latin Dictionary*, rev. ed. (Oxford: Clarendon Press, 1879), s.v. "catholicus," II. For particular examples, see notes 29 and 30 below.

[22]   This language intentionally echoes the explanation of the purpose of "Faith and Order" ecumenism in the by-laws of the Faith and Order Commission of the World Council of Churches: "to proclaim the oneness of the Church of Jesus Christ and to call the churches to the goal of visible unity in one faith and one eucharistic fellowship, expressed in worship and in common life in Christ, in order that the world may believe" (quoted in *Faith and Order: Toward a North American Conference. Study Guide*, ed. Norman A. Hjelm [Grand Rapids: William B. Eerdmans, 2004], vii). This is not, however, intended to suggest that there has ever been such a uniform understanding of the ecclesiological and ecumenical implications of such a qualitative catholicity. As Raymond E. Brown demonstrated in *The Churches the Apostles Left Behind* (New York: Paulist Press, 1984), this was certainly not the case in the New Testament, and despite the clear statement of this vision of the Faith and Order stream of the modern ecumenical movement in the "New Delhi Definition" adopted by The Third Assembly of the World Council of Churches in New Delhi, India, in 1961 and now regarded as the classic definition of the visible unity sought by the ecumenical movement ("Report of the Section on Unity," in *The New Delhi Report: The Third Assembly of the World Council of Churches, 1961* [New York: Association Press, 1962], 116), there is little agreement among the member bodies of the WCC as to what the realization of this ecumenical vision should entail.

One paragraph prior to the description of the church as "catholic" in *Smyrneans* 8, Ignatius warns the church at Smyrna regarding the doctrine and practice of the Docetists, "They abstain from the eucharist and prayer, since they do not confess that the eucharist is the flesh of our savior Jesus Christ, which suffered on behalf of our sins and which the Father raised in his kindness," and then Ignatius exhorts them to "flee divisions as the beginning of evils."[23] It is significant that immediately prior to this section, Ignatius links the doctrinal errors of the Docetists, who lacked a truly embodied Christology, with their failures to embody the Christian way of life: "But take note of those who [are heterodox with reference to] the gracious gift of Jesus Christ that has come to us, and see how they are opposed to the mind of God. They have no interest in love, in the widow, the orphan, the oppressed, the one who is in chains or the one set free, the one who is hungry or the one who thirsts" (*Smyrneans* 6.2).[24] For Ignatius, then, a qualitative catholicity is robustly incarnational. Because it is incarnational it is also sacramental, and because it is incarnational and sacramental it is also socially embodied and therefore concerned with social justice.[25]

Baptist restorationists might have little argument with the incarnational dimensions of a qualitative catholicity, and in the century of their origins Baptists did not reject a sacramental faith,[26] though then and as well as now they might stop short of the confession "the eucharist is the flesh of our savior Jesus Christ." Nor might they necessarily be opposed to a third mark of qualitative catholicity present in this passage, the visible unity of the church: "but flee divisions as the beginning of evils" (*Smyrneans* 7.2).[27]

---

[23] Ignatius of Antioch, *Smyrneans* 7.1–2, in *Apostolic Fathers*, ed. and trans. Ehrman, 1:302–3.

[24] Ignatius of Antioch, *Smyrneans* 6.2, in *Apostolic Fathers*, ed. and trans. Ehrman, 1:303 (modifications in brackets).

[25] Though I grant that in suggesting this I am engaging in a most tendentious theological reading of a specific episode of ecclesiastical history, I wonder if it is not merely coincidental that these connections also manifested themselves in the nineteenth-century Oxford Movement in the Church of England: the recovery of an incarnational sacramentalism went hand-in-hand with the commitment of Anglo-Catholic priests to doing social ministry in the slums of inner-city England. See C. Brad Faught, *The Oxford Movement: A Thematic History of the Tractarians and Their Times* (University Park: Pennsylvania State University Press, 2003), 151–52.

[26] See Anthony R. Cross and Philip E. Thompson, "Introduction: Baptist Sacramentalism," in *Baptist Sacramentalism*, ed. Anthony R. Cross and Philip E. Thompson (Studies in Baptist History and Thought, vol. 5; Carlisle, UK: Paternoster, 2003), 1–7.

[27] Ignatius of Antioch, *Smyrneans* 7.2, in *Apostolic Fathers*, ed. and trans. Ehrman, 1:302–3.

Yet the safeguard of ecclesial unity urged by Ignatius in *Smyrneans* 8 will give many Baptists reason for pause:

> All of you should follow the bishop as Jesus Christ follows the Father; and follow the presbytery as you would the apostles. Respect the deacons as the commandment of God. Let no one do anything involving the church without the bishop. Let that eucharist be considered valid that occurs under the bishop or the one to whom he entrusts it. Let the congregation be wherever the bishop is; just as wherever Jesus Christ is, there also is the [catholic] church. It is not permitted either to baptize or to hold a love feast without the bishop. But whatever he approves is acceptable to God, so that everything you do should be secure and valid.[28]

The precise nature of the office of bishop as portrayed in the Ignatian correspondence is much disputed. On the one hand, there are indications of something approaching a monepiscopate; on the other hand, the bishop and the elders collegially share a ministry of oversight—thus the exhortation to follow the elders as well as the bishop. Regardless of how one reads the role of the bishop in these letters, it is indisputable that we have here a threefold ministry—bishop, elder, deacon—in which the office of bishop is distinguished from the office of elder and in which the episcopate serves to guard the church against various threats to catholic unity.

These four marks of qualitative catholicity—incarnational Christology, sacramental realism, visible unity, and the ministry of oversight—are by no means restricted to *Smyrneans* 6–8 in the Ignatian corpus, for the anti-Docetic polemic is a central theological concern of the letters. This polemic features a radical identification of God with the person of Jesus Christ—hence, such expressions as the "blood of God"[29] and "the suffering of my God"[30]—joined with an insistence on the fleshly history of Jesus: his true human birth from a virgin,[31] his sufferings under Pontius Pilate,[32] and even his eating and drinking as incarnational realities.[33] The

---

[28] Ignatius of Antioch, *Smyrneans* 8.1–2, in *Apostolic Fathers*, ed. and trans. Ehrman, 1:304–5 (modifications in brackets).

[29] Ignatius of Antioch, *Ephesians* 1.1, in *Apostolic Fathers*, ed. and trans. Ehrman, 1:218–19.

[30] Ignatius of Antioch, *Romans* 6.3, in *Apostolic Fathers*, ed. and trans. Ehrman, 1:278–79.

[31] E.g., Ignatius of Antioch, *Smyrneans* 1.1, in *Apostolic Fathers*, ed. and trans. Ehrman, 1:296–97.

[32] E.g., Ignatius of Antioch, *Trallians* 9.1 and *Smyrneans* 1.1, in *Apostolic Fathers*, ed. and trans. Ehrman, 1:264–65 and 296–97.

[33] Ignatius of Antioch, *Trallians* 9.1, in *Apostolic Fathers*, ed. and trans. Ehrman, 1:264–65.

quasi-creedal christological antitheses in *Ephesians* 7.2 approach a fully fledged two-natures Christology:

> There is one physician,
> both fleshly and spiritual,
> begotten and unbegotten,
> come in flesh, God,
> in death, true life,
> both of Mary and of God,
> first passible and then impassible,
> Jesus Christ, our Lord.[34]

A high eucharistic theology is likewise not limited to the unqualified affirmation of the real presence of Christ in the Eucharist in *Smyrneans* 7.1. As William Schoedel observes, "the eucharist is the center of worship for Ignatius and serves as the focus for a sense of the presence of saving power in the Christian community."[35] To be apart from the gathered congregation is to lack "the bread of God" (*Ephesians* 5.2),[36] for the purpose of the congregation's gathering is εἰς εὐχαριστίαν θεοῦ καὶ εἰς δόξαν—"to celebrate the Eucharist[37] of God and to give God glory" (*Ephesians* 13.1).[38] The Eucharist is "the medicine that brings immortality" in *Ephesians* 20,[39] and in *Philadelphians* 4 it is the tangible manifestation and instrument of the unity of the church—"one eucharist" in which "one flesh" and "one cup" bring about "the unity of his blood" on "one altar."[40]

Unity has been identified as the central concern of the Ignatian epistles.[41] This centrality of unity is unsurprising in light of the Docetic threats

---

[34] Translation by Schoedel, *Ignatius of Antioch*, 59.

[35] Schoedel, *Ignatius of Antioch*, 21.

[36] Ignatius of Antioch, *Ephesians* 5.2, in *Apostolic Fathers*, ed. and trans. Ehrman, 1:224–25.

[37] "Eucharist" is perhaps a tendentious translation of εὐχαριστίαν in this context, for the construction naturally translates "for the thanking and glorifying of God," but it is supported by the clearly eucharistic meaning of the term in *Smyrneans* 7.1. Lake (*Apostolic Fathers*, 1:187), Schoedel (*Ignatius of Antioch*, 74), and Ehrman (*Apostolic Fathers*, 233) each note the eucharistic reference as a possibility here in Ephesians 13.1 but opt for the more general "thanksgiving" rendering in their translations.

[38] Ignatius of Antioch, *Ephesians* 13.1, in *Apostolic Fathers*, ed. and trans. Ehrman, 1:232–33.

[39] Ignatius of Antioch, *Ephesians* 20, in *Apostolic Fathers*, ed. and trans. Ehrman, 1:240–41.

[40] Ignatius of Antioch, *Philadelphians* 4, in *Apostolic Fathers*, ed. and trans. Ehrman, 1:286–87.

[41] So Schoedel, *Ignatius of Antioch*, 21.

to catholic unity that partially motivate the letters. Ignatius employs the nouns ἔνωσις and ἑνότης, "union" or "unity," a total of nineteen times in this brief corpus, and the closely related term ὁμονία, "harmony," appears eight times.[42] Their primary referent is the unity of the Christian community, a unity that, according to *Philadelphians*, is "from Jesus Christ" (5.2) and "from God" (8.1).[43]

Ignatius also emphasizes the role of episcopal oversight in maintaining ecclesial unity. There are fifty-seven occurrences of ἐπίσκοπος, and two significant uses of the verb ἐπισκοπέω besides. Regarding the latter, in *Romans* 9.1 it is ultimately Jesus Christ who "will serve as overseer/bishop (ἐπισκοπήσει)" of the church in Syria,[44] and in the inscription of the letter to Polycarp, the recipient's own episcopal authority derives from his having "God the Father and the Lord Jesus Christ as his bishop (ἐπισκοπημένῳ)."[45]

This understanding of the catholicity of the church in qualitative as well as quantitative terms coheres with later patristic uses of καθολικός. By the fourth century Eusebius of Caesarea (d. c. 339), Athanasius (d. 373), and Epiphanius (d. 403) were employing the adjective to denote the orthodoxy of the church's faith,[46] and in his catechetical lectures Cyril of Jerusalem (d. 387) offered an expanded definition of catholicity that is both quantitative and qualitative:

> The Church is called Catholic because it is spread throughout the world, from end to end of the earth; also because it teaches universally and completely all the doctrines which [one] should know concerning things visible and invisible, heavenly and earthly; and also because it subjects to right worship all [hu]mankind, rulers and ruled, lettered and unlettered; further because it treats and heals universally every sort of

---

[42]   Edgar J. Goodspeed, ed., *Index Patristicus* (Peabody, Mass.: Hendrickson, 1993), s.v. "ἔνωσις," "ἑνότητι," and "ὁμονία."

[43]   Schoedel, *Ignatius of Antioch*, 21.

[44]   Ignatius of Antioch, *Romans* 9.1, in *Apostolic Fathers*, ed. and trans. Ehrman, 1:280–81 (the translation of ἐπισκοπήσει here is my own).

[45]   Ignatius of Antioch, *Polycarp* inscrip., in *Apostolic Fathers*, ed. and trans. Ehrman, 1:310–11.

[46]   Eusebius of Caesarea employed καθολικός in contrast to heterodoxy in *Historia Ecclesiastica* 7.30.16 (*Patrologiae Cursus Completus: Series Graecae*, ed. J.-P. Migne [Paris: Garnier, 1857–1866], 20:716 [hereinafter PG]), and in contrast to schism in the same work in 10.6.1 (PG 20:892); cf. Athanasius, *Adversus Arianos* 1.4 (PG 26:20); Epiphanius of Salamis, *Panarion* 73.21 (PG 42:414).

sin committed by soul and body, and it possesses in itself every conceivable virtue, whether in deeds, words or in spiritual gifts of every kind.[47]

Lest we suppose that the Reformers left this perspective on the catholicity of the church on the Roman side of the sixteenth-century division of the church in the West, we should note Philipp Melanchthon's definition of catholicity:

> Why is this epithet added in the article of the creed, so that the Church is called Catholic? Because it is an assembly dispersed throughout the whole earth and because its members, wherever they are, and however separated in place, embrace and externally profess one and the same utterance of true doctrine in all ages from the beginning until the very end. . . . Those are truly called Catholic who embrace the doctrine of the truly Catholic Church . . . that which is supported by the witness of all time, of all ages, which believes what the prophets and apostles taught, and which does not tolerate factions, heresies, and heretical assemblies. We must all be Catholic, i.e., embrace this word which the rightly-thinking Church holds, separate from, and unentangled with, sects warring against that Word.[48]

---

[47] Cyril of Jerusalem, *Catecheses* 18.23 (PG 33:1047; ET, *The Works of Saint Cyril of Jerusalem*, trans. Leo P. McCauley and Anthony A. Stephenson [Fathers of the Church, vol. 64; Washington, D.C.: The Catholic University of America Press, 1970], 2:132). In the Latin West, the same fuller sense of catholicity is reflected in the hymn on the passion of Hippolytus of Rome by the poet Prudentius (d. after 405) in the *Peristephanon* 11.23–32 (PL 60:534–36; *Corpus Christianorum: Series Latina*, vol. 126, *Aurelii Prudentii Clementis Carmina*, ed. Maurice P. Cunningham [Turnhout: Brepols, 1966], 370–71; ET, *The Poems of Prudentius*, trans. M. Clement Eagan [Fathers of the Church, vol. 43; Washington, D.C.: The Catholic University of America Press, 1962], 242–43):

> Nor is it strange that the aged man who once was an apostate
> Should be endowed with the rich boon of the Catholic faith.
> When, triumphant and joyful in spirit, he was being conducted
> By the unmerciful foe onward to death of the flesh,
> He was attended by loving throngs of his faithful adherents.
> Thus he replied when they asked whether his doctrine was sound:
> "Leave, O unhappy souls, the infernal schism of Novatus;
> Rally again to the true fold of the Catholic Church.
> Let the one faith of ancient times in our temples now flourish,
> Doctrines by Paul and the high chair of Peter maintained."

[48] Philipp Melanchthon, "De Appellatione Ecclesiae Catholicae," in *Philippi Melanthonis Opera quae supersunt omnia*, ed. Karl Gottlieb Bretschneider and Heinrich Ernst Bindseil (Corpus Reformatorum, vol. 24; Halis Saxonum, 1834–1860), cols. 397–99; quoted in Dulles, *Catholicity of the Church*, 182.

Melanchthon is representative of the catholic commitments of the first generation of the Reformers that frequently seem counterintuitive to their more recent heirs. The "catholicity of the Reformation" stood in continuity with the patristic conviction, expressed inchoately by Ignatius of Antioch and with greater specificity by Cyril of Jerusalem and other fourth-century Christian writers, that the quantitative inclusion of all Christians in the catholicity of the church is inseparable from a qualitatively catholic pattern of faith and practice that characterizes this church and its members.[49]

Qualitative Catholicity in the New Testament?

For many Free Church Christians, however, it matters not how the fathers, or even the Reformers, understood the catholicity of the church, since it is the purity of New Testament faith and practice that is to be restored. After Russell Reno published an essay in *First Things* in 2006 on the remarkable resurgence of interest in the church fathers, the author of a letter to the editor of *First Things* responded in protest, "Professor Reno should return to the Apostles, not the Fathers," quoting in support the following passage from Old Princeton theologian B. B. Warfield's 1897 address "The Significance of the Westminster Standards as a Creed":

> There is no other such gulf in the history of human thought as that which is cleft between the apostolic and the immediately succeeding ages. To pass from the latest apostolic writings to the earliest compositions of uninspired Christian pens is to fall through such a giddy height that it is no wonder if we rise dazed and almost unable to determine our whereabouts. Here is the great fault . . . in the history of Christian doctrine. There is every evidence of continuity—but, oh, at how much lower a level! The rich vein of evangelical religion has run well-nigh out; and, though there are masses of apostolic origin lying everywhere, they are but fragments, and are evidently only the talus which has fallen from the cliffs above and scattered itself over the lowered surface.[50]

---

[49] Cf. Carl E. Braaten and Robert W. Jenson, eds., *The Catholicity of the Reformation* (Grand Rapids: William B. Eerdmans, 1996).

[50] Russell R. Reno, "The Return of the Fathers," *First Things* 167 (November 2006): 15–20; Frederick Kuhl, "Our Fathers" (letter to the editor), *First Things* 170 (February 2007): 3; Benjamin Breckenridge Warfield, *The Significance of the Westminster Standards as a Creed: An Address Delivered before the Presbytery of New York, November 8, 1897, on the Occasion of the Celebration of the Two Hundred and Fiftieth Anniversary of the Completion of the Westminster Standards* (New York: Scribner, 1898).

Is the gulf between the latest New Testament documents and the Ignatian epistles only a decade later really cleft so widely? In the case of Ignatius we are not only dealing with an early Christian author with close chronological proximity to the New Testament. We are also reading literature that has textual links with some of the very New Testament traditions that norm the restorationist project. Numerous studies of Ignatius and New Testament traditions over the past century have suggested the following conclusions about these connections.[51] First, while Ignatius probably had no written New Testament documents before him as he wrote his letters during his journey toward martyrdom, Ignatius was intimately acquainted with 1 Corinthians, probably knew Ephesians, and possibly had access to 1 and 2 Timothy. Second, Ignatius evidences knowledge of the M-tradition, the distinctively Matthean material in the First Gospel, likely in the form of the continuing oral tradition of the church of Antioch a few decades after the writing of Matthew. Third, while it is unlikely that Ignatius knew a written Gospel of John, the strong conceptual parallels between Ignatius and John make it probable that they shared a common theological milieu. In light of those connections, might we find in the New Testament traditions themselves—in particular, those New Testament traditions known by Ignatius—antecedents of the very marks of qualitative catholicity seen in *Smyrneans* 6–8?

---

[51]   Committee of the Oxford Society of Historical Theology, *The New Testament in the Apostolic Fathers* (Oxford: Clarendon Press, 1905), 67, 69, 71–72, 79, 83; Walter J. Burghardt, "Did Saint Ignatius of Antioch Know the Fourth Gospel?" *Theological Studies* 1, no. 1 (February 1940): 1–26; idem, "Did Saint Ignatius of Antioch Know the Fourth Gospel?" *Theological Studies* 1, no. 2 (May 1940): 130–56; Christian Maurer, *Ignatius von Antiochien und das Johannesevangelium* (Abhandlungen zur Theologie des Alten und Neuen Testaments, no. 18; Zürich: Zwingli-Verlag, 1949), 25–43, 92–93; Édouard Massaux, *Influence de l'Évangile de saint Matthieu sur la littérature chrétienne avant saint Irénée* (Louvain: Publications universitaires de Louvain, 1950); ET, *The Influence of the Gospel of Saint Matthew on Christian Literature before Saint Irenaeus*, bk. 1, *The First Ecclesiastical Writers*, trans. Norman J. Belval and Suzanne Hecht, ed. Arthur J. Bellinzoni (New Gospel Studies, no. 5; Macon, Ga.: Mercer University Press, 1990), 86–96; Helmut Köster, *Synoptische Überlieferung bei den apostolischen Vätern* (Texte und Untersuchungen zur Geschichte der altchristlichen Literatur, no. 17; Berlin: Akademie-Verlag, 1957), 24–61; Heinrich Rathke, *Ignatius von Antiochien und die Paulusbriefe* (Texte und Untersuchungen zur Geschichte der altchristlichen Literatur, no. 99; Berlin: Akademie-Verlag, 1967), 39, 41–47, 64–66, 98–99; Joost Smit Sibinga, "Ignatius and Matthew," *Novum Testamentum* 8, no. 2 (April 1966): 263–83; Richard Bauckham, "The Study of Gospel Traditions outside the Canonical Gospels: Problems and Prospects," in *The Jesus Tradition outside the Gospels*, ed. David Wenham (Gospel Perspectives, vol. 5; Sheffield: JSOT Press, 1984), 398 (369–403).

With regard to the christological mark, it suffices to note that the identification of Jesus Christ with God in both 1 Corinthians (e.g., 1 Cor 1:8, 16:22)[52] and the Gospel of John (e.g., John 1:1, 10:30, 20:28)[53] is only slightly intensified in Ignatius, and John joins clear affirmations of the full divinity of the Son as the preexistent Word of God with an anti-Docetic interest in the true physicality of Jesus' incarnate activities.[54] The incarnational Christology of the New Testament is qualitatively catholic in the Ignatian sense.

The sacramental realism explicit in Ignatius is already implicit in the New Testament itself. The Reformers may have been divided over the precise meaning of "is" in Jesus' declaration "This is my body" in the Synoptic Gospels (Matt 26:26; Mark 14:22; Luke 22:19), but the Fourth Gospel's dominical sayings that have eucharistic functions in the absence of a Johannine institution narrative indicate an incipient doctrine of real presence.[55] In John 6:52-66, the insistence that those who eat Christ's flesh

---

[52]   See David B. Capes, *Old Testament Yahweh Texts in Paul's Christology* (Wissenschaftliche Untersuchungen zum Neuen Testament, 2nd series, vol. 47; Tübingen: J. C. B. Mohr [Paul Siebeck], 1992), 43–47 and 83–84, with reference to 1 Cor 1:8, in which the Old Testament "Day of the Lord" (*yōm YHWH*) becomes "the day of the Lord Jesus Christ," and 1 Cor 16:22, where the prayer μαράνα θά ("Our Lord, come!") addressed to Christ had been addressed to Yahweh in the Qumran literature.

[53]   In this connection, the seven "I am" sayings (John 6:35; 8:12; 10:7; 10:11; 11:25; 14:6; 15:1) may also implicitly identify Jesus with Yahweh, the ἐγώ εἰμι ὁ ὤν of Exod 3:14 (LXX); so, e.g., E. M. Sidebottom, *The Christ of the Fourth Gospel in the Light of First-Century Thought* (London: SPCK, 1961), 43–44.

[54]   See Alois Grillmeier, *Christ in Christian Tradition*, vol. 1, *From the Apostolic Age to Chalcedon (451)*, 2nd rev. ed., trans. John Bowden (Atlanta: John Knox Press, 1975), 26–32; James D. G. Dunn, *Christology in the Making: A New Testament Inquiry into the Origins of the Doctrine of the Incarnation* (Philadelphia: Westminster Press, 1980), 239–47; Rudolf Schnackenburg, *Jesus in the Gospels: A Biblical Christology*, trans. O. C. Dean, Jr. (Louisville, Ky.: Westminster John Knox, 1995), 283–94; Frank J. Matera, *New Testament Christology* (Louisville, Ky.: Westminster John Knox, 1999), 215–37.

[55]   Catholic Scripture scholar Rudolf Schnackenburg, *The Gospel according to St. John*, trans. Cecily Hastings, Francis McDonagh, David Smith, and Richard Foley (New York: Seabury Press, 1980), 2:55–75, made an extensive and compelling case for a eucharistic interpretation of this passage; see also Lutheran New Testament scholar Joachim Jeremias, *The Eucharistic Words of Jesus*, trans. Norman Perrin (The New Testament Library; London: SCM Press, 1966), 107–8, who on the basis of a phrase-by-phrase comparison of John 6:51c with parallel phrases in the earliest attestation to Jesus' words of institution in 1 Cor 11:24b concluded: "The whole sequence of thought in the discourse on the bread of life now becomes clearer: its conclusion (6.53–58) is a eucharistic homily, the theme of which is introduced by the word of interpretation to the bread (6.51c). John therefore, although he does not mention the institution of the Lord's Supper, introduces the word of interpretation to the bread in the context of a discourse by Jesus, without it thereby (as the history of research shows) becoming immediately evident as such" (108). In addition

and drink Christ's blood are those who are one with Christ (v. 56) occasions the departure of some from one eucharistic fellowship (v. 66).

The visible unity of the church is a major concern of three sources of New Testament tradition that influenced Ignatius: 1 Corinthians, the letter to the Ephesians, and the Gospel of John. Paul's first letter to the Corinthians was occasioned by news of divisions in the church in Corinth (1 Cor 1:10-17, 3:1-23). Throughout the letter Paul admonishes members of the Corinthian church to conduct themselves in ways that embody the unity made manifest in the one cup and one bread by which they share in the one blood and body of Christ (1 Cor 10:16-17). In chapter 11 Paul's instructions about the celebration of the Lord's Supper target the divisions they bring to their observances of it (1 Cor 11:17-34), and the following chapter encourages the Corinthian believers to understand themselves as diverse members of a singular body of Christ (1 Cor 12:12-31).[56] The concern for ecclesial unity likewise marks the literature attributed to Paul from a later period, notably the letter to the Ephesians, in which the unity of the people of God in Christ and in the Spirit is the overarching theme.[57] In its first chapter the church as the body of Christ is the instrument of God's plan to unify all things (Eph 1:10, 22-23), and in chapter 2 the purpose of the work of Christ is to create "one new humanity . . . in one body through the cross" (Eph 2:15-16). The epistle's central passage

---

to his own previous study anticipating his treatment of John 6:51–58 in *The Eucharistic Words of Jesus* (idem, "Joh 6, 51c–58—redaktionell?" *Zeitschrift für die neutestamentliche Wissenschaft und die Kunde der älteren Kirche* 44 [1952–1953]: 256 57), Jeremias cited other precedents for his interpretation: John Henry Bernard, *A Critical and Exegetical Commentary on the Gospel according to St. John*, 4th ed. (International Critical Commentary, vol. 29; Edinburgh: T&T Clark, 1953), 1:clxx–clxxi; Ernst Lohmeyer, "Vom urchristlichen Abendmahl (III)," *Theologische Rundschau* n.s. 9 (1937): 308 (273–312); and Nils Johansson, *Det urkristna nattvardsfirandet: Dess religionshistoriska bakgrund, dess ursprung och innebörd* (Lund: Gleerup, 1944). Baptist exegete George R. Beasley-Murray, *John* (Word Biblical Commentary, vol. 36; Waco, Tex.: Word Books, 1987), 94–99, on the other hand, argued against associating these words of the Johannine Jesus with the church's celebration of the Eucharist (unconvincingly, in my opinion).

[56] On the motifs of ecclesial division and unity in 1 Cor, see J. Murphy-O'Connor, "Divisions Are Necessary (1 Corinthians 11:19)," in *Celebrating Paul: Festschrift in Honor of Jerome Murphy-O'Connor, O.P., and Joseph A. Fitzmyer, S.J.*, ed. Peter Spitaler (Catholic Biblical Quarterly Monograph Series, vol. 48; Washington, D.C.: Catholic Biblical Association of America, 2011), 9–14.

[57] On the function of the theme of unity in Ephesians, see Stig Hanson, *The Unity of the Church in the New Testament: Colossians and Ephesians* (Acta Seminarii Neotestamentici Upsaliensis, no. 14; Uppsala: Almquist & Wiksells, 1946); John Paul Heil, *Ephesians: Empowerment to Walk in Love for the Unity of All in Christ* (Society of Biblical Literature Studies in Biblical Literature, no. 13; Atlanta: Society of Biblical Literature, 2007).

at the beginning of chapter 4 highlights as the ground and motivation of the admonition to "maintain the unity of the Spirit" (Eph 4:3) the unifying realities of the faith: "There is one body and one Spirit, just as you were called to the one hope of your calling, one Lord, one faith, one baptism, one God and Father of all" (Eph 4:4-6). The Gospel of John has supplied the biblical *locus classicus* of the varied expressions of the modern ecumenical movement: John 17:11-23.[58] Four times in the course of that passage the Johannine Jesus prays that his disciples and all who later believe through their testimony might have unity (vv. 11, 21, 22, 23) and might be protected from the diabolical source of division (v. 15). John's Jesus roots this unity in the mutually indwelling oneness he shares with the Father (vv. 11, 21-23) and prays that the unity of his followers will be visible, discernible by the world (vv. 21 and 23). The New Testament traditions as Ignatius knew them were concerned with the qualitative catholic mark of visible unity.

The Pastoral Epistles, among which Ignatius may have known 1 and 2 Timothy, were addressed to a situation in which the unity of the church was threatened by those who, in the language of 1 Timothy 1:3, "teach different doctrine (ἑτεροδιδασκαλεῖν)." The Pastorals address this threat in part by calling attention to the responsibility of the bishop to teach sound doctrine (1 Tim 3:2; 2 Tim 1:13; Titus 2:1). Hans von Campenhausen argued that the role of the bishop in the Pastorals was a "monarchical episcopacy,"[59] but the texts do not require this reading. In light of other New Testament texts of late date in which the roles of bishops and elders do not seem to be distinguished and in which there may be a plurality of such leadership within a congregation (e.g., 1 Pet 5:1-5), the proposal of a monepiscopate in the Pastorals seems to be claiming too much. Yet the beginnings of a trajectory that leads to a bona fide monepiscopate are

---

[58] For explorations and reconsiderations of this association, see John F. Randall, "The Theme of Unity in John 17:20–23," *Ephemerides Theologicae Lovanienses* 41, no. 3 (July–October 1965): 373–94; Hellen Mardaga, "Reflection on the Meaning of John 17:21 for Ecumenical Dialogue," *Ecumenical Trends* 34, no. 10 (November 2005): 148–52; Gert J. Malan, "Does John 17:11b, 21–23 Refer to Church Unity?" *HTS Teologiese Studies/Theological Studies* 67, no. 1 (2011): 10 pages (doi: 10.4102/hts.v67i1.857), accessed November 20, 2014, http://hts.org.za/index.php/HTS/article/view/857.

[59] Hans von Campenhausen, *Ecclesiastical Authority and Spiritual Power in the Church of the First Three Centuries*, trans. J. A. Baker (Stanford, Calif.: Stanford University Press, 1969), 107: "In the Pastoral Epistles the 'bishop' is always spoken of in the singular. The simplest explanation of this fact is that monarchical episcopacy is by now the prevailing system, and that the one bishop has already become the head of the presbyterate, even if his supreme position is not nearly so strongly emphasized as it is in the Epistles of Ignatius."

reflected in the Pastorals, and the Ignatian letters stand between the Pastorals and a later full-blown monepiscopacy in the same stream of the development of ecclesiastical order. At any rate, the contribution of the teaching function of the episcopal office to the unity of the church is a feature both of the qualitative catholicity of Ignatius of Antioch and of its New Testament precedents.[60] If Ignatius' concept of the catholicity of the church included an incarnational Christology, sacramental realism, visible unity, and the ministry of oversight, then it must be acknowledged that there are present in the New Testament at least incipient forms of these same marks of a qualitative catholicity.

Qualitative Catholicity and the Fallacies of Restorationism

The questions regarding continuity and discontinuity in the Christian tradition raised by this reading of Ignatius of Antioch are hardly new. They were robustly contested by Protestants and Catholics alike in the sixteenth century, and they have been routinely revisited in modern ecumenical theology. The restorationist impulse of many expressions of Free Church Christianity, however, has long kept this stream of the Christian

---

[60] This observation opens up space for asserting a broad Baptist continuity (rather than discontinuity) with this aspect of the ongoing development of early catholic Christianity. Baptists do typically grant that the teaching office has a responsibility to see to the unity of the church, and inasmuch as they have historically equated the office and function of the pastor with that of the bishop on the basis of New Testament texts, Baptists have understood this to be an exercise of episcopacy. In the report from the second series of conversations between the Baptist World Alliance and the Catholic Church, both a bold-type agreed paragraph and a regular-type paragraph explaining the distinctiveness of the Baptist perspective affirm the connection between the ministry of oversight, its teaching function, and the unity of the church: Baptist World Alliance and Catholic Church, "The Word of God in the Life of the Church: A Report of International Conversations between the Catholic Church and the Baptist World Alliance 2006–2010," §§190 and 192, in *American Baptist Quarterly* 31, no. 1 (Spring 2012): 100–101. It should be noted in this connection that some seventeenth-century English Baptists such as Thomas Grantham argued for a threefold ministry that included, in addition to pastors/elders and deacons, "messengers" who had episcopal functions; see John Inscore Essick, *Thomas Grantham: God's Messenger from Lincolnshire* (James N. Griffith Series in Baptist Studies; Macon, Ga.: Mercer University Press, 2013), 70–111. Furthermore, some contemporary Eastern European Baptists have bishops as a third office of ministry, appealing to the New Testament as warrant for the office and title; Valdis Teraudkalns explores this phenomenon with special reference to Latvian Baptists in his essay "Episcopacy in the Baptist Tradition" in *Recycling the Past or Researching History? Studies in Baptist Historiography and Myths*, ed. Philip E. Thompson and Anthony R. Cross (Studies in Baptist History and Thought, vol. 11; Milton Keynes, UK: Paternoster, 2005), 279–93.

tradition from addressing these questions in a sufficiently self-critical fashion. Toward that end I identify three interrelated fallacies of a restorationist hermeneutic of early Christian history that Baptists and others must avoid as they read the Christian Scriptures and the history of the church to which the Bible belongs.

First, New Testament restorationism may uncritically assume that the pattern of faith and practice embodied by one's own restorationist tradition is in fact the pattern of faith and practice of the New Testament. Since Baptist identity is by virtue of its radical biblicism heavily invested in the project of restoring New Testament Christianity, it is easy for Baptists to assume that the typical Baptist reading of the New Testament is the one that corresponds to the true faith and practice of the New Testament, and then to read that pattern into the New Testament as if it were the self-evident teaching of the biblical text. But this is an ecumenically pervasive tendency that is by no means restricted to Baptists and other Free Church restorationists, for as Raymond Brown observed, "In a divided Christianity we have a long history of using the Scriptures to prove ourselves right, whether as churches or as individuals."[61]

Second, New Testament restorationism has a tendency to regard everything in Christian history that differs from the restorationist understanding of New Testament faith and practice as discontinuous with first-century Christianity. It is of course possible for the patristic church to develop patterns of faith and practice that are discontinuous with the New Testament, but it is also possible that the New Testament may be closer to the supposed discontinuities than one's restorationist tradition has allowed. Baptist symbolic memorialists with theologies of the Lord's Supper influenced by Zwingli may assume that a theology of real presence is a postbiblical development, blinding them to the force of the eucharistic language of John 6, and proponents of congregational polity with a two-fold ministry of a diaconate and overseers who are both pastors and elders may wrongly charge other traditions with the development of nonbiblical forms of governance, when in fact there are antecedents of both presbyterial and episcopal forms of polity in Acts 15 and elsewhere in the New Testament along with the precedents for congregational ecclesiologies long cited by Free Church restorationists.

Third, New Testament restorationism reads the New Testament as a book of the primitive first-century church, when it would be more appropriate to read the New Testament as a book of the patristic church. The

---

[61] Brown, *Churches the Apostles Left Behind*, 149.

New Testament canon did not emerge fully formed at the end of the first century. It is instead the product of the church in the second, third, and fourth centuries as it ruled out Docetism, Ebionitism, a plethora of Gnosticisms, Marcionitism, and Arianism as inadequate narrations of the Christian story. The New Testament canon that funds a program of New Testament restorationism has the patristic rule of faith as the doctrinal principle of its formation and the key to its overarching meaning.[62] To be radically biblical is therefore to be radically catholic, even if one is not conscious of the connection or its implications. Yet because the Bible is intertwined with the qualitatively catholic faith at the root of the tradition, to be less than fully catholic in the qualitative sense of that term is to be less than fully biblical in faith and practice.

There is a proper sort of New Testament restorationism: one that not only seeks renewal by returning to the New Testament sources of the faith but also recognizes that this is a qualitatively catholic pattern of faith and practice formed by the post-first-century rejection of other patterns that do not cohere with the rule of faith. To restore New Testament Christianity is to restore at least some dimensions of the patristic coming of age of Christian faith and practice. Ignatius of Antioch is a witness to the developing catholic faith that issues forth in the New Testament canon, as well as a witness to the broad continuity of patristic catholicity with the primitive Christianity reflected in the New Testament. If Baptists and other Free Church Christians who seek a radical restoration of New Testament faith and practice can come to appreciate this continuity, they may be able to appreciate even the sacramental realism commended in the saying attributed to Abba Daniel the Pharanite quoted at the beginning of this chapter. They might even dare to appropriate it, and to consider themselves New Testament Christians in doing so.[63]

---

[62] Cf. Robert W. Jenson, *Canon and Creed* (Interpretation: Resources for the Use of Scripture in the Church; Louisville, Ky.: Westminster John Knox, 2010).

[63] Baptist discomfort with a doctrine of eucharistic real presence is reflected in the omission from many Baptist hymnals (e.g., hymn 80 in *The Baptist Hymnal*, ed. Wesley L. Forbis [Nashville: Convention Press, 1991]) of this stanza from *Let All Mortal Flesh Keep Silence*, a hymn text translated by Gerard Moultrie (1829–1885) from the fifth-century *Liturgy of St. James*:

> King of kings, yet born of Mary, as of old on earth he stood,
> Lord of lords, in human vesture, in the body and the blood:
> He will give to all the faithful his own self for heavenly food.

This stanza—clearly rooted in a eucharistic reading of John 6:22-59—is, however, included unaltered as stanza 2 of hymn 81, in the *Celebrating Grace Hymnal*, ed. Tom McAfee, John Simons, David Music, Milburn Price, Stanley Roberts, and Mark Edwards

The churches' mutual recognition of the coinherence of radical biblicism and radical catholicity is integral to their progress toward full visible unity. When Baptists are radically biblicistic, relentlessly looking to the Bible as the norming norm that authorizes their faith and practice as they seek to bring their life together ever more fully under the rule of Christ, they are simultaneously identifying with the quantitatively catholic church to which the Scriptures belong and with the qualitatively catholic pattern of faith and practice that is inseparable from the Scriptures canonized by the church catholic. Becoming more conscious of this connection and making it more explicit in their ecclesial life can help Baptists become intentional about their catholicity, for the sake of their formation of Christian disciples within their own communities and for the sake of their relation to the whole church. At the same time, when Baptists offer their radical biblicism as one of their distinctive ecclesial gifts to the rest of the church, they are aiding the whole church in its pilgrim journey toward the ecumenical future by calling the church to return again and again to the sacred story that is both renewing root and shared good of the living catholic tradition that must be contested in the church en route to this future. But this can happen only when Baptists view their distinctive ecclesial identity as a means toward the end of the exchange of ecclesial gifts necessary for the whole church, Baptists included, to become more fully catholic.

(Macon, Ga.: Celebrating Grace, 2010), used by many congregations affiliated with the Cooperative Baptist Fellowship, and of hymn 441 in *Baptist Praise and Worship* (Oxford: Oxford University Press on behalf of the Psalms and Hymns Trust, 1991), a hymnal commissioned by the Baptist Union of Great Britain and utilized by many of its churches. In a review of my book *Towards Baptist Catholicity*, in which I had commended as a principle for Baptist worship the patristic liturgical maxim *lex orandi, lex credendi* (the rule of praying should establish the rule of believing, and vice versa), Charles Scalise suggested that "the transformation of the *lex orandi, lex credendi* liturgical slogan into *lex cantandi, lex credendi* ('the law of *singing* is the law of believing') more accurately reflects the history of Baptists in North America and thus may serve as an appropriate resource for the renewal of Baptist life and thought" (Charles J. Scalise, review of *Towards Baptist Catholicity: Essays on Tradition and the Baptist Vision*, by Steven R. Harmon, in *Perspectives in Religious Studies* 35, no. 4 [Winter 2008]: 435 [433–35]). To the extent that this is true of the relation between what Baptists sing in worship services and what they believe (or may come to believe), Baptists who sing this second stanza of *Let All Mortal Flesh Keep Silence* are affirming a sacramentally realistic reading of this part of the biblical story on which they base their faith and practice. This has the potential to mediate a fuller Baptist reception of a qualitatively catholic sacramental realism, for the faith that is prayed—or sung—is the faith that the church and its members may come to believe through the faith-forming function of the theological content of worship.

PART III

BAPTIST IDENTITY AND RECEPTIVE ECUMENISM

6

The End of Baptist Denominationalism

Is there an ongoing place for denominations as the churches move closer to the ecumenical future? The oft-repeated descriptive observation that this is a postdenominational age—sometimes expressed as a prescriptive exhortation—would seem to render denominationalism irrelevant to ecumenical advance, even an obstacle to it, or at the very least consign it to the same doldrums inhabited by the ecumenical movement itself.[1] My own theological reflections on the applicability of the ecclesiological category "denomination" to the communities denominated "Baptist" and its relevance for Baptist participation in the quest for Christian unity are conditioned by the particularities of my specific ecclesial identity as a member of churches affiliated with the Cooperative Baptist Fellowship (CBF) and professor in institutions that serve as its theological education "partners." This chapter therefore begins with a consideration of what an internal debate within the CBF as to whether it is or should become a "denomination" reveals about broader Baptist perspectives on denominational identity before turning to the ecumenical dimensions of denomination as an ecclesiological category for Baptists.

---

[1]   E.g., William Swatos, "Beyond Denominationalism? Community and Culture in American Religion," *Journal for the Scientific Study of Religion* 20 (September 1981): 217–27; Robert Wuthnow, *The Restructuring of American Religion* (Princeton, N.J.: Princeton University Press, 1988); Donald E. Miller, *Reinventing American Protestantism: Christianity in the New Millennium* (Berkeley: University of California Press, 1999).

The Cooperative Baptist Fellowship as "Denomination"

My Christian nurture from infancy onward, baptism and ongoing Christian formation, discernment of my calling to vocational ministry, ordination, and theological education took place within the denominational framework of the Southern Baptist Convention (SBC). By the time I enrolled as a divinity student in 1989 at one of the official seminaries of the SBC (Southwestern Baptist Theological Seminary in Fort Worth, Texas), however, the denomination was a decade into a bitter public struggle between well-organized political networks of "conservatives" and "moderates" over the control of its institutions and agencies.[2] By the end of my second year of seminary in 1991, Southern Baptist moderates had largely disengaged from these political efforts and formed the CBF as a network for fellowship among churches and individuals that perceived themselves as disaffected from those who now led the SBC and for the support of emerging institutions and agencies that would provide alternatives for key denominational services that the SBC had traditionally provided to local churches: theological education, mechanisms for the cooperative support of missions, literature for Christian education, Baptist-related news media, and public advocacy for Baptist perspectives on matters of religious liberty and ethics. I soon identified myself with the CBF[3] and following

---

[2]   For historical and sociological studies of the controversy in the SBC, see Bill Leonard, *God's Last and Only Hope: The Fragmentation of the Southern Baptist Convention* (Grand Rapids: William B. Eerdmans, 1990); Nancy T. Ammerman, *Baptist Battles: Social Change and Religious Conflict in the Southern Baptist Convention* (New Brunswick, N.J.: Rutgers University Press, 1990); David T. Morgan, *The New Crusades, the New Holy Land: Conflict in the Southern Baptist Convention, 1969–1991* (Tuscaloosa: University of Alabama Press, 1996); and Barry Hankins, *Uneasy in Babylon: Southern Baptist Conservatives and American Culture* (Tuscaloosa: University of Alabama Press, 2002). For a "moderate" recounting of the conflict and the genesis of the Cooperative Baptist Fellowship and related institutions, see Walter B. Shurden, ed., *The Struggle for the Soul of the SBC: Moderate Responses to the Fundamentalist Movement* (Macon, Ga.: Mercer University Press, 1993); idem, *Not an Easy Journey: Some Transitions in Baptist Life* (Macon, Ga.: Mercer University Press, 2005), 248–303. Histories of the conflict written from the perspective of the ultraconservatives are Jerry Sutton, *The Baptist Reformation: The Conservative Resurgence in the Southern Baptist Convention* (Nashville: Broadman & Holman, 2000); and James Hefley, *The Conservative Resurgence in the Southern Baptist Convention* (Hannibal, Mo.: Hannibal Books, 1991).

[3]   An experience that solidified my inclinations toward the CBF that had been developing during the period of its beginnings was my nomination in 1997 to join the faculty of Southwestern Baptist Theological Seminary as the successor of my doctoral mentor James Leo Garrett, Jr., upon his retirement and the withdrawal of that nomination by the seminary president after it became clear that trustee dissatisfaction with my affirmation of the ordination of women to pastoral ministry and other indicators of my incompatibility with the theological positions that were beginning to predominate in the SBC

the completion of my doctoral studies taught theology at two of its part-
ner institutions of theological education, Campbell University Divinity
School in Buies Creek, North Carolina, from 1998 until 2008, and the
School of Divinity at Gardner-Webb University in Boiling Springs, North
Carolina, since 2010.

Throughout the first decade of its existence, the CBF engaged in a public debate over the manner in which it should differentiate itself from the
SBC. The debate tended to be framed in terms of the question "Is the CBF
a denomination?" Some members of the CBF favored official "denominational" status in the hope that it would help CBF churches establish an
identity separate from the SBC, which they believed no longer reflected
or welcomed their version of Baptist identity. Others opposed it: some for
the pragmatic reason that it would be too difficult for many churches to
modify their long-cherished official associations with the SBC (though
Baptist congregational polity does allow for multiple national denominational affiliations), others because they identified "denomination" with
the oppressive forms of institutional authority they had experienced in the
SBC, and still others because they contended that denominations were a
thing of the past that would not be viable in a postmodern world. Almost
everyone involved in this debate regarded a denomination as an institutional organization that assumes a particular sort of bureaucratic structure.
Furthermore, all assumed that whatever its nature, there should be some
sort of identifiable entity beyond the local church that would comprise
other local churches and individuals committed to similar convictions
about Baptist faith and practice.

The CBF "denominational question" surfaced in business sessions at
annual CBF General Assembly meetings and in news articles and op-ed
pieces in Baptist media from 1991 to 1995. In 1995 CBF Moderator Patrick Anderson appointed a five-member committee charged "to study the
CBF denominational question" with the understanding that the committee would not bring a specific recommendation but rather a report that
would "raise our level of conversation and understanding about issues

---

during my prenomination questioning would result in a trustee vote to reject the nom-
ination. The episode and its aftermath were reported, among other places, by Jim Jones,
"Seminary Turns away Professor: Trustees' Hiring Rules Come into Question," *Fort
Worth Star-Telegram* (March 15, 1997): B1, 8; Toby Druin, "Prospective Prof Nixed over
Clergy Gender," *Baptist Standard* 109, no. 12 (March 19, 1997): 6; Jim Jones, "Baptist
Leaders Say Female Pastor Issue Halted Seminary Appointment," *Fort Worth Star-Telegram*
(May 22, 1997): B2; Kit Lively, "Baptist Leaders in Texas Criticize Southwestern Semi-
nary," *Chronicle of Higher Education* (June 6, 1997), accessed November 22, 2014, http://
chronicle.com/article/Baptist-Leaders-in-Texas/75426/.

involved in CBF becoming or not becoming a separate convention."[4] The term "convention" employed in the charge to the committee may require explanation for readers unfamiliar with the context in which the CBF originated. Many Baptists with historic connections to the SBC prefer the designation "convention" to "denomination" or "church" when referring to translocal associations of Baptists at the national level, owing to the reference of "convention" to the group of representatives of local congregations who convene each year in annual session in contrast to a permanent bureaucratic or hierarchical structure. The CBF "denominational question" was therefore frequently framed in terms of whether the CBF should be understood as a convention distinct from the SBC.

In response to this charge the committee commissioned several position papers on the issue by CBF-affiliated theological educators, ministers, and laypersons; interpreted the results of an earlier survey of the CBF constituency conducted by its Coordinating Council; and solicited letters from all who wished to express and elaborate their opinions on the matter. The final report of the committee was issued prior to the 1996 CBF General Assembly in the form of a book of 141 pages that included a summary of the input from surveys and letters along with the full text of the twelve position papers. In keeping with the charge given the committee, it made no specific recommendation, and accordingly the CBF took no action on it other than disseminating the report. The denominational issue continued to be discussed in the aftermath of the report's publication, especially as the CBF took steps to begin endorsing military and hospital chaplains.

The collection of position papers solicited and published by the CBF special study commission provides the best window into the theological dimensions of the question of denominational identity among Cooperative Baptists. Some authors discerned clear advantages for self-identification as a denomination or convention.[5] Others identified denominational status

---

[4]   W. Randall Lolley, Eileen R. Campbell-Reed, Pope A. Duncan, Pete Hill, and Nancy A. Thurmond, eds., *Findings: A Report of the Special Study Commission to Study the Question: "Should the Cooperative Baptist Fellowship Become a Separate Convention?"* (Atlanta: Cooperative Baptist Fellowship, 1996), vi. For fuller historical accounts of the formation and development of the CBF, see Walter B. Shurden, "The Cooperative Baptist Fellowship," in *The Baptist River: Essays on Many Tributaries of a Diverse Tradition*, ed. W. Glenn Jonas, Jr. (Macon, Ga.: Mercer University Press, 2006), 241–68; Pamela R. Durso, *A Short History of the Cooperative Baptist Fellowship Movement* (Brentwood, Tenn.: Baptist History and Heritage Society, 2006).

[5]   E.g., Kenneth Chafin, "Traveling New Roads," in *Findings*, ed. Lolley et al., 69–76. Whereas Chafin's case for separate denominational identity has in mind the features and functions of the "convention" as established by the SBC, Samuel S. Hill's paper "A Discussion of Whether the Cooperative Baptist Fellowship Should Become a Separate

with oppressive forms of institutionalism that would inevitably betray the principles that had given birth to the CBF and urged against becoming a denomination. Carolyn Blevins cited in summary H. Richard Niebuhr's contention in his 1929 book *The Social Sources of Denominationalism* that denominations "tend to: compromise with the world, accommodate to the caste system, seek primarily to preserve themselves, and be influenced by culture more than they influence culture."[6] Blevins granted that those identified with the CBF have principles worth preserving but contended that replicating the features of modern American denominations might prove to be the worst possible way of preserving the distinctive gifts of this expression of Baptist identity.[7] Yet other contributors recognized the need for the CBF to establish an identity of its own but cautioned against making this move too swiftly in light of significant recent shifts in attitudes toward denominations in American Christianity.[8]

A paper by Nancy T. Ammerman representing this last category, "On Being a Denomination: CBF and the Future," offered the best-developed historical, sociological, and theological analysis of the CBF denominational question among the papers collected in the report.[9] Her categories for interpreting the functions of a denomination and their relation to CBF denominational identity provide an ideal point of departure for my own

---

Convention of Baptists" (93–102) argues for envisioning a more "radical" form of Baptist communal life "through embracing the dialectical relationship between a world-affirming theology and a change-minded heartbeat. It ought to be doctrinally better defined, its standards firmer. It must resist the temptation to make freedom its watchword, since freedom is a second-order concept. It ought to refuse 'buying into' 'modern' forms of organization and efficiency, to live more locally and less centrally. I urge that it endeavor to live with a quiet and firm appreciation of such radical stances as pacifism and a simple lifestyle ethic" (102).

[6] Carolyn DeArmond Blevins, "Cooperative Baptist Fellowship: Denominational Move Unwise at This Time," in *Findings*, ed. Lolley et al., 41 (41–48); H. Richard Niebuhr, *The Social Sources of Denominationalism* (New York: Henry Holt, 1929), 3–25 (appropriately for the present context, this first chapter of Niebuhr's book is titled "The Ethical Failure of the Divided Church").

[7] Blevins, "Cooperative Baptist Fellowship: Denominational Move Unwise at This Time," 44–47; cf. Will D. Campbell, "A Personal Struggle with Soul Freedom (Excerpted)," in *Findings*, ed. Lolley et al., 61–67.

[8] E.g., William L. Hendricks, "Cooperative Baptist Fellowship: Some Reflections," in *Findings*, ed. Lolley et al., 77–84; Bill J. Leonard, "Perspectives on Baptist Denominationalism: Anticipating the Future," in *Findings*, ed. Lolley et al., 103–11.

[9] Nancy T. Ammerman, "On Being a Denomination: CBF and the Future," in *Findings*, ed. Lolley et al., 21–31. The CBF Special Study Commission also found Ammerman's treatment definitive and elected to place it first among the position papers published in the report, arranging the remainder alphabetically by authors' surnames.

observations and proposals regarding denomination as a Baptist ecclesiological category.

Ammerman proposes four senses in which transcongregational patterns of ecclesial life function as "denominations." First, denominations may be identified as "agencies," "through which we do missions and from which we get the goods and services that help us do the work of our local churches."[10] Inasmuch as the CBF has from its inception established networks of partnerships with agencies that support and send missionaries, provide graduate–professional theological education, publish literature in support of programs of Christian education in local churches, offer access to denominational news media, voice Baptist convictions about religious liberty and other ethical concerns in the public square, and assist the ministries of local churches in other ways, despite the disavowals of denominational status quoted above, the CBF has long functioned as a denomination in the sense of agency, though in ways that Ammerman labels "postmodern denomination."[11] Second, a denomination functions as a "specific religious tradition that binds us to one another"[12]—that is, a theological identity rooted in the convictions and practices that distinguish Baptist communities from, say, Lutheran or Reformed or Catholic ones. Despite the aversion of many in the CBF to doctrinal specificity, Ammerman insists that the CBF must embrace this aspect of denominational identity as well:

> In Baptist life, theology belongs to the people, and this moment of crisis has offered us a reason to ask theological questions. We pride ourselves on being non-creedal, but what do we believe? What do we want to teach our children about why they should be Baptist? What do we contribute to the larger body of Christ? What ways of being Christian and ideas about God are uniquely treasured by us?[13]

This way of portraying the inescapably theological dimensions of denominational identity parallels the definition of the doctrinal task of the church offered by the James Wm. McClendon, Jr.: "a church teaching as she must teach if she is to be the church here and now."[14] Baptists who identify with the CBF are far from agreed on the content of what it is that their church must teach, but Ammerman insists, "Still we need ways to talk about what

---

[10] Ammerman, "On Being a Denomination," 22.
[11] Ammerman, "On Being a Denomination," 24.
[12] Ammerman, "On Being a Denomination," 25.
[13] Ammerman, "On Being a Denomination," 26.
[14] James Wm. McClendon, Jr., *Doctrine: Systematic Theology, Vol. 2* (Waco, Tex.: Baylor University Press, 2012), 23–24.

we believe. . . . In many ways, to be Baptist is simply to participate in the conversation about what it means to be Baptist."[15] The latter stress on what it means to participate actively in the ongoing formation of a religious tradition is reminiscent of Alasdair MacIntyre's definition of "a living tradition" as "an historically extended, socially embodied argument, and an argument precisely in part about the goods which constitute that tradition"[16]—a connection to which this chapter will return in its proposal for a more intentionally ecumenical understanding of Baptist denominational identity. The third and fourth senses of denominational identity defined by Ammerman likewise have something in common with MacIntyre's description of the "living tradition" that is central to the life of various types of institutions, including denominations: denominations have "cultural identities" that consist in their external perceptions by the larger culture as well as their own internal cultural life, and they are "social institutions" that conform to the way a certain species of social organizational life is ordinarily constructed.[17] This chapter will return to the possibility of developing Ammerman's categories of Baptist denominationalism in a more explicitly MacIntyrean direction in connection with my own proposals for an ecumenical construal of "denomination" as an eccesiological category for Baptists.

While the CBF officially continued to disavow the "denomination" label, it did find it necessary to claim a distinct organizational identity separate from the SBC in connection with its application in 2001 for membership in the Baptist World Alliance (BWA), the Baptist counterpart to the Lutheran World Federation and other world communions. When the CBF was asked to elaborate its case for membership, it formulated a rationale for its distinction from the SBC that exemplified all four meanings of "denomination" in Ammerman's typology. The BWA Membership Committee initially deferred action on the application, requesting from the CBF further evidence that it was not an "integral part" of any other BWA member body, in this case the SBC. In 2002 the CBF Coordinating Council voted to acknowledge officially that the CBF had "separated ourselves from the structures and organization of the SBC, and have a distinctly diverse understanding to the SBC of what it means to be an

---

[15] Ammerman, "On Being a Denomination," 27.

[16] Alasdair MacIntyre, *After Virtue: A Study in Moral Theory*, 2nd ed. (Notre Dame, Ind.: University of Notre Dame Press, 1984), 222.

[17] Ammerman, "On Being a Denomination," 27–30.

organized body of Baptist churches and individuals in covenant relationship,"[18] and in 2003 the BWA General Council voted to accept the application. In addition to this declaration of separate identity, the Coordinating
Council response listed "twenty indications that we are no longer integral
to the SBC," among which the following are germane to our reflections
on what "denomination" means for Baptists:

4. We have our own annual assemblies that routinely draw 3,000 to 5,000 of
   our constituents, at which we elect leadership, pass budgets and conduct
   business. . . .
6. We have substantial organizational documentation, including a Constitution
   and Bylaws, which clearly establishes our unique and separate identity.
7. We have our own organizational structure, including a board of directors, formal annual budgets, and a large group of employed staff and office
   buildings.
8. We have organized autonomous states and regions with their own boards of
   directors, formal budgets, employed staffs, and office buildings.
9. We own and operate our own missions sending agency, foundation and a
   benefits board with over 300 participants.
10. Our 140 missionaries are in partnership with other autonomous entities
    worldwide as representatives of the CBF. . . .
12. We have over 150 partnering churches that have no formal membership
    in the SBC.
13. We have planted over 50 churches that partner only with CBF at the national
    and international level.
14. We are recognized as an official endorsing body for chaplains and pastoral
    counselors by the US Armed Forces Board; national pastoral care, counsel-
    ing and education organizations; and other viable entities. . . .
15. We are recognized as a non-governmental organization (NGO) by the
    United Nations and have participated as such on the world stage. . . .
20. We are recognized by numerous U.S. Baptist state conventions as a legiti-
    mate national Baptist body, including Virginia, Texas, and North Carolina,
    each of which offers a channel for its churches to give to CBF through its
    state budget.

Yet after this list that reflects the traditional features and functions of modern North American denominations, the response insists, "Though fully
independent of the SBC or any other union, we do not declare that we
are a denomination or convention. . . . We have chosen instead to define
ourselves as a 'fellowship,' which means that we are 'a Baptist association of churches and individuals' in partnership for the advancement of
God's Kingdom." As of the writing of this book, the "Frequently Asked

[18] Cooperative Baptist Fellowship, "Response to the Membership Committee
of the Baptist World Alliance by the Coordinating Council of the Cooperative Baptist Fellowship," accessed November 22, 2014, http://assets.baptiststandard.com/
archived/2002/10_28/print/cbf_text.html.

Questions about CBF" portion of the official CBF web site concluded with the question "Is CBF a denomination?" and provided this answer: "CBF is not a denomination but rather a fellowship of churches and Christians"[19]— which nevertheless embodies Ammerman's description of denomination as agency, religious tradition, cultural identity, and social institution.[20]

The Ecclesiality of Baptist Denominations

Presbyterian theologian Barry Ensign-George's definition of denomination as "a structured entity between congregation and church" that "is a contingent, intermediary, inter-dependent, partial and permeable embodiment of the church"[21] likewise largely applies to the self-understanding of CBF as a "fellowship," even if the CBF and its constituent churches and individuals do not claim to be a "denomination." This application requires a significant qualification, however, for while many Baptists have affirmed the existence of an "invisible" universal church that includes all who belong to Christ, they have also tended to regard only the local congregation as the "visible" expression of the church.[22] Thus, for most Bap-

---

[19] Cooperative Baptist Fellowship, "Frequently Asked Questions," accessed November 22, 2014, http://www.thefellowship.info/About-Us/FAQ. In a report to the 2014 General Assembly of the CBF, Executive Coordinator Suzii Paynter spoke of CBF identity in ways that edged closer to denominational description, coining the word "denominetwork" to describe an organization that in its socially embodied connections fulfills many of the traditional functions of denominations while not employing that term to describe itself. See Bob Allen, "CBF a 'Denominetwork,' Paynter Says," *Baptist News Global* (June 26, 2014), accessed November 23, 2014, http://baptistnews.com/ministry/organizations/item/28867-cbf-a-denominetwork-paytner-says; Leadership Education at Duke Divinity, "Suzii Paynter: Leading a Denomi-network," *Faith & Leadership* (April 22, 2014), accessed November 23, 2014, http://www.faithandleadership.com/qa/suzii-paynter-leading-denomi-network.

[20] Interestingly, Ammerman illustrated the manner in which denominations conform to social expectations for what organizations of a certain type "look like" by citing the state's criteria for what constitutes a denomination implemented in the credentialing of military chaplains by the Pentagon—which happens to be part of indication number 14 in the CBF response to the BWA Membership Committee. The Pentagon considers the CBF a separate denomination, so the CBF invokes this as evidence that it is not integral to the SBC even while denying that it is a denomination.

[21] Barry Ensign-George, "Denomination as Ecclesiological Category: Sketching an Assessment," in *Denomination: Assessing an Ecclesiological Category*, ed. Paul M. Collins and Barry Ensign-George (Ecclesiological Investigations, vol. 11; London: T&T Clark International, 2011), 6 (1–21).

[22] According to the Particular Baptist *Second London Confession* (1677/89), §26.1, "The Catholick or universal Church, which (with respect to internal work of the Spirit, and truth of grace) may be called invisible, consists of the whole number of the Elect, that have been, are, or shall be gathered into one, under Christ the head thereof" (*Baptist*

tists a "denomination," or its functional equivalent, will be conceived of as an entity between the (visible) local church and the (invisible) universal church.

Cooperative Baptists and other sorts of Baptists do regard their form of translocal fellowship as "contingent." They hold the local congregation to be the necessary form of life together in Christian community and typically assume the universal church as a spiritual given, but they view denominational structures as connections that the local church may maintain with intentionality as long as the denomination is serving the congregation's needs but that the local church may ignore, supplement with other structures for translocal connections, or dispense with entirely when the denomination is no longer perceived to be of service to the life of the congregation. Yet it must be conceded that many Baptists manifest a triumphalistic perspective on Baptist identity that regards it as anything but contingent: the Baptists have most consistently restored the New Testament church, it is thought, and denominations will no longer be necessary when other denominations recognize this and embrace Baptist principles themselves.[23] Whenever Baptist identity is conserved as an end in itself, in order to preserve in perpetuity a distinctively Baptist pattern of faith and practice that is not regarded as a temporary way-station en route to the full visible unity of the universal church, Baptist denominational identity ceases to be contingent.

Therefore, there are aspects of Baptist conceptions of denominational identity that do not lend themselves easily to Ensign-George's characterization of denominations as "intermediary" between local congregation and church universal. Yet in the case of the CBF, this functionally denominational form of Baptist translocal connections does make available to its constituents various means of connection with the rest of the church. It is now a member body of the BWA through which CBF partnering

---

Confessions of Faith, 2nd rev. ed., ed. William L. Lumpkin, rev. Bill J. Leonard [Valley Forge, Pa.: Judson, 2011], 283). Likewise, the General Baptist *Orthodox Creed* (1678/79) appropriated three of the four Nicaeno-Constantinopolitan *notae ecclesiae* in confessing in article 29, "there is one holy catholick church, consisting of, or made up of the whole number of the elect, that have been, are, or shall be gathered, in one body under Christ, the only head thereof" and in article 30, "we believe the visible church of Christ on earth, is made up of several distinct congregations, which make up that one catholick church, or mystical body of Christ" (*Baptist Confessions of Faith*, ed. Lumpkin, rev. Leonard, 327–28).

[23] E.g., the chapter "Baptists and Christian Union" (chap. 14) in E. Y. Mullins, *The Axioms of Religion: A New Interpretation of the Baptist Faith* (Philadelphia: American Baptist Publication Society, 1908), 221–34. The Baptist triumphalism evident in that chapter takes full flight in chapter 16, "The Contribution of the Baptists to American Civilization," and chapter 17, "Baptists and World Progress."

congregations and individuals are linked in fellowship with Baptists who belong to other Baptist denominational bodies internationally as well as in the United States. Though not yet an official member body of the National Council of the Churches of Christ in the USA or the World Council of Churches, it is a member of Christian Churches Together, and individual members of the CBF have served on commissions of the NCCCUSA and the WCC. Some other Baptist denominational bodies such as the Baptist Union of Great Britain, the American Baptist Churches USA (formerly the Northern Baptist Convention), and the National Baptist Convention have been official members of the World Council of Churches since its inception.[24]

While Baptist congregational polity does imbue the Baptist denominational tradition with a strongly independent spirit, and it is true that there are many Baptist congregations that declare themselves to be Independent Baptist churches and do not belong to any form of translocal fellowship, from their seventeenth-century origins Baptists have also embodied an associational principle that qualifies their congregational independence as an interdependent congregationalism. In this more connectional dimension of Baptist ecclesiology, the independence of local congregations is not absolute. Local Baptist congregations are interdependent in their relations with one another, in local associations but also in various national and international associations of Baptists. When seven local Baptist congregations in London together issued the *London Confession* of 1644, they explained their interdependence in discerning the mind of Christ for their faith and practice in this fashion:

---

[24] James Leo Garrett, Jr., *Baptist Theology: A Four-Century Study* (Macon, Ga.: Mercer University Press, 2009), 595–96, has compiled a list of Baptist unions that have held membership in the WCC from the reports of WCC assemblies from 1948 through 1998. In addition to the Baptist Union of Great Britain, the American Baptist Churches, USA, and three historical African-American unions—the National Baptist Convention, the National Baptist Convention of America, and the Progressive National Baptist Convention—this list includes the following as full member bodies: Baptist Union of Western Congo, Episcopal Baptist Community (Democratic Republic of Congo), Native Baptist Church of Cameroon, Union of Baptist Churches of Cameroon, Nigerian Baptist Convention, Bangladesh Baptist Sangha, Baptist Union of New Zealand, China Baptist Council, Myanmar Baptist Convention, Samavesam of Telugu Baptist Churches (India), Jamaica Baptist Union, Baptist Union of Denmark, Baptist Union of Hungary, Evangelical Christian-Baptist Union of Russia (formerly USSR), Union of Baptist Congregations in the Netherlands, and Baptist Convention of Nicaragua. Three additional unions have held associate member status: Baptist Union of El Salvador, Bengal-Orissa–Bihar Baptist Convention (India), and Evangelical Baptist Union of Italy. Chapter 10 of this book gives attention to these affiliations and other ways Baptists have embodied the ecumenical dimensions of their ecclesial identity.

[B]ecause it may be conceived, that what is here published, may be but the Judgment of some one particular Congregation, more refined than the rest; We do therefore here subscribe it, some of each body in the name, and by the appointment of seven Congregations, who though we be distinct in respect of our particular bodies, for convenience sake, being as many as can well meet together in one place, yet are all one in Communion, holding Jesus Christ to be our head and Lord; under whose government we desire alone to walk, in following the Lamb wheresoever he goeth; and we believe the Lord will daily cause truth more to appear in the hearts of his Saints . . . that so they may with one shoulder, more study to lift up the Name of the Lord Jesus, and stand for his appointments and Laws; which is the desires and prayers of the condemned Churches of Christ in London for all saints.[25]

The rule of Christ in the local congregations in the plural therefore has implications for the efforts of any single local congregation to discern the mind of Christ, and vice versa. Together in their mutual relations they seek to walk under the government of Christ, seeking from him a fuller grasp of the truth, as one ecclesial communion—a communion which, it was hoped by these early Baptists, might extend beyond Baptist churches in association to include all the saints. Baptists do not always conceive of this interdependence as involving non-Baptists, but the interdependence embodied in Baptist forms of denomination has openings for transdenominational expressions of interdependence that can be more fully exploited by Baptists who regard the visible unity of all Christians as an ecclesial good.

Despite the previously noted Baptist triumphalism that has surfaced in the tradition now and then, few if any Baptists would argue that their denomination is the full historical manifestation of the church. The strained historiographical apologetic of "Landmark" Baptists did seek to make the case that Baptists can trace a lineage of direct succession through pre-Reformation sectarian movements all the way back to the baptism of Jesus by John the Baptist,[26] but in the main Baptists regard Baptist denominational identity as a partial embodiment of the church—even if many

---

[25] *London Confession* (1644) pref., in *Baptist Confessions of Faith*, ed. Lumpkin, rev. Leonard, 143 (spelling standardized in quotation herein).

[26] For a historical overview of the development of this approach to Baptist historiography (to which no recognized Baptist historian today holds but which has continued to exert some popular influence among some Baptists in the United States), see James Edward McGoldrick, *Baptist Successionism: A Crucial Question in Baptist History* (ATLA Monograph Series, no. 32; Metuchen, N.J.: Scarecrow Press, 1994).

Baptists may consider some denominations as more partial than others in their approximation of the fullness of the church. Most Baptist conceptions of denomination are likewise permeable, with respect both to membership and to denominational mutability. It would be hard to conceive of a more permeable denomination-like configuration than the self-description of the CBF, for example. Even so, the reluctance of some Baptist congregations to recognize the baptisms of other communions when members of those churches present themselves for Baptist church membership can render Baptist denominationalism less permeable, and many Baptists at all points on the theological spectrum will consider the modification of what they regard as essential Baptist distinctives to be a betrayal of the Baptist heritage rather than something that contributes to its improvement.

In what sense can Baptists affirm denomination as an "embodiment" of the church? While Baptists do not regard a denomination as *ekklēsia* proper in the sense of the church local or universal, Baptist ecclesiology can admit that denominations are ecclesial to the degree that they participate in the qualities of church. Indeed, in a somewhat paradoxical manner Baptist "gathered church" ecclesiology is at least in theory able to grant a substantial degree of ecclesiality not only to various forms of denominational translocal associations of Baptists but even to ecumenical gatherings, for all of these embodiments of the church are instances "where two or three are gathered in my name" (Matt 18:20) for the purpose of bringing their common life under the lordship of Christ. British Baptist theologian Paul Fiddes has made such connections between the location of the church in the gathered congregation and the embodiment of the church in various forms of translocal fellowship, for "since the same rule of Christ [experienced in the gathered local congregation] can be experienced in assemblies of churches together, there is also the basis here for Baptist associational life, and indeed for participating in ecumenical clusters."[27] This recognition of the ecclesiality of ecumenical partnerships is expressed also in the summary of the Baptist perspective on how extracongregational structures for *episkopē* might serve the unity of the church in the report from the second series of conversations between the Baptist World Alliance and the Catholic Church, which contrasts how "Catholics . . .

---

[27] Paul S. Fiddes, *Tracks and Traces: Baptist Identity in Church and Theology* (Studies in Baptist History and Thought, vol. 13; Milton Keynes, UK: Paternoster, 2003), 6. Cf. John Howard Yoder, *The Royal Priesthood: Essays Ecclesiological and Ecumenical*, ed. Michael G. Cartwright (Grand Rapids: William B. Eerdmans, 1994), 236, who makes a similar point regarding the ecclesiality of ecumenical gatherings (a point to which the next chapter of this book returns).

regard this covenanting of church leaders together as an ecumenical rather than an ecclesial structure, while Baptists can regard such covenants as partaking in the characteristics of the church."[28] From the standpoint of Baptist and other expressions of Free Church ecclesiology, the embodiment of the church in the local congregation is the normative expression of church, but it is not the whole church.[29] The local embodiment of the church in its fullness is one in which gatherings of members from multiple congregations—and from other associations of local congregations, perhaps even from those belonging to other Christian communions—may participate. A denomination is ecclesial, though not an *ekklēsia* in Baptist perspective.

Baptist Denominational Identity and the Ecumenical Future

It would be easy to attribute the formation and perpetuation of Baptist denominational entities to a self-serving concern for the preservation and transmission of the Baptist tradition to future generations. Those who formed the CBF were certainly motivated in part by the concern that their perspectives on Baptist identity would no longer be inculcated by the institutions of the SBC. Denominations do have the legitimate function of serving as bearers of a religious tradition (cf. the second category in Ammerman's typology), and this function need not always be self-serving. It can be directed toward the end of the visible unity of the church, and the Baptist associational impulse has at its best suggested surprisingly ecumenical dimensions of Baptist denominational identity. Baptists form various types of translocal fellowships partly out of the recognition that no local congregation possesses in and of itself all the resources it needs for becoming a community of faithful disciples. The local congregations are

---

[28] So Baptist World Alliance and Catholic Church, "The Word of God in the Life of the Church: A Report of International Conversations between the Catholic Church and the Baptist World Alliance 2006–2010," §196, in *American Baptist Quarterly* 31, no. 1 (Spring 2012): 103 (28–122).

[29] This understanding of the relation of the local and universal expressions of church, traceable to Jean-Jacques von Allmen, "L'Église locale parmi les autres Églises locales," *Irénikon* 43 (1970): 512 (512–37), was affirmed by the Symposium on Baptist Identity and Ecclesiology in Elstal, Germany, March 21–24, 2007, sponsored by the Baptist World Alliance in conjunction with the German Union of Free Evangelical (Baptist) Churches, that addressed the question "Are Baptist Churches Autonomous?" See Elizabeth Newman, "Are Local Baptist Churches Wholly Autonomous?" *Baptist News Global* (June 12, 2007), accessed November 23, 2014, http://baptistnews.com/archives/item/2582-opinion-are-local-baptist-churches-wholly-autonomous.

interdependent in their efforts to fulfill the mission of the church—perhaps beginning with those of like faith and order, but potentially extending this recognition to those belonging to other denominations. Interestingly enough, the CBF's closest approximation of a declaration of separate identity as a Baptist denomination, even while disavowing the term, came in an effort to have a channel for wider ecumenical connections with other Baptists worldwide via the Baptist World Alliance, the world communion through which Baptists relate at the international level to other communions (e.g., through its delegations to the joint commissions of bilateral ecumenical dialogues and other forums for ecumenical encounter). Walter Shurden, a Baptist historian who wrote one of the position papers solicited by the CBF Special Study Commission, contended that the CBF should seek denominational status in part so that it would have its own representation in the BWA.[30] Shurden's rationale could also be extended to the need for official representation in ecumenical councils that serve as instruments of Faith and Order contestation and convergence, in particular the World Council of Churches.

In my opinion, only the end of the full visible unity of the church justifies the continued separate ecclesial existence of Baptist denominational identity. When continued denominational existence becomes an end in itself, it perpetuates the division of the church. If visible unity is to be achieved, there must be both an interconfessional contestation of faith and order and an interconfessional exchange of gifts. This can happen only when the denominations see themselves as lacking something essential to what it means to be "church" as long as they remain separated from full communion with the other churches—an insight that is most easily gained from participation in the ecumenical contestation of the matters of faith and order that currently preclude full communion—and it can happen only when the other churches are able to receive the distinctive gifts that each denomination has to offer the rest of the body of Christ. "Receptive ecumenism" therefore complements conciliar Faith and Order ecumenism as an ecumenical paradigm within which it may be envisioned that an embrace of thick denominational identity can contribute to the quest for the visible unity of the church rather than the solidifying of its divisions.

Some older approaches to ecumenism created Baptist resistance to institutional expressions of the quest for Christian unity such as the World Council of Churches by giving the impression that the price of visible

---

[30] Walter B. Shurden, "A Solicited Letter to the Study Commission," in *Findings*, ed. Lolley et al., 126 (123–27).

unity would be the surrender of some of the things held most dear by each church. A newer approach to ecumenical engagement, however, is gaining traction in the international ecumenical community. "Receptive ecumenism" is an approach to ecumenical dialogue according to which the communions in conversation with one another seek to identify the distinctive gifts that each tradition has to offer the other and which each could receive from the other with integrity.[31] This paradigm for ecumenical engagement was given expression by Pope John Paul II in his 1995 encyclical on ecumenism *Ut Unum Sint*: "Dialogue is not simply an exchange of ideas. In some ways it is always an 'exchange of gifts' " (§28).[32] Some bilateral dialogues, such as that between the Catholic Church and the World Methodist Council, have worked toward concrete proposals for the exchange of ecclesial gifts.[33] Yet as an international conference on receptive ecumenism held at Durham University (UK) in 2006 defined the enterprise, "the primary emphasis is on learning rather than teaching. . . . each tradition takes responsibility for its own potential learning from others and is, in turn, willing to facilitate the learning of others as requested but without dictating terms and without making others' learning a precondition to attending to one's own."[34]

The starting place for this receptive ecumenical learning is the denomination as a bearer of a religious tradition, one of Ammerman's categories for the function of denominations. If the denomination is the bearer of a living tradition in the MacIntyrean sense, it will be a contested one. Thus, Ammerman suggests that "to be Baptist is simply to participate in the conversation about what it means to be a Baptist"[35]—in other words, to participate in the argument about the good that constitutes the Baptist tradition. This intraconfessional contestation can help Baptists discover the aspects of the catholicity of the church that are uniquely preserved within the Baptist

[31]   See Paul D. Murray, ed., *Receptive Ecumenism and the Call to Catholic Learning: Exploring a Way for Contemporary Ecumenism* (Oxford: Oxford University Press, 2008).

[32]   John Paul II, *On Commitment to Ecumenism* (*Ut Unum Sint*, May 25, 1995), accessed October 21, 2014, http://www.vatican.va/holy_father/john_paul_ii/encyclicals/documents/hf_jp-ii_enc_25051995_ut-unum-sint_en.html.

[33]   Catholic Church and World Methodist Council, *The Grace Given You in Christ: Catholics and Methodists Reflect Further on the Church. Report of the International Commission for Dialogue between the Roman Catholic Church and the World Methodist Council* (Lake Junaluska, N.C.: World Methodist Council, 2006).

[34]   Quotation from a briefing document distributed to conference participants in Walter Cardinal Kasper's "Foreword" to *Receptive Ecumenism and the Call to Catholic Learning*, ed. Murray, vii.

[35]   Ammerman, "On Being a Denomination," 27.

tradition so that they know what it is they have to offer as gift as well as what they might need to receive in the exchange of ecclesial gifts.

Despite their contingency, it is the denominations that are the primary ways in which the argument about the goods that constitute the living tradition of the church is historically extended and socially embodied. The separate denominational traditions are the historical extensions of the arguments within the larger tradition of the church catholic that led to their separate existence, and they are therefore the pathways along which we must travel in reengaging those arguments en route to ecumenical convergence. The *Joint Declaration on the Doctrine of Justification*, for example, could never have resulted from the reconsideration of theological propositions alone.[36] Its differentiated consensus was possible only because for four decades representatives of the Lutheran and Catholic traditions traveled together back through their respective historical extensions of this sixteenth-century argument and thus were able to contest their differences today in a way that clarified the teaching of both communions and drew them closer together, at least on this matter. The *JDDJ* likewise illustrates the socially embodied nature of this contestation. It was undertaken not by a random assortment of Christian theologians who happened to have adopted either Catholic or Lutheran positions on justification irrespective of the denomination to which they belonged, but rather by theologians who were formed by the social embodiments of those traditions and who also participated over time in the particular socially embodied institution that is a joint ecumenical commission.

Only the existence of the translocal denominations makes it possible for the local churches and their individual members to have a participation in the contestation of their own tradition and in the contestation between the denominational traditions necessary for progress toward the visible embodiment of the spiritual unity of the church universal. This argument reveals not only differences and openings for convergence between them, but the location of the universal church's dispersed gifts and the possibilities for their exchange. Denominations serve the end of visible unity when they foster within and without the denominational tradition both the contestation of divisions and the reception of gifts across the current divides. Even if Cooperative Baptists and some other Baptist unions eschew the label "denomination," their translocal forms of ecclesial association are

---

[36] Lutheran World Federation and Catholic Church, *Joint Declaration on the Doctrine of Justification* (Grand Rapids: William B. Eerdmans, 2000).

their gateway to engagement with the non-Baptist churches so "that they may become completely one" (John 17:23).

Denominational Receptive Ecumenism, Baptist Style

The paradigm of receptive ecumenism, which supplies denominational-ism with its only legitimate ongoing raison d'être in relation to the end of the visible unity of the church, is in many respects friendlier to Baptist participation in ecumenical engagement than some earlier models may have been. It assumes that because Baptists have been entrusted with a unique journey as a people of God, they possess distinctive gifts to be offered to the rest of the body of Christ. It also suggests the possibility that Baptists can incorporate the gifts of others into their own faith and practice without abandoning or distorting the gifts that already define the Baptist identity. Receptive ecumenism may also reveal Baptists as being much more receptive ecumenically than one might assume. Throughout their history and in their ecclesial life today, Baptists have received from other churches much that forms the core of Baptists' identity as Christians while also enriching their distinctive identity as Baptists.

The earliest Baptists received gifts from the English Separatists and Continental Anabaptists that helped distinguish these Free Churches or Believers' Churches from other Christian communities. Yet together with the Separatists and the Anabaptists, the early Baptists received from the pre-Reformation church the canon of Scripture and the core doctrines of orthodox Christianity in light of which they read this canon. These gifts combined with their unique historical experiences as a socially embodied community to form a quintessentially Baptist pattern of faith and practice, at the core of which is ancient catholicity. Early Baptist confessions of faith underscored Baptist indebtedness to these gifts with language and con-cepts drawn directly from the ecumenical creeds, Anabaptist confessions, the Anglican *Thirty-Nine Articles*, and the Reformed *Westminster Confession*.

A pair of important seventeenth-century Baptist confessions of faith illustrates this Baptist reception of the creedal and confessional gifts of the rest of the church. The *Second London Confession* was adopted by English Particular (Calvinistic) Baptists in 1677; the *Orthodox Creed* was issued by English General (Arminian) Baptists in 1678. In keeping with Baptist confessions that preceded them, these two confessions are replete with echoes of Nicaeno-Constantinopolitan trinitarianism and Chalcedonian Christology. In addition, the *Second London Confession* calls the church "Catholick or universal," and the *Orthodox Creed* confesses faith in "one holy catholick church," the language of three of the four marks of the church in the Nicene Creed.[37] The most explicit reception of the ancient catholic tradition among Baptist confessions of faith takes place in the *Orthodox Creed*, which reproduces the text of the Apostles', Nicene, and Athanasian Creeds and encourages Baptists to receive and believe them. Much language of that article on the creeds is lifted almost verbatim from article 8 of the Anglican *Thirty-Nine Articles*.[38] Likewise, when the *Second London Confession* and the *Orthodox Creed* call the church "catholic," they are indebted to chapter 25 of the *Westminster Confession*, which served as the model for the articles on the church in both confessions.[39] Also derived from the *Westminster Confession* are the echoes of the Nicene Creed and the Chalcedonian definition in the trinitarian and christological portions of the *Second London Confession* and the *Orthodox Creed*.[40]

Baptists have also received patterns and practices of worship from other Christians. With other Christians, Baptists have received the overarching pattern of gathering for worship described by Justin Martyr in the middle of the second century: the act of gathering on Sunday, the reading of Scripture, a sermon, prayers, corporate responses, communion (when celebrated), and an offering.[41] Baptist worship in all its variety and the *ordo* of the Roman Mass alike reflect common reception of the essential elements of this ancient pattern of worship—as do other traditions from the Orthodox divine liturgy to Pentecostal and charismatic worship.

By the middle of the twentieth century, the singing of hymns had become such a typical feature of Baptist worship that British Baptist Ernest Payne could describe Baptist worship as "Scripture, prayer and sermon, interspersed with hymns."[42] With some adjustment for the advent of songs and choruses in "contemporary" worship, that description continues to describe the worship of many Baptist churches throughout the world. That was not always the case. The early General Baptists opposed congregational singing of all types on the grounds that such "set forms" hindered

---

[37] *Second London Confession*, §26.1, in *Baptist Confessions of Faith*, ed. Lumpkin, rev. Leonard, 283; *Orthodox Creed*, §29, in *Baptist Confessions of Faith*, ed. Lumpkin, rev. Leonard, 327.

[38] *Orthodox Creed*, §38, in *Baptist Confessions of Faith*, ed. Lumpkin, rev. Leonard, 337–38.

[39] *Second London Confession*, §26.1, in *Baptist Confessions of Faith*, ed. Lumpkin, rev. Leonard, 283; *Orthodox Creed*, §29, in *Baptist Confessions of Faith*, ed. Lumpkin, rev. Leonard, 327.

[40] *Second London Confession*, §§2.3 and 8.1–7, in *Baptist Confessions of Faith*, ed. Lumpkin, rev. Leonard, 237 and 247–50; *Orthodox Creed*, §§3–7, in *Baptist Confessions of Faith*, ed. Lumpkin, rev. Leonard, 301–5.

[41] Justin Martyr, *1 Apology* 67; ET in *Ante-Nicene Fathers*, ed. Alexander Roberts and James Donaldson (New York: Christian Literature, 1885), 1:185–68.

[42] Ernest Payne, *The Fellowship of Believers: Baptist Thought and Practice Yesterday and Today* (London: Carey Kingsgate Press, 1952), 96.

Spirit-led spontaneity. The early Particular Baptists followed the practice of other Calvinistic Dissenters in permitting congregational singing only in the form of metrical psalms. The Baptist practice of hymn singing seems to have been introduced by Benjamin Keach, a former General Baptist who became pastor of a Particular Baptist congregation in Southwark, England, in the 1670s. By 1700 many British Baptist congregations had adopted the practice, which spread rapidly over the next half century. Baptist hymn singing soon crossed the Atlantic, and in 1742 the Phila-delphia Baptist Association issued a confession that added to the *Second London Confession* an article commending congregational hymn singing as a "divine institution."

Baptist hymnals are arguably the most significant ecumenical docu-ments produced by Baptists. They implicitly recognize hymn writers from a wide variety of traditions throughout the history of the church as sisters and brothers in Christ by including their hymns alongside hymns by Bap-tists. Since many Baptist hymnals are produced by denominational com-missions and published by denominational presses, this recognition carries some degree of official Baptist imprimatur. Baptist hymnals functioned as ecumenical documents in this sense from the inception of their use in Bap-tist churches. As Baptist liturgical theologian Christopher Ellis observes, "Despite the existence of Baptist hymn writers, there has never been a cor-pus of 'Baptist hymns' which has expressed or nourished an identity for the denomination in the way that the Wesleys' hymns have done for Method-ists."[43] The most widely used hymnal among Baptists in Great Britain and North America by the late eighteenth and early nineteenth century was John Rippon's *Selection of Hymns.* Most hymns in the collection were not by Baptists, and in the preface Rippon wrote:

> It has given me no small pleasure, to unite, as far as I could, different Denominations of Ministers, and Christians on Earth, in the same noble Work, which shall for ever employ them above. . . . hence it will be seen, that Churchmen and Dissenters, Watts and Tate, Wesley and Toplady, England and America sing Side by Side, and very often join in the same Triumph, using the same Words.[44]

[43]   Christopher J. Ellis, *Gathering: A Theology and Spirituality of Worship in Free Church Tradition* (London: SCM Press, 2004), 152.

[44]   John Rippon, *A Selection of Hymns from the Best Authors: Intended to Be an Appendix to Dr. Watts's Psalms and Hymns* (London: Thomas Wilkins, 1787), preface; quoted in Ellis, *Gathering,* 152.

Baptist hymnals have functioned as key facilitators of receptive ecumenism. They have helped Baptists to sing and receive the theologies of patristic and medieval Christianity, the Protestant Reformation, and a wide denominational variety of more recent hymn writers including post-Reformation Catholics as well as Protestants of all stripes. One significant counterintuitive feature of recent Baptist hymnals is their receptive retrieval of patristic hymnody. *The Baptist Hymnal* published in 1991 by the Southern Baptist Convention (SBC), for example, is the hymnal used for the better part of the past two decades not only by most Southern Baptist congregations but also by those that now identify more closely with the Cooperative Baptist Fellowship (CBF). This hymnal included seven hymns with texts of patristic composition: *Let All Mortal Flesh Keep Silence* from the fifth-century *Liturgy of St. James*; *All Glory, Laud, and Honor* by Theodulph of Orleans; *The Day of Resurrection* by John of Damascus; *Of the Father's Love Begotten* by Aurelius Clemens Prudentius; the fourth-century *Gloria Patri*; and the anonymous Latin hymns *Christ Is Made the Sure Foundation* and *O Christ, Our Hope, Our Heart's Desire*.[45] All but two were the gifts of John Mason Neale, an Anglo-Catholic divine of the nineteenth century whose translations of Greek and Latin patristic and medieval hymns greatly enriched the hymnody of the Church of England en route to their reception by Baptists and other communions. A new *Baptist Hymnal* published in 2008 by the SBC retained four of those seven patristic hymns.[46] *Baptist Praise and Worship*, a hymnal produced in 1991 for the Baptist Union of Great Britain, includes ten hymns with texts of patristic origin (only four of which parallel the patristic contents of *The Baptist Hymnal* [1991]): *Of the Father's Love Begotten* by Prudentius; *All Glory, Praise and Honor* by Theodulph of Orleans (though attributed in *Baptist Praise and Worship* to John Mason Neale, the hymn text was translated rather than authored by Neale); *Sing, My Tongue, the Glorious Battle* and *The Royal Banners Forward Go* by Venantius Fortunatus; *Come, You Faithful, Raise the Strain* and *Come, God's People, Sing for Joy* by John of Damascus; *Father, We Thank You Now for Planting*, versified from a text in the second-century *Didache*; *Let All Mortal Flesh Keep Silence* from the fifth-century *Liturgy of St. James*; *Holy, Holy, Holy, God Almighty Lord*, based on the *Sanctus* that dates from the fourth-century liturgies; and *Christ Is Made the Sure Foundation*, a seventh-century Latin hymn.[47] The *Celebrating Grace Hymnal* published in 2010 by

[45] Wesley L. Forbis, ed., *The Baptist Hymnal* (Nashville: Convention Press, 1991).

[46] Mike Harland, ed., *Baptist Hymnal* (Nashville: Lifeway Worship, 2008).

[47] Psalms and Hymns Trust, *Baptist Praise and Worship* (Oxford: Oxford University Press on behalf of the Psalms and Hymns Trust, 1991). According to a survey of worship

an independent board but closely associated with the CBF includes six of the seven patristic hymns in the 1991 *Baptist Hymnal* and adds three others: the fifth-century Latin hymn *That Easter Day with Joy Was Bright*; *Come, Ye Faithful, Raise the Strain* by John of Damascus; and *Christ Be Near at Either Hand* from the *Breastplate* attributed to St. Patrick.[48] Beyond these patristic hymns, Baptists receive through their hymnals the gifts of Francis of Assisi and Teresa of Jesus, Martin Luther, the post-Reformation Catholic author of the hymn *Fairest Lord Jesus* from the *Münster Gesangbuch*, the Methodist Charles Wesley, and more recently the Pentecostal pastor Jack Hayford, to name a few hymn writers whose ecclesial gifts Baptists have gladly received with their voices and hearts—even if not always aware of the hymns' denominational origins.

Baptists have benefited from the transdenominational liturgical renewal of the late twentieth century, and today a growing number of Baptist congregations have incorporated other liturgical gifts from beyond the Baptist tradition into their worship: the full Christian year and the liturgical colors that accompany its seasons, the lectionary, the imposition of ashes on Ash Wednesday and processions with palm fronds at the start of Holy Week, and even incense and icons here and there. In my Baptist context in the United States, Dayspring Baptist Church in Waco, Texas (affiliated with the Cooperative Baptist Fellowship), for example, describes itself as "a Baptist Church in the contemplative tradition."[49] Visitors to the church's web site are greeted with a quotation from Ambrose of Milan's hymn *Splendor of God's Glory Bright*. The site characterizes worship there as "liturgical" in the sense that "there are 'formal' expressions in every service, forms handed on to us from the past. Litanies, responses, and readings from the Revised Common Lectionary are typical. In addition," the site's worship page says they "are guided by the Church Calendar Year and observe communion monthly." A group from the congregation meets with the pastor for a "Lectionary Breakfast" each Friday. The order of service from the fourth Sunday of Lent in 2010 notes that occasion and includes a prayer from St. Isaac of Nineveh, readings from the lectionary, and a corporate prayer of confession and declaration of pardon, along with

---

practices in churches of the Baptist Union of Great Britain (BUGB) conducted in 1996 and published as Christopher J. Ellis, *Baptist Worship Today* (Didcot, UK: Baptist Union of Great Britain, 1999), cited in Ellis, *Gathering*, 152, this hymnal was utilized by about 25 percent of member churches of the BUGB at the time of the survey.

[48] Tom McAfee, John Simons, David Music, Milburn Price, Stanley Roberts, and Mark Edwards, eds., *Celebrating Grace Hymnal* (Macon, Ga.: Celebrating Grace, 2010).

[49] Dayspring Baptist Church (Waco, Tex.), church web site, accessed December 15, 2014, http://www.ourdayspring.org/.

the hymns and sermon more typical of Baptist worship.[50] They also recite
the ancient creeds as acts of worship now and then and engage together
in the practice of *lectio divina*. While Dayspring Baptist Church is of relatively recent foundation, a more historic Baptist congregation that has
likewise recently been intentional about the practice of liturgical receptive
ecumenism is First Baptist Church in Dayton, Ohio (founded in 1824 and
affiliated with the American Baptist Churches, USA, and the Alliance
of Baptists). First Baptist Church Dayton's web site describes the congregation as "deliberately sacramental," for "we believe in experiencing
our faith in every possible way, and that includes the Sacrament of Holy
Communion."[51] The church celebrates communion monthly in the main
worship service in the sanctuary but offers weekly communion for those
who desire it in an additional Sunday service held in its chapel. Current
pastor Rodney Kennedy has coedited a book of essays and appended worship resources intended to help other Baptists claim such liturgical gifts
of the whole church as the full Christian year, more frequent and more
intentionally meaningful eucharistic observance, and the confession of the
ancient ecumenical creeds.[52] Earlier in the year of the book's publication,
the congregation practiced the eucharistic hospitality and reception of the
liturgical gifts of others commended in the book by holding joint worship
services for several Sundays with a neighboring Episcopal church while
its building underwent renovations. First Baptist celebrated the Eucharist
each of those Sundays, using wine, and incorporated aspects of the *Book of
Common Prayer* eucharistic rite into their Baptist services.[53]

Other Baptist congregations in the United States have been able to
re-receive the *Book of Common Prayer,* which the founders of their movement rejected in the seventeenth century as a mandated liturgy, as a freely
embraced gift that can enrich the worship of Baptist congregations today.
Broadway Baptist Church in Fort Worth, Texas (affiliated with the Cooperative Baptist Fellowship and the Alliance of Baptists), has a long tradition

---

[50] E-mail correspondence with Eric Howell (pastor, Dayspring Baptist Church),
March 17, 2010.

[51] First Baptist Church, Dayton, Ohio, church web site, accessed December 15, 2014,
http://www.fbcdayton.org/?page_id=106.

[52] Rodney W. Kennedy and Derek C. Hatch, *Gathering Together: Baptists at Work in
Worship* (Eugene, Ore.: Pickwick, 2013).

[53] Jeff Brumley, "Baptists Host Episcopalians, Wine," *Baptist News Global* (January 24,
2013), accessed December 15, 2014, http://baptistnews.com/ministry/congregations/
item/8161-baptists-host-episcopalians-wine.

of receiving the liturgical gifts of the wider church in its Sunday worship.[54] But in 2010 the congregation began an experiment to revitalize Wednesday evening midweek services, transforming them from the "prayer meeting and Bible study" format typical of Baptist churches in the region into a service of Vespers based on the *Book of Common Prayer* office of Evening Prayer.[55] Another Baptist church has made the *Book of Common Prayer* the primary resource for its liturgical life. All Souls Charlottesville, a congregation in Charlottesville, Virginia, affiliated with the Baptist General Association of Virginia, was launched in 2009 as a Baptist congregation whose worship stands intentionally in the Anglican tradition.[56]

Connectional associations of Baptist congregations—Baptist denominations—may also serve as agents of ecumenical receptivity. The congregations of the Evangelical Baptist Church of Georgia represent a fascinating case study in Baptist receptive ecumenism that includes striking forms of liturgical as well as ecclesiological reception.[57] In a culture that is historically Eastern Orthodox, the Evangelical Baptist Church of Georgia has maintained "belief in believer's baptism, autonomy of the local church, freedom of conscience and religious liberty,"[58] while adopting an ecclesial structure that is a hybrid of congregational and episcopal governance with a threefold ministry of bishops, presbyters, and deacons. In this structure the local congregations are autonomous in relation to one another and to the structure of the Evangelical Baptist Church of Georgia, but they are presided over by a bishop, whose office is a "symbol of unity" with the "responsibility . . . to provide spiritual guidance to the whole church

---

[54] James Leo Garrett, Jr., *Living Stones: The Centennial History of Broadway Baptist Church, Fort Worth, Texas, 1882–1982*, 2 vols. (Fort Worth, Tex.: Broadway Baptist Church, 1984), 2:906, wrote of a shift in emphasis during the latter years of the church's first century of existence toward "more liturgical worship" and "more emphasis on Holy Week and Advent."

[55] Brent Beasley, "Transforming Wednesday Nights for Adults," Cooperative Baptist Fellowship General Assembly Workshop, June 20–23, 2012, Fort Worth, Texas, *CBF General Assembly Program Book*, accessed December 15, 2014, http://issuu.com/fellowship/docs/2012generalassemblyguide/57.

[56] Jeff Brumley, "Virginia Church May Look Anglican, but It's Fully Baptist," *Baptist News Global* (March 26, 2014), accessed December 15, 2014, http://baptistnews.com/ministry/congregations/item/28506-va-church-is-anglican-leaning-but-fully-baptist?tmpl=component&print=1.

[57] See Malkhaz Songulashvili, *Evangelical Christian Baptists of Georgia: The History and Transformation of a Free Church Tradition* (Studies in World Christianity; Waco, Tex.: Baylor University Press, 2015).

[58] Daniel Buttry, "Baptists amid Georgian Revolutions," *Baptists Today* 23, no. 8 (August 2005): 9.

as prophet, preacher, and teacher of the Gospel."[59] The ministers of the Evangelical Baptist Church wear Orthodox vestments and employ the Orthodox use of the sign of the cross, incense, and icons in their worship services.[60] The Church sponsors monastic orders for men and women[61] and a school of iconography. As their archbishop Malkhaz Songulashvili puts it, they "technically should be considered a Reformed Orthodox Church. On the one hand," he says, "we are committed to the principles of the European Radical Reformation, and on the other hand we hold to our own Orthodox legacy."[62] In other words, they have received the gifts of the Orthodox tradition and incorporated them into their Baptist pattern of faith and practice.

Much Baptist receptive ecumenism is mediated by Baptist educational institutions. Baptist theological educators have long taught Baptist seminarians that the resources they need for the work of the ministry are not exclusively Baptist in origin. Baptist ministers thus routinely glean the riches of non–Baptist biblical scholarship in their sermon preparation. They learn in church history courses that the four-century-long Baptist tradition can be appreciated only as part of the whole history of the whole

[59] W. Benjamin Boswell, "Liturgy and Revolution Part 1: Georgian Baptists and the Non-violent Struggle for Democracy," *Religion in Eastern Europe* 27, no. 2 (May 2007): 59 (48–71).

[60] William E. Yoder, "The Unorthodox Baptist Bishop: How One Church Leader in Georgia Is Breaking the Long-Standing Divide between Protestants and Orthodox," *Christianity Today* 57, no. 5 (June 2013): 48–51.

[61] Monasticism as a Baptist endeavor is not unheard of elsewhere in the Baptist world. Paul R. Dekar, *Community of the Transfiguration: The Journey of a New Monastic Community* (New Monastic Library: Resources for Radical Discipleship, vol. 3; Eugene, Ore.: Cascade Books, 2008), explores the foundation of Holy Transfiguration Monastery by members of Breakwater Baptist Church in Victoria, Australia, and its subsequent development and impact. Many Baptists in North America have participated in communities related to the "New Monasticism" exemplified by Shane Claiborne, *The Irresistible Revolution: Living as an Ordinary Radical* (Grand Rapids: Zondervan, 2006), and Jonathan Wilson-Hartgrove, *New Monasticism: What It Has to Say to Today's Church* (Grand Rapids: Brazos Press, 2008). The term "new monasticism" was appropriated from a book by Wilson-Hartgrove's father-in-law, who is himself a Baptist theologian: Jonathan R. Wilson, *Living Faithfully in a Fragmented World: Lessons for the Church from MacIntyre's "After Virtue"* (Christian Mission and Modern Culture; Harrisburg, Pa.: Trinity Press International, 1997). A revised edition took into account the phenomenon of "New Monastic" communities influenced by the proposals of the first edition: idem, *Living Faithfully in a Fragmented World: From "After Virtue" to a New Monasticism*, 2nd ed. (New Monastic Library: Resources for Radical Discipleship, vol. 6; Eugene, Ore.: Cascade Books, 2010).

[62] Archbishop Malkhaz Songulashvili, interview correspondence quoted in Boswell, "Liturgy and Revolution," 59.

church.[63] Significantly, a remarkable number of younger Baptist historians and historical theologians are now making patristics their specialization. Baptist ministers are enriched by the contemplation of systematic theologies written by theologians of other churches. They learn to incorporate practices of pastoral care forged in other traditions into their own approach to the cure of souls. They are shown how to plan worship and craft programs of Christian education that weave the gifts of other Christians into the fabric of Baptist congregational life.

There is also a Baptist receptive ecumenism that belongs to the sphere of personal piety. Many younger Baptists have a keen interest in spirituality and are drawn to the practice of spiritual disciplines that originated in other communions. These same younger Baptists, along with some more mature ones, are taking up the practice of meditating on Scripture according to the pattern of *lectio divina*, walking labyrinths, and even using the sign of the cross as an embodied act of personal devotion and experimenting with praying the Rosary and using Orthodox chotkis to pray the Jesus Prayer.

Baptists have received the gifts of other Christians through an ecumenism of the confession of faith, an ecumenism of the sanctuary and especially of the hymnal taken in hand therein, an ecumenism of the seminary classroom and pastor's study, and an ecumenism of personal devotion. They have received these gifts from the church in its catholicity *along with* other Christians and more directly *from* other Christians in a contemporary convergence toward our common catholicity.

One of the distinctive gifts of the Baptist tradition may be its unique capacity for receptive ecumenism. Lacking a foundational theologian like Martin Luther or John Calvin, a mandated liturgy, or a binding confession, Baptists and their churches are free to incorporate the gifts of others into their own faith and practice without ceasing to be Baptist—but this ought to be done more intentionally.

Paul Fiddes has identified four specific areas in which Baptists might more intentionally learn something from the wider church through the practice of receptive ecumenism: tradition, episcopacy, infant baptism, and the visibility of the church.[64] Beyond the new Baptist appreciation

---

[63] Cf. E. Glenn Hinson, "Some Things I've Learned from the Study of Early Christian History," *Review and Expositor* 101, no. 4 (Fall 2014): 739 (729–44): "As a seminary professor, I have tried to teach ministers to embrace all of church history as the history of us all."

[64] Paul S. Fiddes, "Learning from Others: Baptists and Receptive Ecumenism," *Louvain Studies* 33, nos. 1–2 (2008): 54–73.

for the coinherence of Scripture and tradition that surfaced in the second series of conversations between the Baptist World Alliance and the Catholic Church,[65] Fiddes suggests that Baptists might intentionally extend the communal interpretation of Scripture that takes place within the local church to the church in its historic and contemporary catholicity. Furthermore, Baptists might incorporate the broad contours of the catholic tradition into their worship through "the more regular use of the creeds" as acts of worship that "celebrate God's drama" and "present the Trinity as the supreme meta-narrative."[66] Regarding episcopacy, Fiddes sees potential for convergence between Anglican conceptions of the episcopate as a sign of apostolic succession and the Baptist practice of appointing translocal or regional ministers, who may similarly serve as "a focus of unity and continuity" in the church.[67] Concerning infant baptism, Fiddes proposes that Baptists might learn from this practice the recognition that God's grace is at work in the lives of very young children, that the faith of the church plays an important role in the formation of Christians, and that infant baptism may be regarded as a legitimate practice within a "whole process of initiation" or "journey of beginnings" (even if Baptists continue to baptize only believing disciples within their own communities).[68] And in dialogue with the Eastern Orthodox tradition, Fiddes suggests that

[65] Fiddes, "Learning from Others," 61–64, refers to papers presented in the first two years of the second series of conversations between the Baptist World Alliance and the Catholic Church (2006–2010), insights from which were incorporated into the section on "The Authority of Christ in Scripture and Tradition" in the final report: Baptist World Alliance and Catholic Church, "The Word of God in the Life of the Church," §§34–71.

[66] Fiddes, "Learning from Others," 63.

[67] Fiddes, "Learning from Others," 66. Earlier in the article (55–56), Fiddes offers as an earlier Baptist anticipation of current receptive ecumenism proposals the example of John Howard Shakespeare, General Secretary of the Baptist Union of Great Britain 1898–1924, who in his book *The Churches at the Cross-Roads: A Study in Unity* (London: Williams and Norgate, 1918), 83, asks of his fellow Baptists, "Is there any reality in the doctrine of the Holy Ghost as the guide and teacher of truth, and if so, can we believe that a form [i.e., episcopacy] which goes back to the beginning of Christian history, and has taken its place 'in the greater part of Christendom as the recognized organ of the unity and continuity of the Church' arose without the guidance of the Spirt?" and of others, "Or, on the other hand, can we believe that the guidance of the Spirit has been so completely withheld from the non-episcopal churches that they have gone quite astray?"

[68] Fiddes, "Learning from Others," 68–70. Baptists have been able to affirm this paradigm as a way of recognizing the legitimacy of infant baptism within the journey of Christian beginnings, while continuing to baptize only believers as a Baptist practice, in the context of international bilateral dialogue with the Anglican Communion and the Catholic Church: see Anglican Consultative Council and Baptist World Alliance, *Conversations around the World 2000–2005: The Report of the International Conversations between the Anglican Communion and the Baptist World Alliance* (London: Anglican Communion Office,

Baptists, who already affirm the visibility of the local church but typically regard the catholic or universal church as the invisible community of all the redeemed of all the ages, might work toward thinking "in terms of a constant *becoming* visible of the whole catholic church."[69] I heartily affirm these proposals for a more intentional receptive ecumenism among Baptists and add two of my own—which can apply to other Christian communions as well.

First, Baptists might take the reports and agreed statements from bilateral ecumenical dialogues in which Baptists have been involved as the basis of congregational study and grassroots ecumenical encounter with neighboring churches from the traditions with which Baptists have been in dialogue. The Baptist World Alliance (BWA) has held such dialogues with the World Alliance of Reformed Churches (1973–1977), the Lutheran World Federation (1986–1989), the World Mennonite Conference (1989–1992), the Anglican Communion (2000–2005), and the Catholic Church (1984–1988 and 2006–2010), each of which has issued a published report; Baptist unions have also engaged in dialogues at the national level that have yielded substantial joint statements.[70] The reports of these conversations recount the stories of the two communions in relation to one another, explain the things the two traditions can affirm together, and name the ongoing matters of disagreement that merit further conversation. Sometimes they propose practical steps that can be taken at the local level to enhance unity between the two communions. The bilateral dialogues accomplish little if they are not received at the local level, and local reception must begin with reading and discussing the reports within Baptist congregations and together with our local ecclesial neighbors. Such discussions can foster receptive ecumenism at the grassroots as the basis for identifying and sharing mutually enriching ecclesial gifts as well as acting locally on the "Lund Principle," according to which churches should "act together in all matters except those in which deep difference of conviction

---

2005), §§42–52 (pp. 46–52); Baptist World Alliance and Catholic Church, "The Word of God in the Life of the Church," §§101–104.

[69]   Fiddes, "Learning from Others," 70–73.

[70]   For documentation and discussion of the international bilateral dialogues with Baptist participation, see chapter 9. Chapter 10 includes additional documentation for the national bilateral conversations between Baptist unions and other churches; later in that chapter I develop further my commendation here of the study of reports from ecumenical dialogues between Baptists and other communions.

compel them to act separately" (Third World Conference on Faith and Order, Lund, Sweden, 1952).[71]

Second, Baptists might intentionally engage the more communal forms of theological and ethical deliberation exemplified by Catholic magisterial teaching, including the *Catechism of the Catholic Church*, the documents of Vatican II, papal encyclicals, and bishops' letters. The place to begin encouraging the consideration of these sources of Christian teaching is graduate/professional theological education. Baptist ministers have much to learn from Catholic processes of conciliar theological and ethical deliberation, even if they may not always agree with what these resources propose as Christian teaching. The communal consultation that funds these proposals has the capacity for transcending the subjectivity of the theological constructions and moral judgments of individual theologians and ethicists, and ought to be weighed accordingly—even if such weighing may result in heavily qualified reception among Baptists. The next chapter will develop more fully the proposal that even magisterium—the authoritative teaching office of the church—belongs to the gifts Baptists need to receive from Catholics and other Christians.

Baptists need the gifts that Catholics and other Christians have to offer, but the Baptist tradition has been entrusted with gifts that the rest of the church needs in order to become fully catholic as well. These gifts include (but are by no means limited to) those named in the first chapter of this book: the zeal of Baptists for guarding conscience from coercion by civil or ecclesiastical powers, their insistence that God's freedom to be God in the life of the church not be constrained, an ecclesiology that emphasizes the mutuality of covenant responsibilities among the members of the church as a corollary of the necessity that each embrace the faith personally, and their healthy aversion to overly realized eschatologies of the church, reflected in their understanding of the church as a pilgrim community seeking to become a community living fully under the rule of Christ. Baptists are able to offer these as ecclesial gifts only because of their relation to the gifts of catholic Christian identity Baptists have received from the churches that preceded their 1609 origins. Baptists have received the gifts of Catholics and other Christians, and they must continue to do so while conserving and offering to the other churches their own distinctive gifts if they are to help the whole church make progress toward the ecumenical future. They will be most

---

[71] World Council of Churches, *The Third World Conference on Faith and Order, Lund 1952*, ed. Oliver S. Tomkins (London: SCM Press, 1953), 15–16.

likely to participate in this exchange of ecclesial gifts when they come to share the conviction of Baptist theologian James Wm. McClendon, Jr., that "such peoplehoods as Baptist, Methodist, and the like are justified only if they serve as provisional means toward that one great peoplehood that embraces all, the Israel of God, the end toward which the biblical story moves."[72]

---

[72] McClendon, *Doctrine*, 365.

7

Receiving the Gift of Magisterium

In 2009 I spoke on the program of a conference on "Evangelicals and the Nicene Faith."[1] That year happened to mark two not-unrelated anniversaries. Ten years earlier evangelical patristics scholar D. H. Williams, then teaching at Loyola University of Chicago, published *Retrieving the Tradition and Renewing Evangelicalism: A Primer for Suspicious Protestants*.[2] In that book and several subsequent publications, Williams has plead passionately for evangelicals to embrace as their own heritage the patristic tradition, with the fourth-century Nicene configuration of faith and practice as its canonical core.[3] Many evangelicals who long for their churches to manifest a more conscious catholicity have enthusiastically applauded Williams' project, but others have raised hard questions about its viability that are not easily answered. In the Spring 2009 issue of the journal *Pro Ecclesia*, Dennis Martin reviewed Williams' more recent book *Evangelicals*

---

[1] Samford University's Beeson Divinity School hosted a conference on the theme "The Will to Believe and the Need for Creed: Evangelicals and the Nicene Faith" on its campus in Birmingham, Alabama, September 28–30, 2009. Versions of papers presented at that conference are among the chapters in *Evangelicals and the Nicene Faith: Reclaiming the Apostolic Witness*, ed. Timothy F. George (Grand Rapids: Baker Academic, 2011).

[2] Daniel H. Williams, *Retrieving the Tradition and Renewing Evangelicalism: A Primer for Suspicious Protestants* (Grand Rapids: William B. Eerdmans, 1999).

[3] Daniel H. Williams, "The Patristic Tradition as Canon," *Perspectives in Religious Studies* 32, no. 4 (Winter 2005): 357–79; idem, *Evangelicals and Tradition: The Formative Influence of the Early Church* (Evangelical Ressourcement: Ancient Sources for the Church's Future, vol. 1; Grand Rapids: Baker Academic, 2005); idem, ed., *The Free Church and the Early Church: Bridging the Historical and Theological Divide* (Grand Rapids: William B. Eerdmans, 2002).

and Tradition: The Formative Influence of the Early Church. I quote here some extended excerpts from Martin's review:

> Following up on several earlier books devoted to a similar thematic, Dan Williams, my former Loyola Chicago colleague, challenges evangelical Protestants to undertake a ressourcement in the writings of the church fathers of the first five centuries, a specifically evangelical Protestant ressourcement that steps around most of the ecclesial issues. . . . Even for its intended readership, *Evangelicals and Tradition* suffers from another nearly insurmountable problem: even if this or that evangelical reader would seek to enter deeply into the patristic world, not by way of guidance from either an Orthodox or Catholic magisterium but as an individual Baptist, Pentecostal, evangelical Lutheran, or independent Bible church leader, would not those persons or groups who thus answer Williams' call end up with widely different, idiosyncratic portraits of the *catholica* [i.e., the things that belong to the catholicity] of the "patristic tradition"? Why should D. H. Williams' portrait be authoritative for any of his readers? . . . Who gets to define, delimit, describe, and characterize the content and characteristics of [the traditional] memory [of the church]? . . . Given the absence of an articulated theology of authority and the absence of a magisterium among evangelicals, could evangelicals who might take up Williams' challenge get very far? Would they do so as amateur historians or as theologians? Such a question is a roundabout way of suggesting that, unless something like a supernaturally guided, indefectible organic ecclesial magisterium exists and is part of Christ's plan for the church, do not all renewers and reformers function essentially as private historians, at most continually reasserting on their own behalf (against rival private historian claimants) that the Holy Spirit has blessed their particular version of ressourcement?[4]

One does not have to affirm that "a supernaturally guided, indefectible organic ecclesial magisterium exists and is part of Christ's plan for the church" to grant that Martin is right on target in naming the unacknowledged elephant present in the room whenever evangelicals talk about retrieving the tradition. What is the tradition that ought to be retrieved? And who decides what the tradition is, and to what degree it is authoritative for us? To ask these questions is to inquire about the location of the authority by which the church may teach something regarding Christian

---

[4] Dennis D. Martin, review of *Evangelicals and Tradition: The Formative Influence of the Early Church*, by Daniel H. Williams, in *Pro Ecclesia* 18, no. 2 (Spring 2009): 216–19.

belief, worship, or practice as the teaching of the church on these matters. The teaching authority of the church is its magisterium, and any time some expression of church proposes something as Christian teaching, magisterium is at work, even if unacknowledged. But since many evangelicals are under the impression that to be Catholic is to have a magisterium and to be Protestant is to reject magisterium, it would doubtless be utterly alien to them to contemplate how they might go about the magisterial implementation of Williams' proposals.

Baptists, Retrieval, and Magisterium

Though Williams addressed these calls for the retrieval of tradition to a broadly evangelical readership, he is a Baptist by denominational tradition, has served as a Baptist pastor, and since 2002 has taught at Baptist-related Baylor University. The year 2009 marked the quadricentennial celebration of the Baptist tradition: in 1609 a group of English expatriates formed in Amsterdam the earliest Baptist congregation. In the years since Williams published *Retrieving the Tradition and Renewing Evangelicalism*, other Baptist theologians have followed suit in contending that Baptists too must reclaim the Nicene faith and other expressions of ancient catholicity for the sake of their future, and that such retrieval is not alien to Baptist identity but very much in continuity with the surprisingly catholic ecclesial outlook of the earliest Baptists.[5] Some Baptists in the United States have vigorously resisted these proposals, contending that they do violence to historic Baptist identity and charging that they will inevitably lead to the creation of some sort of magisterium.[6] Yet, ironically, the very concept of a

---

[5] E.g., Stephen R. Holmes, *Listening to the Past: The Place of Tradition in Theology* (Carlisle, UK: Paternoster/Grand Rapids: Baker Academic, 2002); Steven R. Harmon, *Towards Baptist Catholicity: Essays on Tradition and the Baptist Vision* (Studies in Baptist History and Thought, vol. 27; Milton Keynes, UK: Paternoster, 2006); Barry Harvey, *Can These Bones Live? A Catholic Baptist Engagement with Ecclesiology, Hermeneutics, and Social Theory* (Grand Rapids: Brazos Press, 2008); Elizabeth Newman, *Attending the Wounds on Christ's Body: Teresa's Scriptural Vision* (Eugene, Ore.: Cascade Books, 2012); Curtis W. Freeman, *Contesting Catholicity: Theology for Other Baptists* (Waco, Tex.: Baylor University Press, 2014). See also the other literature cited in Steven R. Harmon, " 'Catholic Baptists' and the New Horizon of Tradition in Baptist Theology," in *New Horizons in Theology*, ed. Terrence W. Tilley (Maryknoll, N.Y.: Orbis Books, 2005), 117–43, and idem, *Towards Baptist Catholicity*, 1–21.

[6] E.g., Bruce Gourley, "Bapto-Catholics Move into the Spotlight in North Carolina," accessed December 17, 2014, http://baptistperspective.brucegourley.com/2010/09/bapto-catholics-move-into-spotlight-in.html.

definable Baptist identity and the possibility that it could be betrayed point in the direction of an unacknowledged Baptist magisterium.

It is not only Baptist academics who encounter the problem of magisterium when they turn to the Christian past for the resources they need in doing theology in the service of the church today. As more and more tradition-starved Baptists sense that there is something in the Great Tradition—and in the ongoing Catholic and Orthodox ecclesial traditions that stand in concrete continuity with it—that their own churches lack, and begin to experiment with retrieving it, they run headlong into the problem of magisterium. This increasingly common phenomenon is exemplified by Gordon Atkinson, former pastor of Covenant Baptist Church near San Antonio, Texas (1992–2010), whom journalist Terry Mattingly profiled for a newspaper story. Atkinson had completed a 13-week pastoral sabbatical, during which he discovered Eastern Orthodox liturgy and began to attend services at Russian, Greek, and Antiochian Orthodox churches. But "now," Mattingly wrote, Atkinson "is returning to his Baptist pulpit, while hearing choirs of voices arguing in his head representing many different eras of church history":

> "What I don't know how to do is rank all of these voices and decide who has authority," [Atkinson] said. "Who is right and who is wrong? . . . And I want to know, where does Gordon Atkinson fit into this whole picture? I know that I can't go back to the old Protestant, evangelical way that I was, but I don't know where I'm supposed to go now. This is a problem."[7]

It is not that Baptists lack magisterium—despite Martin's assertion to the contrary regarding evangelicals in general in his review of D. H. Williams. In a paper presented in the course of the second series of international bilateral conversations between the Baptist World Alliance and the Catholic Church, Baptist delegate Timothy George claimed, "Baptists and Catholics differ on the scope and locus of the *magisterium* but not on whether it exists as a necessary component in the ongoing life of the Church."[8]

---

[7]   Terry Mattingly, "A Baptist Minister's Eye-Opening Sabbatical," *San Angelo Standard-Times* (August 10, 2009), accessed November 27, 2014, http://www.gosanangelo.com/news/2009/aug/10/terry-mattingly-baptist-ministers-eye-opening-sabb/.

[8]   Timothy George, "Scripture and Tradition: An Evangelical Baptist Perspective," paper presented to the first session of the 2006–2010 bilateral conversations between the Baptist World Alliance Doctrine and Interchurch Cooperation Commission and the Pontifical Council for Promoting Christian Unity, Beeson Divinity School, Samford University, Birmingham, Alabama, USA, December 10–15, 2006; cf. idem, "An

Many Baptists would be taken aback by and perhaps vigorously reject George's assertion that Baptists along with Catholics affirm that the magisterium "exists as a necessary component in the ongoing life of the Church." But Baptist churches, like all Christian communities, discover that as they make disciples they must teach something.[9] I have no illusions that here I will definitively solve the problem of magisterium encountered whenever Baptists and others in the Free Church tradition attempt to retrieve the riches of the Nicene faith and other expressions of a fuller catholicity. Instead this chapter aims for the more attainable goal of entertaining a possible configuration of how teaching authority might function in a more intentional manner for Baptists and other Free Church Christians who have not typically thought that they had an authoritative teaching office.

Magisterium—Catholic and Magisterial Protestant Versions

Since many Baptists seem erroneously to assume that the magisterium is whatever the Pope teaches and that Protestants therefore do not have a magisterium, it is appropriate at this point to explain the respective Catholic and Protestant configurations of the teaching office.

Catholic Magisterium

As the late Avery Cardinal Dulles defined it in his book *Magisterium*, "In modern Catholic teaching the term 'Magisterium' generally designates the hierarchical teachers—the pope and the bishops—who by virtue of their office have authority to teach publically in the name of Christ and to judge officially what belongs to Christian faith and what is excluded by it. This concept of the Magisterium," Dulles acknowledged, "is relatively recent."[10] Though rooted in the early patristic conviction that the bishops as successors of the apostles safeguarded the faith against heresy by teaching the faith handed down to them from the apostles, the more

---

Evangelical Reflection on Scripture and Tradition," *Pro Ecclesia* 9, no. 2 (Spring 2000): 206 (184–207).

9   Cf. James Wm. McClendon, Jr.'s definition of doctrine in terms of the church's necessary teaching function: "Doctrine *is* teaching . . . and by *Christian* doctrine I will here mean *a church teaching as she must teach if she is to be the church here and now*" (James Wm. McClendon, Jr., *Doctrine: Systematic Theology, Vol. 2* [Waco, Tex.: Baylor University Press, 2012], 23–24).

10   Avery Dulles, *Magisterium: Teacher and Guardian of the Faith* (Naples, Fla.: Sapientia Press of Ave Maria University, 2007), 35.

fully developed modern Catholic concept of magisterium was historically conditioned by medieval conflict between papal and imperial powers for supremacy in the ecclesiastical and civil orders, rival claims to papal jurisdiction during the "Great Schism," the late medieval debate between those who contended that the bishops in council had authority over the pope and those who maintained that papal proclamations trumped conciliar decisions (a debate the conciliarists lost), the Tridentine responses to the challenges of the Reformation, and the ultramontanist response to the challenges of modernism at the First Vatican Council.[11]

The definitive statements of the modern Catholic understanding of magisterial authority are in two key documents issued by the Second Vatican Council: the Dogmatic Constitution on the Church *Lumen Gentium*, sections 22 through 26, and the Dogmatic Constitution on Divine Revelation *Dei Verbum*, section 10. A pair of quotations from these documents illustrates this Catholic pattern of magisterium. *Lumen Gentium* 25 affirms this about the teaching authority of the church:

> For in such a case [of infallible, irreformable papal teaching] the Roman Pontiff does not utter a pronouncement as a private person, but rather does he expound and defend the teaching of the Catholic faith as the supreme teacher of the universal Church, in whom the church's charism of infallibility is present in a singular way. The infallibility promised to the Church is also present in the body of bishops when, together with Peter's successor, they exercise the supreme teaching office. Now, the assent of the Church can never be lacking to such definitions on account of the same Holy Spirit's influence, through which Christ's whole flock is maintained in the unity of the faith and makes progress in it. Furthermore, when the Roman Pontiff, or the body of bishops together with him, define a doctrine, they make the definition in conformity with revelation itself, to which all are bound to adhere and to which they are obligated to submit.[12]

This is how *Dei Verbum* 10 characterizes the Catholic configuration of magisterium:

---

[11] Johannes Brosseder, "Teaching Office: 1. Roman Catholic," in *Encyclopedia of Christianity*, ed. Erwin Fahlbusch et al., trans. Geoffrey W. Bromiley (Grand Rapids: William B. Eerdmans, 2008), 5:316–19; Dulles, *Magisterium*, 21–34.

[12] Vatican II, *Dogmatic Constitution on the Church (Lumen Gentium)*, §25, November 21, 1964, in *Vatican Council II: The Conciliar and Post Conciliar Documents*, rev. ed., ed. Austin Flannery (Vatican Collection, vol. 1; Northport, N.Y..: Costello, 1992), 380.

By adhering to it [the sacred deposit of the Word of God] the entire holy people, united to its pastors, remains always faithful to the teaching of the apostles, to the brotherhood, to the breaking of bread and the prayers (cf. Acts 2:42 Greek). So, in maintaining, practicing and professing the faith that has been handed on there should be a remarkable harmony between the bishops and the faithful. But the task of giving an authentic interpretation of the Word of God, whether in its written form or in the form of Tradition, has been entrusted to the living teaching office of the Church alone. Its authority in this matter is exercised in the name of Jesus Christ. Yet this Magisterium is not superior to the Word of God, but is its servant. It teaches only what has been handed on to it. At the divine command and with the help of the Holy Spirit, it listens to this devotedly, guards it with dedication and expounds it faithfully. All that it proposes for belief as being divinely revealed is drawn from this single deposit of faith.[13]

In those texts we encounter a decidedly hierarchical conception of teaching authority: it is ultimately defined by the papal exercise of magisterial authority—both the ordinary papal magisterium expressed in encyclicals, letters, addresses, and other forms of papal teaching, and the extraordinary papal magisterium exemplified by the two modern mariological dogmas. And yet in this configuration of teaching authority the pope does not exercise magisterium alone. He does so in association with the bishops. And the bishops, including the bishop of Rome, do not exercise their collective magisterium alone, for there is also a nonhierarchical magisterium in which others in the church participate and on which the bishops depend en route to the formulation of magisterial teaching. The bishops consult theologians—not only dogmatic/systematic theologians and moral theologians, but also Scripture scholars, ecclesiastical historians, and specialists in non-Christian religions. They name to official Vatican commissions and consultations scientists and others with areas of expertise beyond theology that may inform the magisterium's deliberation regarding moral issues, for example. The Vatican II documents illustrate this participatory nature of the Catholic magisterium. The documents are themselves expressions of magisterial teaching, and they underwent a long and often contentious process of formation to which many theologians who were not bishops

---

[13] Vatican II, *Dogmatic Constitution on Divine Revelation (Dei Verbum)*, §10, November 18, 1965, in *Vatican Council II*, ed. Flannery, 755–56.

contributed behind the scenes.[14] Even non-Catholic theologians participated in the Catholic magisterium and contributed to the formulation of its teaching during the Second Vatican Council, for they too were consulted with regard to potential difficulties for the ecumenical reception of the various decrees and constitutions. As *Dei Verbum* emphasizes, all these expressions of Catholic magisterium, hierarchical and nonhierarchical, are subservient to the truth of the gospel; but when the magisterium defines dogma, it does so infallibly.

Magisterial Protestant Magisterium

That Protestants have their own version of magisterium is suggested by George Huntston Williams' use of the label "Magisterial Reformation" to distinguish the "classical Protestant" traditions that include the Lutheran and Reformed churches from churches of the "Radical Reformation" exemplified by the Anabaptists.[15] The Magisterial Reformation was accomplished with the cooperation of the civil power, the magistrates, but it was also magisterial in the sense that it was accomplished through the influence of the *magister*, the authoritative teacher, in association with the magistrate. Though this is a slightly unfair, reductionistic oversimplification, we may explain the difference between the Catholic and Magisterial Protestant conceptions of magisterium in this manner: while for both Catholics and Protestants the teaching office depends upon, serves, and transmits the truth of the gospel, in the Catholic understanding of magisterium the emphasis is on the authority of the teaching office that depends upon, serves, and transmits the truth of the gospel, whereas for Magisterial Protestants the emphasis is on the authority of the truth of the gospel that the teaching office depends upon, serves, and transmits. The Catholic version of magisterium is located in the community of bishops who teach the truth; the Magisterial Protestant version of magisterium is in principle located in the truth that bishops or others in the church who fulfill their function teach.

The statements on the office of bishop in the documents of the Lutheran *Book of Concord* illustrate this Magisterial Protestant approach to

---

[14]   A process evidenced by the conciliar history of Giuseppe Alberigo, *History of Vatican II*, trans. Joseph A. Komonchak, 5 vols. (Maryknoll, N.Y.: Orbis Books, 1995–2006), and the personal involvement in it chronicled by Yves Congar, *My Journal of the Council*, trans. Mary John Ronayne and Mary Cecily Boulding, ed. Denis Minns (Collegeville, Minn.: Liturgical Press, 2012).

[15]   George Huntston Williams, *The Radical Reformation* (Philadelphia: Westminster Press, 1962).

teaching authority. Martin Luther and the other early Lutheran doctors viewed the historical development of the office of bishop, distinguished from and overseeing the office of elder, as an ecclesial structure established by human authority but nevertheless beneficial for the unity and health of the church; they were willing to retain it and even submit themselves to the Catholic bishops if only the bishops would teach the truth and refrain from suppressing the ministry of those who disagreed with their error. In the *Treatise on the Power and Primacy of the Pope* authored by Philip Melanchthon in 1537, for example, he and the other theologians of the Smalcald League were able to appeal to patristic precedent for their perspective on the functional adaptability of *episkopē* in the church:

> The gospel bestows upon those who preside over the churches the commission to proclaim the gospel, forgive sins, and administer the sacraments. . . . It is universally acknowledged, even by our opponents, that this power is shared by divine right by all who preside in the churches, whether they are called pastors, presbyters, or bishops. For that reason Jerome plainly teaches that in the apostolic letters all who preside over the churches are both bishops and presbyters. . . . Jerome goes on to say, "One person was chosen thereafter to oversee the rest as a remedy for schism, lest some individuals draw a following around themselves and divide the church of Christ." . . . Jerome, then, teaches that the distinctions of degree between bishop and presbyter or pastor are established by human authority. That is clear from the way it works, for, as I stated above, the power is the same. One thing subsequently created a distinction between bishops and pastors, and that was ordination, for it was arranged that one bishop would ordain the ministers in a number of churches. However, since the distinction of rank between bishop and pastor is not by divine right, it is clear that an ordination performed by a pastor in his own church is valid by divine right.
>
> As a result, when the regular bishops become enemies of the gospel or are unwilling to ordain, the churches retain their right to do so. For wherever the church exists, there also is the right to administer the gospel.
>
> All this evidence makes clear that the church retains the right to choose and ordain ministers. Consequently, when bishops either become heretical or are unwilling to ordain, the churches are compelled by divine right to ordain pastors and ministers for themselves.[16]

---

[16] Philip Melanchthon, "Treatise on the Power and Primacy of the Pope," §§60–72, in *The Book of Concord: The Confessions of the Evangelical Lutheran Church*, ed. Robert

Elsewhere the *Book of Concord* repeatedly mentions authoritative teaching as belonging to the office of bishop and to these other ministers in
the church who exercise the ministry of oversight. When bishops teach
the truth, they ought to be heeded; when they fail to teach the truth,
their authority must be rejected, and their function is rightfully taken on
by others.

Catholic and Magisterial Protestant Magisterium
in Free Church Perspective

From the vantage point of my own Baptist ecclesial tradition, both the
Catholic and Magisterial Protestant versions of magisterium have strengths
and weaknesses. The Catholic magisterium has the strength of collegial-
ity in the communal formulation of authoritative teaching. The bishops
together, in association with the faithful, seek the mind of Christ on matters of doctrine and moral theology. Individual theological preferences
must make way for communal discernment that seeks consensus under the
lordship of Christ. Even when the pontiff defines doctrine *ex cathedra*, he
does so not as an individual theologian but as one who self-consciously
functions as supreme teacher of the church and therefore must speak with
the voice of the church and not his own personal theological voice. Its
weakness, however, is infallibility. In association with the distinct but
not unrelated concept of the church's impeccability, this can make for an
overly realized eschatology of the church, in which the church has great
difficulty admitting and forsaking past errors in its pilgrim journey toward
the full realization of what Christ wills his church to be.

The Magisterial Protestant configuration of magisterium has the
strength of adaptability. There are situations in which the embodied structures of magisterial authority may fail in their task of "teaching as [the
church] must teach if she is to be the church here and now," as James Wm.
McClendon, Jr., defined the task of Christian doctrine.[17] In such circumstances the Magisterial Protestant paradigm makes it possible to reject the
authority of those who have failed to teach the truth and to point instead to
other teachers whose authority derives from their faithful teaching of the
gospel and to authoritative confessional documents that have definitively
expressed this faithful teaching. It has the weakness, however, of becoming too tied to individual foundational teachers in all their theological

---

Kolb and Timothy J. Wengert, trans. Charles Arand et al. (Minneapolis: Fortress Press,
2000), 340–41.
    [17]   McClendon, *Doctrine*, 24.

idiosyncrasies. Furthermore, despite a commitment to Scripture alone as the infallible rule for faith and practice, the privileged status of foundational confessional documents in this paradigm can make for a "paper magisterium" that is difficult to reform. It is one thing to revise the *Baptist Faith and Message* now and then; it is quite another to revise the *Book of Concord* or the Westminster Standards. The Magisterial Protestant configuration too in its own way can fall prey to an overly realized eschatology of the church. This susceptibility is exemplified by what Stanley Hauerwas suggested, only partly in jest, was the most significant ecumenical agreement reached between Catholics and Magisterial Protestants during the sixteenth century: "that it was a very good thing to kill the Anabaptists."[18] Yet in this connection some of the present-day heirs of the Magisterial Protestant Reformers are seeking to practice ecclesial repentance toward the end of the healing of memories and reconciliation. After the Lutheran World Federation (LWF) and the Mennonite World Conference (MWC) engaged in an international bilateral dialogue from 2005 to 2008, during a service of repentance, forgiveness, and reconciliation at the Eleventh Assembly of the LWF in Stuttgart, Germany, on July 22, 2010, the LWF asked forgiveness for Lutheran persecutions of Anabaptists and subsequent failures to address their legacies. The two communions are jointly implementing an ongoing reconciliation process.[19]

[18] Stanley Hauerwas, "Why Truthfulness Requires Forgiveness: A Commencement Address for Graduates of a College of the Church of the Second Chance (1992)," in *The Hauerwas Reader*, ed. John Berkman and Michael C. Cartwright (Durham, N.C.: Duke University Press, 2001), 314 (307–17).

[19] See Lutheran World Federation and Mennonite World Conference, *Healing Memories: Reconciling in Christ. Report of the Lutheran–Mennonite International Study Commission* (Geneva: Lutheran World Federation and Strasbourg: Mennonite World Conference, 2010), accessed November 28, 2014, http://www.lwf-assembly.org/uploads/media/Report _Lutheran-Mennonite_Study_Commission.pdf; Lutheran World Federation, "Action on the Legacy of Lutheran Persecution of 'Anabaptists' " (July 22, 2010), accessed November 28, 2014, http://www.lwf-assembly.org/uploads/media/Mennonite_Statement-EN_03 .pdf; Mennonite World Conference, "Mennonite World Conference Response to the Lutheran World Federation Action on the Legacy of Lutheran Persecution of Anabaptists" (July 22, 2010), accessed November 28, 2014, https://www.mwc-cmm.org/joomla/ images/files/DialogueFiles/MWC_Response_to_LWF.pdf; Lutheran World Information, "Lutheran–Mennonite Dialogue Moves Closer on Peace Issues, Future Cooperation" (September 17, 2014), accessed November 28, 2014, http://www.lutheranworld .org/news/lutheran-mennonite-dialogue-moves-closer-peace-issues-future-cooperation.

A Free Church Magisterium?

Beyond the Catholic and Magisterial Protestant configurations of magisterium, there is yet a third major pattern according to which the church "teaches as she must teach if she is to be the church here and now." Even if unacknowledged or denied outright, there is a configuration of functional magisterial authority for Baptists and others who belong to the broader Free Church or Believers' Church tradition—those churches that emphasize the authority of the congregation of baptized believers gathered in a covenanted community under the lordship of Christ, which include Mennonites, the Disciples of Christ and Churches of Christ, Bible churches, a great many nondenominational churches, and numerous Pentecostal and charismatic communities, as well as Baptists. This configuration, which for the sake of convenience we will call Free Church magisterium, embodies aspects of the strengths of both the Catholic and Magisterial Protestant paradigms, while in theory avoiding their susceptibilities to overly realized eschatologies of the church—though the Free Church tradition has its own share of those in actual practice.

Authority of the Community Gathered under the Rule of Christ

In my book *Towards Baptist Catholicity*, I tried to articulate a Free Church vision of teaching authority that could be labeled a magisterium of the whole. Inasmuch as Baptists have historically granted that local churches gathered under the lordship of Christ possess an authority that derives from Christ as Lord, I argued that this authority can also be extended to the communion of saints, who constitute a real community under the lordship of Christ that transcends space and time.[20] Drawing also on Alasdair MacIntyre's definition of a "living tradition" as "an historically extended, socially embodied argument, and an argument precisely in part about the goods which constitute that tradition,"[21] and defining the goods that constitute the tradition in terms of the Christian narrative, the biblical story of the Triune God that is told at length and with great particularity in the Scriptures and summarized in the ancient creeds, I portrayed the church's teaching authority as one that is located most broadly in the communion of saints in its entirety in its ongoing argument about what the

---

[20] Harmon, *Towards Baptist Catholicity*, 39–69.
[21] Alasdair MacIntyre, *After Virtue: A Study in Moral Theory*, 2nd ed. (Notre Dame, Ind.: University of Notre Dame Press, 1984), 222.

church "must teach in order to be the church here and now."[22] But again: who decides how the argument should be decided, however provisionally, at various points in the historical extension of the argument? If all members of the communion of saints are participants in this ongoing argument, do they all participate in the same way? Do the voices of all participants carry the same weight, so that the argument is decided by majority? This MacIntyrean magisterium of the whole offers a way for Baptists and other historic dissenters to appreciate the place their dissent has within the larger argument that constitutes the Christian tradition, making positive contributions to the health of the living tradition through their dissent,[23] but it needs greater specificity in its location of socially embodied ecclesial authority.

Perhaps unsurprisingly, I suggest that Free Church magisterial authority is located in the gathered congregation. Though this is a clumsy English coinage, one might call this the "magisterium-hood of all believers"— which seems to be the implication of reading the gospels as manuals of discipleship, which therefore means that all who become disciples of Christ are commissioned by him in Matthew 28:18ff to participate in the church's teaching office.[24] But just as in the Catholic configuration of magisterium the bishops do not exercise magisterium only in association with the bishop of Rome and the other bishops, but also with the faithful who participate in various ways in the nonhierarchical dimension of the magisterium, so in the Free Church practice of teaching authority, it is not the local congregation alone that authorizes its teaching, nor is the membership of the congregation undifferentiated in its participation in this practice. In the best expressions of Baptist ecclesiology, the independence of local congregations is not absolute. Local Baptist congregations are interdependent in their relations with one another, in local associations but also in various national and international associations of Baptists. When seven local Baptist congregations in London together issued the *London Confession* of 1644, they explained their interdependence in discerning the mind of Christ for their faith and practice in this fashion:

> [B]ecause it may be conceived, that what is here published, may be but the Judgment of some one particular Congregation, more refined than

---

[22] McClendon, *Doctrine*, 24.

[23] Cf. Harmon, *Towards Baptist Catholicity*, 66.

[24] This reading of the role of the disciples in Matthew's Gospel is influenced by Andrew T. Lincoln, "Matthew—A Story for Teachers?" in *The Bible in Three Dimensions: Essays in Celebration of Forty Years of Biblical Studies in the University of Sheffield*, ed. David J. A. Clines et al. (JSOT Supplements, no. 87; Sheffield: JSOT Press, 1990), 103–25.

the rest; We do therefore here subscribe it, some of each body in the name, and by the appointment of seven Congregations, who though we be distinct in respect of our particular bodies, for convenience sake, being as many as can well meet together in one place, yet are all one in Communion, holding Jesus Christ to be our head and Lord; under whose government we desire alone to walk, in following the Lamb wheresoever he goeth; and we believe the Lord will daily cause truth more to appear in the hearts of his Saints . . . that so they may with one shoulder, more study to lift up the Name of the Lord Jesus, and stand for his appointments and Laws; which is the desires and prayers of the condemned Churches of Christ in London for all saints.[25]

The rule of Christ in the local congregations in the plural therefore has implications for the efforts of any single local congregation to discern the mind of Christ, and vice versa. Together in their mutual relations they seek to walk under the government of Christ, seeking from him a fuller grasp of the truth, as one ecclesial communion—a communion which, it is hoped, might extend beyond Baptist churches in association to include all the saints.

Within local congregations, discerning the mind of Christ is not a matter of simple majority vote of the congregation, nor is it determined by acquiescence to the will of the congregation's pastor. Paul Fiddes explains the embodied "Baptist experience" that informs Baptist theology in this passage, which provides the fuller context of a sentence quoted in the preceding chapter of this book:

The liberty of local churches to make decisions about their own life and ministry is not based in a human view of autonomy or independence, or in selfish individualism, but in a sense of being under the direct rule of Christ who relativizes other rules. This liberating rule of Christ is what makes for the distinctive "feel" of Baptist congregational life, which allows for spiritual oversight (*episkopē*) both by the *whole* congregation gathered together in church meeting, and by the minister(s) called to lead the congregation. . . . Since the same rule of Christ can be experienced in assemblies of churches together, there is also the basis here

---

[25] *London Confession* (1644) pref., in *Baptist Confessions of Faith*, 2nd rev. ed., ed. William L. Lumpkin, rev. Bill J. Leonard (Valley Forge, Pa.: Judson Press, 2011), 143 (spelling standardized in quotation herein).

for Baptist associational life, and indeed for participating in ecumenical clusters.[26]

Elsewhere Fiddes fleshes out what it means for the whole congregation to seek together the mind of Christ in what British Baptists call "church meeting":

> Upon the whole people in covenant there lies the responsibility of finding a common mind, of coming to an agreement about the way of Christ for them in life, worship and mission. But they cannot do so unless they use the resources that God has given them, and among those resources are the pastor, the deacons and (if they have them) the elders. The church meeting is not "people power" in the sense of simply counting votes and canvassing a majority. . . . The aim is to search for consent about the mind of Christ, and so people should be sensitive to the voices behind the votes, listening to them according to the weight of their experience and insight. As B[arrington] White puts it, "One vote is not as good as another in church meeting," even though it has the same strictly numerical value.[27]

"In all this," Fiddes writes, "the pastor's voice is the one that carries weight"— provided that pastors have created trust in their leadership through service. In this paradigm, pastors are the ones charged with the responsibility of *episkopē*, which carries with it the catechetical task of equipping the members of the congregation with the resources they need from beyond the congregation for seeking the mind of Christ, resources that include the doctrine, worship, and practice of other congregations, other Christian traditions, and indeed the whole Christian tradition. For this reason theological educators also have a key form of participation in Free Church magisterium, for they have the opportunity to supply ministers with these God-given resources from beyond the local congregation and to form them in the skills they need for the discerning use of these resources.

In 1997 Curtis Freeman, James Wm. McClendon, Jr., and others issued a statement titled "Re-envisioning Baptist Identity: A Manifesto for Baptist Communities in North America." This "Baptist Manifesto," as it came to be known, functioned as a sort of Barmen Declaration for Baptists who resisted the pull toward the perilous ideological polarities of the denominational controversy then raging in the Southern Baptist Convention. The

---

[26] Paul S. Fiddes, *Tracks and Traces: Baptist Identity in Church and Theology* (Studies in Baptist History and Thought, vol. 13; Milton Keynes, UK: Paternoster, 2003), 6.

[27] Fiddes, *Tracks and Traces*, 86.

first of the manifesto's five affirmations regarding the nature of freedom, faithfulness, and community was this:

> We affirm Bible Study in reading communities rather than relying on private interpretation or supposed "scientific" objectivity. . . . We thus affirm an open and orderly process whereby faithful communities deliberate together over the Scriptures with sisters and brothers of the faith, excluding no light from any source. When all exercise their gifts and callings, when every voice is heard and weighed, when no one is silenced or privileged, the Spirit leads communities to read wisely and to practice faithfully the direction of the gospel.[28]

Beyond an undifferentiated magisterium of the whole, the way the Baptist Manifesto frames the process by which the church discerns what it must teach on the basis of the word of God envisions well how this more nuanced configuration of Free Church magisterium might work.

Ecumenical Extension of the Community Gathered under the Rule of Christ

What then are the potential sources of light that ought not be excluded as Baptist communities determine what it is they must teach to be the church in the time and place they inhabit? What are the voices that should be heard and weighed without being silenced in their Free Church practice of magisterium? These voices ought to include at least the following nine types of resources.

First, Baptists in their practice of congregational magisterium should hear and weigh and not silence the ancient creeds that stem from the early church's rule of faith. Having pride of place among these are the Nicaeno-Constantinopolitan Creed, which as the baptismal and eucharistic confession of the Eastern churches and the eucharistic confession of churches in the West is the only truly ecumenical confession of the church, and the Apostles' Creed with roots in the Old Roman Symbol, which has functioned with baptismal associations in Western churches. These ancient ecumenical voices

---

[28] Mikael Broadway, Curtis W. Freeman, Barry Harvey, James Wm. McClendon, Jr., Elizabeth Newman, and Phillip E. Thompson, "Re-envisioning Baptist Identity: A Manifesto for Baptist Communities in North America," §1; published in *Baptists Today* (June 1997), 8–10; *Perspectives in Religious Studies* 24, no. 3 (Fall 1997): 303–10; reprinted as appendix 1 in *Towards Baptist Catholicity*, 215–23; also available online (accessed November 28, 2014, http://divinity.duke.edu/sites/divinity.duke.edu/files/documents/faculty-freeman/reenvisioning-baptist-identity.pdf).

should be recovered first and foremost as expressions of worship. The creeds are summaries of the biblical story of the Triune God, drawn from the language of the Bible itself, that in their liturgical use also form worshipers in the faith the church teaches: they declare the story to which Christians commit themselves in baptism; they invite worshipers to locate afresh their individual stories within the larger divine story that is made present in worship; they impress upon them again and again the overarching meaning of the Bible and shape their capacity for hearing and heeding what specific passages of Scripture have to say; they invite worshipers into diachronic solidarity with the saints gone before who for two millennia have confessed this story with these same words and synchronic solidarity with sisters and brothers in Christ throughout the world who today embrace the story of the Triune God.[29] This characterization of the nature and function of the creeds answers to Baptist objections to use of these creeds. The contention that their use in the churches would be inauthentically Baptist owes to the legitimate dissent of early Baptists from coercive uses of creeds and confessions as exclusionary tests of faith. But when the creeds are properly understood in relation to their biblical roots, essentially narrative genre, and primarily liturgical function—especially in relation to the pledges of baptismal candidates to take Christ's story as their own and the renewal of these baptismal pledges by the members of the congregation—and when they are freely confessed by uncoerced consciences as an expression of Baptist freedom to follow the leadership of the Spirit in bringing their ecclesial life under the rule of Christ, the creeds can form the first-order convictions and practices of Baptist communities and fund their second-order theological deliberations as well.

Second, Baptists in their practice of congregational magisterium should hear and weigh and not silence the historic Reformation confessions and catechisms, along with more recent confessional statements from various denominations. Some Baptist confessions of faith from the seventeenth century reflect a hearing and weighing of the confessions of the Baptists' ecclesial neighbors, echoing and excerpting Mennonite confessions, the Reformed *Westminster Confession*, and even the *Articles of Religion* of the Church of England.[30]

---

[29] On this narrative form and function of the source and substructure of the ancient creeds employed in the ongoing liturgical tradition of the church, see Paul M. Blowers, "The *Regula Fidei* and the Narrative Character of Early Christian Faith," *Pro Ecclesia* 6, no. 2 (Spring 1997): 199–228.

[30] On this phenomenon in early Baptist confessions of faith, see Steven R. Harmon, "Baptist Confessions of Faith and the Patristic Tradition," *Perspectives in Religious Studies* 29, no. 4 (Winter 2002): 349–58; idem, *Towards Baptist Catholicity*, 77–80.

Where they found convergences with the teachings of other churches, they incorporated them into their own statements of faith as expressions of Christian solidarity; where Baptists dissented, their confessions articulated the Baptist position, but it was a dissent that depended on the hearing and weighing of these other voices in the church. When Baptist communities seek to bring their faith and practice under the lordship of Christ and to articulate to themselves and the world what that lordship means for their life together today, they likewise should take into account the historic and recent attempts of other communions to do the same thing. The efforts of any part of the church to teach what it must teach to be the church here and now are resources that the whole church must hear and weigh in our mutual efforts to teach the faith.

Third, Baptists in their practice of congregational magisterium should hear and weigh and not silence the confessions of the Baptist tradition. Because the pilgrim character of Baptist communities makes them reluctant to regard any of their historic efforts to teach what they believe the church must teach to be the church in a particular place and time in the form of a confession of faith as definitive, they have felt themselves free to issue new confessions with comparatively great frequency. A recently revised and updated collection of Baptist confessions of faith includes fifty-three of them (excluding the Anabaptist confessions also included as "forerunner confessions").[31] While Baptists need to look beyond their ranks for the voices that need to be heard and weighed in their deliberations about what they must teach as the church to be the church more fully under the rule of Christ, they will be best able to listen to these other voices with discerning openness when they know what their own voices have said and are saying.

Fourth, Baptists in their practice of congregational magisterium should hear and weigh and not silence Catholic magisterial teaching. The sources of such teaching include the *Catechism of the Catholic Church*, the documents of Vatican II, papal encyclicals, and letters and statements issued by conferences of bishops such as the United States Conference of Catholic Bishops. Free Church communities that are becoming more intentional about exercising a communal teaching authority have much to learn from Catholic processes of conciliar theological and ethical deliberation, even if we do not always agree with what these resources propose as Christian teaching. These more communal proposals have the capacity for transcending the subjectivity of the theological constructions and moral judgments of individual

---

[31] *Baptist Confessions of Faith*, ed. Lumpkin, rev. Leonard.

theologians and ethicists, and ought to be weighed accordingly—even if such weighing results in heavily qualified reception.[32]

Fifth, Baptists in their practice of congregational magisterium should hear and weigh and not silence the liturgical texts of other traditions. The patristic maxim *lex orandi, lex credendi* ("the rule of praying is the rule of believing," and vice versa[33]) suggests that some of the most enduringly formative sources of guidance for the church in bringing its faith and practice under the rule of Christ may be the patterns and practices of worship that have formed the Christian identities of the faithful. The Eastern Orthodox churches, which went unmentioned in the foregoing Western-centric treatment of Catholic, Magisterial Protestant, and Free Church configurations of

---

[32] Cf. Michael D. Beaty, Douglas V. Henry, and Scott H. Moore, "Protestant Free Church Christians and *Gaudium et Spes*: A Historical and Philosophical Perspective," *Logos: A Journal of Catholic Thought and Culture* 10, no. 1 (Winter 2007): 136–65. The following quotation from the final paragraph is especially worthy of note: "We remain committed to the special charism of Free Church Christianity. Yet for all of these reasons, we believe that the future of Free Church Protestants does not lie in distancing ourselves from ecumenical resources like *GS*, but rather in re-engaging a longer and larger tradition of Christian discipleship and witness, one that is represented precisely by documents such as *GS*. Therefore, amidst the changing cultural conditions precipitated by modernity and now postmodernity, we are prepared neither to allow our practice of the faith—untethered to a rich tradition and without the resources of a functional *magisterium*—to die the death of continued accommodation to culture, nor to convert to Roman Catholicism. As a viable alternative, we envision a pilgrimage that, without giving rise to full communion, nonetheless involves a critical engagement with Roman Catholicism as a touchstone of vital tradition and teaching authority about Christian faith and practice" (162). The article is a revision of a paper Beaty, Henry, and Moore presented at a Vatican-sponsored conference that marked the fortieth anniversary of *Gaudium et Spes*. When members of their Baptist constituency became aware of the content of their paper thereafter via an abstract posted online, there was considerable public controversy; see Ken Camp, "Debate about Baylor's Future Asks: Should Baptists Learn from Catholics?" *Baptist News Global* (March 9, 2006), accessed December 16, 2014, http://baptistnews.com/archives/item/992 -debate-about-baylors-future-asks-should-baptists-learn-from-catholics?.

[33] The maxim seems to have originated as an abbreviation of a formula that appears in Prosper of Aquitaine (c. 390–after 455). During a period of conflict in the early fifth-century Western church between adherents to the teachings of Augustine on the one hand and followers of Pelagius on the other concerning the relation of divine grace and the human will, Prosper appealed to the church's liturgy as evidence against the position of the Semipelagians: the fact that in the liturgy ministers throughout the Christian world entreat God to bring people to faith is evidence that the church has traditionally associated the experience of salvation with God's gracious initiative rather than human efforts to attain it. In making this argument, Prosper urged that one should "let the rule of prayer lay down the rule of faith" (*lex supplicandi statuat legem credendi*). Prosper of Aquitaine, "Official Pronouncements of the Apostolic See on Divine Grace and Free Will," 8, in *Defense of St. Augustine*, trans. P. de Letter (Ancient Christian Writers, no. 32; Westminster, Md.: Newman Press, 1963), 183 (178–85).

magisterium, epitomize this function of the liturgy. There is a sense in which Orthodox magisterial authority is located in the coinherence of the seven ecumenical councils and the living voice of the Orthodox liturgy.[34]

Here, Orthodoxy provides a paradigm that Baptists in their practice of congregational magisterium might adapt and extend to the whole church and its liturgical gifts. Especially as Baptists exercise their freedom as a communion without a mandated liturgy to enrich their worship by incorporating faith-forming patterns and practices of worship from other traditions into their own liturgical life, they can receive much helpful guidance from the churches that have engaged in diachronic and synchronic trans-local communal deliberation about the liturgies that will best serve all the local churches in their communions. The books of worship published as the fruit of such deliberations offer Baptist communities valuable resources to be heard and weighed as they seek the Spirit's guidance in the ordering of their worship of the God made known in Jesus Christ. They would do well to begin with a book of worship produced by and for Baptists by the Baptist Union of Great Britain. *Gathering for Worship: Patterns and Prayers for the Community of Disciples*, published in 2005,[35] is the closest approximation of the *Book of Common Prayer* issued by any Baptist union to date, though it is a much more flexible and adaptable collection of worship resources than the *BCP*. As the product of the intentional practice of liturgical receptive ecumenism, it does draw on the *BCP* as well as the liturgical resources of many other churches for a number of collects, forms, and other liturgical texts,[36] but in doing so it was guided by the "core worship values" of Baptist communities identified in the rich theological account of Baptist worship elaborated in the book's preface.[37] Baptists might also

[34] See the chapter on "Affirmations of Faith in Eastern Orthodoxy" in Jaroslav Pelikan, *Credo: Historical and Theological Guide to Creeds and Confessions of Faith in the Christian Tradition* (New Haven, Conn.: Yale University Press, 2003), 397–426. Pelikan observes, "A principal reason for this ambivalent position of 'symbolical books' within Eastern Orthodoxy lies, however, in the distinctively Eastern version, articulated in a special way in the *Philokalia*, of the inseparable connection between 'the rule of prayer [*lex orandi*]' and 'the rule of faith [*lex credendi*]' " (405). He goes on to explore the function of *The Divine Liturgy according to Saint John Chrysostom* as an authoritative confession of faith, documenting the parallels between various features of the liturgy and the doctrines treated in each of the seven ecumenical councils (405–19).

[35] Baptist Union of Great Britain, *Gathering for Worship: Patterns and Prayers for the Community of Disciples*, ed. Christopher J. Ellis and Myra Blyth (Norwich, UK: Canterbury Press, 2005).

[36] Baptist Union of Great Britain, *Gathering for Worship*, "Acknowledgements," 414–23.

[37] Baptist Union of Great Britain, *Gathering for Worship*, "Worship in the Community of Disciples: A Preface," xiv–xix.

consider turning to the *BCP* itself as a source for such magisterial liturgical guidance, re-receiving it as a gift of the communion from which they separated, as a step toward the repair of this historic division at the heart of their denominational identity.

Sixth, Baptists in their practice of congregational magisterium should hear and weigh and not silence the reports and agreed statements of bilateral and multilateral ecumenical dialogues, at both the national and international levels. A joint commission of the delegations to a bilateral or multilateral ecumenical dialogue is not a church, but it does possess a socially embodied ecclesiality as a community of persons who represent their churches. It is not a baptizing community, but it is a community of the baptized. Like a church, these bilateral and multilateral communities of the baptized are collaboratively seeking to bring what their churches teach under the lordship of Christ. The late Mennonite theologian John Howard Yoder thought the gathering church ecclesiology of the Free Churches made it possible to envision an ecumenical gathering as a gathered community under the lordship of Christ that gathers for the purpose of seeking his rule in the community:

> This view gives more, not less, weight to ecumenical gatherings. The "high" views of ordered churchdom can legitimate the worship of a General Assembly or a study conference only by stretching the rules, for its rules do not foresee ad hoc "churches"; only thoroughgoing congregationalism fulfills its hopes and definities whenever and wherever it sees "church" happen.[38]

Yoder's observation applies to the ecumenical gatherings that are bilateral and multilateral dialogue commissions. Study of their reports by local congregations from communions involved in such dialogue is an important but much-neglected resource for discerning the mind of Christ on what the church teaches as Christian faith and faithfulness.[39]

Seventh, Baptists in their practice of congregational magisterium should hear and weigh and not silence the contextual theologies that emerge from social locations

---

[38] John Howard Yoder, *The Royal Priesthood: Essays Ecclesiological and Ecumenical*, ed. Michael G. Cartwright (Grand Rapids: William B. Eerdmans, 1994), 236. Regarding the ecclesiality of ecumenical gatherings and organizations in Baptist perspective, cf. Fiddes, *Tracks and Traces*, 6; and Baptist World Alliance and Catholic Church, "The Word of God in the Life of the Church: A Report of International Conversations between the Catholic Church and the Baptist World Alliance 2006–2010," §196, in *American Baptist Quarterly* 31, no. 1 (Spring 2012): 103 (28–122).

[39] See chapters 9 and 10 for documentation of ecumenical dialogues with Baptist participation and exploration of their significance.

other than their own. It is especially important that these theologies be heard and not silenced, for they are a necessary check on the blind spots that may come from the social location of our own community when it is not intentionally interdependent with the global church. For Baptist communities in North America and Europe, this might mean deliberately seeking out and reading the theologies of liberation that emerge not only in Latin America but in many other contexts where oppression is a reality the practices of the church must address; black theology in its American and African developments; the various efforts by Asian theologians to contextualize the faith in non-Western cultures; feminist, womanist, and *mujerista* theologies; and the growing body of theological literature by Christians whose sexual orientations likewise represent differing social locations within which they seek to bring their life under the lordship of Christ. These voices from other social locations must also be weighed, but unless a community hears them and refrains from silencing them, its capacity for weighing its own voices will be diminished.

Eighth, Baptists in their practice of congregational magisterium should hear and weigh and not silence various types of ecclesial resolutions on ethical issues adopted by diverse church bodies. Such resolutions are often issued by Christian world communions, national denominational organizations, and regional conferences. These are various expressions of ecclesial community that are seeking to bring their churches under the rule of Christ, and therefore they must be heard and weighed by other churches—even if, again, this does not always lead to agreement with them. It is especially the matters of Christian ethics/moral theology that are under contestation today in the living tradition of the church, often in ways that threaten to fracture further the divided church, and in many cases the tradition of this contestation is not yet sufficiently long to provide the church with more authoritative guidance. In their pilgrimage toward the church that is fully under the rule of Christ, all its divisions must refrain from silencing any parties to their disagreements as they seek to hear what the Spirit may disclose to the churches about the mind of Christ. Giving consideration to the contradictory ethical resolutions of the churches can help them keep listening.

Ninth, Baptists in their practice of congregational magisterium should hear and weigh and not silence the lived Christian lives of the saints. This enumeration of voices to be heard and weighed and not silenced in congregational magisterium has heretofore been disproportionately weighted toward texts. But the congregational magisterium that represents the authority of the community of all the saints[40] is comprised primarily of people who seek to embody the way of Jesus Christ rather than the theological texts that very few of them produce or read. When the members of this community hear and read Jesus urging them, "Be merciful, just as your Father is merciful" (Luke 6:36), mercy is not for them merely an abstract virtue. They know how to perform the biblical virtue of mercy because they have seen it embodied concretely by the saints, some of whom have shown mercy directly to them.[41] These saints may include those officially recognized as such in the sanctorals of other communions, some of which include Baptists in their calendars of saints,[42] but the saints that help the church learn how to embody the biblical story are not limited to these. They include also saints known only to local communities. These locally known and more widely known saints have this status and function not because they have perfectly lived the Christian life, but rather because they have exemplified this or that dimension of the way of Jesus Christ in a manner worthy of emulation by the rest of Christ's followers. These saints are indispensable to the community in its exercise of the congregational magisterium by which it seeks to bring its life ever more fully under the rule of Christ. In a 1986 lecture, James Wm. McClendon, Jr., gestured toward this magisterial function of the saints—including especially recent and contemporary ones—in teaching the members of the church: "If we remember, and relive, and so tell the stories that great Christians are discovered

[40] Cf. Steven R. Harmon, "The Authority of the Community (of All the Saints): Toward a Postmodern Baptist Hermeneutic of Tradition," *Review and Expositor* 100, no. 2 (Fall 2003): 587–621; idem, *Towards Baptist Catholicity*, 39–69.

[41] Cf. Richard B. Hays and Ellen F. Davis, "Beyond Criticism: Learning to Read the Bible Again," *Christian Century* 121, no. 8 (April 20, 2004): 23–27, who include this among the "theses on interpreting Scripture" they propose: "7. The saints of the church provide guidance in how to interpret and perform Scripture" (26).

[42] The calendar in the 1979 Episcopal Church (USA) edition of the *Book of Common Prayer*, for example, includes an April 4 feast for Martin Luther King, Jr. (Episcopal Church, *The Book of Common Prayer and Administration of the Sacraments and Other Rites and Ceremonies of the Church: Together with the Psalter or Psalms of David according to the Use of the Episcopal Church* [New York: Oxford University Press, 1979], 22). In addition, the Standing Commission on Music and Liturgy of the Episcopal Church (USA) produced in 2010 an updated trial calendar that includes entries also for Walter Rauschenbusch (July 2), William Carey (October 19), and Charlotte Diggs (Lottie) Moon (December 22) as a step toward a projected new volume of commemorations, tentatively titled "A Great Cloud of Witnesses" (Episcopal Church Standing Commission on Liturgy and Music, *Holy Women, Holy Men: Celebrating the Saints* [New York: Church Publishing, 2010]). On the possibility that Baptists might produce their own calendar of saints, including Baptist saints as well as saints from the whole church, see Andrew Goodliff, "Towards a Baptist Sanctoral?" *Journal of European Baptist Studies* 13, no. 3 (May 2013): 24–30.

among us again in our own day, then the saints are alive *and the Spirit once again informs the people of God"* [emphasis added].[43]

These resources that Baptists should hear and weigh and refrain from silencing in their practice of congregational magisterium are not in agreement with one another, and many of them will elicit much Baptist disagreement. That is why these voices must be weighed. But first they must be heard, and not silenced. In much of Baptist life, most of these voices are silent, not because they have been intentionally silenced, but because they have not been intentionally engaged.

Despite the real differences between the Catholic, Magisterial Protestant, and Free Church traditions in the way they configure teaching authority in the church, they share three rather substantial commonalities. First, in all three traditions magisterium is subservient to the word of God. Second, in all three traditions magisterium is a communal practice that in various ways involves the whole body of Christ. Third, in all three traditions those who exercise *episkopē* in the church play a key role in helping the community discern the mind of Christ, in part by bringing these various wider voices to bear on the matters under deliberation (a role for which their theological education should prepare them). Perhaps the ecumenical future will include some form of shared magisterium, or at least the mutual recognition of one another's teaching authorities as they converge toward a genuine unity in the truth, teaching the catholic faith as "a church teaching as she must teach if she is to be the church here and now."[44] In the meantime, each tradition must see to it that the faith it teaches is fully catholic. Baptists will be helped toward that end by including the magisterial teaching of other traditions, along with the insights of the contextual readings of Scripture done in communities unlike their own and the people who embody those readings, among the voices that they hear and weigh within their own church. In that way Baptists can retrieve the catholic tradition, not as "private historians" but as full participants in the living teaching office of the whole church.

---

[43]   James Wm. McClendon, Jr., "Do We Need Saints Today? (1986)," in *The Collected Works of James Wm. McClendon, Jr.*, 2 vols., ed. Ryan Andrew Newson and Andrew C. Wright (Waco, Tex.: Baylor University Press, 2014), 2:285–94. See also idem, *Biography as Theology: How Life Stories Can Remake Today's Theology*, rev. ed. (Philadelphia: Trinity Press International, 1990), appendix, "Christian Worship and the Saints," 172–84.

[44]   McClendon, *Doctrine*, 24.

PART IV

BAPTIST THEOLOGY AND THE ECUMENICAL FUTURE

8

The Ecumenical Task of Theology

Following a Sunday morning worship service at the Baptist church where I served as part-time pastor while in college, a guest thanked me for conducting his mother's funeral service earlier that week and pressed an envelope into my hands. Along with an honorarium check, it contained a letter in which this member of an Assemblies of God congregation shared with me some words of encouragement he believed God had spoken to him during the funeral. Among other things, the letter exhorted me to remember during my years of preparation for ministry that God "does not want you to be imprisoned by the doctrines of man or the dictates of denominationalism." The man who kindly wrote these words to me instinctively held some of the same convictions about the sinfulness of ecclesiastical divisions that have motivated the modern ecumenical movement since the Edinburgh World Missionary Conference in 1910. In an earlier conversation with me he had offered his observations about some of the doctrinal differences between the Baptist tradition in which he had been raised and the Assemblies of God tradition of his adult experience. He took great delight in the essential agreements between the two denominations and attributed their disagreements to the limitations of human understanding. His words in the letter and in our conversation, however, also reflected a more negative perspective on the relation of theology to the worship, work, and witness of the church held widely not only among laypersons but even among clergy and other ecclesiastical professionals: doctrine, the product and object of the work of theological reflection, is merely human in origin in contrast to God's revelation and frequently serves only to confuse and divide Christians, distracting them from the real ministry of the church.[1]

Such suspicions about theology's ecclesial utility are reinforced by the traditional curricular divisions in seminaries and divinity schools, where the future ministers of the church undertake biblical studies, historical studies, theological studies, and practical studies. The designation of the latter division as "practical theology" unintentionally implies that there is something less than practical about the courses in systematic theology. But when properly conceived and practiced, systematic theology is indeed a practical discipline in the service of the church that is necessary for the pursuit of its mission, especially for its devotion to the end of the domini-cal vision of Christian unity expressed in Jesus' prayer in John 17:20-21: "that they may all be one . . . so that the world may believe."

Theology's Manifold Service of the Church

Charges that theology is irrelevant or even injurious to the church and its ministry are not groundless. Some theologians have pursued theological reflection quite apart from active participation in embodied Christian community, sometimes in open antagonism toward the forms of Christian faith and practice that led them to be interested in theology in the first place. Theology done more consciously in the service of the church has sometimes exceeded legitimate polemical concerns and sought to justify the continuation of the separate ecclesial existence of various denominational expressions of the church, furthering its ongoing division. Theology continues to occupy a central place in the educational preparation of ministers, however, because across two millennia the needs of the church have occasioned the writing and teaching of theology.

Baptist theologian James Leo Garrett, Jr., identified seven major reasons for the necessity of systematic theology to the church. First, the *catechetical* reason: theology is "a proper extension of the teaching function of the Christian church." Second, the *exegetical* reason: theology is necessary "for the integrated formulation of biblical truth." Third, the *homiletical* reason: theology is required "for the accurate clarification, the proper under-girding, and the helpful amplification of the gospel message that ought to

---

[1]   Similar sentiments have existed even within the modern ecumenical movement: "Doctrine divides, service unites" was an early slogan of the Life and Work stream of the early-twentieth-century expressions of organized ecumenism that coalesced (along with the Conference on Faith and Order, and eventually the International Missionary Council) in the post–World War II formation of the World Council of Churches.

be preached by Christian preachers and indeed of the total proclamation of the Word of God by all the people of God." Fourth, the *polemical* reason: the church depends upon theology "for the defense of Christian truth against error within the church or from quasi-Christian movements." Fifth, the *apologetic* reason: theology is done "either in response to the challenge of a leading philosophy in a given era, or in response to the entire cultural situation of the time, including prevailing criticisms of Christianity, or in response to questions about ultimate reality allegedly posed by humankind." Sixth, the *ethical* reason: theology functions "as the essential background for the interpretation and application of Christian ethics to personal and social needs and problems." Seventh, the *dialogic* and *missionary* reasons: theology contributes to "the proper encounter of Christianity with other major religions and . . . the more effective propagation of the Christian gospel among all human beings."[2]

The church certainly needs theology for all the reasons named by Garrett. Those needs are in the forefront of my own mind as I teach theology to future ministers as a discipline done in, with, and for the church. Yet in light of the confluence of three dimensions of my work as an ecclesial theologian—teaching theology to a denominationally diverse student body that includes members of a wide variety of Christian traditions in addition to Baptists, doing research and writing in patristic theology and ecumenical theology, and occasionally serving as a Baptist ecumenist through participation in bilateral and multilateral forms of dialogue—I would add an eighth reason for the ecclesial necessity of theology, interrelated with the seven identified by Garrett: the *ecumenical* reason. The church needs theology because the ecclesial future envisioned in the biblical story involves visible Christian unity, and unless its theologians function as stewards of the Christian memory, which is the living tradition to which all the currently divided churches are heirs, the church will be severely crippled in its movements toward this aspect of God's designs for it.[3] The church needs theology in order to remember the ecclesial future for which it works in the present and in order to conserve and cultivate the traditional doctrinal resources necessary for moving toward that future.

---

[2] James Leo Garrett, Jr., *Systematic Theology: Biblical, Historical, and Evangelical*, 2 vols. (Grand Rapids: William B. Eerdmans, 1990), 1:12–15.

[3] Cf. Robert L. Wilken, *Remembering the Christian Past* (Grand Rapids: William B. Eerdmans, 1995), chap. 8, "Memory and the Christian Intellectual Life," 165–80.

Theology and the Ecumenical Crisis of the Church

The second chapter of this book gave attention to the current state of the ecumenical movement, which seems not to be moving much these days in comparison with the decades that followed the Second Vatican Council. Among whatever factors are responsible for the recent paralysis especially of the Faith and Order stream of the modern ecumenical movement, surely the discipline of theology has made its own contributions to the widespread indifference to ecclesial division. One factor is an increasingly common abdication by academic theologians of their responsibilities to the catechetical needs of the church, a disengagement from one of the original reasons for the existence of the discipline with grave consequences for the church's heeding of the ecumenical imperative. Enamored with novelty in the interests of cultural relevance and academic respectability, many theologians have given more attention to the exploration of new philosophical frameworks for theology or the rethinking of Christian theology in light of the theory du jour[4] than to careful stewardship of what "the church of Jesus Christ believes, teaches, and confesses on the basis of the word of God."[5] As a result, they have unwittingly helped form new generations of ministers who do not see catechesis as essential to the exercise of pastoral ministry and who therefore have not actively formed the members of their congregations in the teachings that have sustained the church through two millennia of challenges. This neglect of the catechetical dimension of the discipline of theology both exacerbates the existing ecclesial divisions and obscures the means by which they might be overcome. Joseph Small, who

---

[4]   These assertions should not be understood as a conservative wholesale indictment of the liberal tradition in Christian theology on my part. As Christopher H. Evans argues in *Liberalism without Illusions: Renewing an American Christian Tradition* (Waco, Tex.: Baylor University Press, 2010), this is a venerable theological trajectory that has contributed rich gifts to the life of the church that are vital to ecclesial existence today. My identification with the postliberal trajectory in contemporary theology means that these enduring gifts belong to my own identity as a theologian, even while I critique other aspects of theological liberalism.

[5]   Jaroslav Pelikan, *The Christian Tradition: A History of the Development of Doctrine*, vol. 1, *The Emergence of the Catholic Tradition (100–600)* (Chicago: University of Chicago Press, 1971), 1. Pelikan's definition of doctrine focuses on the content of doctrine, while the definition proposed by James Wm. McClendon, Jr., quoted elsewhere in this book is concerned with the active practice of teaching by the church: "Doctrine *is* teaching . . . and by *Christian* doctrine I will here mean *a church teaching as she must teach if she is to be the church here and now*" (James Wm. McClendon, Jr., *Doctrine: Systematic Theology, Vol. 2* [Waco, Tex.: Baylor University Press, 2012], 23–24).

served as coordinator of the Office of Theology and Worship for the Presbyterian Church (U.S.A.) prior to his retirement, has observed:

> There have been times in the church's life when oppressive orthodoxy
> was a painful problem. Ours is not one of those times. Our problem is
> a *laissez faire* approach to dogma that produces ecclesial cacophony. The
> solution does not lie in a revival of oppressive orthodoxy, but in a fitting
> reception of the rule of faith coupled with suitable conversation about
> unsettled or ambiguous matters. The *regula fidei* does not squelch theo-
> logical exploration in the church, but rather enables it.[6]

The ecumenical reason for theology as a discipline in the service of the
church, then, depends especially upon proper attention to its catechetical
rationale and to the relationship of theology as the explication of Christian
teachings to other sorts of theologizing.

What Sort of Theology the Divided Church Needs

The church's current inability to make a common confession of the apostolic faith calls for a theology that develops and emphasizes the coinherence
of the catechetical and ecumenical rationales for the necessity of systematic
theology to the life of the church. Properly understood, these reasons the
church needs the discipline of systematic theology function as interrelated
expressions of systematic theology that together assist the church in its
journey toward the ecumenical future.

Systematic Theology as Dogmatic Theology

The divided church needs a theology that makes a proper distinction
between theological reflection that has the teaching of the church as its primary object, beneficiary, and set of parameters, and theological reflection
that carefully ventures beyond these parameters and creatively addresses
other concerns while remaining rooted in the teaching of the church. In
other words, the church needs a renewal of the writing and teaching of
what used to be called "dogmatic theology"—not in the sense of the more
recently acquired connotation of "dogmatic" as "asserting or imposing
dogmas or opinions in an authoritative, imperious, or arrogant manner,"

---

[6] Joseph D. Small, "Theology's Passive Voice," *Perspectives: A Journal of Reformed
Thought* 20, no. 9 (October 2005), accessed November 29, 2014, https://www.pcusa.org/
site_media/media/uploads/theologyandworship/pdfs/passivevoice.pdf.

but rather as a synonym of "doctrinal"[7] linked etymologically with the early Christian usage of the Greek adjective *dogmatikos* to refer to that which is "concerned with doctrine."[8] In this classical sense "dogmatics" designates a species of theology that reflects upon and gives expression to the church's teachings.

From the thinkers of the patristic era to those recognized as their modern equivalents, Christianity's finest theologians have been dogmaticians in the sense that they carefully distinguished between their efforts to give voice to the teaching of the church and their individual musings beyond it, even while exercising creativity in doing both dogmatic theology and theology of other sorts. Novelty and creativity do have a proper place within and alongside dogmatic theology, for the dogmatic theologian is comparable to "the scribe who has been trained for the kingdom of heaven," who "is like the master of a household who brings out of his treasure what is new and what is old" (Matt 13:52). The scribes, the theologians of Jesus' day, drew upon the traditional resources of the "old things" of the Torah but also brought forth the "new things" of the application of the Torah to the emergences of daily living centuries after the giving of the Torah. Just as the scribes "trained for the kingdom of heaven" connected these "old things" with the "new things" now experienced in Christ,[9] so the church's dogmatic theologians have creatively configured the "old things" of the traditional teaching of the church to address the "new things" of the life of the church in another time and place.

Origen (d. AD 254) is sometimes identified as the church's first systematic theologian on the basis of his coherent treatment of all the major doctrinal rubrics in a single work, *On First Principles*, something not accomplished in the extant Christian literature that antedates Origen. In the preface to that treatise, Origen declares that as Christian believers hold "conflicting opinions" on matters of great as well as trivial importance, "it seems necessary first to lay down a definite line and unmistakable rule (*regulam*) in regard to each of these, and to postpone the inquiry into other

---

[7]   *The Oxford English Dictionary*, 2nd ed., ed. J. A. Simpson and E. S. C. Weiner (Oxford: Clarendon Press, 1989), s.v. "dogmatic" (definitions A.2 and A.4).

[8]   *A Patristic Greek Lexicon*, ed. G. W. H. Lampe (Oxford: Clarendon Press, 1961), s.v. "*dogmatikos*" (definition 3).

[9]   This reading of the role of the scribes in this enigmatic parable is influenced by Andrew T. Lincoln, "Matthew—A Story for Teachers?" in *The Bible in Three Dimensions: Essays in Celebration of Forty Years of Biblical Studies in the University of Sheffield*, ed. David J. A. Clines et al. (JSOT Supplements, no. 87; Sheffield: JSOT Press, 1990), 107–8 (103–25).

matters until afterwards."[10] Some of the apostolic doctrines are "necessary ones," while "there were other doctrines . . . about which the apostles simply said that things were so, keeping silence as to the how or why."[11] This distinction allowed a proper role for speculative theology as inquiry into "the how or why" that respects the broad boundaries of the "unmistakable rule." For Origen, the apostolic rule included within an overarching trinitarian structure a series of summary narrative affirmations regarding the oneness of the God of the Old Testament and New Testament who created all things and revealed himself in Jesus Christ; the preexistence, incarnation, virginal conception, crucifixion, death, resurrection, and ascension of Jesus Christ; the unity "in honor and dignity with the Father and the Son" of the Holy Spirit, who inspired the prophets and the apostles; the judgment of the soul after its departure from this world and the resurrection of the dead; the freedom of the human will and the reality of its struggle against the evil powers and assistance by the angelic powers; the creation of this world "at a definite time"—an affirmation of *creatio ex nihilo*; and the divine inspiration of the Scriptures and the existence within them of both "obvious" and "hidden" levels of meaning.[12] These are the "first principles" to which the title of the treatise refers, and they provide guidance for the consideration of other matters. Origen carefully noted in his summary of the apostolic rule the points at which "no clear statement . . . is set forth in the Church teaching."[13] On such points—the nature of the resurrection body, precisely what sorts of creatures are the celestial bodies, and the extent to which God's saving work will be universally realized among rational creatures being notable examples—Origen was free to speculate, but always in an effort to relate them to the "elementary and foundation principles" in "a connected body of doctrine."[14] The later scholastic Origenists did not preserve this distinction between the "foundation principles" and speculation beyond them, for which failure their teachings were anathematized in AD 553 at the Fifth Ecumenical Council (Constantinople II). Nevertheless, the church's first systematic theologian provides an ancient precedent for Joseph Small's contention that "the *regula*

---

[10] Origen, *On First Principles*, I.pref.2 (*Origen On First Principles*, trans. G. W. Butterworth [Gloucester, Mass.: Peter Smith, 1973], 1–2; for the extant text of the passage in Rufinus' Latin translation, see *Origène Traité des Principes*, vol. 1, ed. Henri Crouzel and Manlio Simonetti [Sources Chrétiennes, no. 252; Paris: Éditions du Cerf, 1978], 78).

[11] Origen, *On First Principles*, I.pref.3 (*On First Principles*, trans. Butterworth, 2).

[12] Origen, *On First Principles*, I.pref.4–10 (*On First Principles*, trans. Butterworth, 2–6).

[13] Origen, *On First Principles*, I.pref.7 (*On First Principles*, trans. Butterworth, 5).

[14] Origen, *On First Principles*, I.pref.10 (*On First Principles*, trans. Butterworth, 6).

fidei does not squelch theological exploration in the church, but rather enables it."[15]

More recently the Swiss Reformed theologian Karl Barth (1886–1968), regarded by many as a "modern church father," rediscovered the centrality of dogmatic theology to the church's theological needs as a result of his encounter with the dogmatic theologians of post-Reformation orthodoxy. Daunted by the opportunity to teach a course in dogmatics in 1924 following the third academic year of his initial professorship at Göttingen, Barth—who lacked a *Doktor der Theologie*, not to mention the postdoctoral *Habilitation* expected of professors in the German university system—was desperate not only for help in lecture preparation but especially for an approach that would help him and his students to read the Bible through the lenses of the church in a way not accomplished by any of the reigning theological paradigms. In the midst of a frenetic effort during the break between terms to work through the major dogmatic works of the patristic period and later, Barth happened upon the *Reformed Dogmatics* of Heinrich Heppe (1820–1879).[16] There Barth discovered a stage in the evolution of Protestant theology at which the breakthrough insights of Luther, Calvin, and the other early Reformers had been carefully evaluated by the church and incorporated into a truly "ecclesial hermeneutic." Although Barth went on to read other Protestant orthodox dogmaticians of the mid-nineteenth century, in particular the Lutheran theologian Heinrich Schmid (1811–1885),[17] Heppe remained the most influential, and the *Göttingen Dogmatics* that emerged from these lectures (delivered 1924–1926) reads like a running commentary on Heppe's *Dogmatics*.[18] Bruce McCormack has argued cogently that it was this discovery—rather than the much-cited later engagement with Anselm's thought in 1930—that marked the turning point that determined the ultimate shape of the *Church*

[15]   Small, "Theology's Passive Voice."

[16]   Heinrich Heppe, *Die Dogmatik der evangelisch-reformierten Kirche* (Elberfeld: R. L. Friedrichs, 1861); ET, *Reformed Dogmatics*, trans. G. T. Thomson (London: Allen & Unwin, 1950; repr., Grand Rapids: Baker Book House, 1978).

[17]   Heinrich Schmid, *Die Dogmatik der Evangelisch-lutherischen Kirche, dargestellt und aus den Quellen belegt*, 7th ed. (Gütersloh: C. Bertelsmann, 1893); ET, *The Doctrinal Theology of the Evangelical Lutheran Church*, 3rd rev. ed., trans. Charles A. Hay and Henry E. Jacobs (Minneapolis: Augsburg, 1961).

[18]   Karl Barth, *Unterricht in der christlichen Religion (1924–1926)*, 3 vols., ed. Hannelotte Reiffen and Hinrich Stoevesandt (Karl Barth-Gesamtausgabe, pt. 2, vols. 9, 10, 13; Zürich: Theologischer Verlag, 1985–2003); partial ET, *The Göttingen Dogmatics: Instruction in the Christian Religion*, ed. Hannelotte Reiffen, trans. Geoffrey W. Bromiley (Grand Rapids: William B. Eerdmans, 1991).

Dogmatics published from 1932 to 1965.[19] In the prolegomena volume of the *Church Dogmatics*, Barth identified its genre as "regular dogmatics," which is "an enquiry into dogma which aims at the completeness appropriate to the special task of the school, of theological instruction" that prepares ministers to do their own independent theological work and so "must cover the whole field in respect of the range of concepts and themes that are significant for church proclamation."[20]

On a first reading, Barth's *Church Dogmatics* seems to be mostly concerned with the "old things" suggested by Matthew 13:52. Barth did not so much create a new theology as reengage decidedly old expressions of theology, and much of the substance of the *Church Dogmatics* consists of extended fine print excurses in which Barth does biblical exegesis and mines the resources of the doctrinal tradition of the church. Yet in the manner in which Barth draws these "old things" into a coherent whole in the service of the proclamation of the church of his own age, the *Church Dogmatics* gives expression to "new things." A clue to the place of creative novelty in Barth's reclamation of dogmatic theology is supplied by the much-commented-upon juxtaposition of two portraits in his Basel study: John Calvin, the great Reformed theologian, and Wolfgang Amadeus Mozart, the great classical composer. In light of this pairing of paintings, one might understand Barth the dogmatic theologian as a theological artist.[21]

As artists, musical composers normally work with certain givens that they did not themselves create: tones, keys, scales, rhythms, even formal and stylistic traditions that make the composition recognizable as music and as music of a certain type, and yet out of these given media the composer fashions something novel. Sometimes received media mandate fixed repetition, as in the baroque passacaglia, a dance form with a short melodic figure repeated over and over again and variations arranged around the fixed figure. In the *Passacaglia for Solo Violin* that concludes the *Rosary Sonatas* by Heinrich Ignaz Franz von Biber (1644–1704), for example, the violinist repeats the same four descending notes in each measure of the ten-minute-long piece, yet Biber's haunting ornamentations of the

---

[19] Bruce L. McCormack, *Karl Barth's Critically Realistic Dialectical Theology: Its Genesis and Development 1909–1936* (Oxford: Oxford University Press, 1997), especially 23, 334–37, 349–50.

[20] Karl Barth, *Church Dogmatics*, trans. G. W. Bromiley (Edinburgh: T&T Clark, 1975), I/1:275–76.

[21] Cf. Theodore A. Gill, "Barth and Mozart," *Theology Today* 43, no. 3 (October 1986): 403–11.

recurrent figure make this passacaglia anything but monotonous. Like the composer of a passacaglia, Barth worked with the Scriptures and the doctrines that he received from the church—unchanging "old things." In giving faithful voice to a tradition that he did not create, he nevertheless exercised a delightfully creative aesthetic sensibility in arranging the "notes" and "rhythms" of the tradition so that the *Church Dogmatics* offered the church "new things" in the form of artfully crafted theological compositions.

A renewal of dogmatic theology in seminaries and divinity schools, in which theologians would function primarily as catechists whose writing and teaching equip ministers to do catechesis themselves in local churches, will not consign the discipline of theology to antiquarian irrelevance, nor will it prevent those who do dogmatic theology from making ad hoc use of new developments in philosophy and social or literary theory to explicate Christian doctrines and ponder them in light of fresh perspectives. Rather, it will make available to the contemporary church the resources it needs to confess its faith with the oneness that the currently unbelieving world will find compelling in the ecclesial future envisioned by Jesus. Teaching the doctrines a specific ecclesial communion holds in common with all Christians, such as the trinitarian character of God and the full humanity and full divinity of Jesus Christ, strengthens the basis upon which the divided churches may move closer to a common confession of the apostolic faith. Teaching the doctrines that a particular Protestant communion holds in common with other churches of the Reformation (and thus not with Catholicism or Orthodoxy), as well as the doctrines unique to that denomination, helps foster clarity about the remaining doctrinal divisions and therefore contributes to the earnest ecumenical contestation of what it means to be the "one, holy, catholic, and apostolic church" necessary for seeking a visible unity of faith and order that is not merely an insipid affirmation of all existing differences as varying expressions of an invisible oneness.[22]

Systematic Theology as Ecumenical Theology

Dogmatic theology has long been recognized as a species of systematic theology, as the traditional systematic loci are nothing other than the major doctrines taught by the church. Ecumenical theology, on the other

---

[22] Fisher Humphreys, *The Way We Were: How Southern Baptist Theology Has Changed and What It Means to Us All*, rev. ed. (Macon, Ga.: Smyth & Helwys, 2002), 15–58, has effectively utilized this ecumenical approach to defining Baptist identity.

hand, has not usually been regarded in this way. It is often categorized as a subtheme of one of the doctrinal loci, ecclesiology, for its concern is especially with the largely ecclesiological church-dividing theological issues.

The church in its ecumenical expressions, however, has not been content to consign ecumenical theology to a subtheme of one of the systematic rubrics. There is now an ecumenically shared commitment to ecumenical formation as indispensable to preparation for pastoral ministry, evidenced by the *Directory for the Application of the Principles and Norms of Ecumenism* published by the Pontifical Council for Promoting Christian Unity (1993) and the World Council of Churches Programme on Ecumenical Theological Education working document "Magna Charta on Ecumenical Formation in Theological Education in the 21st Century" (2008).[23] Despite this development, ecumenical formation remains difficult to spot in the formal curricula of most Protestant denominational and interconfessional institutions of theological education. The compulsory course in ecumenism recommended by the *Directory* for Catholic seminarians has no parallel in the typical Master of Divinity curriculum requirements in a Protestant seminary or divinity school.[24] In theory the insistence of the *Directory* that an ecumenical approach should be taken to every individual discipline of the body of divinity is heeded by Protestant theological educators as well, and often this is true in their actual practice. Yet in the absence of more intentional efforts in ecumenical formation, the average ordinand is either unaware of the significant strides toward visible unity in faith and order that have emerged from the bilateral and multilateral dialogues or else regards them as mildly interesting but of little relevance to the practice of congregational ministry.

While the institutions of theological education await this needed curricular revision, professors of the individual biblical, historical, theological, and practical disciplines can reenvision their courses so that their learning outcomes include ecumenical formation as it relates to the subject matter. As a theologian, I am convinced that this can best be accomplished in my

---

[23] Pontifical Council for Promoting Christian Unity (Catholic Church), *Directory for the Application of the Principles and Norms of Ecumenism* (March 25, 1993), accessed November 29, 2014, http://www.vatican.va/roman_curia/pontifical_councils/chrstuni/general -docs/rc_pc_chrstuni_doc_19930325_directory_en.html; Dietrich Werner, "Magna Charta on Ecumenical Formation in Theological Education in the 21st Century—10 Key Convictions," *International Review of Mission* 98, no. 1 (2009): 161–70.

[24] There are of course exceptions to this generalization. At the Evangelical Lutheran Church in America–sponsored Lutheran Theological Southern Seminary in Columbia, South Carolina, for example, the M.Div. course in Ecumenical Theology that I taught there during the Spring 2012 semester is required of all seminarians.

own discipline if ecumenical theology is understood as a specific form of systematic theology that is systematic in its own right, is informed by other expressions of systematic theology, and in turn can serve as a source for systematic theological construction.

What Qualifies as "Systematic" Theology?

Definitions of systematic theology abound, and they are almost as varied as they are numerous.[25] For the purposes of this chapter, I propose that a particular theological proposal or practice of theological reflection qualifies as systematic theology if it fulfills the following three criteria.

First, systematic theology is *comprehensive*. It is comprehensive in its treatment of all the loci of doctrinal theology, and it draws comprehensively from its sources of authority, in particular the canon of Scripture and the tradition of what "the church of Jesus Christ has believed, taught, and confessed" on its basis in the church's task of "teaching as she must teach if she is to be the church here and now."[26] Second, systematic theology is *coherent*. It is coherent in the sense that it is not a treatment of a series of discrete doctrinal rubrics considered in isolation from one another but rather a presentation of their interdependence. A systematic theology may fulfill this criterion by employing a specific integrative motif, core doctrine, or methodological approach, or it may appropriate a particular philosophical or theoretical framework as a means of making explicit the interdependence of the loci. Third, systematic theology is *constructive*. It does not merely receive and reiterate past formulations of theology, however authoritative they may be. At the same time, systematic theological construction cannot be entirely de novo. Rather, systematic theology offers constructive proposals that stand in continuity with a tradition while giving it a fresh voice in a particular time and place and with particular purposes in mind. In terms of an analogy similar to one employed above in connection with the catechetical dimension of Barth's *Church Dogmatics*, this constructive dimension of systematic theology involves a creativity comparable to that of an artist, who does not create out of thin air the media with which he or she works but takes given things like canvas and oil paint in a range of colors and constructs of these familiar givens something that has never previously existed as a visual rendering of the world.

---

[25] Recently, e.g., Nicholas M. Healy, "What Is Systematic Theology?" *International Journal of Systematic Theology* 11, no. 1 (January 2009): 24–39.

[26] Pelikan, *Christian Tradition*, 1:1; McClendon, *Doctrine*, 23–24.

The Deficiencies of Modern Systematic Theology in Systematic Comprehensiveness

Modern systematic theology has not been lacking in intellectual coherence and constructive creativity, but much of it has not been fully comprehensive in the sense that it fails to listen comprehensively to the theological voice of the whole church en route to making constructive theological proposals that are otherwise coherent and comprehensive in their treatment of all the doctrinal rubrics. In many systematic theologies, the engagement of other theological constructions as conversational partners tends to function as a conversation between individual theologians who make constructive theological proposals in dialogue principally with the proposals of other individual theologians past and present, frequently with little reference to key communal expressions of the church's theology.[27]

We return to Barth as a significant exception to this characterization of the deficiencies of modern systematic theology in systematic comprehensiveness. While some definitions of systematic theology differentiate

---

[27] The comparative lack of substantive interaction with communal expressions of Christian doctrine does not, however, always indicate disregard for it. It is possible for a theologian to affirm and assume the broad outlines of the dogmatic tradition yet focus on the contributions of individual Christian thinkers whose thought creatively thickens an account of what "the church of Jesus Christ believes, teaches, and confesses on the basis of the word of God" (Pelikan, *Christian Tradition*, 1:1) in order to retrieve unrecognized or underappreciated possibilities in the tradition that can fund fresh articulations and applications of doctrine, helping the church teach "as she must teach if she is to be the church here and now" (McClendon, *Doctrine*, 23–24). Sarah Coakley, for example, scarcely refers to the ancient ecumenical councils or their creeds and definitions in her otherwise wide-ranging patristic engagement in the first installment of her projected four-volume systematic theology *On Desiring God*. In *God, Sexuality, and the Self: An Essay "On the Trinity"* (Cambridge: Cambridge University Press, 2013), she refers to conciliar expressions of patristic theology on only five occasions. But this represents neither disregard for nor disagreement with these voices: Coakley's announced intention is to "query or complexify" the "conciliar-based narrative," namely, the "accounts of early trinitarianism that give sole attention to the status of the 'Son' vis-à-vis the 'Father' up to the mid fourth century." This is necessary because they "miss most of the drama: *at one and the same time* the crucial prayer-based logic of emergent trinitarianism is missed, and the related, and complicated entanglements with questions of human gender, power, and desire mutely disregarded" (Coakley, *God, Sexuality, and the Self*, 4; emphasis in original). In this connection it is the individual voices, especially Augustine, Gregory of Nyssa, Origen, and Pseudo-Dionysius among patristic theologians, that provide Coakley access to the "drama" that one misses when conciliar orthodoxy is the primary frame of reference. See Steven R. Harmon, "Ressourcement Totale: Sarah Coakley's Patristic Engagement in *God, Sexuality, and the Self*," *Perspectives in Religious Studies* 41, no. 4 (Winter 2014): 413–17.

it from dogmatic theology,[28] the *Church Dogmatics* fully embodies the comprehensive, coherent, and constructive character of a truly systematic theology—even though it dispensed with traditional systematic prolegomena and remained unfinished, eschewed philosophical coherence, and avoided conscious efforts toward constructive originality. This passage from the section on "Authority under the Word" in *Church Dogmatics* I/2 points to another manner in which a theology may be comprehensively, coherently, and constructively systematic:

> But it is obvious that before I myself make a confession I must myself have heard the confession of the Church, i.e., the confession of the rest of the Church. In my hearing and receiving of the Word of God I cannot separate myself from the Church to which it is addressed. I cannot thrust myself into the debate about a right faith which goes on in the Church without first having listened. . . . If I am to confess my faith generally with the whole Church and in that confession be certain that my faith is the right faith, then I must begin with the community of faith and therefore hear the Church's confession of faith as it comes to me from other members of the Church. And for that very reason I recognise an authority, a superiority in the Church: namely, that the confession of others who were before me in the Church and are beside me in the Church is superior to my confession if this really is an accounting and responding in relation to my hearing and receiving of the Word of God, if it really is my confession as that of a member of the body of Christ.[29]

Barth's project is unparalleled in its effort to listen comprehensively to the tradition en route to doing systematic theological construction. Its methodological coherence derives in part from Barth's attention in the extensive "fine print" sections not only to the individual confessions of others who preceded him in the church, notable as well as obscure, but especially to the church's communal confessions of its faith. In this Barth anticipated the insistence of Jaroslav Pelikan that "the history of tradition requires that we listen to the choruses and not only to the soloists—nor

---

[28]   E.g., in the Baptist tradition, Augustus Hopkins Strong, *Systematic Theology: A Compendium*, 3 vols. in 1 (Valley Forge, Pa.: Judson Press, 1907), 41–42: "Dogmatic theology is, in its strict usage, the systematizing of the doctrines as expressed in the symbols of the church, together with the grounding of these in the Scriptures, and the exhibition, so far as may be, of their rational necessity. Systematic theology begins, on the other hand, not with the symbols, but with the Scriptures. It asks first, not what the church has believed, but what is the truth of God's revealed word."

[29]   Barth, *Church Dogmatics*, I/2:589.

only to the virtuosi among the soloists."[30] Thus, Barth privileged "general ecclesiastical doctrinal decisions" over the proposals of individual theologians,[31] and in his hearing of the church's confession as it came to him from other members of the church in the patristic period he located the ecclesial "chorus" in the patristic conciliar and credal documents collected in the Denzinger *Enchiridion Symbolorum*.[32]

When Barth then made his own constructive "confession as that of a member of the body of Christ," it was comprehensive in receiving and voicing anew the confession of the whole church and not merely that of a few of its members, and comprehensive in giving attention to the full range of matters addressed in the ecclesial confession that preceded him. It was methodologically coherent in its rigorous application of an ecclesial theological hermeneutic that yielded a coherent presentation of the interdependence of the doctrines because it discerned the trinitarian shape and Christocentric core of the church's confession. And it was constructive in that Barth creatively gave fresh voice to this confession as a theological proposal crafted to assist the church in its ongoing efforts to confess its faith compellingly.

Ecumenical Theology as Systematic Theology

Like Barth's *Church Dogmatics*, ecumenical theology has the potential for correcting the deficiencies of modern theology in systematic comprehensiveness by shifting the focus from the proposals of individual theologians to the church's efforts to confess its faith communally. As a form of systematic theological reflection that serves the particular purpose of furthering the quest for the visible unity of the church, ecumenical theology functions as constructive systematic theology, even while it is informed

[30] Jaroslav Pelikan, *The Vindication of Tradition* (New Haven, Conn.: Yale University Press, 1984), 17.

[31] Barth had articulated this methodological principle already in the *Göttingen Dogmatics*: see Barth, *Göttingen Dogmatics*, 229.

[32] Barth's references correspond to the section numbering of the fourteenth/fifteenth edition: Heinrich Denzinger, Clemens Bannwart, and Johann Baptist Umberg, eds., *Enchiridion Symbolorum: Definitionum et declarationum de rebus fidei et morum*, 14th and 15th ed. (Freiburg im Breisgau: Herder, 1922). On this feature of Barth's interaction with patristic dialogue partners, see Steven R. Harmon, "Karl Barth's Conversation with the Fathers: A Paradigm for *Ressourcement* in Baptist and Evangelical Theology," *Perspectives in Religious Studies* 33, no. 1 (Spring 2006): 7–23, especially 16 and 19; idem, *Towards Baptist Catholicity: Essays on Tradition and the Baptist Vision* (Studies in Baptist History and Thought, vol. 27; Milton Keynes, UK: Paternoster, 2006), 129–50, especially 140 and 144–46.

by other constructive systematic proposals. Furthermore, the ecumenical theology done in the context of the interconfessional dialogues of the past four decades offers a wealth of largely untapped resources that can fund the work of individual systematic theologians who follow Barth in hearing the confession of the whole church on the way to making constructive proposals that benefit the church.

Since the beginnings of the modern ecumenical movement, there has been substantial overlap between systematic theology and ecumenical theology. The close relationship between ecumenical and systematic theology is epitomized by the career of Wolfhart Pannenberg, who long served in the dual role of professor of Systematic Theology and director of the Institute of Ecumenical Theology at the University of Munich, participated actively in various forums for ecumenical dialogue, wrote extensively on ecumenical themes, and treated each of the systematic loci with ecumenical comprehensiveness in his three-volume *Systematic Theology* with the purpose of contributing to the ecumenical goal of the visible unity of the church clearly in mind.[33] Similarly, Jürgen Moltmann's constructive work as a systematic theologian went hand-in-hand with his active service as a member of the Faith and Order Commission of the World Council of Churches from 1963 to 1983, as a direct consequence of which he "began to do theology for 'the whole of Christendom on earth,' no longer only for our own church and our own country."[34] The six volumes of "system-

---

[33] Wolfhart Pannenberg, *Systematic Theology*, 3 vols., trans. Geoffrey W. Bromiley (Grand Rapids: William B. Eerdmans, 1991–1998).

[34] Jürgen Moltmann, *A Broad Place: An Autobiography*, trans. Margaret Kohl (Minneapolis: Fortress Press, 2008), 85 (pp. 84–87 are devoted to Moltmann's reflections on his ecumenical work in connection with the WCC Faith and Order Commission). On Moltmann's instrumental role in the work of the WCC Faith and Order Commission working group that worked in 1978 and 1979 on possible ways forward beyond the East–West divisions over the *Filioque* controversy and published Lukas Vischer, ed., *Spirit of God, Spirit of Christ: Ecumenical Reflections on the Filioque Controversy* (Faith and Order Paper no. 103; Geneva: World Council of Churches, 1981), see Steven R. Harmon, "Ecumenical Reception of Ecumenical Perspectives on the *Filioque*," foreword in *Ecumenical Perspectives on the Filioque for the 21st Century*, ed. Myk Habets (London: T&T Clark International, 2014), xiii–xiv (xiii–xviii).

atic contributions to theology"[35] that followed Moltmann's earlier trilogy[36] reflect the reenvisioning of systematic theology as ecumenical theology resulting from these and other ecumenical encounters, even if some of the solutions to ecumenical problems he proposed therein have not been met with broad ecumenical reception.

If other systematic theologians will embrace more intentionally the systematic character of ecumenical theology in their classroom instruction and constructive theological projects, they will bolster their discipline's contributions to the ecumenical formation of the ministers of the church—and ultimately of its members—and therefore will make their own contributions to ecumenical convergence and reception. They can easily do so because ecumenical theology is marked by systematic comprehensiveness, coherence, and constructive possibilities.

The Systematic Comprehensiveness of Ecumenical Theology

Given the nature of the matters that continue to divide the churches, it is unsurprising that much of the attention of the agreed texts and reports issued by the bilateral and multilateral interconfessional dialogues is to various sub-loci of ecclesiology. Yet all the rubrics of systematic theology receive enough attention in these documents that they may serve as significant sources for comprehensive systematic theological reflection that supplement the creedal and confessional tradition as essential aids to discerning the communal voice of the church in its confession. The ancient creeds do give expression to the confession of the church in ways that are determinative for the confessions of the divided communions, even when these creeds are not explicitly recognized as authoritative, and the

---

[35] Jürgen Moltmann, *The Trinity and the Kingdom: The Doctrine of God*, trans. Margaret Kohl (San Francisco: Harper & Row, 1981); idem, *God in Creation: A New Theology of Creation and the Spirit of God*, trans. Margaret Kohl (San Francisco: Harper & Row, 1985); idem, *The Way of Jesus Christ: Christology in Messianic Dimensions*, trans. Margaret Kohl (San Francisco: HarperSanFrancisco, 1990); idem, *The Spirit of Life: A Universal Affirmation*, trans. Margaret Kohl (Minneapolis: Fortress Press, 1992); idem, *The Coming of God: Christian Eschatology*, trans. Margaret Kohl (Minneapolis: Fortress Press, 1996); idem, *Experiences in Theology: Ways and Forms of Christian Theology*, trans. Margaret Kohl (Minneapolis: Fortress Press, 2000).

[36] Jürgen Moltmann, *Theology of Hope: On the Ground and Implications of a Christian Eschatology*, trans. James W. Leitch (New York: Harper & Row, 1967); idem, *The Crucified God: The Cross as the Foundation and Criticism of Christian Theology*, trans. R. A. Wilson and John Bowden (New York: Harper & Row, 1974); idem, *The Church in the Power of the Spirit: A Contribution to Messianic Ecclesiology*, trans. Margaret Kohl (New York: Harper & Row, 1977).

confessions of specific communions in the wake of the divisions of the Western church in the sixteenth century and later are of course indispensable for hearing the distinctive communal confessions that each of these traditions has to offer the rest of the church. Only the interconfessional dialogues, however, are ecclesially sanctioned international forums in which the church as an institution with the sort of "living tradition" described by Alasdair MacIntyre can enter into a "historically extended, socially embodied argument . . . about the goods which constitute [the] tradition" of the church across its divisions.[37] This dialogical contestation of the church's confession enables larger portions of the divided church to confess with one voice what they discover they are able to confess together, and to the degree that many of the parties to these dialogues have been able to confess the apostolic faith in explicit agreement with one another, they set forth a fundamental consensus on Christian doctrine that ranges across the major systematic rubrics. The identification and articulation of such expressions of interconfessional consensus is a communal practice of doing systematic theology in its comprehensive dimension, and this practice in turn depends upon intraconfessional practices of collaborative systematic theological reflection by each delegation in dialogue with its own tradition.

Beyond the rich ongoing exploration of baptism, Eucharist, ordination, oversight, and other ecclesiological issues throughout the dialogues, the agreed statements have addressed the other major doctrines of systematic theology. Each of the dialogues—from the Anglican–Lutheran, Anglican–Orthodox, Anglican–Catholic, Lutheran–Catholic, and Methodist–Catholic conversations initiated in the 1960s through the second phase of Baptist–Catholic dialogue of 2006–2010—has found it necessary to address extensively the interrelationship of divine revelation and the sources of authority in Scripture and tradition on the basis of which the churches respond to this revelation in their configurations of faith and practice.[38]

---

[37] Alasdair MacIntyre, *After Virtue: A Study in Moral Theory*, 2nd ed. (Notre Dame, Ind.: University of Notre Dame Press, 1984), 222.

[38] Lutheran World Federation and Anglican Communion, "Pullach Report" (1972), §§17–50, in *Growth in Agreement: Reports and Agreed Statements of Ecumenical Conversations on a World Level*, ed. Harding Meyer and Lukas Vischer (Faith and Order Paper no. 108; New York: Paulist Press/Geneva: World Council of Churches, 1984), 16–20 (14–32); Anglican Communion and Orthodox Churches, "Moscow Statement" (1976), §§4–18, in *Growth in Agreement*, 41–44 (41–49); Anglican Communion and Catholic Church, "Authority in the Church I (Venice Statement)" (1976), "Authority in the Church—Elucidation" (1981), and "Authority in the Church II (Windsor Statement)" (1981), in *Growth in Agreement*, 88–118; Lutheran World Federation and Catholic Church, "The

In addition, the dialogues have produced consensual expressions of trinitarian doctrine (e.g., the Reformed–Orthodox "Agreed Statement on the Holy Trinity"), Christology (e.g., the Anglican–Oriental Orthodox "Agreed Statement on Christology"), pneumatology (e.g., the Reformed–Pentecostal "Word and Spirit, Church and World" report), soteriology (e.g., the Anglican–Catholic "Salvation and the Church" statement), and even eschatology (e.g., the Old Catholic–Eastern Orthodox text "Eschatology").[39]

Even if a particular dialogue may not treat all the loci, the dialogues are interdependent inasmuch as they represent convergences toward greater unity in faith and order within the one, holy, catholic, and apostolic church. Collectively they represent the effort of the whole church to articulate its faith comprehensively across its divisions. Furthermore, the theology done in the dialogues is comprehensive in its attention to the churches' sources of authority in Scripture and tradition, for the dialogues require a joint reading of the Bible and a mutual exploration of the resources of their respective and shared traditions. Considered together, the dialogue reports collected in the *Growth in Agreement* volumes published under the auspices of the World Council of Churches (as well as those published elsewhere and not yet included in that series) offer the

---

Gospel and the Church ('Malta Report')" (1972), §§14–34, in *Growth in Agreement*, 172–76 (168–89); World Methodist Council and Catholic Church, "Denver Report" (1971), §§99–118, in *Growth in Agreement*, 330–36 (308–39); Anglican Communion and Baptist World Alliance, "Conversations around the World: International Conversations between the Anglican Communion and the Baptist World Alliance, 2000–2005," §§18–25, in *Growth in Agreement III: International Dialogue Texts and Agreed Statements, 1998–2005*, ed. Jeffrey Gros, Thomas F. Best, and Lorelei F. Fuchs (Faith and Order Paper no. 204; Geneva: WCC Publications/Grand Rapids: William B. Eerdmans, 2007), 333–37 (319–74); Baptist World Alliance and Catholic Church, "The Word of God in the Life of the Church: A Report of International Conversations between the Catholic Church and the Baptist World Alliance 2006–2010," §§34–71, in *American Baptist Quarterly* 31, no. 1 (Spring 2012): 48–61 (28–122).

[39] World Alliance of Reformed Churches and Orthodox Churches, "Agreed Statement on the Holy Trinity" (1992), in *Growth in Agreement II: Reports and Agreed Statements of Ecumenical Conversations on a World Level, 1982–1998*, ed. Jeffrey Gros, Harding Meyer, and William G. Rusch (Faith and Order Paper no. 187; Geneva: WCC Publications/Grand Rapids: William B. Eerdmans, 2000), 280–84; Anglican Communion and Oriental Orthodox Churches, "Agreed Statement on Christology" (2002), in *Growth in Agreement III*, 35–38; World Alliance of Reformed Churches and Classical Pentecostals, "Word and Spirit, Church and World: International Pentecostal–Reformed Dialogue, 1996–2000," in *Growth in Agreement III*, 477–97; Anglican Communion and Catholic Church, "Salvation and the Church" (1986), in *Growth in Agreement II*, 315–25; Old Catholic Church and Eastern Orthodox Churches, "Eschatology" (1987), in *Growth in Agreement II*, 264–66.

theologian the opportunity to hear comprehensively the confession of the whole church, a possibility to which this chapter will return.

The Systematic Coherence of Ecumenical Theology

As a distinctive type of systematic theology, ecumenical theology possesses a methodological coherence that derives from being rooted in concrete ecclesial communities of reference, each of which has a living tradition that is a "historically extended, socially embodied argument . . . about the goods which constitute [the] tradition" (MacIntyre). Through their dialogue these living ecclesial traditions are able to bring their continuities of conflict into constructive encounter with one another. Thus the dialogue itself becomes a concrete instantiation of the living tradition of the church in its historically extended, socially embodied contestation of its tradition. The dialogues also manifest a more conscious methodological consistency in their approach to their theological work: discernment of matters of fundamental consensus and differentiated consensus, identification of issues of disagreement that merit ongoing dialogue, and recommendation of ways in which the two communions might embody in their current relations the steps toward visible unity that have already been achieved in the dialogue. Some of the resulting bilateral convergences do not yet seem fully consistent with one another, but they nevertheless have underlying pneumatic-ecclesiological theological connections. For the members of the delegations belong to the one body of Christ and share one Spirit, the same Spirit who guided the church in the formation and recognition of its Scriptures and who is the source of "the unity of the Spirit" (Eph 4:4) that is the goal of ecumenical encounter. The joint reports and agreed statements should therefore be read as interdependent doctrinal constructions, even if they have not been conceived in conscious dependence on the results of all previous and current interconfessional dialogues.

Systematic Construction in and on the Basis of Ecumenical Theology

Since the interconfessional dialogues make possible a MacIntyrean contestation of the Christian tradition across its divisions, any convergences that emerge from this dialectical process will be inherently constructive theological proposals. These constructions have not heretofore existed, and they could not have come into existence apart from the constructive theological work of the joint commissions. The *Joint Declaration on the Doctrine of Justification* issued by the Lutheran World Federation and Catholic Church in 1999 and joined by the World Methodist Council in 2006, for example, is nothing less than a constructive soteriological proposal, fully comprehensive and coherent in its development, which will have to be taken into account by all future efforts at constructive soteriology.[40] The recent systematic theologies of Wolfhart Pannenberg and Robert Jenson are noteworthy for their reception of the texts of the Lutheran–Catholic dialogues that preceded the *Joint Declaration*, along with the reports of numerous other ecumenical dialogues, as constructive theological proposals in their own right.[41]

The engagement of interconfessional ecumenical theology in the projects of Pannenberg and Jenson suggests the possibility that a constructive systematic theology might draw upon the results of the dialogues in a much more thoroughgoing manner, as a particular way of implementing Barth's methodological principle of hearing the confession of the whole church en route to making one's own confession as a systematic theologian. Indeed, it is theoretically possible to write a comprehensive systematic theology that engages the agreed texts of the bilateral and multilateral dialogues as its principal dialogue partners for each of the systematic loci. But whether or not such a systematic theology sees publication, ecumenical theology can be incorporated more extensively into the teaching of systematic theology in support of the ecumenical formation of Baptist seminarians.

What Sort of Theologians the Divided Church Needs

The renewal of systematic theology through attention to its coinherent dogmatic and ecumenical expressions in the service of the divided church will not come about merely through the adoption of a new set of methodological commitments by those who write and teach theology. Such renewal requires theologians who have been deeply formed by the church, who actively participate in its local ministries, and who in their vocational self-understanding are *ecclesial* theologians whose function is to serve as *doctores ecclesiae*—teachers of the church as well as the academy, teachers of the church in its ecumenicity as well as its local and denominational expressions, teachers of laity as well as future clergy. The church has been hurt by theological teachers who pursue their careers as avenues of escape from engagement with the church in all its shortcomings. The church will be helped toward healing if we encourage students with promise for

---

[40] Lutheran World Federation and Catholic Church, *Joint Declaration on the Doctrine of Justification* (Grand Rapids: William B. Eerdmans, 2000); Geoffrey Wainwright, "World Methodist Council and the Joint Declaration on the Doctrine of Justification," *Pro Ecclesia* 16, no. 1 (Winter 2007): 7–13.

[41] Pannenberg, *Systematic Theology*; Robert W. Jenson, *Systematic Theology*, 2 vols. (New York: Oxford University Press, 1997–1999).

a ministry of theological education to live "in the ruins of the church" as ecclesial theologians, remaining in and devoting their lives to the service of the ecclesial communions of their nurture and calling, even if there is much that is undesirable about these ecclesial dwellings.[42]

When Baptist ministers are formed in this sort of theology by that sort of academic theologian, Baptists will be helped further along in their journey toward the ecumenical future. But distinctively Baptist theology has its own contributions to make to this pilgrim journey of the church catholic. Those contributions are the concern of the next chapter.

---

[42] This image is suggested by Russell R. Reno, *In the Ruins of the Church: Sustaining Faith in an Age of Diminished Christianity* (Grand Rapids: Brazos Press, 2002). I remain convinced of the appropriateness of the book's thesis and argument, even if Reno himself subsequently came to view it as just the kind of theory distancing one from ecclesial concreteness he had criticized in the book (idem, "Out of the Ruins," *First Things* 150 [February 2005]: 11–16).

9

The Theology of a Pilgrim Church

Whatever the ecumenical future will be will happen in God's own time and in God's own way, so it is something that ecumenists can neither predict nor plan. But if the prayer of the Johannine Jesus for the unity of his followers is any indication, it will be a unity the world can see. In John 17 Jesus prays that his followers may be one as he and the Father are one, "so that the world may believe" and "so that the world may know" that the Father has sent Jesus and loves the world (John 17:21-23). The emphasis is on visible unity, because if it is merely a spiritual unity that leaves the churches still visibly divided, it is not yet a unity the world can see.

What might it look like for the church to have a unity the world can see? At their 1961 assembly in New Delhi, the World Council of Churches approved a definition of the unity sought by the modern ecumenical movement that has stood the test of time as the clearest statement of the goal of the movement:

> We believe that the unity which is both God's will and his gift to his Church is being made visible as all in each place who are baptized into Jesus Christ and confess him as Lord and Savior are brought by the Holy Spirit into one fully-committed fellowship, holding the one apostolic faith, preaching the one Gospel, breaking the one bread, joining in common prayer, and having a corporate life reaching out in witness and service to all and who at the same time are united with the whole Christian fellowship in all places and all ages, in such wise that ministry

and members are accepted by all, and that all can act and speak together as occasion requires for the tasks to which God calls his people.[1]

According to the New Delhi definition, the church lacks a unity the world can see if (1) all churches do not recognize baptisms performed by other churches as expressions of the one baptism that belongs to the one body of Christ, (2) all Christians cannot celebrate the Eucharist together in one another's churches, (3) all churches cannot confess together the essence of the apostolic faith, (4) all churches do not accept the ministers and members of one another's churches as their own, (5) the churches cannot share the gospel and serve the needy and work to liberate the oppressed together, and (6) Christians cannot speak prophetic words to the world with a unified voice whenever God calls them to do so. Since the whole church does not currently fulfill any of these six criteria, the church falls short of a unity the world can see.

How might the particular traditions in their diverse distinctiveness move together toward the ecumenical future of the visible unity the church presently lacks? The conservation of the identity of any particular Christian tradition can become an end in itself, and whenever it does so the denominations perpetuate division. But as chapter 6 argued, cultivating a consciousness of denominational identity can serve as a means to the ecumenical end when it facilitates the exchange of ecclesial gifts among the divided churches. Until the day that all the particular traditions have fully received the gifts of the other traditions and by these gifts have been renewed toward the full catholicity that belongs to visible unity, there will need to be particular traditions for there to be gifts to be shared and received.

These gifts include the theological dimension of what is distinctive in denominational identity. Is there anything distinctive about theology in the Baptist tradition that constitutes some portion of the ecclesial gifts that the rest of the church might contemplate receiving from Baptists? Beyond the obvious systematic rubric of ecclesiology, the locus of so many of the theological roots of Christian division, is there a distinctively Baptist approach to doing theology that might enrich the whole church's efforts to think and confess the apostolic faith together? British Baptist theologian Stephen Holmes of the University of St. Andrews takes up that question in his recent book *Baptist Theology* and answers in the negative. At the end of

---

[1]   World Council of Churches, "Report of the Section on Unity," in *The New Delhi Report: The Third Assembly of the World Council of Churches, 1961* (New York: Association Press, 1962), 116 (116–35).

the chapter "Baptist Perspectives on Ecumenical Theology," he concludes: "On average, Baptists are perhaps a little more conservative and evangelical than other Protestant groups, but there is nothing distinctive in their theology other than their beliefs about the nature and role of the church, and its officers and sacraments."[2] Holmes' point is well taken. There is a sense in which there is no such thing as a Baptist doctrine of the Trinity or a Baptist Christology. Yet even with these core ecumenically shared doctrines, there is a distinctively Baptist way of approaching them that functions as one of the tradition's ecclesial gifts.

The Dialogical Discovery of Baptist Theological Gifts

The best place to look for a distinctive account of Baptist theological identity is not necessarily the confessions of faith produced in abundance during the four centuries of Baptist existence, though these confessions certainly had the function of testifying to the convictions Baptists shared in common with the orthodox Christian tradition as well as to the convictions that distinguished the Baptists from other communions. Nor is it necessarily the systematic theologies published by Baptist systematic theologians, though these likewise have served the purpose of relating Baptist doctrinal perspectives to the larger Christian theological tradition.

An underappreciated source of ordered expressions of a Christian communion's theological convictions is the ecumenical theology hammered out in bilateral and multilateral ecumenical dialogue. The previous chapter contended that these expressions of ecclesial theology constitute a specific form of systematic theology, systematic in its own right by virtue of its comprehensive, coherent, and constructive character. This understanding of the systematic nature of ecumenical theology applies to the theological convergences articulated by the reports issued by the bilateral ecumenical dialogues in which the Baptist World Alliance (BWA) has been involved. To date joint reports have been published from the dialogues between the BWA and the World Alliance of Reformed Churches (1973–1977), the Lutheran World Federation (1986–1989), the World Mennonite Conference (1989–1992), the Anglican Consultative Council (2000–2005), and the Catholic Church (1984–1988 and 2006–2010). Baptist participation in these instruments for dialogue yields a Baptist constructive theology that draws deeply from the Baptist theological tradition while creatively identifying openings for theological convergence with

---

[2]   Stephen R. Holmes, *Baptist Theology* (Doing Theology; London: T&T Clark International, 2012), 87.

other traditions that previously have been unnoticed or undeveloped. This holds true for all the major systematic loci from prolegomena and theology proper through eschatology, but it is especially matters of prolegomena that account for dialogical theological constructions that situate the Baptist vision ecumenically as one that is radically biblical, radically catholic, and relentlessly pilgrim.

There is a sense in which theological prolegomena is peripheral to the task of ecumenical theology. Ecumenical theology as a species of systematic theology is nonfoundational in that it does not seek to establish a theoretical framework within which theological differences may be negotiated. Individual theologians may and do propose theories of ecumenical convergence,[3] but actual ecumenical dialogues do not proceed on the basis of such theoretical foundations. Their starting point and basis is Christian faith and faithfulness itself in the form of the first-order convictions and practices of the concrete communities that enter into dialogue with each other. The second-order task of discerning commonalities and possibilities for convergence is a collaborative enterprise that necessarily transcends any theoretical or philosophical inclinations of the individual theologians involved.

Yet ecumenical theology cannot entirely dispense with theological prolegomena. While it does not appeal to an external philosophical or theoretical justification for its dogmatic claims, ecumenical theology necessarily engages the presuppositional question of authority often treated under the rubric of prolegomena. Many of the most intractable ecumenical difficulties are ultimately traceable to differing configurations of the authorizing sources of each tradition's convictions and practices. As noted in the previous chapter, most of the international bilateral dialogues over the past four decades therefore have given early and substantial attention to the authority question.

The tension between the biblicism typical of Baptists and the appeal of some of their dialogue partners to tradition and other sources of authority has stretched these joint commissions toward articulating some of the most richly nuanced ecumenical treatments of authority published to date. Baptists are routinely stereotyped as holding to a radicalized version of the *sola scriptura* hermeneutic of the Reformation that amounts to *nuda scriptura* (Scripture all by itself). Yet in the context of international ecumenical

---

[3]　E.g., Erin M. Brigham, "A Habermasian Approach to Ecumenical Ecclesiology," *Journal of Ecumenical Studies* 44, no. 4 (Fall 2009): 587–98, which draws on philosopher Jürgen Habermas' theory of "communicative action" as a framework that suggests a method for discerning a consensus among multiple seemingly divergent perspectives.

dialogue, Baptists have consistently affirmed what individual Baptist theologians have increasingly insisted is a more faithful account of what Baptists actually do whenever they turn to the Bible for guidance in bringing their convictions and practices under the lordship of Christ. For Baptists and other Christians, the Bible functions in a pattern of authority in which Christ as the revelation of the Triune God is the ultimate source of authority, Scripture is the supreme earthly source of authority that discloses the ultimate authority of Christ for Christian faith and faithfulness, and the traditioned teaching of the church in its diachronic continuity along with the mind and experience of the church in its synchronic solidarity are indispensable guides for discerning Christ's lordship through the practice of reading Scripture. In other words, as the report of the conversations between the BWA and the Anglican Consultative Council puts it, "it would be more accurate to regard the Baptist view of Scripture as *suprema scriptura* rather than *sola scriptura*,"[4] a conclusion echoed in the report of the most recent series of conversations with the Catholic Church.[5]

One might expect to encounter less explicit distancing of Baptist theology from an unqualified adherence to *sola scriptura* in the dialogue with the close Free Church kindred of Baptists in the Mennonite World Conference. Indeed, the section "Baptist Perspectives on Authority" in the report of those conversations includes this statement: "Baptists therefore have no difficulty in embracing the Reformation dictum of *sola scriptura*: in contrast to many Reformation churches, Baptists do not accord any official authority to creeds."[6] In light of two related statements in the same section, however, this seeming reiteration of the stereotype in fact points in the direction of a thick ecclesial embodiment of a *suprema scriptura* pattern of authority. First, immediately prior to the affirmation of *sola scriptura* is an acknowledgment that "Scripture is also an important source of authority for Baptists" (note the indefinite article). It is important because

---

[4] Anglican Consultative Council and Baptist World Alliance, *Conversations around the World 2000–2005: The Report of the International Conversations between the Anglican Communion and the Baptist World Alliance* (London: Anglican Communion Office, 2005), §26 (pp. 37 and 108, n. 46).

[5] Baptist World Alliance and Catholic Church, "The Word of God in the Life of the Church: A Report of International Conversations between the Catholic Church and the Baptist World Alliance 2006–2010," §62, in *American Baptist Quarterly* 31, no. 1 (Spring 2012): 58 and 117, n. 57 (28–122).

[6] Baptist World Alliance and Mennonite World Conference, "Theological Conversations, 1989–1992," in *Growth in Agreement III: International Dialogue Texts and Agreed Statements, 1998–2005*, ed. Jeffrey Gros, Thomas F. Best, and Lorelei F. Fuchs (Faith and Order Paper no. 204; Geneva: WCC Publications/Grand Rapids: William B. Eerdmans, 2007), 434 (426–48).

of its relationship to the ultimate source of authority: "Thoroughly trinitarian, Baptists affirm in all matters of faith and practice the Lordship of Christ," which is "revealed in Scripture and present in the church."[7] Second, the presence of Christ in the church means that there is an ecclesial embodiment of authority beyond the text of Scripture. Two paragraphs after the affirmation of *sola scriptura* is the insistence on the part of the Baptist delegation that an "emphasis among Baptists is the church's role as a vehicle of authority."[8] This description of how ecclesial authority functions for Baptists then follows:

> Among Baptists, the mind of Christ is sought through prayerful submission of the individual to the community which seeks the will of the Spirit through scripture. The commanding impulse is personal but never private. Liberty of conscience, a vital plan in Baptist doctrine, is never meant to imply privatized religion. . . . Liberty of conscience is sometimes misconstrued as freedom from the church rather than freedom in the church.[9]

That specifically Baptist perspective on authority is subsequently reaffirmed as something Baptists were able to affirm together with Mennonites: a summary of convergences on authority includes "'the gathered congregation' as [the] primary locus of discernment and decision-making."[10]

Baptists have been able to join the World Alliance of Reformed Churches in naming "Holy Scripture as the normative source for faith and practice"—not the sole source, but the normative source that norms any other source that may play a role in norming faith and practice.[11] The report from the dialogue with the Lutheran World Federation similarly situates

[7]   Baptist World Alliance and Mennonite World Conference, "Theological Conversations," 433.

[8]   Baptist World Alliance and Mennonite World Conference, "Theological Conversations," 434.

[9]   Baptist World Alliance and Mennonite World Conference, "Theological Conversations," 434.

[10]   Baptist World Alliance and Mennonite World Conference, "Theological Conversations," 435.

[11]   Baptist World Alliance and World Alliance of Reformed Churches, "Report of Theological Conversations Sponsored by the World Alliance of Reformed Churches and the Baptist World Alliance, 1977," §2, in *Growth in Agreement: Reports and Agreed Statements of Ecumenical Conversations on a World Level*, ed. Harding Meyer and Lukas Vischer (Faith and Order Paper no. 108; New York: Paulist Press/Geneva: World Council of Churches, 1984), 135–36 (132–51). Additional documentation for this dialogue appears in Baptist World Alliance and World Alliance of Reformed Churches, *Baptists and Reformed in Dialogue: Documents from the Conversations Sponsored by the World Alliance of Reformed*

Scripture within a pattern of authority in which "Authority for preaching and teaching . . . resides ultimately in God who has revealed himself in Jesus Christ, and who is present with us in the saving and liberating power of the Spirit."[12] In this report Baptists join Lutherans in affirming *sola scriptura*, but the Baptist–Lutheran joint commission heavily qualifies the concept in two significant ways. First, it makes the connection between Scripture and revelation dynamic and participatory rather than static and absolute: "Authority is necessarily linked to the Bible"—not exclusively located in the Bible—"because the biblical testimonies witness to God's saving and liberating activity in the history of humanity."[13] Second, the report clearly defines the relationship between Scripture and tradition as one of coinherence. Scripture and tradition are inseparable, for, in the words of the report, "The scriptures belong to the Tradition of the Christian church."[14] Interestingly and perhaps significantly, "Tradition" in the singular is capitalized throughout the report, while the plural "traditions" is lowercase. This usage likely reflects the influence of the 1963 World Council of Churches Faith and Order paper on *Tradition and traditions*.[15] In continuity with that multilateral study text, the Baptist–Lutheran report simultaneously grants that the biblical documents and the canon to which they belong are the products of tradition even while they norm the tradition: "Within that Tradition the scriptures function to protect the gospel of Jesus as the Christ against influences foreign to the gospel and to the Bible."[16] Thus, on the one hand, the report insists, "We owe much to Tra-

---

Churches and the Baptist World Alliance, ed. Larry Miller (Studies from the World Alliance of Reformed Churches, no. 4; Geneva: World Alliance of Reformed Churches, 1983).

[12] Baptist World Alliance and Lutheran World Federation, "A Message to Our Churches," §1, in *Growth in Agreement II: Reports and Agreed Statements of Ecumenical Conversations on a World Level, 1982–1998*, ed. Jeffrey Gros, Harding Meyer, and William G. Rusch (Faith and Order Paper no. 187; Geneva: WCC Publications/Grand Rapids: William B. Eerdmans, 2000), 156 (155–75).

[13] Baptist World Alliance and Lutheran World Federation, "A Message to Our Churches," §2 (p. 156).

[14] Baptist World Alliance and Lutheran World Federation, "A Message to Our Churches," §3 (p. 156).

[15] World Council of Churches, *Report of the Theological Commission on Tradition and traditions* (Faith and Order Paper no. 40; Geneva: World Council of Churches, 1963). Cf. Yves Congar, *La Tradition et les traditions*, 2 vols. (Paris: Arthème Fayard, 1960–1963); ET, *Tradition and Traditions: An Historical and a Theological Essay*, trans. Michael Naseby and Thomas Rainborough (London: Burns & Oates, 1966). The same distinction between uppercase-"T" Tradition and lowercase-"t" traditions is also made in Baptist World Alliance and Catholic Church, "The Word of God in the Life of the Church," §59.

[16] Baptist World Alliance and Lutheran World Federation, "A Message to Our Churches," §3 (p. 156). The following section (§4) is also significant in this connection:

dition [uppercase] and therefore do not want to deprecate it."[17] But on the other hand, it continues:

> We recognize, however, that not all traditions are in harmony with the ground and content of our faith, Jesus Christ. . . . Sola scriptura is not directed against Tradition as such, but against a tradition that departs from the biblical witness to Jesus Christ, or attempts to identify the living reality of the gospel with dogmatic formulations.[18]

In the course of a first series of conversations between the Baptist World Alliance and the Catholic Church in the 1980s, Baptists and Catholics were able to affirm together a *suprema scriptura* pattern of authority: "the scriptures are our primary source for the revelation of God in Jesus."[19] Yet the report from those conversations sharply differentiated the Baptist perspective—in which, vis-à-vis councils and creeds as expressions of tradition, the "scriptures alone" are normative—from the Catholic articulation of the coinherence of Scripture and tradition in the Vatican II Dogmatic Constitution on Revelation *Dei Verbum*.[20] In a concluding section on "areas needing continued exploration," however, the Baptist–Catholic joint commission agreed that their "differences [on the relation of Scripture and tradition] are not as sharp as this formulation would suggest," for in the nuanced formulation of *Dei Verbum* the roles of Scripture and tradition in presenting the truth of Jesus Christ are not identical, while

---

"In the development of the biblical canon (the determination of which writings are included in the holy scriptures) the church sees the work of God's Spirit. By recognizing the canon, the church confesses that the scriptures, i.e. the biblical part of Tradition, are the measure of the rest of Tradition. The scriptures alone can ascertain that the Tradition remains true to the gospel. They alone can assure that the tradition continues to tell the story of Jesus as Redeemer and Liberator. This is the meaning of the Reformation emphasis on sola scriptura which both Lutherans and Baptists affirm. This formula is open for misunderstanding, however, and therefore calls for interpretation" (156).

[17] Baptist World Alliance and Lutheran World Federation, "A Message to Our Churches," §5 (p. 157).

[18] Baptist World Alliance and Lutheran World Federation, "A Message to Our Churches," §6 (p. 157).

[19] Baptist World Alliance and Catholic Church, "Summons to Witness to Christ in Today's World: A Report on Conversations 1984–1988," §12, in *Growth in Agreement II*, 376 (373–85).

[20] Baptist World Alliance and Catholic Church, "Summons to Witness to Christ in Today's World: A Report on Conversations 1984–1988," §§45–46 (p. 382); cf. Vatican II, *Dogmatic Constitution on Divine Revelation (Dei Verbum)*, §9, November 18, 1965, trans. Robert Murray, in *Decrees of the Ecumenical Councils*, ed. Norman P. Tanner, vol. 2, *Trent to Vatican II* (London: Sheed & Ward/Washington, D.C.: Georgetown University Press, 1990), 974–75.

"on the other hand, Baptists invoke the Baptist heritage as decisively as Roman Catholics cite Tradition, usually disclaiming that it bears the same authority as scripture but holding on to it vigorously nonetheless."[21]

When Baptists and Catholics reengaged the relation of Scripture and tradition in a second series of conversations concluded in December 2010, the new joint commission was able to articulate convergences on Scripture, tradition, and authority that, while maintaining deep continuity with the Baptist theological tradition, are creatively nuanced in such a manner that they constitute theological constructions rather than descriptions. The report introduces these convergences with this statement:

> When the Catholic and Baptist delegations met eighteen years later for a new series of conversations, participants were able to identify a deepened and striking convergence on the nature of Scripture as the inspired Word of God and its central place in the life of the church, along with a mutual welcome for two developments that surfaced during this new phase of dialogue: a more appreciative assessment of the value of tradition and its relation to Scripture by the *Baptist* participants and a more critical approach to tradition in its relation to Scripture by the *Catholic* participants.[22]

The report intentionally takes up the paradigm of "differentiated consensus" exemplified by the 1999 Lutheran–Catholic *Joint Declaration on the Doctrine of Justification*.[23] As applied to the relationship of Scripture and tradition, this yields a consensus that includes the centrality of the Scriptures to the life of the church, the primarily liturgical location of the normativity of Scripture, the divine authorship of Scripture, the traditioned nature of the biblical documents and the canon to which they belong and thus the coinherence of Scripture and tradition, the distinction between Scripture as the word of God and tradition as that which hands on the word of God, the Christocentricity of the whole Bible as a coherent story that requires a Christocentric interpretation, the affirmation of the individual reading of Scripture coupled with the insistence that this reading should not be isolated from the ecclesial interpretive community, and the conviction that the proper reading of Scripture should be connected with

---

[21] Baptist World Alliance and Catholic Church, "Summons to Witness to Christ in Today's World: A Report on Conversations 1984–1988," §§45–46 (p. 382).

[22] Baptist World Alliance and Catholic Church, "The Word of God in the Life of the Church," §34.

[23] Lutheran World Federation and Catholic Church, *Joint Declaration on the Doctrine of Justification* (Grand Rapids: William B. Eerdmans, 2000).

the proper behavior of those who read it.[24] This consensus on authority is differentiated, however, by a stronger Baptist emphasis on the Scriptures as the normative root of the tradition—in other words, a radical biblicism that is relentlessly pilgrim in its aversion to overly realized eschatologies of the church and of the doctrines that the church teaches on the basis of the word of God.

Beyond the construction of a pattern of authority that has a place not only for Scripture but also for the tradition to which Scripture belongs and the resources of the community in which Scripture and tradition authorize Christian faith and faithfulness, in these dialogues Baptists have also been able to join their dialogue partners in articulating the broad contours of the shape of the normative tradition in the form of the shared doctrinal heritage of the church. The Baptist portion of the section on authority in the dialogue with the Mennonites insists that Baptists are "thoroughly trinitarian."[25] At every stage in the dialogue with the Anglican Communion that included separate regionalized meetings in England, Myanmar, Kenya, Chile, the Bahamas, and Nova Scotia, these diverse segments of the global Baptist community insisted that while Baptists may be distinctive ecclesiologically, they confess the doctrines of the apostolic faith together with Anglicans and other Christians. The report then names several notable exceptions to the typical description of Baptists as noncreedal: the General Baptist *Orthodox Creed* of 1679 that affirms the Apostles' Creed, Nicene Creed, and Athanasian Creed and urges that they be believed, received, and taught in Baptist churches; the twentieth-century German-language confession used by Baptists in Germany, Austria, and Switzerland that begins with an affirmation of the Apostles' Creed as the common confession of Christians; the confession of Norwegian Baptists that affirms the content of the Apostles' Creed and the Nicene Creed; a covenant service produced by the Baptist Union of Great Britain in 2001 that includes the Apostles' Creed and Nicene Creed as texts for the liturgical confession of the apostolic faith; and the recitation of the Apostles' Creed by participants in the inaugural Baptist World Congress in 1905.[26]

While Baptists are able to confess the shared doctrinal heritage of the church as having normative status within the tradition, they are also

---

[24] Baptist World Alliance and Catholic Church, "The Word of God in the Life of the Church," §§35, 37, 41, 46, 48, 53, 56, 58.

[25] Baptist World Alliance and Mennonite World Conference, "Theological Conversations," 433.

[26] Anglican Consultative Council and Baptist World Alliance, *Conversations around the World 2000–2005*, §21 (pp. 33–34).

careful to guard against substituting the condensed narratives that are the church's traditional doctrines for the normativity of the entirety of Scripture in its rich narrative fullness. This distinction between Scripture and the doctrines that summarize Scripture is also a matter of consensus between Baptists and Catholics, though a differentiated one. The report from the recently completed second series of conversations with the Vatican expresses the differentiated consensus in this way:

> While Catholics often profess their common faith by means of creeds, especially the Apostles' Creed and the Nicene-Constantinopolitan Creed, this is not a frequent practice among Baptists. Both Catholics and Baptists understand the words of the Creeds as short expressions of the truth expressed in the Scriptures, but neither would put them on the same level as the Scriptures. Because of their connection to the official teaching office, however, creeds enjoy a normative authority for Catholics. For their part, Baptists affirm the contents of the creeds, and have explicitly commended them in some of their confessions of faith as reliable witnesses. . . . Baptists do not generally regard creeds as binding in the same way as Catholics do; however, both believe that the authority of creeds depends on their ability to reflect Scripture.[27]

Inasmuch as the attention to patterns of theological authority in all of these dialogues leads Baptists to identify the shared doctrinal heritage they are able to confess with other Christians even while articulating the Baptist resistance to reducing the faith to doctrinal formulations, these dialogical constructions of Baptist ecumenical theology fall under the rubric of theological prolegomena, not only in the presuppositional sense but also in the sense in which Karl Barth did an unapologetic approach to prolegomena—it is a theology in advance, articulated in summary at the beginning. In this case it is a theology in advance that affirms the content of the ancient rule of faith in common with the rest of the church, even while it refuses to be content with any reduction of the faith to creedal formulations that can diminish the richness of Scripture or make the church too content with the status quo of its second-order accounts of its first-order convictions and practices. The Baptist constructive theology that emerges from the dialogues may therefore be characterized as both radically biblical and radically catholic and yet relentlessly pilgrim. In this construction of Baptist theological identity, Baptists are radically biblicisitic Reformers

---

[27] Baptist World Alliance and Catholic Church, "The Word of God in the Life of the Church," §188.

who insist that when the gathered community turns to the Scriptures for the guidance of the Spirit in bringing its life together more fully under the rule of Christ, the church encounters the powerful means by which it is always being reformed. Baptists are also radical catholics in that this turn to the canon of Scripture leads them to affirm the rule of catholic faith that is both drawn from Scripture and norms its canonical contents but that also serves to critique subsequent developments in the tradition that they may regard as distortions of or departures from this radical catholicity. Baptists are also shown to be a relentlessly pilgrim community whose vision of what it means for a community to come fully under the rule of Christ is thoroughly eschatological: the source of its ecclesial vision is not any particular past or present instantiation of the church but its future goal, a future that it seeks to embody ever more fully in the present. The same Baptist vision is discernible well beyond the dialogues' expected engagement with ecclesiological issues. When Baptists are able to say something together with other communions about trinitarian theology and Christology, for example, they do so with a Baptist accent, marked by the cadences and inflections of the radically biblical, radically catholic, and relentlessly pilgrim Baptist vision.

The Discovery of a Pilgrim Church Theology

In dialogue with the whole church, the Baptist communion discovers that it has a pilgrim church theology—a theology from and for a church on pilgrimage, a community striving to bring its life together ever more fully under the rule of Christ, renewing itself by fresh reappropriations of the normative biblical and catholic roots of Christian faith and faithfulness. While there have been many Baptist failures to embody the ideals of this vision, a pilgrim church theological orientation is one of the gifts this tradition has to offer the whole church. A consciousness of being a church on pilgrimage may even be a necessary precondition for engaging in receptive ecumenism. Unless all churches are willing to acknowledge the possibility that they currently lack something they need to be more fully catholic, more fully under the rule of Christ, they will not be receptive to the gifts currently found elsewhere in the body of Christ. Without pilgrim openness to receiving what they need for renewal from one another, the divided churches cannot make further progress in their shared pilgrimage toward the ecumenical future.

Baptist churches at their best are relentlessly pilgrim communities that resist all overly realized eschatologies of the church. Their ecclesial ideal is the church that is fully under the rule of Christ, which they locate somewhere ahead of them rather than in any past or present instantiation of the church. Baptists are relentlessly dissatisfied with the present state of the church in their pilgrim journey toward the community that will be fully under the reign of Christ. As Mennonite John Howard Yoder observed about the broader tradition to which Baptists belong, "the Free Church position is intrinsically unfinished."[28]

That opens up the possibility that Baptist and Free Church communities that take seriously their pilgrim identity may find the church that is under the rule of Christ somewhere beyond what is traditionally understood to be a Baptist or Free Church identity. That possibility was realized by some of the earliest leaders of the Baptist movement. John Smyth was the founder of the very first Baptist congregation of historical record in Amsterdam in 1609. Earlier in Smyth's journey he had been an Anglican priest, became persuaded by Puritan perspectives, then concluded that congregational polity was scriptural and became a Separatist. In 1609 Smyth and a group of fellow Separatists left England for the Netherlands with the intent of forming a pure church by covenanting with God and one another to bring their life together under the rule of Christ according to what they understood to be the apostolic pattern of faith and practice. By 1609 Smyth had not only rejected his baptism in the Church of England as a false baptism; having concluded that no communion in Amsterdam was qualified as a true church to administer a true baptism, not even the believer-baptizing Mennonites, Smyth proceeded to baptize himself and the other members of his congregation. Smyth came to regret this action, however, when he later concluded that the Mennonites were indeed a true church after all and then sought to lead his congregation to be received into the Mennonite fellowship—which occasioned the first Baptist church split. Thomas Helwys and a number of other congregants refused to repudiate their baptisms by Smyth, and in 1611 they returned to England to form the first Baptist church established on British soil. Meanwhile, Smyth and the remaining larger portion of the congregation had proceeded to seek union with the Mennonite community. Smyth died of tuberculosis in 1612 while his congregation awaited a final judgment regarding their application to the Mennonites for membership, meeting in the meantime in a bakery owned by one of the members of the Mennonite fellowship. Finally, in January 1615, Smyth's group was admitted to membership without being rebaptized, and today John Smyth is identified

---

[28] John Howard Yoder, "Karl Barth: How His Mind Kept Changing," in *How Karl Barth Changed My Mind*, ed. Donald K. McKim (Grand Rapids: William B. Eerdmans, 1986), 171 (166–71).

as an elder of the Mennonite congregation in a listing of congregational leaders in the entryway of the Singel Mennonite Church in Amsterdam, even though his membership was unresolved at the time of his death.[29]

Roger Williams, founder of the first Baptist church in America, in Providence in what became Rhode Island, has a similar story (though perhaps a more disappointing one from an ecclesiological standpoint). Like John Smyth, Williams was ordained as a priest of the Church of England but became a convinced Puritan during his studies at Cambridge. Despairing of the possibility of further reform of the Church of England under archbishop of Canterbury William Laud, Williams sailed with his wife to join the Puritan settlement in Boston. After his arrival he was offered and refused a position as "teaching minister" in the Puritan church there, finding it insufficiently separated from the Church of England. Williams had similar perspectives on the churches in Salem and Plymouth, where he lived and worked for a time, and ultimately was banished from Massachusetts by its General Court. Williams settled in Providence, where he met for church services in his home with a group of Separatists and eventually concluded that infant baptism was unscriptural. Sometime in 1638 Williams received believer's baptism from another member of his house church, returned the favor, and baptized around ten others, thus constituting what continues to be known as the First Baptist Church in America. But Williams remained a Baptist for only a few months longer. He became convinced that there were no true churches left on earth and no true ministers qualified to lead them. Williams withdrew from the Baptist congregation he founded and refrained from affiliating with any other church for the rest of his life, devoting himself instead to prayer for Christ to send new apostles to restore the church.[30] Even though John

---

[29]   Abe Dueck, "Baptists and Mennonites Meet in Amsterdam," *Mennonite Historian* 18, no. 3 (September 1992), accessed December 3, 2014, http://www.mennonitechurch .ca/programs/archives/mennonitehistorian/mhsep92.htm#7. For a critical examination of the historical sources for this emergence of the Baptists and the relationship of the Smyth congregation to the Mennonites, see James Robert Coggins, *John Smyth's Congregation: English Separatism, Mennonite Influence, and the Elect Nation* (Studies in Anabaptist and Mennonite History, no. 32; Waterloo, Ont.: Herald Press, 1991), 61–65. Smyth set forth the theological rationale for his rejection of the baptisms of other churches as "anti-Christian" in his 1609 treatise *The Character of the Beast or the False Constitution of the Church* (printed in *The Works of John Smyth, Fellow of Christ's College, 1594–8*, 2 vols., ed. William Thomas Whitley [Cambridge: Cambridge University Press, 1915], 2:563–680).

[30]   For recent treatments of Williams' life and thought, see John M. Barry, *Roger Williams and the Creation of the American Soul: Church, State, and the Birth of Liberty* (New York: Viking, 2012); Edwin S. Gaustad, *Roger Williams* (Lives and Legacies; New York: Oxford University Press, 2005); idem, *Liberty of Conscience: Roger Williams in America* (Grand

Smyth and Roger Williams in differing ways ended their earthly lives on the periphery of the Baptist churches they helped establish, there was something quintessentially Baptist about the pilgrim journeys of Smyth among the English expatriates in the Netherlands and Williams in colonial America that led them to the conclusion that the church they sought was somewhere beyond the confines of their existing Baptist communities.

This pilgrim church vision, however, is by no means limited to Baptists. The earliest monastic communities blossomed in the fourth century as persecution ceased and Christianity became assimilated into the institutions of Greco-Roman society, leading many Christians to long for more radically committed patterns of Christian living. In the monastic communities they sought to bring their life together ever more fully under the rule of Christ as pilgrim communities. The same can be said about the later religious orders. In the *City of God* Augustine characterized the earthly sojourn of the heavenly city as a "society of pilgrims."[31] Avery Cardinal Dulles observed that Augustine's pilgrim characterization of the earthly church was representative of patristic as well as medieval thought in its distinction between an imperfect earthly church and a perfected heavenly church toward which the church journeys as a pilgrim community.[32] Thus, when Martin Luther among the Magisterial Reformers advocated a form of ecclesial community that would embrace a pilgrim vision of the church as its organizing principle, he had precedent in the tradition. Though it was never actually realized in practice, Martin Luther envisioned in his preface to the 1526 "German Mass and Order of Service" a community in which "those who want to be Christians in earnest and who profess the gospel with hand and mouth should sign their names and meet alone to pray, to read, to baptize, to receive the sacrament, and to do

---

Rapids: William B. Eerdmans, 1991); James P. Byrd, *The Challenges of Roger Williams: Religious Liberty, Violent Persecution, and the Bible* (Macon, Ga.: Mercer University Press, 2002). For a Baptist critique of certain Baptist perspectives on Williams and his relation to the American experiment in religious liberty (which would apply to aspects of Barry's treatment of Williams as well), see Curtis W. Freeman, "Roger Williams, American Democracy, and the Baptists," *Perspectives in Religious Studies* 34, no. 3 (Fall 2007): 267–86.

[31] Augustine of Hippo, *De Civitate Dei* 19.17 (*Saint Augustine: The City of God against the Pagans*, trans. William Chase Greene [Loeb Classical Library, no. 416; Cambridge, Mass.: Harvard University Press, 1960], vol. 6, 196). The translation of "*perigrinam . . . societatem*" as "society of pilgrims" is from Marcus Dods' translation of *City of God* in *Nicene and Post-Nicene Fathers: First Series*, ed. Philip Schaff (New York: Christian Literature, 1887), vol. 2, 412 (1–511).

[32] Avery Dulles, *Models of the Church*, expanded ed. (New York: Doubleday, 1987), 104–5 and 111. Significantly, Dulles treats patristic, medieval, and modern variants of the pilgrim church vision in the chapter "The Church and Eschatology" (103–22).

other Christian works" and "those who do not lead Christian lives could be known, reproved, corrected, cast out, or excommunicated according to the rule of Christ."[33]

To the degree that Donald Durnbaugh's "Believers' Church" designation can be associated with a pilgrim church vision, the pilgrim church identity is also embodied by the communities Durnbaugh treats in his 1968 book *The Believers' Church: The History and Character of Radical Protestantism*: among medieval sectarians, the Waldensians and Unity of Brethren (and their Moravian descendants); among the Anabaptist Radical Reformers, the Swiss and Hutterite Brethren; the Separatist Puritans, of which Durnbaugh treats the Baptists and Quakers as representative; the Church of the Brethren and Methodists as Free Church Pietists; the Disciples of Christ and the Plymouth Brethren, communities Durnbaugh designates as New Testament Restorationists; the Confessing Church under the Nazi regime in Germany; and as examples of then-contemporary "new forms of the church," the Church of the Saviour in Washington, D.C., the East Harlem Protestant Parish, and what journalists in the late 1960s were calling "underground churches" that carried forward certain trajectories from Vatican II in forming Catholic communities not officially recognized as such.[34] To Durnbaugh's examples could be added some more recent ones: the basic communities associated with the Latin American liberation theology movement, nondenominational churches, independent Pentecostal or charismatic congregations, and now the communities associated with the emergent or emerging church movement, as well as the intentional communities founded in connection with the "new monasticism."

The pilgrim church identity also belongs to the Catholic Church. The Vatican II Dogmatic Constitution on the Church *Lumen Gentium* describes the earthly journey of the people of God in eschatological terms. In a chapter titled "The Eschatological Nature of the Pilgrim Church and Her Union with the Heavenly Church," *Lumen Gentium* insists that the church "will receive its perfection only in the glory of heaven, when will come the time of the renewal of all things."[35] Because the pilgrim church is the body of Christ, it participates now in the final restoration of

---

[33]   Martin Luther, "German Mass and Order of Service," in *Luther's Works*, ed. Jaroslav Pelikan, vol. 53, *Hymns and Liturgy* (Philadelphia: Fortress Press, 1965), 63–64 (61–90).

[34]   Donald F. Durnbaugh, *The Believers' Church: The History and Character of Radical Protestantism* (New York: Macmillan, 1968).

[35]   Vatican II, *Dogmatic Constitution on the Church (Lumen Gentium)*, §48, November 21, 1964, in *Vatican Council II: The Conciliar and Post Conciliar Documents*, rev. ed., ed. Austin Flannery (Vatican Collection, vol. 1; Northport, N.Y.: Costello, 1992), 407.

all things in Christ and thus "is endowed already with a sanctity that is real though imperfect"[36] (language which, it is worth noting, is similar to the Decree on Ecumenism's affirmation of a "certain, though imperfect, communion" that non-Catholic baptized Christian believers have with the Catholic Church[37]). Yet "until there be realized new heavens and a new earth in which justice dwells . . . the pilgrim church, in its sacraments and institutions, which belong to this present age, carries the mark of this world which will pass, and she herself takes her place among the creatures which groan and travail yet and await the revelation of the children of God."[38] *Lumen Gentium* invokes the pilgrim image explicitly six times in the document. One instance is especially germane to the constructive proposals that are developed later in this chapter: "On earth, still as pilgrims in a strange land, following in trial and in oppression the paths [Christ] trod, we are associated with his sufferings as the body with its head, suffering with him, that with him we may be glorified."[39] Pontifex Emeritus Benedict XVI echoed this pilgrim church language in his final general audience on February 27, 2013, when he referred to the difficulties of "the Church's pilgrim way" in the world.[40] If Yves Cardinal Congar was on target, Yoder's contention that "the Free Church position is intrinsically unfinished" is true also of the Catholic Church, for in his essay "Moving towards a Pilgrim Church," reflecting on the ecclesiological developments of Vatican II, Congar wrote: "This reborn Church is not the only form that a Pilgrim Church can take. . . . That pilgrim way has been open in principle since the Son of God became man and sent us, from the Father, the Spirit who makes us proclaim God's glory in every human language."[41]

The pilgrim church identity also belongs to the modern ecumenical movement and all churches that participate in it. The concept is clearly expressed in reports and documents issued in connection with assemblies of the World Council of Churches that preceded and followed the Second

---

[36] Vatican II, *Lumen Gentium*, §48, in *Vatican Council II*, ed. Flannery, 408.

[37] Vatican II, *Decree on Ecumenism (Unitatis Redintegratio)*, §3, November 21, 1964, in *Vatican Council II*, ed. Flannery, 456.

[38] Vatican II, *Lumen Gentium*, §48, in *Vatican Council II*, ed. Flannery, 408.

[39] Vatican II, *Lumen Gentium*, §7, in *Vatican Council II*, ed. Flannery, 356.

[40] Benedict XVI, "Final General Audience," February 27, 2013, accessed December 3, 2014, http://www.news.va/en/news/pope-final-general-audience-full-text.

[41] Yves Congar, "Moving towards a Pilgrim Church," trans. David Smith, in *Vatican II Revisited: By Those Who Were There*, ed. Alberic Stacpoole (Minneapolis: Winston Press, 1986), 148 (129–52). These developments were also treated at length by Catholic ecumenist George H. Tavard in his book *The Pilgrim Church* (New York: Herder & Herder, 1967).

Vatican Council—Evanston in 1954 and New Delhi in 1961, as well as Uppsala in 1968. The New Delhi assembly issued a Report on Witness that urged "a reappraisal of the patterns of church organization and institutions inherited by the younger churches" so that "outdated forms . . . may be replaced by strong and relevant ways of evangelism." It offered this as an example of "How the Church may become the Pilgrim Church, which goes forth boldly as Abraham did into the unknown future, not afraid to leave behind the securities of its conventional structure, glad to dwell in the tent of perpetual adaptation, looking to the city whose builder and maker is God." The New Delhi assembly also proposed a vision of the ecumenical future toward which the pilgrim church journeys in its definition of the unity sought by the modern ecumenical movement quoted earlier in this chapter.[42]

The ecumenical movement that embraces this vision knows painfully well that there can be no realized eschatology of the ecumenical movement. The kind of visible unity the New Delhi definition envisions does not exist even within the denominational communions, much less between the divided churches. Only a pilgrim church vision can sustain the quest for the visible unity of the church. It recognizes that each church lacks something it needs to receive to be visibly united with the other churches and perhaps retains something it must relinquish for visible unity to be realized. It refuses to be content with the status quo of the ecumenical movement, though it has achieved much, and it regards the nonetheless significant expressions of spiritual ecumenism as only partial embodiments of what ought to be. Until there is a unity within the church that the world without the church can see, the church's pilgrim journey must continue.

The Pilgrim Possibilities of a Narrative-Christological Ecclesiology

If a pilgrim church perspective on theological constructions in general is both a gift the Baptist and broader Free Church tradition may offer to the rest of the church and at the same time a perspective that is ecumenically shared, can it suggest in particular a constructive ecclesiology that might help the divided churches to embrace more intentionally their pilgrim church identity? A somewhat unusual entrée to a pilgrim church ecclesiology is suggested by the Christology of the late Baptist theologian James Wm. McClendon, Jr. It is unusual partly because of its stance toward what

---

[42] World Council of Churches, "Report of the Section on Unity," 116.

many might regard as an essential ecumenically shared doctrine, and yet that stance also exemplifies the pilgrim church theological orientation in its Baptist expression.

McClendon's own theological career has the character of pilgrim journey. He received his early Christian nurture and theological education from Southern Baptists, among whom he served as a pastor and then professor of theology at the Golden Gate Baptist Theological Seminary. There McClendon experienced an early exile from his Southern Baptist community, fired despite having tenure when he encouraged student involvement in Martin Luther King, Jr.'s efforts in Selma, Alabama. That experience was fortuitous and perhaps providential, for it led to a sojourn that involved teaching in Catholic institutions, including the University of Notre Dame, where his relationship with Mennonite theologian John Howard Yoder contributed to McClendon's reclamation of his Free Church heritage even while the Catholic context led him to relate this heritage to the larger Christian tradition. Eventually he landed another tenure-track position at the (Episcopal) Church Divinity School of the Pacific and then taught until his death at the broadly evangelical Fuller Theological Seminary. Along the way McClendon made an early contribution to the postliberal narrative theology movement with his 1974 book *Biography as Theology*.[43]

McClendon's magnum opus was his three-volume *Systematic Theology*, in which he sought to give voice to what he discerned as a distinctively Baptist way of doing theology—not only from the uppercase-"B" Baptist tradition, but also from the broader Free Church tradition that he references as lowercase-"b" baptist.[44] This concrete community of reference led McClendon to write the first volume, on ethics, dealing with what it means for a community of disciples to walk together in the way of Jesus.[45] Since such a community must form disciples in this way by teaching what the church must teach to be a community of faithful disciples of Jesus

---

[43] James Wm. McClendon, Jr., *Biography as Theology: How Life Stories Can Remake Today's Theology* (Nashville: Abingdon Press, 1974); a revised edition was published by Trinity Press International in 1990.

[44] James Wm. McClendon, Jr., *Systematic Theology*, 3 vols. (Nashville: Abingdon Press, 1986–2000). An edition with a new introduction by Curtis W. Freeman in the frontal matter of each volume was published by Baylor University Press in 2012 (the pagination of the main text is identical to the Abingdon Press edition).

[45] James Wm. McClendon, Jr., *Ethics: Systematic Theology, Vol. 1* (Nashville: Abingdon Press, 1986). A second revised and enlarged edition was published by Abingdon Press in 2002.

Christ, he devoted the second volume to doctrine.[46] Such a community exists not for its own sake but to testify to the world that salvation is found in Jesus and his way, so volume 3 deals with the church's witness.[47] Accordingly, the three volumes are individually titled *Ethics*, *Doctrine*, and *Witness*.

In the *Doctrine* volume, McClendon surveys three rival christological models—the pre-Nicene Logos model, the two-natures model of the trajectory from Nicaea through Chalcedon, and the historical model influenced by the modern quest of the historical Jesus—to which he addresses three "persistent questions" intended to probe their adequacy: first, "What right has Jesus Christ to absolute Lordship—the Lordship that Scripture assigns to God alone?"; second, "How can monotheists . . . tell the Jesus story as their own?"; and third, "How Christ-like . . . are disciples' lives to be?" McClendon finds the culmination of the two-natures trajectory in the Chalcedonian Definition deficient especially in regard to the third question, asking whether that Jesus provides a paradigm for discipleship that disciples can really put into practice. Later he concludes, "Two-natures Christology has had its day, and we need not return to it save as a monument to what has gone before. All honor to Athanasius and Basil and Leontius, but they did not write Scripture, and it is to Scripture that we must return in fashioning our convictions."[48]

Seemingly as a replacement for the two-natures Christology that since 451 has defined the orthodox center for much of the church in its teaching about the person of Christ, McClendon proposes a "two-narrative

[46] James Wm. McClendon, Jr., *Doctrine: Systematic Theology, Vol. 2* (Nashville: Abingdon Press, 1994).

[47] James Wm. McClendon, Jr., with Nancey C. Murphy, *Witness: Systematic Theology, Vol. 3* (Nashville: Abingdon Press, 2000). An autobiographical account of his life and theological career was published the year of McClendon's death: James Wm. McClendon, Jr., "The Radical Road One Baptist Took," *Mennonite Quarterly Review* 74 (2000): 503–10, republished in *The Collected Works of James Wm. McClendon, Jr.*, 2 vols., ed. Ryan Andrew Newson and Andrew C. Wright (Waco, Tex.: Baylor University Press, 2014), 1:17–25. For a helpful orientation to the *Systematic Theology* as well as the biographical context of its genesis and development, see Curtis W. Freeman, "A Theology for Brethren, Radical Believers, and Other Baptists: A Review Essay of James McClendon's *Systematic Theology*," *Brethren Life and Thought* 50, nos. 1–2 (Winter/Spring 2006): 106–15, revised and expanded as "Introduction: A Theology for Radical Believers and Other Baptists," in McClendon, *Ethics*, vii–xxxviii (Baylor University Press edition; also included as the introduction to the *Doctrine* and *Witness* volumes). A brief biography of McClendon is also provided by Mikael N. Broadway, "Introduction" (James Wm. McClendon, Jr., *Festschrift* issue), *Perspectives in Religious Studies* 27, no. 1 (Spring 2000): 5–9.

[48] McClendon, *Doctrine*, 276.

Christology."[49] In this account, one's identity is located not in one's classification according to abstract categories of "natures." One's identity is nothing other than one's story. A person's story in its totality and particularity is the thickest possible description one can offer of a person's identity.[50] For Christ, this narrative identity is both twofold and singular. McClendon proposes:

> Therefore we have these two stories, of divine self-expense and human investment, of God reaching to people even before people reach to God, of a God who gives in order to be able to receive, and a humanity that receives so that it shall be able to give. Together, they constitute the biblical story in its fullness. *And now the capstone word is this: these two stories are at last indivisibly one.* We can separate them for analysis, but we cannot divide them; there is but one story there to be told. Finally, this story becomes gospel, becomes good news, when we discover that it is our own.[51]

Here is my own interpretive summary of McClendon's proposal, intentionally echoing the two-natures-in-one-person template of the Chalcedonian Definition. *The story of Christ fully encompasses and discloses the story of the Triune God, which is God's identity. At the same time the story of Christ fully encompasses and discloses the story of humanity, which is our identity. Yet these two distinguishable stories, these two identities, are in Jesus Christ one indivisible narrative identity.* Notwithstanding McClendon's declaration that "two-natures Christology has had its day, and we need not return to it,"[52] his two-narrative alternative should be seen not as a replacement for Chalcedon but as an extension and enrichment of it. McClendon's Christology teases out additional implications of the incarnation beyond what could be expressed within the constraints of the Chalcedonian categories by rereading the

---

[49] McClendon, *Doctrine*, 263–79.

[50] Cf. F. Michael McLain, "Narrative Interpretation and the Problem of Double Agency," in *Divine Action: Studies Inspired by the Philosophical Theology of Austin Farrer*, ed. Brian Hebblethwaite and Edward Henderson (Edinburgh: T&T Clark, 1990), 143 (143–72): "If God is an agent who acts in the world so as to disclose divine character and purpose, then narrative is the appropriate form in which to render God's identity." Daniel L. Migliore cites McLain in connection with his own observations on the connection between narrative, identity, and revelation: "[O]ur identity as persons is often rendered in narrative form. If this is true of our self-disclosure to each other, by analogy it is also true of the self-disclosure of God" (Migliore, *Faith Seeking Understanding: An Introduction to Christian Theology*, 2nd ed. [Grand Rapids: William B. Eerdmans, 2004], 37).

[51] McClendon, *Doctrine*, 276–77 (emphasis in original).

[52] McClendon, *Doctrine*, 276.

council's insights in light of a new set of questions and categories that belong to a context other than the Hellenism of late antiquity—namely, the West after modernity. Just as McClendon compared the diverse historical atonement theories to the Jewish rabbinical midrashim that reinterpreted rather than replaced the biblical stories,[53] so we might regard McClendon's two-narrative proposal as a sort of midrashic reinterpretation rather than replacement of Chalcedon. Furthermore, McClendon's qualifications regarding the relation of the two narratives to each other correspond to those of the Chalcedonian Definition: the two narrative identities may be separated for analysis ("without confusion"), but they cannot be divided ("without division or separation").

It is true that "to the objection that all this talk of twoness and oneness in narrative does not correspond very well to classic two-natures-in-one-being Christology," McClendon himself replied, "It does not."[54] Thus it might initially seem that McClendon's proposal is just as much of an ecumenical nonstarter as would be the suggestion of scrapping trinitarian faith, which is the minimal doctrinal basis for membership in the broadly inclusive World Council of Churches.[55] Yet there is good ecumenical precedent for considering the Chalcedonian two-nature Christology and McClendon's two-narrative account fundamentally compatible. The Vatican II Decree on Ecumenism *Unitatis Redintegratio* allowed that differing doctrinal formulations, including the relation of Chalcedonian Christology to the Christologies of the non-Chalcedonian churches of the East, may be "mutually complementary rather than conflicting."[56] John Paul II's encyclical "On Commitment to Ecumenism" *Ut Unum Sint* likewise posited the essential unity of "different ways of looking at the same reality,"

---

[53]   McClendon, *Doctrine*, 230–33.

[54]   McClendon, *Doctrine*, 276.

[55]   Affirmation of a basically trinitarian doctrine of God—one God who exists as three distinct persons, Father, Son, and Holy Spirit—seems to be the implication of the basis adopted by the World Council of Churches at its Third Assembly in New Delhi, India, in 1961: "The World Council of Churches is a fellowship of churches which confess the Lord Jesus Christ as God and Saviour according to the scriptures and therefore seek to fulfill together their common calling to the glory of the one God, Father, Son and Holy Spirit" (World Council of Churches, "Theological and Historical Background of the WCC Basis," accessed December 11, 2014, http://www.oikoumene.org/en/resources/documents/other/theological-and-historical-background-of-the-wcc-basis).

[56]   Vatican II, *Decree on Ecumenism (Unitatis Redintegratio)*, §17, November 21, 1964, in *Decrees of the Ecumenical Councils*, ed. Norman P. Tanner, vol. 2, *Trent to Vatican II* (London: Sheed & Ward/Washington, D.C.: Georgetown University Press, 1990), 917. In context, the reference to "mutually complementary rather than conflicting" theological formulations has in mind ecumenical relations with the Eastern Orthodox churches.

offering as evidence that such is possible the common declarations on Christology signed by Catholic popes and patriarchs of non-Chalcedonian churches.[57] The progress made in the several bilateral dialogues between the non-Chalcedonian churches of the East and Catholic, Orthodox, and Protestant churches shows what a pilgrim church stance toward the theological formulations of one's own communion can make possible ecumenically,[58] in addition to opening up the possibility that McClendon's non-Chalcedonian Christology could nonetheless be regarded as consistent with what Chalcedon affirmed about the relation of the singular person of the incarnation to God's divinity and our humanity.[59] It may be

[57] John Paul II, *On Commitment to Ecumenism* (*Ut Unum Sint*), May 25, 1995), §38, accessed October 21, 2014, http://www.vatican.va/holy_father/john_paul_ii/encyclicals/documents/hf_jp-ii_enc_25051995_ut-unum-sint_en.html.

[58] The documents from these bilateral dialogues are gathered in the second and third volumes of the *Growth in Agreement* series published under the auspices of the World Council of Churches Faith and Order Commission. Frequently these involve multiple communiqués and memoranda included in a volume section designated here by inclusive pagination. In *Growth in Agreement II*, ed. Gros, Meyer, and Rusch: "Anglican–Oriental Orthodox Dialogue," 108–112; "Eastern Orthodox–Oriental Orthodox Dialogue," 187–99; "Reformed–Oriental Orthodox Dialogue," 291–94; "Oriental Orthodox–Roman Catholic Dialogue," 688–708; "Assyrian Church of the East–Roman Catholic Dialogue," 709–12. In *Growth in Agreement III*, ed. Gros, Best, and Fuchs: "Eastern Orthodox–Oriental Orthodox Dialogue," 2–11; "Anglican–Oriental Orthodox," 33–38; "Reformed–Oriental Orthodox Dialogue," 39–57; "Oriental Orthodox–Roman Catholic Dialogue," 190–96; "Assyrian Church of the East/Chaldean Church–Roman Catholic Dialogue," 197- 205. The following quotation from the "Agreed Statement on Christology" issued in 2002 by the Anglican–Oriental Orthodox International Commission is representative of what these dialogues have achieved in overcoming the christological divisions of the fifth century, in this case between those who affirm the Chalcedonian Definition and the Monophysites anathematized by it: "[T]hose among us who speak of two natures of Christ are justified in doing so since they do not thereby deny their inseparable indivisible union; similarly, those among us who speak of one incarnate nature of the Word of God are justified in doing so since they do not thereby deny the continuing dynamic presence in Christ of the divine and the human. . . . We recognize the limit of all theological language and the philosophical terminology of which it makes and has made use. We are unable to confine the mystery of God's utter self-giving in the incarnation of the divine Word in an ineffable, inexpressible and mysterious union of divinity and humanity, which we worship and adore" (Anglican–Oriental Orthodox International Commission, "Agreed Statement on Christology" [Holy Etchmiadzin, Armenia, November 5–10, 2002], in *Growth in Agreement III*, 36 [35–38]).

[59] A lingering question debated in the reception of McClendon's two-narrative Christology has been whether it is consistent with orthodox christological formulations. See, e.g., Jonathan R. Wilson, "Can Narrative Christology Be Orthodox?" *International Journal of Systematic Theology* 8, no. 4 (October 2006): 371–81, which answers the question posed in the article's title in the affirmative, contra critics of McClendon's proposal cited therein. For a more critical assessment of the relation of McClendon's two-narrative

that McClendon has successfully articulated in narrative terms rather more directly the essential event that other christological formulations reference in less-direct ways. Events like the incarnation, after all, *are* stories. Narrations of events have a more direct relationship to the events themselves; explanations of the events are more distant. Fidelity to the same first-order narrative that gives the community its identity may nevertheless yield differing second-order explications that are, in the words of *Unitatis Redintegratio*, "mutually complementary rather than conflicting."[60] McClendon's narrative approach to Christology highlights the shared first-order narrative in ways that render differing explications less exclusive of one another; it might also be applicable to other doctrinal roots of the church's current divisions.

McClendon's willingness to revisit and revise the outcome of the Council of Chalcedon exemplifies the radically biblical, radically catholic, relentlessly pilgrim approach to doing theology highlighted earlier in this chapter, according to which in Baptist perspective the church's doctrinal formulations are considered revisable in light of "fresh light that may yet break forth from the Word."[61] Yet that is not the primary reason for introducing his novel christological proposal at this point. In the course of elaborating his two-narrative proposal, McClendon drops but does not develop the tantalizing hint that features of his Christology may be extended ecclesiologically. He writes that "*in resurrection light*, apostolic Christianity can be construed as the continuation of the Jesus story already begun."[62] This narrative approach to Christology has unexplored implications for a christological approach to ecclesiology that in turn has implications for the quest for the church's visible unity. A

Christology to the "monument to what has gone before" from which he distanced his proposal, see Kimlyn J. Bender, "Theology for Pilgrims: McClendon and the Future of Baptist Theology," *Perspectives in Religious Studies* 40, no. 3 (Fall 2013): 288–91 (283–91).

[60] Vatican II, *Unitatis Redintegratio*, §17, in *Decrees of the Ecumenical Councils*, ed. Tanner, vol. 2, *Trent to Vatican II*, 917.

[61] These much-quoted words attributed to English Separatist John Robinson (1575/76–1625) in a farewell address delivered to the Mayflower Pilgrims at their departure from the Netherlands in 1620 are frequently offered as a concise articulation of this pilgrim hermeneutical stance toward received interpretations of Scripture. Robinson's address was recounted by Edward Winslow (1595–1655) in *Hypocrisie Unmasked: A true relation of the proceedings of the Governor and company of the Massachusetts against Samuel Gorton of Rhode Island* (1646; repr., Providence, R.I.: Club for Colonial Reprints, 1916). As scholarship on Robinson has noted, however, the quotation in question may be apocryphal; so, e.g., Timothy George, *John Robinson and the English Separatist Tradition* (NABPR Dissertation Series, no. 1; Macon, Ga.: Mercer University Press, 1982), vii.

[62] McClendon, *Doctrine*, 272.

narrative-christological ecclesiology may help in reenvisioning the whole church as a pilgrim community, on pilgrimage to the ecumenical future as the body of Christ that embodies the story of Jesus.

The New Testament itself offers a christological approach to ecclesiology, for as Paul Minear demonstrated in his well-known book *Images of the Church in the New Testament*, the Pauline "body of Christ" is the central image that provides the interpretive key to the function of the ninety-six images of the church his book explores.[63] In the opening chapter of 1 Corinthians, Paul invokes the body image in order to persuade the Corinthian Christians that they ought to be "in agreement," with "no divisions among" them, "united in the same mind and the same purpose" (1 Cor 1:10). "Has Christ been divided?" Paul asks in response to reports of their divisions. The implication, of course, is what Paul makes explicit later in the letter: there is only one Christ, who can have only one body, which is the church. To divide the church is to divide Christ. Christology, then, should be the governing principle of ecclesiology.

To suggest the systematic coinherence of Christology and ecclesiology is nothing new. Karl Barth's theology of the church has been called a "christological ecclesiology,"[64] for example, and Orthodox theologian George Florovsky insisted that the church is the locus of "the continuing presence of the divine Redeemer."[65] But Barth and Florovsky simply echo something long established in the tradition. Augustine had cemented the connection in his memorable formula *totus Christus, caput et corpus*—"the whole Christ, head and body"—which he employed especially in his polemics against the Donatists who would divide the whole Christ.[66]

A christological ecclesiology, especially one rooted in a narrative Christology in which the church continues the story of Jesus, therefore has significant implications for the pilgrim journey toward the ecumenical future. The remainder of this chapter proposes seven theses regarding

[63] Paul S. Minear, *Images of the Church in the New Testament* (Philadelphia: Westminster Press, 1960), 221–49.

[64] Kimlyn J. Bender, *Karl Barth's Christological Ecclesiology* (Barth Studies; Burlington, Vt.: Ashgate, 2005).

[65] George Florovsky, "As the Truth Is in Jesus," *Christian Century* 68, no. 51 (December 19, 1951): 1459 (1457–59).

[66] E.g., Augustine of Hippo, *Sermo* 341.1.1 (*Patrologiae Cursus Completus: Series Latina*, ed. J.-P. Migne [Paris: Garnier, 1844–1864], 39:1493); ET, "Sermon 341: On the Three Ways of Understanding Christ in Scripture," in *Sermons 341–400*, trans. Edmund Hill, ed. John E. Rotelle (The Works of Saint Augustine: A Translation for the 21st Century, pt. III, vol. 10; Hyde Park, N.Y.: New City Press, 1995), 19.

what it might mean ecumenically for the church to embody the story of Jesus as a pilgrim people.[67]

First thesis: The church's identity is the identity of Christ. If the church is identified with the whole Christ as the body of Christ, the church's identity can be nothing other than Christ's identity. The divided church is a church that is separated from the fullness of its common identity in Christ. Its pilgrim journey to the ecumenical future progressively recovers this identity.

Second thesis: The church's identity is the identity of Christ, which is the story of Christ. If Christ's identity is most fully described in terms of his story, and the church derives its identity from Christ, then unless head and body are severed, Christ's story is the church's story, and thus its identity. The divided church is a church that has lost its unifying story. Its pilgrim journey to the ecumenical future entails a recovery of Christ's story as its own—as the narrative world in and out of which it lives, as the narrative in light of which it understands the world to which it bears witness.

Third thesis: The church's identity is the identity of Christ, which is the story of Christ, which is the story of the church's baptism. It is in baptism that Christ's identity becomes the church's identity, and it is baptism that discloses this identity as the story of Christ. In baptism the story of Jesus' death and resurrection becomes the story of those who follow him (Rom 6:3-11), making them participants in a new story in which characters have new roles: because they have taken on Christ's story in baptism, "There is no longer Jew or Greek, there is no longer slave or free, there is no longer male and female; for all of you are one in Christ Jesus" (Gal 3:27-28). The origin of the ancient rule of faith in baptismal confession underscores baptism's conferral of narrative identity. In the eventual forms of the Nicaeno-Constantinopolitan Creed, the baptismal confession of the Eastern Churches, and the Apostles' Creed, the baptismal confession of the Western churches, the rule of faith rehearses in brief the story in Christ told in full by the Bible. In baptism Christians embrace this narrative identity as theirs, and it embraces them. The divided church is a church that has not fully recognized this baptismal identity as one baptism into the one body of Christ. Its pilgrim journey to the ecumenical future must involve mutual recognition of one another's baptisms, for not to recognize

---

[67] While he developed it differently from the narrative-christological approach proposed in this chapter, George Lindbeck has also offered a narrative account of ecclesiology in his essay "The Story-Shaped Church: Critical Exegesis and Theological Interpretation," in *Scriptural Authority and Narrative Interpretation*, ed. Garrett Green (Philadelphia: Fortress Press, 1987), 161–78.

a person's baptism "in the name of the Father and of the Son and of the Holy Spirit" (Matt 28:19) is to deny Christ as that person's identity.[68]

Fourth thesis: The church's identity is the identity of Christ, which is the story of Christ, which is the story of the Triune God. The divine story that is the story of Christ is not the story of generic, abstract divinity, but the inescapably triadic story of the God of Abraham, Isaac, and Jacob who has taken on flesh in Jesus Christ and given God's Spirit to the church in Pentecost. This triadic divine story is the one that members of the church embrace and that embraces them in their tripartite baptismal confession. Yet there is a proper distinction between the story of the creator and the story of the creature.[69] For the church as God's creature, Christ is the key to this distinction. As the one in whom "all the fullness of God was pleased to dwell" (Col 1:19), Christ's story is directly the story of the Triune God. As the body that has Christ as head (Col 1:18), the church's story is derivatively the story of the Triune God. By virtue of the church's *koinonia*, its participation, in Christ as Christ's body, it has a participation in the life of the Triune God. This is the point at which Christology has an advantage over trinitarian theology as the organizing principle of an ecclesiology. Ecclesiologies developed along the lines of social trinitarian thought such as Jürgen Moltmann's have contributed important insights regarding the ecclesial life that ought to be, but the church's identity in the story of the Triune God does not come from the church's imitation of the mutuality that characterizes the Triune life.[70] The church's identity in the story of the Triune God comes from its participation in the life of the Triune God through Christ. The divided church has an attenuated trinitarian identity because it is bodily diminished

[68]   Two documents offered to the churches as the fruit of decades of multilateral dialogue through the World Council of Churches Commission on Faith and Order have proposed possible pathways to convergence in mutual baptismal recognition: World Council of Churches, *Baptism, Eucharist and Ministry* (Faith and Order Paper no. 111; Geneva: World Council of Churches, 1982); World Council of Churches, *One Baptism: Towards Mutual Recognition. A Study Text* (Faith and Order Paper no. 210; Geneva: World Council of Churches, 2011). For a Baptist perspective on the proposals of the latter document, see Steven R. Harmon, "'One Baptism': A Study Text for Baptists," *Baptist World: A Magazine of the Baptist World Alliance* 58, no. 1 (January/March 2011): 9–10.

[69]   A distinction McClendon makes in *Doctrine*, 275.

[70]   E.g., Jürgen Moltmann, *The Trinity and the Kingdom: The Doctrine of God*, trans. Margaret Kohl (San Francisco: Harper & Row, 1981); and Leonardo Boff, *Trinity and Society*, trans. Paul Burns (Theology and Liberation Series; Maryknoll, N.Y.: Orbis Books, 1988). Miroslav Volf offers appropriate cautions regarding the pitfalls of rooting an ecclesiology or political theology in human imitation of the intratrinitarian relations in his article "'The Trinity Is Our Social Program': The Doctrine of the Trinity and the Shape of Social Engagement," *Modern Theology* 14, no. 3 (July 1998): 403–23.

in relationship to its head. The church's pilgrim journey to the ecumenical future requires taking up ecclesial practices that invite its members into deeper participation in the life of the Triune God, including especially the ecclesial practices of spiritual ecumenism—worshiping together and praying together for Christian unity and engaging in common work and witness wherever possible. As Christians participate more fully in the life of the Triune God, the mutuality of the Triune God's oneness-in-distinct-otherness becomes more fully manifest in ecclesial life. Visible unity is the fruit it yields.

Fifth thesis: The church's identity is the identity of Christ, which is the story of Christ, which is the story of our humanity. Here the emphasis is on *our* humanity. McClendon's insistence that the story of Christ fully encompasses and discloses the story of humanity means that in Christ's humanity is the story of humanity as it ought to be—seen in the New Testament emphasis on the sinlessness of Jesus, or positively expressed as his "full faithfulness"[71]—as well as the story of humanity in opposition to God's intentions for human life. In regard to the latter, McClendon seems to suggest that the humanity that Jesus embraces is not unfallen humanity but our humanity inclined toward sin—an inclination that Jesus shared in his solidarity with our human condition but which Jesus faithfully resisted at every stage in his human moral development.[72] When Christ's story as the story of our humanity becomes the church's story, it is in this two-fold sense. It discloses the church as it ought to be—the spotless bride of Christ. But it also exposes the church's distance from that in its existence in the eschatological tension between the "already" and the "not yet." The church is a pilgrim community because of its earthly distance from its not-yet-realized goal—a distance that includes what Karl Rahner named as ecclesial sin.[73] Certainly, the church's divisions and refusals to overcome

---

[71]   McClendon, *Doctrine*, 273.

[72]   McClendon, *Doctrine*, 262 and 273. Karl Barth, whose anticipations of a narrative Christology McClendon applauded, had also insisted that it is this sort of sinful humanity that Christ assumed in *Church Dogmatics*, I/2, trans. G. T. Thomson and Harold Knight (Edinburgh: T&T Clark, 1956), 151–55.

[73]   Karl Rahner, "The Sinful Church in the Decrees of Vatican II," in *Theological Investigations*, vol. 6, *Concerning Vatican Council II*, trans. Karl-H. and Boniface Kruger (Baltimore: Helicon Press, 1969), 270–94. See also Rahner, "The Church of Sinners," in *Theological Investigations*, vol. 6, 253–69; these two essays, along with the chapter "The Church and the Parousia of Christ" (*Theological Investigations*, vol. 6, 295–312), belong to a section of this volume of the *Theological Investigations* titled "The Pilgrim Church." In this connection, it is significant that in the essay "Justified and Sinner at the Same Time" placed two chapters prior to this section (*Theological Investigations*, vol. 6, 218–30), Rahner offers a qualified Catholic affirmation of Luther's formula in the sense that the person who

them are among these ecclesial sins. The pilgrim church, whose narrative identity is that of Christ, shares especially in the story of our sin-inclined humanity that Jesus's story encompasses. The church's pilgrim journey to the ecumenical future therefore involves owning its temporal identity as a penitential community, called to repentance for sins of division and its perpetuation.[74]

Sixth thesis: The church's identity is the identity of Christ, which is the story of Christ, which is the story of all the members of Christ's body. The way to the ecumenical future entails the recovery of the common narrative-christological identity the church receives in baptism, but that does not require the relinquishing of the stories of the divided communities in their historic and ongoing journeys. While the denominational stories are in part stories of ecclesial sin, they also serve as bearers of the distinctive ecclesial gifts that are distributed throughout the divided church and that no one church completely possesses. In recognition of both dimensions of the stories of particular communions—ecclesial sin as well as ecclesial giftedness—the five-year international dialogue between the Baptist World Alliance and the Anglican Consultative Council gave significant attention to the sharing of local stories of Baptist communities, of Anglican communities, and of the local relationships between them.[75] The story of Christ includes such particular stories, for Christ is present in them. And if these stories belong to the story of Christ, they are the one church's stories, too. The church's pilgrim journey to the ecumenical future involves the sharing of the particular stories that belong to the story of the whole church—as acts of confession, repentance, and reconciliation, and as acts of receptive ecumenism that receive as gifts from one another the missing pieces of the particular churches' stories.

Seventh thesis: The church's identity is the identity of Christ, which is the story of Christ, which is the story of the eschatological community. Story is inherently eschatological—a story goes somewhere. If it is a story, it has a plot, driven by conflict and resolution. Jesus himself discloses a dimension of the conclusion to the church's story in John 17 when he prays for the visible unity of those who follow him. The story's plot is driven in part by the conflict

---

is justified "remains a pilgrim," who in this pilgrim state is properly regarded as *simil justus et peccator* (229–30).

[74]   This point is forcefully argued by Ephraim Radner, *The End of the Church: A Pneumatology of Christian Division in the West* (Grand Rapids: William B. Eerdmans, 1998).

[75]   Anglican Consultative Council and Baptist World Alliance, *Conversations around the World 2000–2005: The Report of the International Conversations between the Anglican Communion and the Baptist World Alliance* (London: Anglican Communion Office, 2005), 82–97.

of division, introduced already in the New Testament chapter of the story. The church's pilgrim journey to the ecumenical future takes place in the tension between the present conflict of division and the future resolution of visible unity. But because the church knows the story's conclusion, the church participates in the quest for Christian unity in hope, no matter how dismal the present prospects for visible unity may seem.

In early 2013 the *Washington Post* published a story about the circumstances of Catholic Christians in China. The story quoted Anthony Lam, a researcher affiliated with the Holy Spirit Research Centre of the Catholic Diocese of Hong Kong. "As Catholics, we're trained to be optimistic," Lam said. "For more than 2,000 years, the church has survived all manner of difficulty, from the Roman Empire to modern ones. We live in hope."[76] Indeed the church does. The Christian church lives in hope because of its story—because its story is the story of Christ, because of what the church has already experienced in this story, and because of what the church anticipates and works toward as the conclusion of its pilgrim journey toward the ecumenical future. The theology of the pilgrim people called Baptist has important contributions to make toward that end.

---

[76] William Wan, "For China's Catholics, New Pope Brings Hope," *Washington Post* (February 24, 2013), accessed December 4, 2014, http://www.washingtonpost.com/world/asia_pacific/for-chinas-catholics-new-pope-brings-hope/2013/02/24/15df5676 −7c42−11e2−9a75-dab0201670da_story.html.

10

The Baptist Eschatological Vision
and the Ecumenical Future

The title of this final chapter will strike some readers as incongruous. What may be for some the most conspicuous incongruity applies to the whole book: its association of Baptists, sometimes perceived as the problem children of the modern ecumenical movement, with a concern for Christian unity. Baptists have a history of declaring other traditions to be false churches that begins with the foundation of the earliest identifiable Baptist congregation in Amsterdam in 1609. The previous chapter recounted cofounder John Smyth's pilgrim quest for a true church fully under the rule of Christ. That pilgrimage led him to reject his baptism in the Church of England as a false baptism administered by a false church. He then identified with the Separatists and their congregational ecclesiology as a truer expression of church. But eventually in Amsterdam, Smyth reached the conclusion that no communion there could be considered a true church that administered a true baptism, so he baptized himself and then the other members of his community. Notwithstanding his subsequent questions about the legitimacy of his self-baptism and efforts to unite himself and a portion of his congregation with the local Mennonite fellowship now that he regarded them a true church, Smyth's ecclesiological basis for Baptist beginnings foreshadowed the refusal of some of his present-day ecclesiastical progeny to embrace ecumenical proposals for the mutual recognition of one baptism. Baptists also have been quick to divide among themselves whenever some Baptists have become convinced that other Baptists have developed unbiblical patterns of faith and practice. This happened in the earliest community of Baptists in Amsterdam when a small group of its members led by Thomas Helwys insisted on the validity of their baptisms as administered by Smyth and in 1611 or 1612 returned to

England to establish Baptist ecclesial life in their homeland.[1] Baptists ever since, especially in the United States, have tended to follow this fissiparous precedent for intra-Baptist relations in local congregations, associations, national denominational organizations, and international Baptist bodies.[2]

The Baptist Ecclesial Vision and Ecumenism

Given their seeming acceptance of the multiplication of intra-Baptist ecclesial divisions, it comes as no surprise that many Baptists have had serious reservations about various institutional expressions of the modern ecumenical movement. The Baptist tradition has not been a major ecclesial source of leadership, energy, or funding for the modern ecumenical movement in its heyday and has tended toward suspicion as its default perspective on conciliar ecumenism. But as Ernest Payne, who served as General Secretary of the Baptist Union of Great Britain 1951–1967 and whose leadership roles in the World Council of Churches will be noted later in this chapter, observed, "Baptists are not all of one mind about the Ecumenical Movement."[3] On the one hand, there is the perspective represented by the Southern Baptist Convention. This largest of all Baptist unions has steadfastly resisted official participation in institutional expressions of the modern ecumenical movement such as national and international councils of churches in ways that have influenced the perspectives of some Baptists elsewhere. When in 1962 E. Roberts-Thomson, a theological educator among Baptists in New Zealand and Australia, commented on this resistance in his own book on Baptists and the ecumenical movement, he noted that "the Baptist world, ecumenically, can be divided into two groups: those who are of the Southern Baptist point of view, or are closely influenced by it, and those who are not."[4] Thus, on the other hand,

---

[1]   James Robert Coggins, *John Smyth's Congregation: English Separatism, Mennonite Influence, and the Elect Nation* (Studies in Anabaptist and Mennonite History, no. 32; Waterloo, Ont.: Herald Press, 1991), 77–81.

[2]   According to the *Handbook of Denominations in the United States*, 13th ed., ed. Craig D. Atwood, Frank S. Mead, and Samuel S. Hill (Nashville: Abingdon Press, 2010), 161–91, there are at least twenty-nine national-level Baptist conventions or denomination-like organizations in the United States. Many other countries have multiple Baptist unions rather than a unified expression of Baptist ecclesial life.

[3]   Ernest Alexander Payne, "Baptists and the Ecumenical Movement," *Baptist Quarterly* 8, no. 6 (April 1960): 258 (258–67).

[4]   E. Roberts-Thomson, *With Hands Outstretched: Baptists and the Ecumenical Movement* (London: Marshall, Morgan & Scott, 1962), 94. There have certainly been exceptions to Roberts-Thomson's generalization about Southern Baptist attitudes toward the ecumenical movement, but a wariness about Faith and Order approaches to ecumenism has

among Baptists there have been "those who are not" anti-ecumenical—including even a good many Southern Baptists along the way.[5] There have been and are today Baptists whose embrace of the ecumenical movement embodies their pilgrim church ecclesiological vision of a church whose marks of being fully under the rule of Christ include the visible unity of his followers. Lest this book be seen as a merely theoretical proposal unable to point to a concrete community that seeks to live into this vision, it is time to root its construal of the Baptist vision in the history that leads to its realization in the ecumenical future.

---

marked this largest of Baptist unions long before its turn in a more uniformly theologically conservative direction in the 1980s and 1990s, in part owing to the lingering influence of "Landmarkism," a movement exemplified by James Robinson Graves (1820–1893) and James Madison Pendleton (1811–1891). Their insistence that only Baptist churches were true churches and stood in an unbroken historic succession of such churches reaching back to Jesus and his apostles gained traction during the first half century of the Southern Baptist Convention's existence (see James Edward McGoldrick, *Baptist Successionism: A Crucial Question in Baptist History* [ATLA Monograph Series, no. 32; Metuchen, N.J.: Scarecrow Press, 1994]). The successful dissemination of the ecclesiological exclusivism of Landmarkism gave the SBC such lasting resistance to the notion of visible unity with non-Baptists that even Southern Baptist historians and theologians in the second half of the twentieth century who might be expected to be more open to ecumenical engagement, inasmuch as they disavowed Landmarkism on the one hand and would have considerably more theologically conservative successors when the convention moved in that direction late in the century on the other hand, nevertheless tended to stand distant from the institutional expressions of the modern ecumenical movement. Southwestern Baptist Theological Seminary (Fort Worth, Texas) church historian William R. Estep's largely negative book-length assessment of Faith and Order ecumenism in the wake of the New Delhi Assembly of the World Council of Churches and the Second Vatican Council, *Baptists and Christian Unity* (Nashville: Broadman Press, 1966), illustrates this tendency; yet his contemporary fellow Southern Baptist theological educators on the faculty of The Southern Baptist Theological Seminary (Louisville, Kentucky), theologian Dale Moody and church historian E. Glenn Hinson, served as members of the WCC Faith and Order Commission. Moody's ecumenical sensitivity is reflected in Dale Moody, *Baptism: Foundation for Christian Unity* (Philadelphia: Westminster Press, 1967), and Hinson recounts his involvement with the WCC Faith and Order Commission 1978–1987 in his autobiography *A Miracle of Grace: An Autobiography* (Macon, Ga.: Mercer University Press, 2012), 202–16.

[5]   Cf. James Wm. McClendon, Jr.'s encouragement of ecumenical perspectives and practices latent among Southern Baptists in a lecture delivered in 1968 at his alma mater, the SBC-sponsored Southwestern Baptist Theological Seminary, and published as "What Is a Southern Baptist Ecumenism?" *Southwestern Journal of Theology* 10, no. 2 (1968): 73–78, republished in *The Collected Works of James Wm. McClendon, Jr.*, 2 vols., ed. Ryan Andrew Newson and Andrew C. Wright (Waco, Tex.: Baylor University Press, 2014), 1:237–43.

The Ecumenical Orientation of
Baptist Ecclesiology—Embodied

A more ecumenical orientation to Baptist ecclesiology is discernible from the beginnings of the Baptist movement. John Smyth, for example, did search for other "true churches" with which to find fellowship, lest his Amsterdam congregation be devoid of connections with the larger body of Christ. Baptist theologian Stephen Holmes characterizes Smyth's action on the new conclusion that the Mennonite fellowship was indeed a true church in this fashion: "Smyth, perceiving a true church in existence, believed he had no option but to join it; separation from a true church was not an option."[6] The surprisingly ecumenical impulse at the heart of this quest for the true church manifests itself again in the origins of Baptist associational life. In the first half century of Baptist existence, their communities began to form associations of multiple local congregations, in part out of the recognition that a single congregation did not possess in and of itself all the resources it needed to be most fully church, and that these resources are found not only among neighboring Baptist churches but in the whole body of Christ. When seven local Baptist congregations in London together issued the *London Confession* of 1644, they explained their congregational interdependence in discerning the mind of Christ for their faith and practice as a corollary of being "one in Communion, holding Jesus Christ to be our head and Lord; under whose government we desire alone to walk, in following the Lamb wheresoever he goeth" and insisted that inclusion in such an interdependent communion was their hope "for all [the] saints."[7] This early Baptist consciousness of ecclesial interdependence in walking together under the rule of Christ is what would later give rise not only to larger associations of Baptist churches in the form of national Baptist conventions and unions and in 1905 the formation of the Baptist World Alliance as a Christian world communion, but also to various forms of Baptist participation in the modern ecumenical movement.

The Baptist Presence in the Modern Ecumenical Movement

The Baptist pilgrim church vision of a church that moves toward being fully under the rule of Christ through ecclesial interdependence is embodied in

---

[6]   Stephen R. Holmes, *Baptist Theology* (Doing Theology series; London: T&T Clark International, 2012), 17.

[7]   *London Confession* (1644), pref., in *Baptist Confessions of Faith*, 2nd rev. ed., ed. William Lumpkin, rev. Bill J. Leonard (Valley Forge, Pa.: Judson, 2011), 143 (spelling standardized in quotation herein).

the numerous ways in which Baptist history and the history of the modern ecumenical movement are intertwined. Many (though not all) Baptists and their churches and associations have participated actively in the modern ecumenical movement from its beginnings. The 1910 Edinburgh World Missionary Conference that led to the founding of the ongoing International Missionary Conference in 1921 was anticipated a century earlier by a wish expressed in 1806 by William Carey (1761–1834), a Baptist missionary to India, that "a general association of all denominations of Christians from the four quarters of the earth" meet each decade at the Cape of Good Hope.[8] When Carey's "pleasant dream" was realized in the gathering of the World Missionary Conference in Edinburgh in 1910, Baptists, including members of the Southern Baptist Convention, were among the participants. Baptists were likewise involved, again with some limited Southern Baptist representation, in the foundation and early development of the three institutional predecessors of the World Council of Churches: the International Missionary Council (London, 1921), the Conference on Life and Work (Stockholm, 1925), and the World Conference on Faith and Order (Lausanne, 1927), each of which would eventually merge into the World Council of Churches.

When the World Council of Churches held its inaugural assembly in Amsterdam in 1948, eight Baptist unions participated as founding members: the Baptist Union of Great Britain, the Northern Baptist Convention (now American Baptist Churches, USA), the National Baptist Convention (USA), the Seventh Day Baptist General Conference (USA), the Baptist Union of New Zealand, the Union of Baptist Congregations in the Netherlands, the Burma Baptist Missionary Convention, and the China Baptist Council.[9] Though there have been withdrawals from as well as additions to this list, the membership roster of the World Council of Churches now includes twenty-five Baptist unions: American Baptist Churches in the USA, Bangladesh Baptist Church Sangha, Baptist Association of El Salvador, Baptist Convention of Haiti, Baptist Convention of Nicaragua, Baptist Union of Denmark, Baptist Union of Great Britain, Baptist Union of Hungary, Baptist Union of New Zealand, Bengal-Orissa-Bihar Baptist Convention, Church of Christ in Congo-Baptist Community of Congo, Church of Christ in Congo-Protestant Baptist Church in Africa, Episcopal Baptist Community in Africa, Convention of Philippine Baptist Churches, Evangelical Baptist Church in Angola, Evangelical Baptist

---

[8]   E. Glenn Hinson, "William Carey and Ecumenical Pragmatism," *Journal of Ecumenical Studies* 17, no. 2 (Spring 1980): 76–77 (73–83).

[9]   Payne, "Baptists and the Ecumenical Movement," 263.

Union of Italy, Jamaica Baptist Union, Myanmar Baptist Convention, National Baptist Convention of America, National Baptist Convention USA, Native Baptist Convention of Cameroon, Nigerian Baptist Convention, Progressive National Baptist Convention, Samavesam of Telugu Baptist Churches, and Union of Baptist Churches in Cameroon.[10] Most of these unions are also members of their respective national councils of churches, while there are some Baptist unions that are not members of the World Council of Churches but nevertheless belong to a national council. Many Baptists have served as members of the commissions of the World Council of Churches, including some Baptists whose own Baptist union is not an official member of the WCC. The most notable Baptist participating in the leadership of the World Council of Churches has been Ernest Payne, whose position as general secretary of the Baptist Union of Great Britain (1951–1967) overlapped with his service as vice chairman of the Central Committee of the World Council of Churches from 1954 to 1968, the year in which Payne was elected one of six co-presidents at the fourth assembly of the World Council of Churches in Uppsala, Sweden.

Baptists in Bilateral and Multilateral Dialogue

The formation of the Baptist World Alliance as a Christian world communion overlapped with the institutional beginnings of the modern ecumenical movement. It is something of an expression of Baptist ecumenism in its own right, bringing into dialogue with one another the diverse expressions of the global Baptist community. The BWA has also functioned as a means of ecumenical relations at the international level. When on July 5, 1905, the Baptist World Alliance met in London for its first congress, its newly elected president Alexander Maclaren invited congress participants to demonstrate Baptists' relation to the larger Christian tradition by reciting together the Apostles' Creed, "not as a piece of coercion or discipline, but as a simple acknowledgment of where we stand and what we believe."[11] In 1975, at the thirteenth congress of the Baptist World Alliance in Stockholm, Sweden, the BWA adopted a new constitution that explicitly named

---

[10] World Council of Churches, "Member Churches: Church Families: Baptist Churches," accessed December 5, 2014, http://www.oikoumene.org/en/church-families/baptist-churches.

[11] John Howard Shakespeare, ed., *The Baptist World Congress, London, July 11–19, 1905: Authorised Record of Proceedings* (London: Baptist Union Publication Dept., 1905), 20.

seeking "understanding and unity among Baptists and with fellow Christians" as one of its purposes.[12]

Baptists have been well represented in the bilateral and multilateral dialogues that have blossomed in the decades since the Second Vatican Council. The previous chapter explored the international-level bilateral conversations between the BWA and the World Alliance of Reformed Churches (1973–1977), the Lutheran World Federation (1986–1989), the World Mennonite Conference (1989–1992), the Anglican Communion (2000–2005), and the Catholic Church (1984–1988 and 2006–2010). A dialogue with the World Methodist Council is currently under way.[13] Conversations have also been planned with the Pentecostal World Fellowship,[14] and there have been exploratory "pre-conversations" with representatives of the Ecumenical Patriarchate of Constantinople in 1994, 1996–1997, and again in 2011. Baptists have also made significant contributions to international multilateral dialogue in connection with the Faith and Order Commission of the World Council of Churches. The process that led to the Faith and Order convergence text *Baptism, Eucharist and Ministry (BEM)*[15] was preceded by a consultation with Baptist theologians and representatives of other traditions that practice believer's baptism, held at The Southern Baptist Theological Seminary in Louisville, Kentucky, March 28–April 1, 1979.[16] Baptists were represented in the membership of the Faith and Order Commission that issued the final text in 1982, and Baptist unions and individuals participated in the process of reception

---

[12]   Cyril E. Bryant, ed., *New People for a New World—through Christ: Official Report of the Thirteenth Congress, Baptist World Alliance, Stockholm, Sweden, July 8–13, 1975* (Nashville: Broadman Press, 1976), 292.

[13]   Baptist World Alliance, "Baptists and Methodists Conclude First Session of Dialogue" (February 11, 2014), accessed December 6, 2014, http://www.bwanet.org/news/news-releases/354-baptists-and-methodists-conclude-first-session-of-dialogue.

[14]   Baptist World Alliance, "Callam Names BWA Team for Dialogue with Pentecostals" (May 24, 2012), accessed December 6, 2014, http://www.bwanet.org/news/news-releases/130-baptist-pentecostal-dialogue; Bob Allen, "Baptist–Pentecostal Talks Postponed," *Baptist News Global* (August 8, 2012), accessed December 6, 2014, http://baptistnews.com/ministry/organizations/item/7694-baptist-pentecostal-talks-postponed#.UCSFW02PXyg.

[15]   World Council of Churches, *Baptism, Eucharist and Ministry* (Faith and Order Paper no. 111; Geneva: World Council of Churches, 1982).

[16]   Lukas Vischer, "The Convergence Texts on Baptism, Eucharist and Ministry: How Did They Take Shape? What Have They Achieved?" *Ecumenical Review* 54, no. 4 (October 2002): 442–43 (431–54); World Council of Churches, *Louisville Consultation on Baptism* (Faith and Order Paper no. 97; Louisville, Ky.: The Southern Baptist Theological Seminary, 1980), published as *Review and Expositor* 77, no. 1 (Winter 1980).

through the submission of responses to *BEM*.[17] A notable positive Baptist response to *BEM* came from the Myanmar (Burma) Baptist Convention, which has origins in the early-nineteenth-century missionary work of Adoniram and Ann Judson. This historic association of Baptists not only publicly affirmed the call of *BEM* to refrain from the re-baptism of those previously baptized as infants but also commended the document to the churches of the Convention to use as a study guide to help Baptists appreciate the theological significance of infant baptism in other communions.[18] Baptist members of the WCC Faith and Order Commission have likewise contributed to the significant Faith and Order study texts

[17]   Among Baptists, nine Baptist communions have issued responses to *BEM*, published in *Churches Respond to "Baptism, Eucharist and Ministry,"* 6 vols., ed. Max Thurian (Geneva: World Council of Churches, 1986–1988): Baptist Union of Great Britain and Ireland (1:70–77), All-Union Council of Evangelical Christians-Baptists in the USSR (3:227–29), Baptist Union of Scotland (3:230–45), Baptist Union of Denmark (3:246–53), Covenanted Baptist Churches in Wales (3:254–56), American Baptist Churches, USA (3:257–63), Burma Baptist Convention (4:184–90), Union of the Evangelical Free Churches in the GDR (Baptists) (4:191–99), and Baptist Union of Sweden (4:200–13). For a response commissioned by the Baptist World Alliance, see William R. Estep, "A Response to *Baptism, Eucharist and Ministry*: Faith and Order Paper No. 111," in *Faith, Life and Witness: The Papers of the Study and Research Division of the Baptist World Alliance 1986–1990*, ed. William H. Brackney and R. J. Burke (Birmingham, Ala.: Samford University Press, 1990), 2–16. The responses from all the churches are surveyed in World Council of Churches, *Baptism, Eucharist and Ministry 1982–1990: Report of the Process and the Responses*, (Faith and Order Paper no. 149; Geneva: World Council of Churches, 1990). The variety of Baptist perspectives on baptismal recognition in relation to church membership is described by Thorwald Lorenzen, "Baptism and Church Membership: Some Baptist Positions and Their Ecumenical Implications," *Journal of Ecumenical Studies* 18, no. 4 (Fall 1981): 561–74.

[18]   In the course of the Anglican–Baptist International Conversations, representatives of the Myanmar Baptist Convention reported that their convention "had embarked on a process of 'conscientization' among the churches, using *BEM* as a study guide, to enable Baptist church members to understand the place of baptism in infant-baptism churches," and agreed "to refrain from what could be understood by others as a 'second baptism' " (Anglican Consultative Council and Baptist World Alliance, *Conversations around the World 2000–2005: The Report of the International Conversations between the Anglican Communion and the Baptist World Alliance* [London: Anglican Communion Office, 2005], 50–51). The official response of the Myanmar (then identified as Burma) Baptist Convention to *BEM* declared, "We do not respond simply because it is expected of us. We respond because of our commitment to unity and the ongoing mission of the whole church in the whole world" ("Response of the Burma Baptist Convention," in *Churches Respond to "BEM,"* ed. Thurian, 4:185). It noted in conclusion, "BEM is important. It is a matter of our 'faith' as well as our 'order.' But we must treat it as more than a matter of faith and order. It is targeted towards unity and mission. . . . There are crucial problems facing humanity today. If our response is to have any validity, it must be life-giving" (4:190).

One Baptism: Towards Mutual Recognition (2011) and *The Church: Towards a Common Vision* (2012).[19]

Baptists have participated in numerous national and regional bilateral dialogues. These have included several series of conversations with representatives of the Catholic Church. The American Baptist Churches USA (1967–1973) and the Southern Baptist Convention (1978–1999) have engaged in dialogues with the United States Conference of Catholic Bishops.[20] Baptists and Catholics in France have held a series of dialogues that have produced notable reports, including a commentary on the report of the first series of dialogues between the BWA and the Catholic Church and reports of subsequent thematic dialogues on baptism, the Eucharist, the church, and Mary.[21] In 2009 Italian Baptists and Catholics issued "A Common Document for a Pastoral Approach to Marriages between Catholics and Baptists in Italy."[22] Substantial national-level dialogue has also taken place with Lutheran churches: the North American Baptist Fellowship (a regional fellowship of the BWA) and the Lutheran Council

---

[19]   World Council of Churches, *One Baptism: Towards Mutual Recognition. A Study Text* (Faith and Order Paper no. 210; Geneva: World Council of Churches, 2011); idem, *The Church: Towards a Common Vision* (Faith and Order Paper no. 214; Geneva: World Council of Churches, 2013).

[20]   American Baptist Churches, USA, and United States Conference of Catholic Bishops, "Growing in Understanding: A Progress Report on American Baptist–Roman Catholic Dialogue," in *Building Unity: Ecumenical Dialogues with Roman Catholic Participation in the US*, ed Joseph Burgess and Jeffrey Gros (Mahwah, N.J.: Paulist Press, 1989), 39–44; Department of Interfaith Witness of the Home Mission Board of the Southern Baptist Convention and United States Conference of Catholic Bishops, "Summary Statement of the Second Triennium in the Dialogue between Southern Baptist and Roman Catholic Scholars (1982–1984)," in *Building Unity*, ed. Burgess and Gros, 45–51; idem, "How We Agree/How We Differ: Roman Catholic–Southern Baptist Scholars' Dialogue (1986–88)," in *Growing Consensus: Church Dialogues in the United States, 1962–1991*, ed. Joseph A. Burgess and Jeffrey Gros (Ecumenical Documents, no. 5; New York: Paulist Press, 1995), 557–65; idem, "Report on Sacred Scripture: Southern Baptist–Roman Catholic Conversation, 1999," in *Growing Consensus II: Church Dialogues in the United States, 1992–2004*, ed. Lydia Veliko and Jeffrey Gros (Washington, D.C.: Bishop's Committee for Ecumenical and Interreligious Affairs, United States Conference of Catholic Bishops, 2005), 334–38.

[21]   Comité mixte baptiste-catholique en France, *Rendre témoinage au Christ* (Documents d'Église; Paris: Les Éditions du Cerf, 1992); idem, *Du Baptême à l'Eglise: Accords et divergences actuels* (Documents d'Église; Paris: Les Éditions du Cerf, 2006); idem, *Marie* (Documents episcopat, no. 10; Paris: Le secretariat général de la conférence des évêques de France, 2009).

[22]   Klaus Rösler, "Italy: When Baptists Marry Catholics," *European Baptist Federation News* (July 7, 2009), accessed December 12, 2014, http://ebf.org/italy-when-baptists-marry-catholics.

in the United States of America, the Baptist Union of Norway and the (Lutheran) Church of Norway, and Baptists and Lutherans in Bavaria in Germany.[23] Australian Baptists have engaged in dialogue with the Uniting Church in Australia.[24] In addition, ongoing dialogue between the Baptist Union of Great Britain and the Church of England yielded a book-length study text.[25] A dialogue held in 1979–1980 between Baptists and the Orthodox Church in what was then the Soviet Republic of Georgia was previously little noticed in the larger ecumenical world, but it produced a remarkable agreed text that has recently been published with introduction and commentary.[26] Its most striking feature is a novel proposal of a common practice of initiation involving something of a synthesis of the Orthodox rite of infant baptism, seemingly reconceived as a rite of infant blessing rather than baptism proper, and the Baptist practice of the baptism of those who embrace the faith personally at a more mature age, seemingly now regarded as baptism proper for both communions[27]—but the agreement seems not to have been acted upon subsequently. While some of

[23] Joseph A. Burgess and Glenn A. Igleheart, eds., *Lutheran–Baptist Dialogue* (Rochester, N.Y.: American Baptist Historical Society, 1982), published in *American Baptist Quarterly* 1, no. 2 (December 1982): 98–216; Bavarian Lutheran–Baptist Working Group, *Learning from One Another—Believing Together: 'One Lord, One Faith, One Baptism' (Eph 4,5). Convergence Document of the Bavarian Lutheran–Baptist Working Group* (Munich: Bavarian Lutheran–Baptist Working Group, 2009), accessed December 12, 2014, http://www.gftp.de/press/public/weitere/Bavarian%20Baptists%20and%20Lutherans%20Final%20Report.pdf; Church of Norway and Baptist Union of Norway, *One Lord—One Faith—One Church: A Longing for One Baptism. The Report from the Bilateral Dialogue between The Church of Norway and The Baptist Union of Norway 1984–1989*, 2nd ed. (1994), accessed December 12, 2014, http://www.gammel.kirken.no/english/doc/baptist_lutheran_1989.doc.

[24] Australian Baptist Ministries and Uniting Church in Australia, *Church Membership: Dialogue Report* (Melbourne: Uniting Church in Australia National Assembly, 2012). Australian Baptist Ministries was formerly identified as the Baptist Union of Australia.

[25] Faith and Unity Executive Committee of the Baptist Union of Great Britain and the Council for Christian Unity of the Church of England, *Pushing at the Boundaries of Unity: Anglicans and Baptists in Conversation* (London: Church House, 2005).

[26] Paul S. Fiddes and Malkhaz Songulashvili, "A Dialogue between the Orthodox Church of Georgia and the 'Evangelical Christians-Baptists' of Georgia (1979–1980) with Its Wider Baptist Context," *International Journal for the Study of the Christian Church* 13, no. 3 (2013): 222–54; the agreed text itself in English translation is appended to the article (pp. 244–54).

[27] The section on baptism concludes with this summary statement: "Therefore, the common Christian faith will administer infant blessing with full observance of the national-religious ceremony. By this action the sense of national and Christian citizenship will enter the child. At a mature age he or she may deepen his or her understanding of the Christian religion, get educated, be filled with the Holy Spirit, and will be baptized consciously in water and the Spirit. If the first stage is the birth of the individual into a Christian society (nation), the second stage is birth into a truly Christian life" (Fiddes and

the details of this baptismal agreement remain problematic in ecumenical perspective (and for many Baptists, problematic also in terms of its relation of Christian initiation to a particular church–state arrangement), its approach anticipates *BEM* and some recent bilateral dialogues in locating the possibility of mutual baptismal recognition in comparable journeys of initiation in which baptism functions in relation to other essential features of the whole process of initiation.[28]

Other national and regional discussions have worked toward mutual recognition of baptisms and ordained ministry. The American Baptist Churches USA and the Church of the Brethren established an "associated relationship" in 1973 and reached an agreement on the mutual recognition of membership and ministry in 1976, as a consequence of which there are now a few local congregations that are dually affiliated with both bodies.[29] In 1990 Baptists in Italy joined the Waldensian and Methodist churches in that country in a mutual recognition agreement.[30] The European Baptist Federation and the Community of Protestant Churches in Europe (the churches that have fellowship on the basis of the Leuenberg Agreement of 1973) engaged in a dialogue on the doctrine and practice of baptism that, while not reaching agreement on the mutual recognition of baptism, paved the way for a 2010 agreement to become "mutually cooperating bodies."[31]

Songulashvili, "Dialogue between the Orthodox Church of Georgia and the 'Evangelical Christians-Baptists' of Georgia," 249).

[28] Fiddes and Songulashvili, "Dialogue between the Orthodox Church of Georgia and the 'Evangelical Christians-Baptists' of Georgia," 232–34.

[29] Carl Desportes Bowman and Donald F. Durnbaugh, *Church of the Brethren: Yesterday and Today* (Elgin, Ill.: Brethren Press, 1986), 193; American Baptist Churches USA, *Yearbook of the American Baptist Churches in the U.S.A. 1976* (Valley Forge, Pa.: American Baptist Churches in the U.S.A., 1976), 16. As of 2004 there were seven congregations dually affiliated with the American Baptist Churches USA and the Church of the Brethren (Richard Schramm, "ABCUSA–Church of the Brethren Relationship Reaffirmed," *American Baptist News Service* [February 26, 2004], accessed December 12, 2014, http://archive.wfn.org/2004/02/msg00214.html).

[30] Evangelical Baptist Union of Italy and Union of Methodist and Waldensian Churches, "Agreement on Mutual Recognition between the Waldensian, Methodist and Baptist Churches in Italy (1990)," in *Wachsende Kirchengemeinschaft: Gespräche und Vereinbarungen zwischen envangelischen Kirchen in Europa*, ed. C. Nussberger (Bern: Evang. Arbeitsstelle Ökumene Schweiz, 1992), 155–67.

[31] Wilhelm Hüffmeier and Tony Peck, eds., *Dialogue between the Community of Protestant Churches in Europe and the European Baptist Federation on the Doctrine and Practice of Baptism* (Leuenberg Documents, vol. 9; Frankfurt am Main: Verlag Otto Lembeck, 2005).

Baptist Participation in Church Union Discussions

A few Baptist unions have been party to discussions that look beyond forms of mutual recognition to the possibility of church union, the seeds of which may be seen in John Smyth's desire to merge the original Baptist congregation in Amsterdam with the Mennonite community there. When some Baptists have discerned that convictions are similar enough to permit life together in ecclesial community, they have on occasion concluded that a continued separate existence is unjustified and pursued mergers with other denominations or have joined united churches.

In 1797 several Baptist and Congregational churches in England formed the Bedfordshire Union of Christians, which in 1910 changed its name to the Bedfordshire Union of Baptist and Congregational Churches. Early in the twentieth century some congregations were planted by the Bedfordshire Union as "union churches." Though the Bedfordshire Union was dissolved in 1968, a number of congregations continue to maintain dual Baptist and Congregational (now United Reformed Church) affiliations.[32]

In the 1920s Baptist churches in North China affiliated with the Church of Christ in China, a union of non-episcopal churches.[33] The Baptist Churches of Northern India in 1970 joined in the formation of the United Church of North India along with Anglican, Congregational, Disciples of Christ, Methodist, Brethren, and Presbyterian churches; Baptists had been involved in consultations laying the groundwork for such a united church from the beginnings of talks in 1929. In the Democratic Republic of Congo, both the Baptist Community of Congo and the Protestant Baptist Church in Africa belong to the Church of Christ in Congo, a united church formed by sixty-two Protestant denominations.[34]

The American Baptist Churches USA held exploratory conversations about the possibility of union with the Disciples of Christ in the middle of the twentieth century. While the two communions elected not to pursue formal union, the conversations did have the outcome of cooperation in the publication of jointly sponsored hymnals.[35] There were parallel con-

---

[32] Baptist Union of Great Britain and Ireland, *Baptists and Unity*, 3rd ed. (London: Baptist Union of Great Britain and Ireland, 1967), 12–13.

[33] Baptist Union of Great Britain and Ireland, *Baptists and Unity*, 9.

[34] World Council of Churches, "Member Churches: Democratic Republic of Congo," accessed December 13, 2014, http://www.oikoumene.org/en/member-churches/africa/democratic-republic-of-congo.

[35] Northern Baptist Convention and Disciples of Christ, *Christian Worship: A Hymnal*, ed. William P. Shelton and Luther Wesley Smith (St. Louis: Christian Board of

versations between the Baptist Union of Great Britain and the Churches of Christ (Disciples) from 1941 until 1952, with similar results.[36]

In Sweden, a number of congregations have long been aligned with both the Baptist Union of Sweden and the Mission Covenant Church. In 2011 the Baptist Union of Sweden joined a merger of three of the Free Church denominations in Sweden along with the Mission Covenant Church and the United Methodist Church to form the Uniting Church in Sweden. All three denominations, which had intermittent exploratory conversations regarding the possibility of some form of union with one another throughout the twentieth century, already jointly owned and operated the Stockholm School of Theology; the youth organizations of the three churches merged in 2008.[37]

The congregational ecclesiology of Baptist churches opens up the possibility of forms of church union at the local church level that may not involve the union of national or regional denominational organizations. In the United States, some Baptist churches are affiliated with the United Church of Christ (a 1957 merger of the Evangelical and Reformed Church and the Congregational Christian Churches) as well as Baptist unions such as the American Baptist Churches USA, the Progressive National Baptist Convention, and the Alliance of Baptists. Owing to these relationships and to similar relationships between congregations of the United Church of Christ and the Christian Church (Disciples of Christ), the Alliance of Baptists, an organization of progressive Baptists in the United States that emerged from conflict within the Southern Baptist Convention during the 1980s and 1990s, has an "Ecumenical Agreement" with the United Church of Christ and the Christian Church (Disciples of Christ) that does not formalize mutual recognition or full communion but functions as a collaborative relationship that includes "the continuation of theological conversation on matters of ministry, ordinances/sacraments, theology, and polity" and facilitates joint participation in various expressions of the

---

Publication, Bethany Press, 1941); American Baptist Convention and Disciples of Christ, *Christian Worship: A Hymnal*, ed. B. Fred Wise (St. Louis: Christian Board of Publication, Bethany Press, 1953); American Baptist Churches and Disciples of Christ, *Hymnbook for Christian Worship*, ed. Charles Huddleston Heaton (St. Louis: Bethany Press, 1970).

[36] Baptist Union of Great Britain and Ireland, *Baptists and Unity*, 19.

[37] Baptist World Alliance, "Baptists Form Joint Church Body with Methodist and Covenant Denominations," *Baptist World: A Magazine of the Baptist World Alliance* 59, no. 3 (July/September 2012): 22; Karin Wiborn, "Joint Future: On the Way to a Uniting Church," *Baptist World: A Magazine of the Baptist World Alliance* 59, no. 3 (July/September 2012): 23.

mission of the church.[38] In the UK numerous churches have been planted as "Local Ecumenical Partnerships" (LEPs) that from the beginning are in full communion with multiple sponsoring denominations.[39] In principle, nothing prohibits a local Baptist church from initiating affiliation with more than one Christian communion—a form of church union that moves from the grassroots upward rather than from a merger of denominational structures incumbent on the local churches that belong to them. All of these instances of Baptist participation in various expressions of the quest for Christian unity are embodiments of the ecumenical dimension of a Baptist pilgrim church ecclesiology. The church that is fully under the rule of Christ is fully and visibly united as his body; the Baptist vision of a church fully under the rule of Christ mandates ecumenical engagement so long as such unity is lacking.

Eschatology and Ecumenism

A second seemingly incongruous combination in the title of this chapter is ecumenism and eschatology. Some varieties of Christian eschatology have fostered outright opposition to ecumenical alliances, while some other forms of eschatology have been detrimental to robust ecumenical engagement in ways that are less obvious. The pessimism of premillennialism did little to encourage hopes for any progress toward visible Christian unity prior to the second advent of Christ and his subsequent millennial kingdom, and dispensational premillennialism in particular branded the Catholic Church as "the whore of Babylon" and viewed the modern ecumenical movement as a precursor to a "one world church" supposedly foretold in the Apocalypse. The historical optimism of postmillennialism went hand-in-hand with the beginnings of the modern ecumenical movement, but it also tended to make some ecumenically inclined mainline Protestants impatient with church-dividing doctrinal differences. When these have been regarded as unnecessary obstacles to ecumenical advance that broad-minded modern (and now postmodern) Christians should

---

[38] Alliance of Baptists, United Church of Christ, and Christian Church (Disciples of Christ), "Ecumenical Agreement between the Alliance of Baptists, United Church of Christ, and the Christian Church (Disciples of Christ), April 25, 2003," accessed December 13, 2014, http://allianceofbaptists.org/documents/EcumencialAgreement withUCC2003.pdf.

[39] On the nature and significance of Local Ecumenical Partnerships, see Baptist Union of Great Britain Faith and Society Team, *Baptists and Ecumenism* (Didcot, UK: Baptist Union of Great Britain, 2013), accessed December 6, 2014, http://www.baptist.org.uk/Publisher/File.aspx?ID=113632&view=browser.

easily be able to move beyond, the churches have tended to lose interest in the earnest contestation of differences of faith and order that must precede any lasting strides toward visible unity. While Eastern Orthodoxy and post–Vatican II Catholicism are fully committed to the goals of Faith and Order ecumenism, from the perspective of Free Church Christians and many other Protestants these communions have in the past fallen prey to an overly realized eschatology of the church that leads them to insist that other churches and ecclesiastical communities are deficient in aspects of faith and order while remaining insufficiently critical of the failures of their own churches.

Baptists have had their own share of entanglements with eschatologies that have not encouraged the healthiest ecumenical perspectives. While it is true that many early English Baptists eventually distanced themselves from the millenarian fervor of the Fifth Monarchists despite (or perhaps because of) early overlap between the two movements,[40] and that the most influential Baptist confessions in England and North America have offered simple affirmations of hope in the return of Christ that eschewed millennial speculation,[41] from the late nineteenth century onward Baptist churches and other Free Church communions have been fertile fields for the cultivation and propagation of dispensational premillennialism and thus also for its denunciation of ecumenism.[42] At the same time, many other nondispensationalist Baptists nevertheless reacted strongly against the initiatives of the Faith and Order movement on account of a sort of Baptist triumphalism that paralleled the overly realized eschatologies of the church they critiqued in Catholic and Orthodox ecclesiology, with similar, or perhaps worse, effects on Baptist attitudes toward other churches.[43] Yet at the core of the Baptist vision is a healthier sort of essential

---

[40] Mark Robert Bell, *Apocalypse How? Baptist Movements during the English Revolution* (Macon, Ga.: Mercer University Press, 2000), 174–75.

[41] The article on "Last Things" in the *Baptist Faith and Message* adopted by the Southern Baptist Convention in 1963, for example, affirms that "God, in His own time and in His own way, will bring the world to its appropriate end" (*Baptist Confessions of Faith*, ed. Lumpkin, rev. Leonard, 414). This language is retained in the most recent revision of this confession in 2000 (*Baptist Confessions of Faith*, ed. Lumpkin, rev. Leonard, 517).

[42] Most of the individuals, institutions, and denominations noted in a section titled "The Rise and Spread of Dispensationalism" in Craig A. Blaising and Darrell L. Bock, *Progressive Dispensationalism* (Grand Rapids: Baker Books, 2000), 10–13, have Baptist and Free Church connections.

[43] A confidence that Free Church patterns of ecclesial life represent the ecumenical future is evident in two apologies for Baptist identity from the first decade of the twentieth century: Walter Rauschenbusch, *Why I Am a Baptist* (Philadelphia: Baptist Leader, 1958; originally published as a series of articles in *Rochester Baptist Monthly* 20

eschatological orientation that has the potential to help Baptists both to heed the biblical imperative of visible Christian unity and to offer their best gifts to the rest of the church through their participation in Faith and Order ecumenism. The same eschatology inherent in the Baptist vision is the eschatology that is embodied in two crucial ecumenical practices by which the divided church seeks the ecumenical future of one eucharistic fellowship: the practice of ecumenical reception of convergences in faith and order arrived at through dialogue, and the practice of praying for unity—an endeavor of "spiritual ecumenism" that even Baptists who have reservations about Faith and Order ecumenism can embrace.

The Baptist Eschatological Vision and Ecumenism

It has been claimed that "there is no Baptist doctrine . . . of eschatology, which is not shared with other Christian communities."[44] Yet James Wm. McClendon, Jr., has persuasively contended that the distinctively baptist vision at its best is fundamentally eschatological. McClendon's three-volume *Systematic Theology* is the most serious effort undertaken thus far to discern and articulate afresh the distinctiveness of the "baptist" vision, with the lowercase-"b" spelling inclusive of Baptists proper and other Free Church communions from the sixteenth-century Anabaptists to contemporary Pentecostal communities.[45] In the second volume titled *Doctrine*, which addressed the question "What must the church teach to be the church now?" eschatology appears not at the end of the book but as the first rubric treated, and it is not so much a separate doctrine as it is the key category "that can lead us to the whole of Christian doctrine."[46] The hermeneutical motto by which McClendon summarizes the baptist vision highlights its eschatological orientation: "this is that" and "then is now"—in other words, the story of the biblical people of God is the story

---

[1905–1906]), and E. Y. Mullins, *The Axioms of Religion: A New Interpretation of the Baptist Faith* (Philadelphia: American Baptist Publication Society, 1908). By the time William R. Estep published *Baptists and Christian Unity* (1966), it was manifest that representatives of the Free Church tradition constituted an ecclesiological minority within the Faith and Order movement. This factor has contributed to the widespread conviction that Baptist participation in any form of organic unity would require the surrender of key Baptist ecclesiological distinctives.

[44] Holmes, *Baptist Theology*, 7.

[45] James Wm. McClendon, Jr., *Systematic Theology*, 3 vols. (Nashville: Abingdon Press, 1986–2000; republished with new introduction, Waco, Tex.: Baylor University Press, 2012).

[46] McClendon, *Doctrine*, 68.

of the present-day community of faith, and the future disclosed in that story is to be embodied by the community now.[47]

The church's efforts to embody here and now the eschatological future disclosed in the biblical story ought to include heeding the imperative of visible Christian unity. Two features of McClendon's treatment of the eschatology at the core of the baptist vision support this assertion. First, McClendon echoes and builds upon Paul Althaus in defining eschatology as the division of theology that is "about what lasts; it is also about what comes last, and about the history that leads from the one to the other."[48] Second, McClendon draws from Ludwig Wittgenstein in developing the eschatological introduction to *Doctrine* in terms not of a linear chronology of eschatological events, but rather a series of interconnected "concrete end-pictures" suggested by the New Testament: the Last Judgment, the return of Jesus Christ, resurrection, death, hell, heaven, and the rule of God.[49] To these focal concrete end-pictures identified by McClendon we should add the visible unity of the followers of Christ, for that is precisely the concrete end-picture envisioned by Jesus in his prayer for those who believe in him in John 17.[50] This is a perichoretic unity that participates in the life of the Triune God (vv. 11 and 21-23a), is in the process of being brought to full completion (v. 23b), and is a visible witness to the world of the love of God (v. 23c).[51] This prayer discloses a concrete end-picture

---

[47]   McClendon, *Ethics*, rev. ed., 26–34; see especially p. 30: "Scripture in this vision effects a link between the church of the apostles and our own. So the vision can be expressed as a hermeneutical principle: shared awareness of the present Christian community as the primitive community and the eschatological community. In a motto, the church now is the primitive church and the church on judgment day."

[48]   McClendon, *Doctrine*, 96; cf. 75, where McClendon cites Paul Althaus, *Die Letzen Dinge: Lehrbuch der Eschatologie* (Gütersloh: Gerd Mohr, 1948), 29, as "a longstanding interpretation of Christian eschatology [which] says that it is concerned about **what lasts** and with **what comes last**" (bold text as employed by McClendon). McClendon continues, "to this we may add its concern with the relation of these two, and thus with the course of **history under the eyes of God**. These are the things about which we wish to know: about the last things in the sense of what abides, of what will remain when all else is done, and of what constitutes the path into that lasting future."

[49]   McClendon, *Doctrine*, 75–89; see also idem, "Picture Eschatology (1995)," in *Collected Works of James Wm. McClendon, Jr.*, 2:355–64.

[50]   McClendon himself regarded Christian unity as that which lasts and comes last, for he insisted in the quotation from *Doctrine* that concluded chapter 6 of this book, "such peoplehoods as Baptist, Methodist, and the like are justified only if they serve as provisional means toward that one great peoplehood that embraces all, the Israel of God, the end toward which the biblical story moves" (McClendon, *Doctrine*, 365).

[51]   On the use of this passage in major ecumenical texts associated with dialogue between the Catholic Church and other ecclesial bodies, see Hellen Mardaga, "Reflection

in that it represents the eschatological hope of the person of God's self-disclosure. Such unity is therefore what lasts and what comes last, and its process of being brought to completion belongs to the history that leads from the one to the other.[52] If McClendon has characterized the eschatological essence of the baptist vision rightly, and if the quest for the visible unity of the church rightly belongs to the fullness of this vision as John 17 suggests, then Baptists are being true to their historic ecclesial vocation when they devote themselves to the quest for visible unity in faith and order. The forms of positive Baptist participation in the multiple expressions of the ecumenical movement summarized earlier in this chapter belong to the history ("under the eyes of God," as McClendon put it[53]) that leads from the eschatologically abiding efforts toward unity in the present to the full realization of the unity in the ecumenical future.

How might the eschatology of ecumenism implicit in Jesus' prayer in John 17 inform Baptist participation in this quest? The eschatology embedded in this prayer is that of the narrative substructure of the New Testament as a whole: the reign of God that has come near in Christ is already a present reality but is not yet fully realized.[54] The concrete end-picture of visible Christian unity partakes of this already-but-not-yet character of the reign of God. Christians already possess a unity that is christological, in that they belong to the one body of Christ, and pneumatological, in that they are indwelt by one Spirit. But as the current divisions of the church attest, this unity is not yet fully realized, for its fullness is not visible. Indeed, to join Jesus in praying that believers may be one is to confess our current lack of unity. If unity, however, is conceived primarily as a spiritual reality, as Baptists have tended to do whenever they define the catholicity of the church in quantitative terms (i.e., as the universal church to which all Christians belong),[55] then Baptists may see little reason to

---

on the Meaning of John 17:21 for Ecumenical Dialogue," *Ecumenical Trends* 34, no. 10 (November 2005): 148–52.

[52] Cf. Yves Congar, *My Journal of the Council*, trans. Mary John Ronayne and Mary Cecily Boulding, ed. Denis Minns (Collegeville, Minn.: Liturgical Press, 2012), 53: "Ecumenism is also a will of God for his Church in the twentieth century. And taking it into account belongs to the fidelity of the Church."

[53] McClendon, *Doctrine*, 75.

[54] Cf. Oscar Cullmann, *Christ and Time: The Primitive Christian Conception of Time and History*, trans. F. V. Filson (London: SCM Press, 1950).

[55] When Baptists have affirmed catholicity as a mark of the church, they have tended to understand catholicity in terms of the church's invisible or "mystical" oneness. The *Orthodox Creed*, a confession adopted by a group of English General Baptist congregations in 1678, exemplifies this understanding in article 30: "[W]e believe the visible church of Christ on earth, is made up of several distinct congregations, which make up that one

devote their energies to the earnest contestation of church-dividing issues of faith and order that must precede visible unity, for this christological and pneumatological unity is already a present reality quite apart from any visible manifestations of this unity. Likewise, if visible unity is fully realized only in the age to come, then there may be little motivation to seek it in the present age. Not only Baptists but many other Protestants have insisted that the four *notae ecclesiae* of the Nicaeno-Constantinopolitan Creed, including the oneness of the church, are *eschatological* marks of the church. This is true enough, but one legacy of this insistence is an aversion to efforts to realize these marks, especially the mark of visible oneness, in the present. If the oneness, holiness, catholicity, and apostolicity of the church will fully be realized only eschatologically, that does not mean that the church should not seek to attain to those marks in the present.

The inadequacy of both of these patterns of relating eschatology to the ecumenical task is apparent in light of an analogous relation of eschatology to the saints' quest for holiness of life. Even now in this earthly life, the saints already are what their designation suggests—"holy ones" (Eph 1:1) who are "seated with him in the heavenly places in Christ Jesus" (Eph 2:6). But in this earthly life the saints are not yet fully holy in person or practice. The completion of sanctification awaits the "eternal weight of glory beyond all measure" (2 Cor 4:17), even if one grants the possibility of "entire sanctification" according to Wesleyan theology or of the earthly realization of divinization in the Orthodox tradition. Just as the present positional holiness of the saints in Christ does not warrant a refusal of the sanctifying work of the Spirit in the present, and just as the deferral of the glorification of the saints until the resurrection should not demotivate the present pursuit of the sanctification that will be completed in the eschaton, so it is with the already/not-yet nature of Christian unity. It is precisely because the church has already been entrusted with the lasting reality of oneness in Christ and in the Spirit that the church must seek to make this oneness visible to the world in advance of the age to come, and it is precisely because visible unity is a concrete end-picture disclosed by Jesus himself that the church can be confident that it is joining God in what God intends to do in and through the church in the culmination of God's goals for all things when it participates in the kind of quest for visible unity envisioned by the New Delhi statement on the goals of Faith

---

catholick church, or mystical body of Christ" (*Baptist Confessions of Faith*, ed. Lumpkin, rev. Leonard, 327–28).

and Order ecumenism.[56] Like the baptist vision at its best, Faith and Order ecumenism at its best is concerned with what lasts, what comes last, and the history that leads from the one to the other.

The Eschatological Practices of Ecumenical Reception

Baptists can live into this eschatological vision more fully by attending to the practices of ecumenical reception with greater intentionality. Not to be confused with the "receptive ecumenism" treated in chapter 7, ecumenical reception refers to the process by which worldwide Christian communions, denominations at the national level, local churches, and individual Christians become informed about, consider, and act upon the proposals and agreements that result from bilateral and multilateral ecumenical dialogue.[57] This practice presents challenges that are particular to Baptists, even while Baptists have some resources among their distinctive ecclesial gifts that should help them prioritize reception as an ecumenical practice—especially when these gifts and this practice are framed eschatologically.

Baptist ecclesiology entails that whenever Baptists participate in ecumenical dialogues with other Christian communions beyond sister Free Church denominations such as the Mennonites, there is an inherent asymmetry between the respective delegations to a joint commission. The Baptist members do not officially speak for their churches or unions, nor is there a singular expression of Baptist confessional commitments for them to articulate to their dialogue partners. Furthermore, any convergences or agreements reached in the dialogue have no ecclesial force for the churches associated with the Baptist communions involved in the dialogue, even if they might in theory for churches of the other communion with which Baptists are in dialogue. This means that a report or agreed text from an ecumenical dialogue with Baptist participation can function as a study text commended to Baptists and their churches, but its agreements do

---

[56] World Council of Churches, *The New Delhi Report: The Third Assembly of the World Council of Churches 1961* (New York: Association Press, 1962), 116. The text of this classic definition of the unity sought by the ecumenical movement is quoted in the opening of the previous chapter.

[57] Adapted from Steven R. Harmon, *Ecumenism Means You, Too: Ordinary Christians and the Quest for Christian Unity* (Eugene, Ore.: Cascade Books, 2010), 116 ("Appendix B: Glossary of Key Ecumenical Terms," s.v. "reception"). For a book-length treatment of ecumenical reception, see William G. Rusch, *Ecumenical Reception: Its Challenge and Opportunity* (Grand Rapids: William B. Eerdmans, 2007); cf. also Rusch's earlier, shorter book *Reception: An Ecumenical Opportunity* (Philadelphia: Fortress Press, 1988).

not directly alter the status of relationships between the involved communities. Attention to reception is necessary if any Christian tradition is to incorporate the fruit of ecumenical dialogue into its embodied ecclesial life. But for Baptists, intentionality about ecumenical reception is the only way the convergences identified in dialogue will have any impact or significance other than as historical texts documenting what particular groups of Baptists discussed with representatives of other communions on specific occasions.

It is possible to root the ecumenical practice of reception in the historic Baptist opposition to the coercion of conscience by either civil or ecclesiastical powers, which is one of the distinctive ecclesial gifts Baptists have to offer the rest of the church. In turn, this can be connected to another eschatological end-picture: the final *shalom* of the reign of God, which is sought in the present order by shunning violence and making peace. Not all Baptists have joined their Free Church kindred in the Mennonite tradition as pacifists,[58] but inasmuch as the coercion of conscience is a form of violence, Baptists are shunning violence and making peace, seeking the *shalom* of the reign of God, when they work to safeguard the consciences of people without and within the church from coercion. Baptists have expressed this respect for conscience in terms of religious liberty, liberty of conscience, "soul competency" and "soul liberty," and sometimes as a dimension of the priesthood of believers. It has parallels, it should be noted, in the Catholic concept of the primacy of the conscience.[59] Furthermore, in Catholic understanding religious liberty, as a safeguard against the coercion of conscience, is a precondition of

---

[58] Baptist World Alliance and Mennonite World Conference, "Theological Conversations, 1989–1992," in *Growth in Agreement III: International Dialogue Texts and Agreed Statements, 1998–2005*, ed. Jeffrey Gros, Thomas F. Best, and Lorelei F. Fuchs (Faith and Order Paper no. 204; Geneva: WCC Publications/Grand Rapids: William B. Eerdmans, 2007), 447 (426–48), summarized the typical divergence between Baptists and Mennonites on this matter: "Mennonites are one of the historic peace churches and most Mennonites see peace and non-resistance as a fundamental aspect of the gospel, whereas Baptists generally identify with the just-war tradition." Yet there have been and are significant Baptist exceptions to this generalization: see Paul R. Dekar, *For the Healing of the Nations: Baptist Peacemakers* (Macon, Ga.: Smyth & Helwys, 1993); idem, *Building a Culture of Peace: Baptist Peace Fellowship of North America, the First Seventy Years* (Eugene, Ore.: Pickwick, 2010).

[59] E.g., Vatican Council II, *Declaration on Religious Liberty (Dignitatis Humanae)*, December 7, 1965, §3, in *Vatican Council II: The Conciliar and Post Conciliar Documents*, rev. ed., ed. Austin Flannery (Vatican Collection, vol. 1; Northport, N.Y.: Costello, 1992), 801–2 (799–812): "It is through his conscience that man sees and recognizes the demands of the divine law. He is bound to follow this conscience faithfully in all his activity so that he may come to God, who is his last end. Therefore, he must not be forced to act contrary

ecumenism.[60] Baptists too can connect their opposition to the coercion of conscience to the practice of ecumenical reception, which especially for them depends on persuasion rather than mandate. No Baptist union, congregation, minister, or church member is bound by any agreement reached in ecumenical dialogue; the consciences of Baptist congregations and their members may object to what their dialogue commissions recommend and what their commissioning unions approve, and they have the freedom to do so. But the reports and agreed statements produced by dialogues can be commended to Baptist unions, congregations, ministers, and church members for study and discussion of their implications for how they relate to other churches and their members. If Baptists are to give their consciences to the consideration of ecumenical convergences, they must be persuaded that they should.

How might Baptists persuasively encourage ecumenical reception? There are two principal loci for Baptist attention to ecumenical reception: institutions of theological education and local churches. Baptist theological educators, especially theologians and church historians, can introduce seminarians to the documents of multilateral dialogue and bilateral dialogues with Baptist participation. When reports or agreed statements from such dialogues are issued, Baptist-related seminaries, divinity schools, and universities can sponsor symposia on the documents and invite members of the communions that have been in conversation with Baptists as program personalities and guests. Unless the institutions of theological education responsible for the educational preparation of Baptist ministers and their postgraduate continuing education take the lead in encouraging ecumenical reception, it is unlikely to happen in the local churches.[61] In local churches, pastors can study reports of ecumenical dialogues with

---

to his conscience. Nor must he be prevented from acting according to his conscience, especially in religious matters."

[60] John Paul II's encyclical on ecumenism *Ut Unum Sint* §8 insisted that the Decree on Ecumenism *Unitatis Redintegratio* "takes into account everything affirmed in the Council's Declaration on Religious Freedom *Dignitatis Humanae*" (John Paul II, *On Commitment to Ecumenism* [*Ut Unum Sint*, May 25, 1995], accessed October 21, 2014, http://www.vatican.va/holy_father/john_paul_ii/encyclicals/documents/hf_jp-ii_enc_25051995_ut-unum-sint_en.html). Significantly, in the preliminary schemas drafted for the Second Vatican Council, a statement on religious liberty was originally conceived not as a separate decree but as a chapter of the decree on ecumenism.

[61] On the responsibility of institutions of theological education for fostering reception of the fruits of ecumenical dialogue, see World Council of Churches, "International Dialogues in Dialogue: Context and Reception," Tenth Forum on Bilateral Dialogues, Dar es Salaam, Tanzania, March 8–14, 2012, accessed December 14, 2014, http://www.oikoumene.org/en/folder/documents-pdf/TheDarEsSalaamReportMay2012.pdf.

Baptist participation as part of their ongoing ecumenical formation. They can share them with ministers from the churches of Baptists' dialogue partners along with fellow Baptist pastors and perhaps form local clergy discussion groups to work through the texts together. Ministers can share these dialogue texts also with church members, who have day-to-day relationships with members of other churches in which they live out visible Christian unity—and who may already be doing so in the context of their marriages and other family relationships.[62] As proposed in chapter 6, reports and agreed statements from ecumenical dialogues can easily serve as the basis of local church formation study groups, which ideally might also involve members of a neighboring church affiliated with a dialogue partner communion. Reception of ecumenical convergences may involve recognition that a concretely altered relationship is possible

---

Baptist World Alliance General Secretary Neville Callam was among the twenty-four forum participants who issued this report, which urged in §11:

> We encourage all churches to find ways of integrating the results of dialogues with theological institutions training clergy and lay people. The training and formation of church leaders, who are likely to have a significant influence on relationships between local congregations, appears to be a particularly valuable locus for promoting reception. We would welcome deeper engagement by such institutions, for example through in depth case studies of particular dialogues in the light of changes in global Christianity (p. 3).

The concluding section of the report (§23, p. 6) included this as the seventh of eight recommendations regarding "Communicating and Evaluating the Results of the Bilateral Dialogues":

> 7. Communions are encouraged to find ways to communicate the results of the dialogues with theological institutions training clergy and lay leaders, and to have their content and methods integrated into the curriculum. Such institutions can also be appropriate places for consultation as the work develops.

Two previous documents, one Catholic and one representing conciliar ecumenism, have broadly attended to the role of institutions of theological education in ecumenical formation: Pontifical Council for Promoting Christian Unity, *Directory for the Application of the Principles and Norms of Ecumenism* (March 25, 1993), accessed November 29, 2014, http://www.vatican.va/roman_curia/pontifical_councils/chrstuni/general-docs/rc_pc_chrstuni_doc_19930325_directory_en.html; Dietrich Werner, "Magna Charta on Ecumenical Formation in Theological Education in the 21st Century—10 Key Convictions," *International Review of Mission* 98, no. 1 (2009): 161–70.

[62] See Association of Interchurch Families, *Interchurch Families and Christian Unity: A Paper Adopted by the Second World Gathering of Interchurch Families from Eleven Countries Held in Rome in July 2003* (London: British Association of Interchurch Families, 2003); published also online as "Interchurch Families and Christian Unity: Rome 2003," accessed December 13, 2014, http://www.interchurchfamilies.org/confer/rome2003/documents/roma2003_en.pdf.

between neighboring churches. On the basis of that recognition and in light of the rich tradition of covenant-making as a Baptist ecclesial practice, it may be possible to formalize a local ecumenical covenant between neighboring churches, with members and ministers pledging to abide by it in their local relations and in the calling of future ministers, who will pledge to continue the pattern of ecumenical relationships specified by the covenant as a condition of accepting their calling to serve in these congregations.[63] All of these are opportunities for making persuasive cases for why ecumenical convergence should matter to the life of the church and the Christian life of its members and for persuading congregationally governed churches to live into the ecumenical convictions they embrace as a matter of conscience.

The Eschatological Practices of Spiritual Ecumenism

Baptists also seek the ecumenical future that their vision helps them see through practices of what has been called "spiritual ecumenism." Spiritual ecumenism begins with the already-present spiritual realities shared by all Christians, such as those named in Ephesians 4:4-6: one body, one Spirit, one hope, one Lord, one faith, one baptism, one God. It is embodied in practices of shared worship and devotion involving Christians whose present church-dividing differences preclude eucharistic fellowship and other manifestations of full visible communion.[64] The practice of praying with other Christians for the unity of the church is a core practice of spiritual ecumenism.

Whenever Baptists observe the Week of Prayer for Christian Unity[65] (and many Baptist congregations do so) or engage in other forms of corporate and individual prayer in which they join their Lord and his body in praying for the visible unity of his church, they embody these connections between the Baptist vision, eschatology, and ecumenism. Prayer in general, and prayer for the church's unity in particular, is an inherently eschatological practice: it participates in the refrain of the first three petitions of

---

[63] A practice commended in Michael Kinnamon, *Can a Renewal Movement Be Renewed? Questions for the Future of Ecumenism* (Grand Rapids: William B. Eerdmans, 2014), 15–16, 83–84.

[64] Adapted from Harmon, *Ecumenism Means You, Too*, 117 ("Appendix B: Glossary of Key Ecumenical Terms," s.v. "spiritual ecumenism").

[65] For accounts of the genesis and historical development of the Week of Prayer for Christian Unity and explorations of its significance from the perspectives of various traditions, see Catherine E. Clifford and James F. Puglisi, eds., *A Century of Prayer for Christian Unity* (Grand Rapids: William B. Eerdmans, 2009).

the Lord's Prayer—"on earth, as it is in heaven" (Matt 6:10). Reflection on Baptist practices of praying for Christian unity suggests the following four observations regarding the significance of such acts in light of the foregoing claims about the eschatology of ecumenism.

First, praying for Christian unity moves Baptists to confess as sin their own contributions to division in the body of Christ. To ask God to grant unity to the church is to admit that the church does not yet have the unity God intends, and the appropriate first response to this admission for any Christian communion is to ask, "Is it I, Lord?" All churches have their own particular sins against the unity of the church to confess, and Baptists are certainly no exception. Prayer for Christian unity exposes the sinfulness of the energies Baptists have devoted to their own internal divisions, of their preoccupation with preserving Baptist distinctives while neglecting to form the faithful in Christian essentials, of failing to recognize the one who is the Truth in the faith and practice of non-Baptist churches with which they disagree, and of all manner of other transgressions against the unity of the body of Christ known only by the Spirit in whom they offer prayer for Christian unity.

Second, praying for Christian unity helps Baptists have the proper attitude toward the distinctive gifts they have to offer to the larger body of Christ through their participation in the quest for visible unity. If asking God to grant unity to the church involves an admission that the church is not yet unified, this admission may also lead to the humble identification of the legitimate points of dissent that are involved in the present divisions and that must be maintained until mutual ecclesial conversion to the church's Lord makes possible closer convergences of faith and practice. These points of dissent are intertwined with Baptist ecclesial distinctiveness and therefore function as both challenges to and gifts for the rest of the church. For example, the eschatological character of the Baptist vision makes Baptists wary of identifying any earthly institution with the full realization of the unity for which Christ prayed. This pilgrim church aversion to overly realized eschatologies of the church is manifest especially in what Baptist theologian Nigel Wright has called "the disavowal of Constantine," by which he means the Baptist witness against symbiotic patterns of relationships between the church and the civil power that have resulted in the compromise of the church's countercultural stance vis-à-vis the powers that be and that have sometimes resulted in the civil power's coercion of the church to do the bidding of the state.[66] It must be acknowledged that circumstances have changed this side of the historical experiences that shaped Baptist convictions regarding religious liberty. The Catholic Church committed itself to the principle of religious liberty in the Vatican II Declaration on Religious Liberty *Dignitatis Humanae*,[67] and the church in its various expressions has become legally and/or culturally disestablished in much of the Western world. Yet Baptists have their origin in dissent from what they see as church-corrupting relationships between church and state, and they still have this witness to offer to the rest of the church—and to themselves, inasmuch as Baptists too have sometimes fallen prey to the temptations of Christendom. Baptists at their best have also dissented from the wielding by the church of what Wright calls "sacred power," by means of which ecclesiastical hierarchies have sometimes coerced the faithful—though there are certainly instances in which Baptists have succumbed to this temptation internally as well.[68] Inasmuch as there are forms of church life that do not easily admit themselves to correction by a radical application of the Vincentian criterion of consent by the faithful (*ab omnibus creditum est*—"that which has been believed *by all*") for discerning that which is truly authoritative in the teaching of the church,[69] therefore also embodying an overly realized eschatology of the church that does not reckon seriously enough with its not-yet-perfected

---

[66] Nigel G. Wright, *Disavowing Constantine: Mission, Church and the Social Order in the Theologies of John Howard Yoder and Jürgen Moltmann* (Carlisle, UK: Paternoster, 2000); idem, *Free Church, Free State: The Positive Baptist Vision* (Milton Keynes, UK: Paternoster, 2005), especially 204–50.

[67] Vatican II, *Dignitatis Humanae*, in *Vatican Council II*, rev. ed., ed. Flannery, 799–812. Karl Barth, however, detected a hint of vestigial Constantinianism even in this declaration, as reflected in the critical question raised in *Ad Limina Apostolorum: An Appraisal of Vatican II*, trans. Keith R. Crim (Richmond, Va.: John Knox Press, 1968), 40: "When or where did the witnesses in the Old and New Testaments demand a legally assured scope for their life and the proclamation of their faith, and for the presentation of other religions?" It must be conceded that the same critical question could also be addressed to Baptist arguments for the constitutional separation of church and state in the United States.

[68] Wright, *Free Church, Free State*, xviii–xx.

[69] Vincent of Lérins *Commonitorium* 2.1–3 (G. Rauschen and P. B. Albers, eds., *Florilegium Patristicum*, vol. 5, *Vincentii Lerinensis Commonitoria*, ed. G. Rauschen [Bonn: P. Hanstein, 1906], 12; ET in *Nicene and Post-Nicene Fathers: Second Series*, ed. Philip Schaff and Henry Wace [A Select Library of the Christian Church; New York: Christian Literature, 1887–1894; repr., Peabody, Mass.: Hendrickson, 1994], 11:132). This insistence on the consent of the faithful might also be construed as a radical extension to the whole communion of saints of the Conciliar Movement by means of which the church reformed itself prior to and in the wake of the Protestant Reformation. On this now-neglected tradition of ecclesial authority, see Paul Avis, *Beyond the Reformation? Authority, Primacy and Unity in the Conciliar Tradition* (London: T&T Clark, 2006).

character, Baptists continue to insist that those dimensions of ecclesiology must be earnestly contested before visible unity is possible. Praying for unity can help Baptists contribute to the quest for visible unity by steering them, however indirectly, toward reclaiming their ecclesial vocation as dissenting catholics even while fostering humility in the practice of their dissent, prayerfully expressing their gratitude for the particularities of their historical pilgrimage as a community of faith that have shaped the distinctive convictions and practices they offer as gifts to the rest of Christ's body.[70]

Third, praying for Christian unity embodies the Baptist emphasis on the priesthood of all believers by inviting all members of the church to participate actively in the foundational ecumenical practice upon which all other forms of ecumenical engagement depend. The concept of the priesthood of all believers is not unique to Baptists. It is, after all, a biblical concept (1 Pet 2:9), and though the Protestant Reformers of the sixteenth century emphasized it, the universal priestly ministry of believers is taught also in the *Catechism of the Catholic Church*.[71] Baptists have nevertheless lent to the priesthood of believers an emphasis on the responsibility of all members of the congregation to do the ministry of the local church in accordance with congregational polity. Applied to the quest for the visible unity of the church, the cherished Baptist principle of the priesthood of all believers means that heeding the ecumenical imperative is the task not only of theologians and ecumenists, and not only of the pastors whose office should entail maintaining the unity of the church in an ecclesiology that equates the biblical offices of bishop and pastor, but also of the laity. Laypersons are the ones who truly embody the quest for Christian unity in their relationships with other Christians who belong to other communions, and it is most appropriate that they constitute the majority of those who are called to prayer during the Week of Prayer for Christian Unity and at other times when the church follows the lead of her Lord in

---

[70] On the possibility that the dissent of the Free Churches has in fact made positive contributions to the quest for unity, see James Wm. McClendon, Jr., and John Howard Yoder, "Christian Unity in Ecumenical Perspective: A Response to David Wayne Layman," *Journal of Ecumenical Studies* 27, no. 3 (Summer 1990): 561–80 (see especially the subsection "How Free Churches Have Made for Unity," 576–78), republished in *Collected Works of James Wm. McClendon, Jr.*, 1:245–67.

[71] Catholic Church, *Catechism of the Catholic Church* (Liguori, Mo.: Liguori, 1994), §2.2.3.6.2.1546 (p. 386): "Christ, high priest and unique mediator, has made of the Church 'a kingdom, priests for his God and Father.' The whole community of believers is, as such, priestly. The faithful exercise their baptismal priesthood through their participation, each according to his own vocation, in Christ's mission as priest, prophet, and king."

praying "that they may all be one."[72] Given the resistance of many Baptists to Faith and Order initiatives that they regard as "organic union schemes," the practice of praying for unity may also be the most appropriate way for most Baptists to begin participating in the one ecumenical movement—and it is the ecumenical practice that is most crucial for the success of the movement, if indeed we believe with the authors of the New Delhi report that "unity is God's gift to God's church."[73]

Fourth, praying for Christian unity provides Baptists and other Christians with a proper perspective on their participation in the quest for visible Christian unity. Praying for unity reminds the church that unity is God's gift: it comes about as the divided churches are converted to Christ by the work of the Holy Spirit in their midst, not through the human efforts of the church to bring about its own unity. Furthermore, if such prayer is oriented toward what lasts, what comes last, and the history that leads from the one to the other, then what is sought by those who pray for unity may not be granted during their earthly lives. The already-inaugurated-but-not-fully-realized character of the reign of God presupposed by such prayer is a proper motivation for the rigorous but patient contributions of theologians, ecumenists, and all members of their churches to the ecumenical goal of "one eucharistic fellowship," a goal that in all likelihood will not be realized in their lifetimes and indeed may require centuries of ecclesial commitment to the contestation of faith and order—apart from unforeseen actions of the Spirit that may yet initiate long-awaited eschatological emergences. Praying for unity keeps the church from losing heart in what increasingly seems from a human point of view to be a losing struggle.[74]

Two profound experiences of hope-renewing prayer for the realization of the ecumenical future served as bookends for the year I published my book *Towards Baptist Catholicity*.[75] In January 2006 I was a member of the consultation convened by the Foundation for a Conference on Faith and Order in North America described in chapter 2. We met for three

---

[72] In addition to the annual Week of Prayer for Christian Unity, following the Ecumenical Prayer Cycle during prayers of intercession in weekly corporate worship provides congregations with a regular opportunity to participate in the unifying practice of prayer for sisters and brothers in Christ who are members of other churches.

[73] World Council of Churches, *New Delhi Report*, 116.

[74] The beginning of chapter 2 surveys the factors that have contributed to the current ecumenical malaise and retrenchment.

[75] Steven R. Harmon, *Towards Baptist Catholicity: Essays on Tradition and the Baptist Vision* (Studies in Baptist History and Thought, vol. 27; Milton Keynes, UK: Paternoster, 2006).

days at the Graymoor Spiritual Life Center of the Franciscan Friars of the Atonement in Garrison, New York, to offer postmortem analyses of the failure of the envisioned Second Conference on Faith and Order in North America, but we also contemplated the possibilities for such a conference in the future. While some of the presentations and discussions evidenced a remarkable degree of ecumenical energy among the constituencies represented at the consultation, the gathering seemed like a funeral for the death of an ecumenical dream. And yet when we joined in common worship each morning and evening, singing Taizé chants and praying together for the unity of the church, we experienced the rekindling of a hope that did not seem warranted by the circumstances. In December 2006 I began my service as a member of the Baptist World Alliance delegation to the second series of conversations with the Pontifical Council for Promoting Christian Unity (2006–2010). We launched that renewed bilateral dialogue with a week of conversations at Beeson Divinity School, an interdenominational evangelical divinity school at Baptist-related Samford University in Birmingham, Alabama. In contrast to the Graymoor consultation, the mood of these conversations was far from somber, yet all participants were acutely aware of the inevitable ecclesiological impasses that lay ahead. Even so, when the delegates gathered for morning and evening prayer each day in Beeson's Andrew Gerow Hodges Chapel, where Thomas Aquinas and Martin Luther significantly stand side-by-side facing worshipers among the sixteen representatives of the communion of saints whose frescoes encircle the chapel's dome, those who were not yet able to be united at the Lord's table were nevertheless able to be united in praying together along with their Lord that they might one day be made one. Both of these experiences of praying for unity at the boundaries of the church's divisions underscore the eschatology of ecumenism that makes this a most appropriate grassroots ecumenical practice for Baptists—and for all other Christians.

My own hope as I join in such prayers is that in some unforeseen way, Baptists might one day come to have the same function in one visibly united church that their pre-Reformation predecessors as "believers' churches," namely the communities and orders that emerged from the patristic and medieval renewal movements of monasticism, have had as committed fellowships that call the one church to renewal from within. While Baptists remain separated ecclesial communities in the not-yet-realized aspect of the church's eschatology, they can join those from whom they are otherwise separated in the common labor of praying for unity. The Baptist eschatological vision that helps Baptists strive to be a pilgrim community, relentlessly seeking the church fully under the rule of Christ, is embodied in prayer that the church might realize its ecumenical future.

A recent book of worship published by the Baptist Union of Great Britain includes a service of reconciliation for the Week of Prayer for Christian Unity. After a prayer of confession acknowledging and asking forgiveness for complicity in the church's divisions and a prayer of intercession for a divided world that asks also that God might grant the church a renewed vision of its unity, a prayer of commitment asks the Spirit to guide and strengthen the whole church in its mission, "strangers no longer but pilgrims together on the way to your kingdom."[76] May it be so for Baptists and their fellow pilgrims throughout the one, holy, catholic, and apostolic church.

---

[76] Baptist Union of Great Britain, *Gathering for Worship: Patterns and Prayers for the Community of Disciples*, ed. Christopher J. Ellis and Myra Blyth (Norwich, UK: Canterbury Press, 2005), 369–70.

Bibliography

Alberigo, Giuseppe. *A Brief History of Vatican II*. Translated by Matthew Sherry. Maryknoll, N.Y.: Orbis Books, 2006.

————. *History of Vatican II*. 5 vols. Translated by Joseph A. Komonchak. Maryknoll, N.Y.: Orbis Books, 1995–2006.

Allen, Bob. "Baptist–Pentecostal Talks Postponed." *Baptist News Global* (August 8, 2012). Accessed December 6, 2014. http://baptistnews.com/ministry/organizations/item/7694-baptist-pentecostal-talks-postponed#.UCSFW02PXyg.

————. "CBF a 'Denominetwork,' Paynter Says." *Baptist News Global* (June 26, 2014). Accessed November 23, 2014. http://baptistnews.com/ministry/organizations/item/28867-cbf-a-denominetwork-paytner-says.

Alliance of Baptists, United Church of Christ, and Christian Church (Disciples of Christ). "Ecumenical Agreement between the Alliance of Baptists, United Church of Christ, and the Christian Church (Disciples of Christ), April 25, 2003." Accessed December 13, 2014. http://allianceofbaptists.org/documents/EcumencialAgreementwithUCC2003.pdf.

Allmen, Jean-Jacques von. "L'Église locale parmi les autres Églises locales." *Irénikon* 43 (1970): 512–37.

Althaus, Paul. *Die Letzen Dinge: Lehrbuch der Eschatologie*. Gütersloh: Gerd Mohr, 1948.

American Baptist Churches and Disciples of Christ. *Hymnbook for Christian Worship*. Edited by Charles Huddleston Heaton. St. Louis: Bethany Press, 1970.

American Baptist Churches USA. *Yearbook of the American Baptist Churches in the U.S.A. 1976*. Valley Forge, Pa.: American Baptist Churches in the U.S.A., 1976.

American Baptist Churches USA, and United States Conference of Catholic Bishops. "Growing in Understanding: A Progress Report on American Baptist–Roman Catholic Dialogue." In *Building Unity: Ecumenical Dialogues with Roman Catholic Participation in the US*, ed. Joseph Burgess and Jeffrey Gros, 39–44. Mahwah, N.J.: Paulist Press, 1989.

American Baptist Convention and Disciples of Christ. *Christian Worship: A Hymnal.* Edited by B. Fred Wise. St. Louis: Christian Board of Publication, Bethany Press, 1953.

Ammerman, Nancy T. *Baptist Battles: Social Change and Religious Conflict in the Southern Baptist Convention.* New Brunswick, N.J.: Rutgers University Press, 1990.

————. "On Being a Denomination: CBF and the Future." In *Findings: A Report of the Special Study Commission to Study the Question: "Should the Cooperative Baptist Fellowship Become a Separate Convention?"* ed. W. Randall Lolley, Eileen R. Campbell-Reed, Pope A. Duncan, Pete Hill, and Nancy A. Thurmond, 21–31. Atlanta: Cooperative Baptist Fellowship, 1996.

Anglican Communion and Baptist World Alliance. "Conversations around the World: International Conversations between the Anglican Communion and the Baptist World Alliance, 2000–2005." In *Growth in Agreement III: International Dialogue Texts and Agreed Statements, 1998–2005,* ed. Jeffrey Gros, Thomas F. Best, and Lorelei F. Fuchs, 319–74. Faith and Order Paper no. 204. Geneva: WCC Publications/Grand Rapids: William B. Eerdmans, 2007.

Anglican Communion and Catholic Church. "Authority in the Church I (Venice Statement)" (1976). In *Growth in Agreement: Reports and Agreed Statements of Ecumenical Conversations on a World Level,* ed. Harding Meyer and Lukas Vischer, 88–99. Faith and Order Paper no. 108. New York: Paulist Press/Geneva: World Council of Churches, 1984.

————. "Authority in the Church—Elucidation" (1981). In *Growth in Agreement: Reports and Agreed Statements of Ecumenical Conversations on a World Level,* ed. Harding Meyer and Lukas Vischer, 99–105. Faith and Order Paper no. 108. New York: Paulist Press/Geneva: World Council of Churches, 1984.

————. "Authority in the Church II (Windsor Statement)" (1981). In *Growth in Agreement: Reports and Agreed Statements of Ecumenical Conversations on a World Level,* ed. Harding Meyer and Lukas Vischer, 106–18. Faith and Order Paper no. 108. New York: Paulist Press/Geneva: World Council of Churches, 1984.

————. "Salvation and the Church" (1986). In *Growth in Agreement II: Reports and Agreed Statements of Ecumenical Conversations on a World Level, 1982–1998,* ed. Jeffrey Gros, Harding Meyer, and William G. Rusch, 315–25. Faith and Order Paper no. 187. Geneva: WCC Publications/Grand Rapids: William B. Eerdmans, 2000.

Anglican Communion and Oriental Orthodox Churches. "Agreed Statement on Christology" (2002). In *Growth in Agreement III: International Dialogue Texts and Agreed Statements, 1998–2005,* ed. Jeffrey Gros, Thomas F. Best, and Lorelei F. Fuchs, 35–38. Faith and Order Paper no. 204. Geneva: WCC Publications/Grand Rapids: William B. Eerdmans, 2007.

Anglican Communion and Orthodox Churches. "Moscow Statement" (1976). In *Growth in Agreement: Reports and Agreed Statements of Ecumenical Conversations on a World Level,* ed. Harding Meyer and Lukas Vischer, 41–49. Faith and

Order Paper no. 108. New York: Paulist Press/Geneva: World Council of Churches, 1984.

Anglican Consultative Council and Baptist World Alliance. *Conversations around the World 2000–2005: The Report of the International Conversations between the Anglican Communion and the Baptist World Alliance.* London: Anglican Communion Office, 2005.

Anglican–Oriental Orthodox International Commission. "Agreed Statement on Christology" (Holy Etchmiadzin, Armenia, November 5–10, 2002). In *Growth in Agreement III: International Dialogue Texts and Agreed Statements, 1998–2005,* ed. Jeffrey Gros, Thomas F. Best, and Lorelei F. Fuchs, 35–38. Faith and Order Paper no. 204. Geneva: WCC Publications/Grand Rapids: William B. Eerdmans, 2007.

Association of Interchurch Families. *Interchurch Families and Christian Unity: A Paper Adopted by the Second World Gathering of Interchurch Families from Eleven Countries Held in Rome in July 2003.* London: British Association of Interchurch Families, 2003.

———. "Interchurch Families and Christian Unity: Rome 2003." Accessed December 13, 2014. http://www.interchurchfamilies.org/confer/rome2003/documents/roma2003_en.pdf.

Athanasius. *Adversus Arianos.* In *Patrologiae Cursus Completus: Series Graecae,* ed. J.-P. Migne, 26:12–468. Paris: Garnier, 1857–1866.

Atherstone, Andrew. *Oxford's Protestant Spy: The Controversial Career of Charles Golightly.* Studies in Evangelical History and Thought. Milton Keynes, UK: Paternoster, 2007.

Atwood, Craig D., Frank S. Mead, and Samuel S. Hill, eds. *Handbook of Denominations in the United States.* 13th ed. Nashville: Abingdon Press, 2010.

Augustine. *City of God.* In *Nicene and Post-Nicene Fathers: First Series,* ed. Philip Schaff, 2:1–511. Translated by Marcus Dods. New York: Christian Literature, 1887.

———. *Saint Augustine: The City of God against the Pagans.* 7 vols. Translated by George E. McCracken, William McAllen Green, David S. Wiesen, Philip Levine, Eva Matthews Sanford, and William Chase Greene. Loeb Classical Library, no. 411–17. Cambridge, Mass.: Harvard University Press, 1960–1981.

———. *Sermo 341.* In *Patrologiae Cursus Completus: Series Latina,* ed. J-P. Migne, 39:1493-1501. Paris: Garnier, 1844–1864.

———. *Sermons 341–400.* Translated by Edmund Hill. Edited by John E. Rotelle. The Works of Saint Augustine: A Translation for the 21st Century, pt. III, vol. 10. Hyde Park, N.Y.: New City Press, 1995.

Australian Baptist Ministries and Uniting Church in Australia. *Church Membership: Dialogue Report.* Melbourne: Uniting Church in Australia National Assembly, 2012.

Avis, Paul. *Beyond the Reformation? Authority, Primacy and Unity in the Conciliar Tradition.* London: T&T Clark, 2006.

————. "Foreword." In *Towards Baptist Catholicity: Essays on Tradition and the Baptist Vision*, by Steven R. Harmon, xvii–xviii. Studies in Baptist History and Thought, vol. 27. Milton Keynes, UK: Paternoster, 2006.

Baker, Robert A., ed. *A Baptist Source Book: With Particular Reference to Southern Baptists*. Nashville: Broadman Press, 1966.

Baptist Union of Great Britain. *Baptist Praise and Worship*. Oxford: Oxford University Press, 1991.

————. *Gathering for Worship: Patterns and Prayers for the Community of Disciples*. Edited by Christopher J. Ellis and Myra Blyth. Norwich, UK: Canterbury Press, 2005.

Baptist Union of Great Britain and Ireland. *Baptists and Unity*. 3rd ed. London: Baptist Union of Great Britain and Ireland, 1967.

Baptist Union of Great Britain Faith and Society Team. *Baptists and Ecumenism*. Didcot, UK: Baptist Union of Great Britain, 2013. Accessed December 6, 2014. http://www.baptist.org.uk/Publisher/File.aspx?ID=113632&view=browser.

Baptist World Alliance. *Baptist World Alliance Annual Gathering, Accra, Ghana, July 2–7, 2007*. Falls Church, Va.: Baptist World Alliance, 2007.

————. "Baptists and Methodists Conclude First Session of Dialogue" (February 11, 2014). Accessed December 6, 2014. http://www.bwanet.org/ news/news-releases/354-baptists-and-methodists-conclude-first-session-o -dialogue.

————. "Baptists Form Joint Church Body with Methodist and Covenant Denominations." *Baptist World: A Magazine of the Baptist World Alliance* 59, no. 3 (July/September 2012): 22.

————. "Callam Names BWA Team for Dialogue with Pentecostals" (May 24, 2012). Accessed December 6, 2014. http://www.bwanet.org/news/news -releases/130-baptist-pentecostal-dialogue.

————. "Minutes of the Commission on Doctrine and Interchurch Cooperation, Buenos Aires, Argentina, July 19, 1983." Folder ff, Baptist World Alliance Records. American Baptist Historical Society Archives Center, Atlanta.

Baptist World Alliance and Catholic Church. "Summons to Witness to Christ in Today's World: A Report on Conversations 1984–1988." In *Growth in Agreement II: Reports and Agreed Statements of Ecumenical Conversations on a World Level, 1982–1998*, ed. Jeffrey Gros, Harding Meyer, and William G. Rusch, 373–85. Faith and Order Paper no. 187. Geneva: WCC Publications/Grand Rapids: William B. Eerdmans, 2000.

————. "The Word of God in the Life of the Church: A Report of International Conversations between the Catholic Church and the Baptist World Alliance 2006–2010." *American Baptist Quarterly* 31, no. 1 (Spring 2012): 28–122.

————. "The Word of God in the Life of the Church: A Report of International Conversations between the Catholic Church and the Baptist World Alliance 2006–2010." *Pontifical Council for Promoting Christian Unity Information Service* 142 (2013): 20–65.

————. "The Word of God in the Life of the Church: A Report of International Conversations between the Catholic Church and the Baptist World Alliance 2006–2010." Accessed November 14, 2014. http://www.vatican.va/roman_curia/pontifical_councils/chrstuni/Bapstist%20alliance/rc_pc_chrstuni_doc_20101213_report-2006–2010_en.html.

Baptist World Alliance and Lutheran World Federation. "A Message to Our Churches." In *Growth in Agreement II: Reports and Agreed Statements of Ecumenical Conversations on a World Level, 1982–1998*, ed. Jeffrey Gros, Harding Meyer, and William G. Rusch, 155–75. Faith and Order Paper no. 187. Geneva: WCC Publications/Grand Rapids: William B. Eerdmans, 2000.

Baptist World Alliance and Mennonite World Conference. "Theological Conversations, 1989–1992." In *Growth in Agreement III: International Dialogue Texts and Agreed Statements, 1998–2005*, ed. Jeffrey Gros, Thomas F. Best, and Lorelei F. Fuchs, 426–48. Faith and Order Paper no. 204. Geneva: WCC Publications/Grand Rapids: William B. Eerdmans, 2007.

Baptist World Alliance and World Alliance of Reformed Churches. *Baptists and Reformed in Dialogue: Documents from the Conversations Sponsored by the World Alliance of Reformed Churches and the Baptist World Alliance.* Edited by Larry Miller. Studies from the World Alliance of Reformed Churches, no. 4. Geneva: World Alliance of Reformed Churches, 1983.

————. "Report of Theological Conversations Sponsored by the World Alliance of Reformed Churches and the Baptist World Alliance, 1977." In *Growth in Agreement: Reports and Agreed Statements of Ecumenical Conversations on a World Level*, ed. Harding Meyer and Lukas Vischer, 132–51. Faith and Order Paper no. 108. New York: Paulist Press/Geneva: World Council of Churches, 1984.

Barry, John M. *Roger Williams and the Creation of the American Soul: Church, State, and the Birth of Liberty.* New York: Viking, 2012.

Barth, Karl. *Ad Limina Apostolorum: An Appraisal of Vatican II.* Translated by Keith R. Crim. Richmond, Va.: John Knox Press, 1968.

————. *Church Dogmatics.* 4 vols./13 parts. Translated by Geoffrey W. Bromiley et al. Edinburgh: T&T Clark, 1956–1975.

————. *The Göttingen Dogmatics: Instruction in the Christian Religion.* Edited by Hannelotte Reiffen. Translated by Geoffrey W. Bromiley. Grand Rapids: William B. Eerdmans, 1991.

————. *Unterricht in der christlichen Religion (1924–1926).* 3 vols. Edited by Hannelotte Reiffen and Hinrich Stoevesandt. Karl Barth-Gesamtausgabe, pt. 2, vols. 9, 10, 13. Zürich: Theologischer Verlag, 1985–2003.

Basil of Caesarea. *St. Basil the Great: On the Holy Spirit.* Translated by David Anderson. Crestwood, N.Y.: St. Vladimir's Seminary Press, 1980.

Bauckham, Richard. "The Study of Gospel Traditions outside the Canonical Gospels: Problems and Prospects." In *The Jesus Tradition outside the Gospels*, ed. David Wenham, 369–403. Gospel Perspectives, vol. 5. Sheffield: JSOT Press, 1984.

Bauer, Walter. *Orthodoxy and Heresy in Earliest Christianity.* Translated by the Philadelphia Seminar on Christian Origins. Edited by Robert A. Kraft and Gerhard Krodel. Philadelphia: Fortress Press, 1979.

―――. *Rechtgläubigkeit und Ketzerei im ältesten Chrisentum.* Beiträge zur historischen Theologie, no. 10. Tübingen: Mohr, 1934.

Bavarian Lutheran–Baptist Working Group. *Learning from One Another—Believing Together: 'One Lord, One Faith, One Baptism' (Eph 4,5). Convergence Document of the Bavarian Lutheran–Baptist Working Group.* Munich: Bavarian Lutheran–Baptist Working Group, 2009. Accessed December 12, 2014. http://www .gftp.de/press/public/weitere/Bavarian%20Baptists%20and%20Lutherans %20Final%20Report.pdf.

Beasley, Brent. "Transforming Wednesday Nights for Adults." Cooperative Baptist Fellowship General Assembly Workshop, June 20–23, 2012, Fort Worth, Texas. *CBF General Assembly Program Book.* Accessed December 15, 2014. http://issuu.com/fellowship/docs/2012generalassemblyguide/57.

Beasley-Murray, George R. *John.* Word Biblical Commentary, vol. 36. Waco, Tex.: Word Books, 1987.

Beaty, Michael D., Douglas V. Henry, and Scott H. Moore. "Protestant Free Church Christians and *Gaudium et Spes*: A Historical and Philosophical Perspective." *Logos: A Journal of Catholic Thought and Culture* 10, no. 1 (Winter 2007): 136–65.

Bebbington, David W. *Evangelicalism in Modern Britain: A History from the 1730s to the 1980s.* London: Routledge, 1989.

Bell, Mark Robert. *Apocalypse How? Baptist Movements during the English Revolution.* Macon, Ga.: Mercer University Press, 2000.

Belyea, Gordon Lansdowne. "Living Stones in a Spiritual House: The Priesthood of the Saint in the Baptist *Sanctorum Communio*." Th.D. thesis, Wycliffe College/University of Toronto, 2012.

Bender, Kimlyn J. *Karl Barth's Christological Ecclesiology.* Barth Studies. Burlington, Vt.: Ashgate, 2005.

―――. "Theology for Pilgrims: McClendon and the Future of Baptist Theology." *Perspectives in Religious Studies* 40, no. 3 (Fall 2013): 283–91.

Benedict XVI. "Address of His Holiness Benedict XVI to the Participants in the International Congress Organized to Commemorate the 40th Anniversary of the Dogmatic Constitution on Divine Revelation *Dei Verbum*" (September 16, 2005). Accessed November 13, 2014. http://www.vatican .va/holy_father/benedict_xvi/speeches/2005/september/documents/hf _ben-xvi_spe_20050916_40-dei-verbum_en.html.

―――. "Final General Audience." February 27, 2013. Accessed December 3, 2014. http://www.news.va/en/news/pope-final-general-audience-full-text.

Bernard, John Henry. *A Critical and Exegetical Commentary on the Gospel according to St. John.* 4th ed. 2 vols. International Critical Commentary, vol. 29. Edinburgh: T&T Clark, 1953.

Black, Andrew Donald. "A 'Vast Practical Embarrassment': John W. Nevin, the Mercersburg Theology, and the Church Question." Ph.D. diss., University of Dayton, 2013.

Blaising, Craig A., and Darrell L. Bock. *Progressive Dispensationalism*. Grand Rapids: Baker Books, 2000.

Blevins, Carolyn DeArmond. "Cooperative Baptist Fellowship: Denominational Move Unwise at This Time." In *Findings: A Report of the Special Study Commission to Study the Question: "Should the Cooperative Baptist Fellowship Become a Separate Convention?"* ed. W. Randall Lolley, Eileen R. Campbell-Reed, Pope A. Duncan, Pete Hill, and Nancy A. Thurmond, 41–48. Atlanta: Cooperative Baptist Fellowship, 1996.

Blowers, Paul M. "The *Regula Fidei* and the Narrative Character of Early Christian Faith." *Pro Ecclesia* 6, no. 2 (Spring 1997): 199–228.

Boff, Leonardo. *Trinity and Society*. Translated by Paul Burns. Theology and Liberation Series. Maryknoll, N.Y.: Orbis Books, 1988.

Boring, M. Eugene. *Disciples and the Bible: A History of Disciples Biblical Interpretation in North America*. St. Louis: Chalice Press, 1997.

Boswell, W. Benjamin. "Liturgy and Revolution Part 1: Georgian Baptists and the Non-violent Struggle for Democracy." *Religion in Eastern Europe* 27, no. 2 (May 2007): 48–71.

Bowman, Carl Desportes, and Donald F. Durnbaugh. *Church of the Brethren: Yesterday and Today*. Elgin, Ill.: Brethren Press, 1986.

Braaten, Carl E. *Mother Church: Ecclesiology and Ecumenism*. Minneapolis: Fortress Press, 1998.

Braaten, Carl E., and Robert W. Jenson, eds. *The Catholicity of the Reformation*. Grand Rapids: William B. Eerdmans, 1996.

———. *In One Body through the Cross: The Princeton Proposal for Christian Unity*. Grand Rapids: William B. Eerdmans, 2003.

Briggs, John H. Y. *The English Baptists of the Nineteenth Century*. A History of the English Baptists, vol. 3. Didcot: Baptist Historical Society, 1994.

Brigham, Erin M. "A Habermasian Approach to Ecumenical Ecclesiology." *Journal of Ecumenical Studies* 44, no. 4 (Fall 2009): 587–98.

Broadway, Mikael N. "Introduction" (James Wm. McClendon, Jr., *Festschrift* issue). *Perspectives in Religious Studies* 27, no. 1 (Spring 2000): 5–9.

Broadway, Mikael N., Curtis W. Freeman, Barry Harvey, James Wm. McClendon, Jr., Elizabeth Newman, and Philip E. Thompson. "Re-envisioning Baptist Identity: A Manifesto for Baptist Communities in North America." *Baptists Today* (June 1997): 8–10.

———. "Re-envisioning Baptist Identity: A Manifesto for Baptist Communities in North America." *Perspectives in Religious Studies* 24, no. 3 (Fall 1997): 303–10.

———. "Re-envisioning Baptist Identity: A Manifesto for Baptist Communities in North America." In *Towards Baptist Catholicity: Essays on Tradition and the Baptist Vision*, by Steven R. Harmon, 215–23. Studies in Baptist History and Thought, vol. 27. Milton Keynes, UK: Paternoster, 2006.

————. "Re-envisioning Baptist Identity: A Manifesto for Baptist Communities in North America." Accessed November 28, 2014. http://divinity.duke.edu/ sites/divinity.duke.edu/files/documents/faculty-freeman/reenvisioning -baptist-identity.pdf.

Brosseder, Johannes. "Teaching Office: 1. Roman Catholic." In *Encyclopedia of Christianity*, ed. Erwin Fahlbusch, Lukas Vischer, Jan Milič Lochman, John Samuel Mbiti, and Jaroslav Pelikan, trans. Geoffrey W. Bromiley, 5:316–19. Grand Rapids: William B. Eerdmans, 2008.

Brown, Dan. *The Da Vinci Code: A Novel*. New York: Doubleday, 2003.

Brown, J. Newton. *The Baptist Church Manual: Containing the Declaration of Faith, Covenant, Rules of Order and Brief Forms of Church Letters*. Philadelphia: American Baptist Publication Society, 1853.

Brown, Raymond E. *The Churches the Apostles Left Behind*. New York: Paulist Press, 1984.

Brumley, Jeff. "Baptists Host Episcopalians, Wine." *Baptist News Global* (January 24, 2013). Accessed December 15, 2014. http://baptistnews.com/ministry/ congregations/item/8161-baptists-host-episcopalians-wine.

————. "Virginia Church May Look Anglican, but It's Fully Baptist." *Baptist News Global* (March 26, 2014). Accessed December 15, 2014. http://baptistnews .com/ministry/congregations/item/28506-va-church-is-anglican-leaning -but-fully-baptist?tmpl=component&print=1.

Bryant, Cyril E., ed. *New People for a New World—through Christ: Official Report of the Thirteenth Congress, Baptist World Alliance, Stockholm, Sweden, July 8–13, 1975*. Nashville: Broadman Press, 1976.

Buckley, James J. and David S. Yeago, eds. *Knowing the Triune God: The Work of the Spirit in the Practices of the Church*. Grand Rapids: William B. Eerdmans, 2001.

Bullard, Scott W. "A Re-membering Sign: The Eucharist and Ecclesial Unity in Baptist Ecclesiologies." Ph.D. diss., Baylor University, 2009.

————. *Re-membering the Body: The Lord's Supper and Ecclesial Unity in the Free Church Traditions*. Free Church, Catholic Tradition. Eugene, Ore.: Cascade Books, 2013.

Burgess, Joseph A., and Glenn A. Igleheart, eds. *Lutheran–Baptist Dialogue*. Rochester, N.Y.: American Baptist Historical Society, 1982. Published in *American Baptist Quarterly* 1, no. 2 (December 1982): 98–216.

Burghardt, Walter J. "Did Saint Ignatius of Antioch Know the Fourth Gospel?" *Theological Studies* 1, no. 1 (February 1940): 1–26.

————. "Did Saint Ignatius of Antioch Know the Fourth Gospel?" *Theological Studies* 1, no. 2 (May 1940): 130–56.

Burrage, Champlin. *The Early Dissenters in the Light of Recent Research (1550– 1641)*. 2 vols. Cambridge: Cambridge University Press, 1912.

Bush, L. Russ, and Thomas J. Nettles. *Baptists and the Bible*. Rev. ed. Nashville: Broadman & Holman, 1999.

Buttry, Daniel. "Baptists amid Georgian Revolutions." *Baptists Today* 23, no. 8 (August 2005): 9.

Byrd, James P. *The Challenges of Roger Williams: Religious Liberty, Violent Persecu-tion, and the Bible.* Macon, Ga.: Mercer University Press, 2002.

Caesarius of Arles. *Saint Caesarius of Arles: Sermons, Volume I.* Translated by Mary Magdeleine Mueller. Fathers of the Church, vol. 31. Washington, D.C.: The Catholic University of America Press, 1956.

Camp, Ken. "Debate about Baylor's Future Asks: Should Baptists Learn from Catholics?" *Baptist News Global* (March 9, 2006). Accessed December 16, 2014. http://baptistnews.com/archives/item/992-debate-about-baylors-future -asks-should-baptists-learn-from-catholics?.

Campbell, Will D. "A Personal Struggle with Soul Freedom (Excerpted)." In *Findings: A Report of the Special Study Commission to Study the Question: "Should the Cooperative Baptist Fellowship Become a Separate Convention?"* ed. W. Randall Lolley, Eileen R. Campbell-Reed, Pope A. Duncan, Pete Hill, and Nancy A. Thurmond, 61–67. Atlanta: Cooperative Baptist Fellowship, 1996.

Campenhausen, Hans von. *Ecclesiastical Authority and Spiritual Power in the Church of the First Three Centuries.* Translated by J. A. Baker. Stanford, Calif.: Stanford University Press, 1969.

Capes, David B. *Old Testament Yahweh Texts in Paul's Christology.* Wissenschaft-liche Untersuchungen zum Neuen Testament, 2nd series, vol. 47. Tübingen: J. C. B. Mohr (Paul Siebeck), 1992.

Cary, Jeffrey W. "Authority, Unity and Truthfulness: The Body of Christ in the Theologies of Robert Jenson and Rowan Williams with a View toward Impli-cations for Free Church Ecclesiology." Ph.D. diss., Baylor University, 2010.

———. *Free Churches and the Body of Christ: Authority, Unity, and Truthfulness.* Free Church, Catholic Tradition. Eugene, Ore.: Cascade Books, 2012.

Catholic Church. *Catechism of the Catholic Church.* Liguori, Mo.: Liguori, 1994.

———. *Rite of Christian Initiation of Adults.* Washington, D.C.: United States Catholic Conference, 1988.

Catholic Church and World Methodist Council. *The Grace Given You in Christ: Catholics and Methodists Reflect Further on the Church. Report of the International Commission for Dialogue between the Roman Catholic Church and the World Method-ist Council.* Lake Junaluska, N.C.: World Methodist Council, 2006.

Chafin, Kenneth. "Traveling New Roads." In *Findings: A Report of the Special Study Commission to Study the Question: "Should the Cooperative Baptist Fellowship Become a Separate Convention?"* ed. W. Randall Lolley, Eileen R. Campbell-Reed, Pope A. Duncan, Pete Hill, and Nancy A. Thurmond, 69–76. Atlanta: Cooperative Baptist Fellowship, 1996.

Chapman, Mark D. *Ernst Troeltsch and Liberal Theology: Religion and Cultural Syn-thesis in Wilhelmine Germany.* Christian Theology in Context. Oxford: Oxford University Press, 2001.

Church of Norway and Baptist Union of Norway. *One Lord—One Faith—One Church: A Longing for One Baptism. The Report from the Bilateral Dialogue between The Church of Norway and The Baptist Union of Norway 1984–1989.* 2nd ed. 1994.

Accessed December 12, 2014. http://www.gammel.kirken.no/english/doc/baptist_lutheran_1989.doc.

Claiborne, Shane. *The Irresistible Revolution: Living as an Ordinary Radical.* Grand Rapids: Zondervan, 2006.

Clifford, Catherine E., and James F. Puglisi, eds. *A Century of Prayer for Christian Unity.* Grand Rapids: William B. Eerdmans, 2009.

Coakley, Sarah. *God, Sexuality, and the Self: An Essay "On the Trinity."* Cambridge: Cambridge University Press, 2013.

Coggins, James Robert. *John Smyth's Congregation: English Separatism, Mennonite Influence, and the Elect Nation.* Studies in Anabaptist and Mennonite History, no. 32. Waterloo, Ont.: Herald Press, 1991.

Collins, Paul M., and Barry Ensign-George, eds. *Denomination: Assessing an Ecclesiological Category.* Ecclesiological Investigations, vol. 11. London: T&T Clark, 2011.

Colwell, John E. *Promise and Presence: An Exploration of Sacramental Theology.* Milton Keynes, UK: Paternoster, 2006.

Comité mixte baptiste-catholique en France. *Du Baptême à l'Eglise: Accords et divergences actuels.* Documents d'Église. Paris: Les Éditions du Cerf, 2006.

―――. *Marie.* Documents episcopat, no. 10. Paris: Le secretariat général de la conférence des évêques de France, 2009.

―――. *Rendre témoinage au Christ.* Documents d'Église. Paris: Les Éditions du Cerf, 1992.

Committee of the Oxford Society of Historical Theology. *The New Testament in the Apostolic Fathers.* Oxford: Clarendon Press, 1905.

Conference on Biblical Inerrancy. *The Proceedings of the Conference on Biblical Inerrancy, 1987.* Nashville: Broadman Press, 1987.

Congar, Yves. *Chrétiens désunis: Principes d'un "oecuménisme" catholique.* Unum Sanctam, no. 1. Paris: Éditions du Cerf, 1937.

―――. *Divided Christendom: A Catholic Study of the Problem of Reunion.* Translated by M. A. Bousfield. London: Geoffrey Bles/Centenary, 1939.

―――. *I Believe in the Holy Spirit.* 3 vols. Translated by David Smith. New York: Seabury Press, 1983.

―――. "Moving towards a Pilgrim Church." Translated by David Smith. In *Vatican II Revisited: By Those Who Were There,* ed. Alberic Stacpoole, 129–52. Minneapolis: Winston Press, 1986.

―――. *My Journal of the Council.* Translated by Mary John Ronayne and Mary Cecily Boulding. Edited by Denis Minns. Collegeville, Minn.: Liturgical Press, 2012.

―――. *Tradition and Traditions: An Historical and a Theological Essay.* Translated by Michael Naseby and Thomas Rainborough. London: Burns & Oates, 1966.

―――. *La Tradition et les traditions.* 2 vols. Paris: Arthème Fayard, 1960–1963.

Congregation for the Doctrine of the Faith (Catholic Church). "Declaration 'Dominus Iesus' on the Unicity and Salvific Universality of Jesus Christ and the Church" (August 6, 2000). Accessed October 21, 2014. http://www

.vatican.va/roman_curia/congregations/cfaith/documents/rc_con_cfaith
_doc_20000806_dominus-iesus_en.html.

———. "Instruction *Donum Veritatis* on the Ecclesial Vocation of the Theologian" (May 24, 1990). Accessed November 14, 2014. http://www.vatican
.va/roman_curia/congregations/cfaith/documents/rc_con_cfaith_doc
_19900524_theologian-vocation_en.html.

———. "Responses to Some Questions regarding Certain Aspects of the Doctrine of the Church" (July 10, 2007). Accessed October 21, 2014. http://www.vatican.va/roman_curia/congregations/cfaith/documents/rc_con_cfaith_doc_20070629_responsa-quaestiones_en.html.

Conner, W. T. *Revelation and God: An Introduction to Christian Doctrine*. Nashville: Broadman Press, 1936.

Consultation on Common Texts. *The Revised Common Lectionary*. Nashville: Abingdon Press, 1992.

Cooperative Baptist Fellowship. "Frequently Asked Questions." Accessed November 22, 2014. http://www.thefellowship.info/About-Us/FAQ.

———. "Response to the Membership Committee of the Baptist World Alliance by the Coordinating Council of the Cooperative Baptist Fellowship." Accessed November 22, 2014. http://assets.baptiststandard.com/archived/2002/10_28/print/cbf_text.html.

Crane, Richard. "Explosive Devices and Rhetorical Strategies: Appreciation for Steven R. Harmon's *Towards Baptist Catholicity*." *Pro Ecclesia* 18, no. 4 (Fall 2009): 367–70.

Cross, Anthony R. *Baptism and the Baptists: Theology and Practice in Twentieth-Century Britain*. Paternoster Biblical and Theological Monographs. Carlisle, UK: Paternoster, 2000.

———. "The Myth of English Baptist Anti-Sacramentalism." In *Recycling the Past or Researching History? Studies in Baptist Historiography and Myths*, ed. Philip E. Thompson and Anthony R. Cross, 128–62. Studies in Baptist History and Thought, vol. 11. Milton Keynes, UK: Paternoster, 2005.

———. *Recovering the Evangelical Sacrament: Baptisma Semper Reformandum*. Eugene, Ore.: Pickwick, 2013.

Cross, Anthony R., and Philip E. Thompson, eds. *Baptist Sacramentalism*. Studies in Baptist History and Thought, vol. 5. Carlisle, UK: Paternoster, 2003.

Cullmann, Oscar. *Christ and Time: The Primitive Christian Conception of Time and History*. Translated by F. V. Filson. London: SCM Press, 1950.

Cunningham, David S. *And These Three Are One: The Practice of Trinitarian Theology*. Cambridge: Cambridge University Press, 1998.

Cyril of Jerusalem. *Catecheses*. In *Patrologiae Cursus Completus: Series Graecae*, ed. J.-P. Migne, 33:331–1180. Paris: Garnier, 1857–1866.

———. *The Works of Saint Cyril of Jerusalem*. 2 vols. Translated by Leo P. McCauley and Anthony A. Stephenson. Fathers of the Church, vols. 61 and 64. Washington, D.C.: The Catholic University of America Press, 1969–1970.

D'Ambrosio, Marecellino. "Ressourcement Theology, Aggiornamento, and the Hermeneutics of Tradition." *Communio* 18 (Winter 1991): 530–55.

Dayspring Baptist Church (Waco, Tex.). Church web site. Accessed December 15, 2014. http://www.ourdayspring.org/.

Dekar, Paul R. *Building a Culture of Peace: Baptist Peace Fellowship of North America, the First Seventy Years.* Eugene, Ore.: Pickwick, 2010.

————. *Community of the Transfiguration: The Journey of a New Monastic Community.* New Monastic Library: Resources for Radical Discipleship, vol. 3. Eugene, Ore.: Cascade Books, 2008.

————. *For the Healing of the Nations: Baptist Peacemakers.* Macon, Ga.: Smyth & Helwys, 1993.

Denzinger, Heinrich, Clemens Bannwart, and Johann Baptist Umberg, eds. *Enchiridion Symbolorum: Definitionum et declarationum de rebus fidei et morum.* 14th and 15th ed. Freiburg im Breisgau: Herder, 1922.

Department of Interfaith Witness of the Home Mission Board of the Southern Baptist Convention and United States Conference of Catholic Bishops. "How We Agree/How We Differ: Roman Catholic–Southern Baptist Scholars' Dialogue (1986–88)." In *Growing Consensus: Church Dialogues in the United States, 1962–1991*, ed. Joseph A. Burgess and Jeffrey Gros, 557–65. Ecumenical Documents, no. 5. New York: Paulist Press, 1995.

————. "Report on Sacred Scripture: Southern Baptist–Roman Catholic Conversation, 1999." In *Growing Consensus II: Church Dialogues in the United States, 1992–2004*, ed. Lydia Veliko and Jeffrey Gros, 334–38. Washington, D.C.: Bishop's Committee for Ecumenical and Interreligious Affairs, United States Conference of Catholic Bishops, 2005.

————. "Summary Statement of the Second Triennium in the Dialogue between Southern Baptist and Roman Catholic Scholars (1982–1984)." In *Building Unity: Ecumenical Dialogues with Roman Catholic Participation in the US*, ed. Joseph Burgess and Jeffrey Gros, 45–51. Mahwah, N.J.: Paulist Press, 1989.

Donahue, John R. "Scripture: A Roman Catholic Perspective." *Review and Expositor* 79, no. 2 (Spring 1982): 231–44.

Donahue, John R., and William L. Hendricks. "Scripture: An Epilogue." *Review and Expositor* 79, no. 2 (Spring 1982): 258.

Druin, Toby. "Prospective Prof Nixed over Clergy Gender." *Baptist Standard* 109, no. 12 (March 19, 1997): 6.

Dueck, Abe. "Baptists and Mennonites Meet in Amsterdam." *Mennonite Historian* 18, no. 3 (September 1992). Accessed December 3, 2014. http://www.men nonitechurch.ca/programs/archives/mennonitehistorian/mhsep92.htm#7.

Dulles, Avery. *The Catholicity of the Church.* Oxford: Clarendon Press, 1985.

————. *Magisterium: Teacher and Guardian of the Faith.* Naples, Fla.: Sapientia Press of Ave Maria University, 2007.

————. *Models of the Church.* Expanded ed. New York: Doubleday, 1987.

————. "Two Languages of Salvation: The Lutheran–Catholic Joint Declaration." *First Things* 98 (December 1999): 25–30.

Dunn, James D. G. *Christology in the Making: A New Testament Inquiry into the Origins of the Doctrine of the Incarnation.* Philadelphia: Westminster Press, 1980.

Durnbaugh, Donald F. *The Believers' Church: The History and Character of Radical Protestantism.* New York: Macmillan, 1968.

Durso, Pamela R. *A Short History of the Cooperative Baptist Fellowship Movement.* Brentwood, Tenn.: Baptist History and Heritage Society, 2006.

Ehrman, Bart D. *Lost Christianities: The Battle for Scripture and the Faiths We Never Knew.* New York: Oxford University Press, 2003.

———. *Misquoting Jesus: The Story behind Who Changed the Bible and Why.* New York: HarperSanFrancisco, 2005.

Elliott, Ralph H. *The 'Genesis Controversy' and Continuity in Southern Baptist Chaos: A Eulogy for a Great Tradition.* Macon, Ga.: Mercer University Press, 1992.

———. *The Message of Genesis.* Nashville: Broadman Press, 1961.

Ellis, Christopher J. *Baptist Worship Today.* Didcot, UK: Baptist Union of Great Britain, 1999.

———. *Gathering: A Theology and Spirituality of Worship in Free Church Tradition.* London: SCM Press, 2004.

Ensign-George, Barry. "Denomination as Ecclesiological Category: Sketching an Assessment." In *Denomination: Assessing an Ecclesiological Category,* ed. Paul M. Collins and Barry Ensign-George, 1–21. Ecclesiological Investigations, vol. 11. London: T&T Clark International, 2011.

Epiphanius of Salamis. *Panarion.* In *Patrologiae Cursus Completus: Series Graecae,* ed. J.-P. Migne, vols. 41–42. Paris: Garnier, 1857–1866.

Episcopal Church Standing Commission on Liturgy and Music. *Holy Women, Holy Men: Celebrating the Saints.* New York: Church Publishing, 2010.

Episcopal Church (USA). *The Book of Common Prayer and Administration of the Sacraments and Other Rites and Ceremonies of the Church: Together with the Psalter or Psalms of David according to the Use of the Episcopal Church.* New York: Oxford University Press, 1979.

Essick, John Inscore. *Thomas Grantham: God's Messenger from Lincolnshire.* James N. Griffith Series in Baptist Studies. Macon, Ga.: Mercer University Press, 2013.

Estep, William R. Estep, *Baptists and Christian Unity.* Nashville: Broadman Press, 1966.

———. "A Response to *Baptism, Eucharist and Ministry:* Faith and Order Paper No. 111." In *Faith, Life and Witness: The Papers of the Study and Research Division of the Baptist World Alliance 1986–1990,* ed. William H. Brackney and R. J. Burke, 2–16. Birmingham, Ala.: Samford University Press, 1990.

Eusebius of Caesarea. *Historia Ecclesiastica.* In *Patrologiae Cursus Completus: Series Graecae,* ed. J.-P. Migne, 20:45–906. Paris: Garnier, 1857–1866.

Evangelical Baptist Union of Italy and Union of Methodist and Waldensian Churches. "Agreement on Mutual Recognition between the Waldensian, Methodist and Baptist Churches in Italy (1990)." In *Wachsende Kirchengemeinschaft: Gespräche und Vereinbarungen zwischen evangelischen Kirchen in Europa,* ed. C. Nussberger, 155–67. Bern: Evang. Arbeitsstelle Ökumene Schweiz, 1992.

Evans, Christopher H. *Liberalism without Illusions: Renewing an American Christian Tradition.* Waco, Tex.: Baylor University Press, 2010.

Faith and Unity Executive Committee of the Baptist Union of Great Britain and the Council for Christian Unity of the Church of England. *Pushing at the Boundaries of Unity: Anglicans and Baptists in Conversation.* London: Church House, 2005.

Faught, C. Brad. *The Oxford Movement: A Thematic History of the Tractarians and Their Times.* University Park: Pennsylvania State University Press, 2003.

Fiddes, Paul S. "Learning from Others: Baptists and Receptive Ecumenism." *Louvain Studies* 33, nos. 1–2 (2008): 54–73.

———. *Participating in God: A Pastoral Doctrine of the Trinity.* Louisville, Ky.: Westminster John Knox, 2000.

———. *Tracks and Traces: Baptist Identity in Church and Theology.* Studies in Baptist History and Thought, vol. 13. Milton Keynes, UK: Paternoster, 2003.

Fiddes, Paul S., Brian Haymes, and Richard Kidd. *Baptists and the Communion of Saints: A Theology of Covenanted Disciples.* Waco, Tex.: Baylor University Press, 2014.

Fiddes, Paul S., and Malkhaz Songulashvili. "A Dialogue between the Orthodox Church of Georgia and the 'Evangelical Christians-Baptists' of Georgia (1979–1980) with Its Wider Baptist Context." *International Journal for the Study of the Christian Church* 13, no. 3 (2013): 222–54.

First Baptist Church, Dayton, Ohio. Church web site. Accessed December 15, 2014. http://www.fbcdayton.org/?page_id=106.

Fitzmyer, Joseph A. *The Biblical Commission's Document "The Interpretation of the Bible in the Church": Text and Commentary.* Subsidia Biblica, vol. 18. Rome: Pontifical Biblical Institute, 1995.

Flannery, Austin, ed. *Vatican Council II: The Conciliar and Post Conciliar Documents.* Rev. ed. Vatican Collection, vol. 1. Northport, N.Y.: Costello, 1992.

Florovsky, George. "As the Truth Is in Jesus." *Christian Century* 68, no. 51 (December 19, 1951): 1457–59.

Fonseca, Josué. "A Response to the Report of International Conversations between the Catholic Church and the Baptist World Alliance." *American Baptist Quarterly* 31, no. 1 (Spring 2012): 123–37.

Forbis, Wesley L., ed. *The Baptist Hymnal.* Nashville: Convention Press, 1991.

Foucault, Michel. *Power/Knowledge: Selected Interviews and Other Writings, 1972–1977.* Translated by Colin Gordon, Leo Marshall, John Mepham, and Kate Soper. New York: Pantheon Books, 1980.

Fowler, Stanley K. *More Than a Symbol: The British Baptist Recovery of Baptismal Sacramentalism.* Studies in Baptist History and Thought, vol. 2. Carlisle, UK: Paternoster, 2002.

Freeman, Curtis W. "Baptists & Catholics Together? Making Up Is Hard to Do." *Commonweal* (January 16, 2009): 18–21.

————. "A Confession for Catholic Baptists." In *Ties That Bind: Life Together in the Baptist Vision*, ed. Garry A. Furr and Curtis W. Freeman, 83–97. Macon, Ga.: Smyth & Helwys, 1994.

————. *Contesting Catholicity: Theology for Other Baptists.* Waco, Tex.: Baylor University Press, 2014.

————. "God in Three Persons: Baptist Unitarianism and the Trinity." *Perspectives in Religious Studies* 33, no. 3 (Fall 2006): 323–44.

————. "Introduction: A Theology for Radical Believers and Other Baptists." In *Ethics: Systematic Theology, Vol. 1*, by James Wm. McClendon, Jr., vii–xxxviii. Waco, Tex.: Baylor University Press, 2012.

————. "Roger Williams, American Democracy, and the Baptists." *Perspectives in Religious Studies* 34, no. 3 (Fall 2007): 267–86.

————. "A Theology for Brethren, Radical Believers, and Other Baptists: A Review Essay of James McClendon's *Systematic Theology.*" *Brethren Life and Thought* 50, nos. 1–2 (Winter/Spring 2006), 106–115.

————. "'To Feed upon by Faith': Nourishment from the Lord's Table." In *Baptist Sacramentalism*, ed. Anthony R. Cross and Philip E. Thompson, 194–210. Studies in Baptist History and Thought, vol. 5. Carlisle, UK: Paternoster, 2003.

Garrett, James Leo, Jr. "The Authority of the Bible for Baptists." *Southwestern Journal of Theology* 41, no. 2 (Spring 1999): 4–40.

————. "Baptist Identity and Christian Unity: Reflections on a Theological Pilgrimage." *American Baptist Quarterly* 24, no. 1 (March 2005): 53–66.

————. *Baptist Theology: A Four-Century Study.* Macon, Ga.: Mercer University Press, 2009.

————, ed. *The Concept of the Believers' Church: Addresses from the 1967 Louisville Conference.* Scottdale, Pa.: Herald Press, 1969.

————. *Living Stones: The Centennial History of Broadway Baptist Church, Fort Worth, Texas, 1882–1982.* 2 vols. Fort Worth, Tex.: Broadway Baptist Church, 1984.

————. "Major Emphases in Baptist Theology." *Southwestern Journal of Theology* 37, no. 3 (Summer 1995): 36–46.

————. "Protestant Writings on Roman Catholicism in the United States between Vatican Council I and Vatican Council II: An Analysis and Critique in View of the Contemporary Protestant–Roman Catholic Confrontation." Ph.D. diss., Harvard University, 1966.

————. "Sources of Authority in Baptist Thought." *Baptist History and Heritage* 13 (1978): 41–49.

————. *Systematic Theology: Biblical, Historical, and Evangelical.* 2 vols. Grand Rapids: William B. Eerdmans, 1990–1995.

————. "Thomas Aquinas' Doctrine of Penance: A Critical Analysis." Th.M. thesis, Princeton Theological Seminary, 1949.

Garrett, James Leo, Jr., E. Glenn Hinson, and James E. Tull. *Are Southern Baptists "Evangelicals"?* Macon, Ga.: Mercer University Press, 1983.

Gaustad, Edwin S. *Liberty of Conscience: Roger Williams in America*. Grand Rapids: William B. Eerdmans, 1991.

————. *Roger Williams*. Lives and Legacies. New York: Oxford University Press, 2005.

Geiselmann, Josef Rupert. *Die Heilige Schrift und die Tradition: Zu den neueren Kontroversen über das verhältnis der Heiligen Schrift zu den nichtgeschriebenen Traditionen*. Quaestiones Disputatae, vol. 18. Freiburg: Herder, 1962.

————. *The Meaning of Tradition*. Translated by W. J. O'Hara. Quaestiones Disputatae, vol. 15. New York: Herder & Herder, 1966.

————. "Das Missverständnis über das Verhältnis von Schrift und Tradition und seine Überwindung in der katholischen Theologie." *Una Sancta* 2 (1956): 131–50.

————. "Schrift—Tradition—Kirche: Ein ökumenisches Problem." In *Begegnung der Christen: Studien evangelischer und katholischer Theologen*, ed. Maximilian Roesle and Oscar Cullmann, 131–59. Stuttgart: Evangelisches Verlagswerk, 1959.

————. "Scripture and Tradition in Catholic Theology." *Theology Digest* 6 (1958): 73–78.

————. "Scripture, Tradition, and the Church: An Ecumenical Problem." In *Christianity Divided: Protestant and Roman Catholic Theological Issues*, ed. Daniel J. Callahan, Heiko A. Oberman, and Daniel J. O'Hanlon, 39–72. New York: Sheed & Ward, 1961.

General Assembly of the Christian Church (Disciples of Christ). *The Design of the Christian Church (Disciples of Christ)*. Revised 2013. Accessed October 20, 2014. http://disciples.org/our-identity/the-design/.

George, Timothy. "An Evangelical Reflection on Scripture and Tradition." *Pro Ecclesia* 9, no. 2 (Spring 2000): 184–207.

————, ed. *Evangelicals and the Nicene Faith: Reclaiming the Apostolic Witness*. Grand Rapids: Baker Academic, 2011.

————. *John Robinson and the English Separatist Tradition*. NABPR Dissertation Series, no. 1. Macon, Ga.: Mercer University Press, 1982.

————. "Scripture and Tradition: An Evangelical Baptist Perspective." Paper presented to the first round of the 2006–2010 bilateral conversations between the Baptist World Alliance and the Catholic Church, Beeson Divinity School, Samford University, Birmingham, Alabama, December 10–15, 2006.

————. "The Unity of Faith: Evangelicalism and 'Mere Christianity.'" *Touchstone* 16, no. 6 (July/August 2003): 58–66.

Gill, Theodore A. "Barth and Mozart." *Theology Today* 43, no. 3 (October 1986): 403–11.

Glare, P. G. W., ed. *Oxford Latin Dictionary*. New York: Oxford University Press, 1982.

Goodliff, Andrew. "Towards a Baptist Sanctoral?" *Journal of European Baptist Studies* 13, no. 3 (May 2013): 24–30.

Goodspeed, Edgar J., ed. *Index Patristicus*. Peabody, Mass.: Hendrickson, 1993.

Gourley, Bruce. "Bapto-Catholics Move into the Spotlight in North Carolina." Accessed December 17, 2014. http://baptistperspective.brucegourley.com/2010/09/bapto-catholics-move-into-spotlight-in.html.

―――. "Editorial: Baptists and Theology―Broad, Deep, and Diverse." *Baptist History and Heritage* 47, no. 2 (Summer 2012): 2–3.

Grantham, Thomas. *Christianismus Primitivus: Or the Ancient Christian Religion, in Its Nature, Certainty, and Excellency, above Any Other Religion in the World.* London: Francis Smith, 1678.

Grenz, Stanley J. *The Named God and the Question of Being: A Trinitarian Theo-ontology.* Louisville, Ky.: Westminster John Knox, 2005.

―――. *Rediscovering the Triune God: The Trinity in Contemporary Theology.* Minneapolis: Fortress Press, 2004.

―――. *The Social God and the Relational Self: A Trinitarian Theology of the Imago Dei.* Louisville, Ky.: Westminster John Knox, 2001.

Grillmeier, Alois. *Christ in Christian Tradition.* Vol. 1. *From the Apostolic Age to Chalcedon (451).* 2nd rev. ed. Translated by John Bowden. Atlanta: John Knox Press, 1975.

―――. "Die Wahrheit der Heilegen Schrift und ihre Erschließung: Zum dritten Kapitel der Dogmatischen Konstitution 'Dei Verbum' des Vaticanum II." *Theologie und Philosophie* 41 (1966): 161–81.

Gros, Jeffrey. "What Are the Factors Necessary for a Conference on Faith and Order in North America?" *Ecumenical Trends* 35, no. 4 (April 2006): 7/55–9/57.

Gros, Jeffrey, Thomas F. Best, and Lorelei F. Fuchs, eds. *Growth in Agreement III: International Dialogue Texts and Agreed Statements, 1998–2005.* Faith and Order Paper no. 204. Geneva: WCC Publications/Grand Rapids: William B. Eerdmans, 2007.

Gros, Jeffrey, Harding Meyer, and William G. Rusch, eds. *Growth in Agreement II: Reports and Agreed Statements of Ecumenical Conversations on a World Level, 1982–1998.* Faith and Order Paper no. 187. Geneva: WCC Publications/Grand Rapids: William B. Eerdmans, 2000.

Gunton, Colin E. *Father, Son, and Holy Spirit: Essays toward a Truly Trinitarian Theology.* London: T&T Clark, 2003.

Gushee, David P. "Blurry Vision and How We Got Here: The Ex-SBC, Part II." *Baptist News Global* (March 4, 2014). Accessed November 23, 2014. http://baptistnews.com/news/item/28413-blurry-vision-how-we-got-here-the-ex-sbc-part-ii#.UzV2OfldWSo.

―――. "Integrating Faith and Learning in an Ecumenical Context." In *The Future of Baptist Higher Education*, ed. Donald Schmeltekopf and Dianna Vitanza, 25–51. Waco, Tex.: Baylor University Press, 2006.

―――. Review of *The Rebirth of Orthodoxy: Signs of New Life in Christianity*, by Thomas Oden. In *Christian Ethics Today* 9, no. 5 (December 2003): 25.

Habets, Myk. *The Anointed Son: A Trinitarian Spirit Christology.* Princeton Theological Monograph Series, vol. 129. Eugene, Ore.: Pickwick, 2010.

Hankins, Barry. *Uneasy in Babylon: Southern Baptist Conservatives and American Culture.* Tuscaloosa: University of Alabama Press, 2002.

Hanson, Stig. *The Unity of the Church in the New Testament: Colossians and Ephesians.* Acta Seminarii Neotestamentici Upsaliensis, no. 14. Uppsala: Almquist & Wiksells, 1946.

Harland, Mike, ed. *Baptist Hymnal.* Nashville: Lifeway Worship, 2008.

Harmon, Steven R. "*Apokatastasis* and Exegesis: A Comparative Analysis of the Use of Scripture in the Eschatological Universalism of Clement of Alexandria, Origen, and Gregory of Nyssa." Ph.D. diss., Southwestern Baptist Theological Seminary, 1997.

———. "The Authority of the Community (of All the Saints): Toward a Postmodern Baptist Hermeneutic of Tradition." *Review and Expositor* 100, no. 2 (Fall 2003): 587–621.

———. "Baptist Confessions of Faith and the Patristic Tradition." *Perspectives in Religious Studies* 29, no. 4 (Winter 2002): 349–58.

———. "Baptist Understandings of Authority, with Special Reference to Baptists in North America." Paper presented to the Anglican–Baptist International Commission—North American Phase, Acadia University, Wolfville, Nova Scotia, September 12, 2003.

———. "Baptists, Praying for Unity, and the Eschatology of Ecumenism." In *A Century of Prayer for Christian Unity*, ed. Catherine E. Clifford and James F. Puglisi, 115–26 and 140–44. Grand Rapids: William B. Eerdmans, 2009.

———. "Baptist Understandings of Theological Authority: A North American Perspective." *International Journal for the Study of the Christian Church* 4, no. 1 (2004): 50–63.

———. "'Catholic Baptists' and the New Horizon of Tradition in Baptist Theology." In *New Horizons in Theology*, ed. Terrence W. Tilley, 117–43. Maryknoll, N.Y.: Orbis Books, 2005.

———. "*Dei Verbum* §9 in Baptist Perspective." *Ecclesiology* 5, no. 3 (September 2009): 299–321.

———. "*Dei Verbum* §9 in Baptist Perspective." Paper presented to the bilateral conversations between the Baptist World Alliance and the Catholic Church, Rome/Vatican City, December 2–8, 2007.

———. "The Ecumenical Dimensions of Baptist Denominational Identity." In *Denomination: Assessing an Ecclesiological Category*, ed. Paul M. Collins and Barry A. Ensign-George, 34–49. Ecclesiological Investigations, vol. 11. London: T&T Clark, 2011.

———. "Ecumenical Reception of Ecumenical Perspectives on the *Filioque*." Foreword in *Ecumenical Perspectives on the Filioque for the 21st Century*, ed. Myk Habets, xiii–xviii. London: T&T Clark International, 2014.

———. "Ecumenical Theology and/as Systematic Theology." *Ecumenical Trends* 38, no. 9 (October 2009): 6/134–9/137, 15/143.

———. *Ecumenism Means You, Too: Ordinary Christians and the Quest for Christian Unity.* Eugene, Ore.: Cascade Books, 2010.

————. *Every Knee Should Bow: Biblical Rationales for Universal Salvation in Early Christian Thought*. Lanham, Md.: Rowman & Littlefield, 2003.

————. "Free Church Theology, the Pilgrim Church, and the Ecumenical Future." *Journal of Ecumenical Studies* 49, no. 3 (Summer 2014): 420–42.

————. "How Baptists Receive the Gifts of Catholics and Other Christians." *Ecumenical Trends* 39, no. 6 (June 2010): 1/81–5/85.

————. "James Wm. McClendon, Jr.'s Narrative Theology in Ecumenical/ Ecclesiological Perspective." *Pacific Journal of Baptist Research* 9, no. 2 (November 2014): 1–10.

————. "Karl Barth's Conversation with the Fathers: A Paradigm for *Ressourcement* in Baptist and Evangelical Theology." *Perspectives in Religious Studies* 33, no. 1 (Spring 2006): 7–23.

————. "The Nicene Faith and the Catholicity of the Church: Evangelical Retrieval and the Problem of Magisterium." In *Evangelicals and the Nicene Faith: Reclaiming the Apostolic Witness*, ed. Timothy F. George, 74–92. Grand Rapids: Baker Academic, 2011.

————. "'One Baptism': A Study Text for Baptists." *Baptist World: A Magazine of the Baptist World Alliance* 58, no. 1 (January/March 2011): 9–10.

————. "Praying and Believing: Retrieving the Patristic Interdependence of Worship and Theology." *Review and Expositor* 101, no. 4 (Fall 2004): 667–95.

————. "Qualitative Catholicity in Ignatius of Antioch—and the New Testament: The Fallacies of a Restorationist Hermeneutic." *Perspectives in Religious Studies* 38, no. 1 (Spring 2011): 33–45.

————. "Remembering the Ecclesial Future: Why the Church Needs Theology." In *Theology in the Service of the Church: Essays Presented to Fisher H. Humphreys*, ed. Timothy George and Eric F. Mason, 82–95. Macon, Ga.: Mercer University Press, 2008.

————. "Ressourcement Totale: Sarah Coakley's Patristic Engagement in *God, Sexuality, and the Self*." *Perspectives in Religious Studies* 41, no. 4 (Winter 2014): 413–17.

————. "The Sacramentality of the Word in Gregory of Nyssa's *Catechetical Oration*: Implications for a Baptist Sacramental Theology." In *Baptist Sacramentalism 2*, ed. Anthony R. Cross and Philip E. Thompson, 239–53. Studies in Baptist History and Thought, vol. 25. Milton Keynes, UK: Paternoster, 2008.

————. "Scripture in the Life of the Baptist Churches: Openings for a Differentiated Catholic–Baptist Consensus on Sacred Scripture." *Pro Ecclesia* 18, no. 2 (Spring 2009): 187–215.

————. "Scripture in the Life of the Baptist Churches: Opportunities for a Differentiated Catholic–Baptist Consensus on Sacred Scripture." Paper presented to the first round of the 2006–2010 bilateral conversations between the Baptist World Alliance and the Catholic Church, Beeson Divinity School, Samford University, Birmingham, Alabama, December 10–15, 2006.

————. *Towards Baptist Catholicity: Essays on Tradition and the Baptist Vision.* Studies in Baptist History and Thought, vol. 27. Milton Keynes, UK: Paternoster, 2006.

————. "Why Baptist Catholicity, and by What Authority?" *Pro Ecclesia* 18, no. 4 (Fall 2009): 386–92.

Harnack, Adolf von. *History of Dogma.* 3 vols. Translated by Neil Buchanan. Gloucester, Mass.: Peter Smith, 1961.

————. *Lehrbuch der Dogmengeschichte.* 4th ed. 3 vols. Tübingen: J. C. B. Mohr, 1909–1910.

————. *What Is Christianity?* New York: Harper, 1957.

————. *Das Wesen des Christentums: Sechzehn Vorlesungen vor Studierenden aller Facultäten im Wintersemester 1899/1900 an der Universität Berlin gehalten.* Leipzig: Hinrichs, 1900.

Harvey, Barry. *Can These Bones Live? A Catholic Baptist Engagement with Ecclesiology, Hermeneutics, and Social Theory.* Grand Rapids: Brazos Press, 2008.

Hatch, Derek C. "E. Y. Mullins, George W. Truett, and a Baptist Theology of Nature and Grace." Ph.D. diss., University of Dayton, 2011.

Hauerwas, Stanley. "Why Truthfulness Requires Forgiveness: A Commencement Address for Graduates of a College of the Church of the Second Chance (1992)." In *The Hauerwas Reader,* ed. John Berkman and Michael C. Cartwright, 307–17. Durham, N.C.: Duke University Press, 2001.

Hays, Richard B., and Ellen F. Davis, eds. *The Art of Reading Scripture.* Grand Rapids: William B. Eerdmans, 2003.

————. "Beyond Criticism: Learning to Read the Bible Again." *Christian Century* 121, no. 8 (April 20, 2004): 23–27.

Healy, Nicholas M. "Traditions, Authorities, and the Individual Christian." *Pro Ecclesia* 18, no. 4 (Fall 2009): 371–74.

————. "What Is Systematic Theology?" *International Journal of Systematic Theology* 11, no. 1 (January 2009): 24–39.

Hefley, James. *The Conservative Resurgence in the Southern Baptist Convention.* Hannibal, Mo.: Hannibal Books, 1991.

Heil, John Paul. *Ephesians: Empowerment to Walk in Love for the Unity of All in Christ.* Society of Biblical Literature Studies in Biblical Literature, no. 13. Atlanta: Society of Biblical Literature, 2007.

Helwys, Thomas. *A Short Declaration of the Mistery of Iniquity.* London: Thomas Helwys, 1611.

Hendricks, William L. "Cooperative Baptist Fellowship: Some Reflections." In *Findings: A Report of the Special Study Commission to Study the Question: "Should the Cooperative Baptist Fellowship Become a Separate Convention?"* ed. W. Randall Lolley, Eileen R. Campbell-Reed, Pope A. Duncan, Pete Hill, and Nancy A. Thurmond, 77–84. Atlanta: Cooperative Baptist Fellowship, 1996.

————. "Scripture: A Southern Baptist Perspective." *Review and Expositor* 79, no. 2 (Spring 1982): 245–57.

Heppe, Heinrich. *Die Dogmatik der evangelisch-reformierten Kirche.* Elberfeld: R. L. Friedrichs, 1861.

―――. *Reformed Dogmatics.* Translated by G. T. Thomson. London: Allen & Unwin, 1950; repr., Grand Rapids: Baker Book House, 1978.

Hill, Samuel S. "A Discussion of Whether the Cooperative Baptist Fellowship Should Become a Separate Convention of Baptists." In *Findings: A Report of the Special Study Commission to Study the Question: "Should the Cooperative Baptist Fellowship Become a Separate Convention?"* ed. W. Randall Lolley, Eileen R. Campbell-Reed, Pope A. Duncan, Pete Hill, and Nancy A. Thurmond, 93–102. Atlanta: Cooperative Baptist Fellowship, 1996.

Hinson, E. Glenn. "Bapto . . . Catholic." In *Tradition and the Baptist Academy,* ed. Roger A. Ward and Philip E. Thompson, 31–45. Studies in Baptist History and Thought, vol. 11. Milton Keynes, UK: Paternoster, 2011.

―――. "Editorial Introduction." *Review and Expositor* 79, no. 2 (Spring 1982): 195–97.

―――. *A Miracle of Grace: An Autobiography.* Macon, Ga.: Mercer University Press, 2012.

―――. "Some Things I've Learned from the Study of Early Christian History." *Review and Expositor* 101, no. 4 (Fall 2014): 729–44.

―――. "William Carey and Ecumenical Pragmatism." *Journal of Ecumenical Studies* 17, no. 2 (Spring 1980): 73–83.

Hjelm, Norman A., ed. *Faith and Order: Toward a North American Conference. Study Guide.* Grand Rapids: William B. Eerdmans, 2004.

Hobbs, Herschel H. *The Baptist Faith and Message.* Nashville: Convention Press, 1971.

Holmes, Stephen R. *Baptist Theology.* Doing Theology series. London: T&T Clark International, 2012.

―――. *The Holy Trinity: Understanding God's Life.* Milton Keynes, UK: Paternoster, 2011.

―――. *Listening to the Past: The Place of Tradition in Theology.* Carlisle, UK: Paternoster and Grand Rapids: Baker Academic, 2002.

―――. *The Quest for the Trinity: The Doctrine of God in Scripture, History and Modernity.* Downers Grove, Ill.: IVP Academic, 2012.

Hüffmeier, Wilhelm, and Tony Peck, eds. *Dialogue between the Community of Protestant Churches in Europe and the European Baptist Federation on the Doctrine and Practice of Baptism.* Leuenberg Documents, vol. 9. Frankfurt am Main: Verlag Otto Lembeck, 2005.

Humphreys, Fisher. *Baptist Theology: A Really Short Version.* Brentwood, Tenn.: Baptist History and Heritage Society, 2007.

―――. *The Way We Were: How Southern Baptist Theology Has Changed and What It Means to Us All.* Rev. ed. Macon, Ga.: Smyth & Helwys, 2002.

Hütter, Reinhard. *Suffering Divine Things: Theology as Church Practice.* Grand Rapids: William B. Eerdmans, 2000.

Ignatius of Antioch. "Letters of Ignatius." In *The Apostolic Fathers*, ed. and trans. Bart D. Ehrman, 1:218–321. Loeb Classical Library, vol. 24. Cambridge, Mass.: Harvard University Press, 2003.

———. "The Epistles of St. Ignatius." In *The Apostolic Fathers*, ed. and trans. Kirsopp Lake, 1:172–277. Loeb Classical Library, vol. 24. Cambridge, Mass.: Harvard University Press, 1912.

International Council on Biblical Inerrancy. "Chicago Statement on Biblical Inerrancy." *Journal of the Evangelical Theological Society* 21 (December 1978): 289–96.

James, Aaron. "Analogous Uses of Language, Eucharistic Identity, and the Baptist Vision." Ph.D. diss., University of Dayton, 2010.

James, Robison B., ed. *The Unfettered Word: Southern Baptists Confront the Authority-Inerrancy Question*. Waco, Tex.: Word Books, 1987.

Jedin, Hubert. *A History of the Council of Trent*. Translated by Ernest Graf. 2 vols. St. Louis: B. Herder, 1957–1961.

Jenson, Robert W. *Canon and Creed*. Interpretation: Resources for the Use of Scripture in the Church. Louisville, Ky.: Westminster John Knox, 2010.

———. "God's Time, Our Time: An Interview with Robert W. Jenson." *Christian Century* 123, no. 9 (May 2, 2006): 31–35.

———. *Systematic Theology*. 2 vols. New York: Oxford University Press, 1997–1999.

Jeremias, Joachim. *The Eucharistic Words of Jesus*. Translated by Norman Perrin. The New Testament Library. London: SCM Press, 1966.

———. "Joh 6, 51c-58—redaktionell?" *Zeitschrift für die neutestamentliche Wissenschaft und die Kunde der älteren Kirche* 44 (1952–1953): 256–57.

Johansson, Nils. *Det urkristna nattvardsfirandet: Dess religionshistoriska bakgrund, dess ursprung och innebörd*. Lund: Gleerup, 1944.

John Paul II. *On Commitment to Ecumenism* (*Ut Unum Sint*, May 25, 1995). Accessed October 21, 2014. http://www.vatican.va/holy_father/john_paul_ii/encyclicals/documents/hf_jp-ii_enc_25051995_ut-unum-sint_en.html.

———. *On the Eucharist in Its Relationship to the Church* (*Ecclesia de Eucharistia*, April 17, 2003). Accessed October 18, 2014. http://www.vatican.va/holy_father/johnpaul_ii/encyclicals/documents/hf_jp-ii_enc_20030417_eccl-de-euch_en.html.

Johnson, W. B. "The Southern Baptist Convention, To the Brethren in the United States; To the Congregations Connected with the Respective Churches; and to All Candid Men." In *Proceedings of the Southern Baptist Convention in Augusta, Georgia, 8–12 May 1845*, 17–20. Richmond: H. K. Ellyson, 1845.

Jones, Jim. "Baptist Leaders Say Female Pastor Issue Halted Seminary Appointment." *Fort Worth Star-Telegram* (May 22, 1997): B2.

———. "Seminary Turns away Professor: Trustees' Hiring Rules Come into Question." *Fort Worth Star-Telegram* (March 15, 1997): B1, 8.

Jones, Keith. Review of *Towards Baptist Catholicity: Essays on Tradition and the Baptist Vision*, by Steven R. Harmon. In *Journal of European Baptist Studies* 7, no. 2 (January 2007): 51–52.

Jorgenson, Cameron H. "Bapto-Catholicism: Recovering Tradition and Reconsidering the Baptist Identity." Ph.D. diss., Baylor University, 2008.

Justin Martyr. *1 Apology*. In *Ante-Nicene Fathers of the Christian Church*, ed. Alexander Roberts and James Donaldson, 1:163–87. Buffalo, N.Y.: Christian Literature, 1885–1896; repr., Peabody, Mass.: Hendrickson, 1994.

Kasper, Walter. *The God of Jesus Christ*. Translated by Matthew J. O'Connell. New York: Crossroad, 1984.

Kennedy, Rodney W., and Derek C. Hatch. *Gathering Together: Baptists at Work in Worship*. Eugene, Ore.: Pickwick, 2013.

Kerr, Feargus. "French Theology: Yves Congar and Henri de Lubac." In *The Modern Theologians: An Introduction to Christian Theology in the Twentieth Century*, 2nd ed., ed. David F. Ford, 105–17. Cambridge, Mass.: Blackwell, 1997.

Kingsolver, Barbara. *The Poisonwood Bible*. New York: HarperCollins, 1998.

Kinnamon, Michael. *Can a Renewal Movement Be Renewed? Questions for the Future of Ecumenism*. Grand Rapids: William B. Eerdmans, 2014.

———. *The Vision of the Ecumenical Movement and How It Has Been Impoverished by Its Friends*. St. Louis: Chalice Press, 2003.

Kobler, John F. "On D'Ambrosio and Ressourcement Theology." *Communio* 19 (Summer 1992): 321–25.

Kolb, Robert, and Timothy J. Wengert, eds. *The Book of Concord: The Confessions of the Evangelical Lutheran Church*. Translated by Charles Arand et al. Minneapolis: Fortress Press, 2000.

Köster, Helmut. *Synoptische Überlieferung bei den apostolischen Vätern*. Texte und Untersuchungen zur Geschichte der altchristlichen Literatur, no. 17. Berlin: Akademie-Verlag, 1957.

Kuhl, Frederick. "Our Fathers" (letter to the editor). *First Things* 170 (February 2007): 3.

LaCugna, Catherine Mowry. *God for Us: The Trinity and Christian Life*. San Francisco: HarperSanFrancisco, 1991.

Lam, Joseph Cong Quy. "Joseph Ratzinger's Contribution to the Preparatory Debate of the Dogmatic Constitution *Dei Verbum*." *Gregorianum* 94, no. 1 (2013): 35–54.

Lampe, G. W. H., ed. *A Patristic Greek Lexicon*. Oxford: Clarendon Press, 1961.

Leadership Education at Duke Divinity. "Suzii Paynter: Leading a Denomi-network." *Faith & Leadership* (April 22, 2014). Accessed November 23, 2014. http://www.faithandleadership.com/qa/suzii-paynter-leading-denomi-network.

Lennerz, Heinrich. "Scriptura et tradition in decreto 4. sessionis Concilii Tridentini." *Gregorianum* 42, no. 3 (1961): 517–22.

———. "Scriptura sola?" *Gregorianum* 40, no. 1 (1959): 38–53.

———. "Sine scripto traditions." *Gregorianum* 40, no. 4 (1959): 624–35.

Leonard, Bill J. *God's Last and Only Hope: The Fragmentation of the Southern Baptist Convention*. Grand Rapids: William B. Eerdmans, 1990.

———. "Perspectives on Baptist Denominationalism: Anticipating the Future." In *Findings: A Report of the Special Study Commission to Study the Question: "Should the Cooperative Baptist Fellowship Become a Separate Convention?"* ed. W. Randall Lolley, Eileen R. Campbell-Reed, Pope A. Duncan, Pete Hill, and Nancy A. Thurmond, 103–11. Atlanta: Cooperative Baptist Fellowship, 1996.

Lewis, Charlton T., and Charles Short, eds. *A Latin Dictionary*. Rev. ed. Oxford: Clarendon Press, 1955.

Lincoln, Andrew T. "Matthew—A Story for Teachers?" In *The Bible in Three Dimensions: Essays in Celebration of Forty Years of Biblical Studies in the University of Sheffield*, ed. David J. A. Clines et al., 103–25. JSOT Supplements, no. 87. Sheffield: JSOT Press, 1990.

Lindbeck, George A. "Ecumenisms in Conflict." In *God, Truth, and Witness: Engaging Stanley Hauerwas*, ed. L. Gregory Jones, Reinhard Hütter, and C. Rosalee Velloso da Silva, 212–28. Grand Rapids: Brazos Press, 2005.

———. *The Nature of Doctrine: Religion and Theology in a Postliberal Age*. Louisville, Ky.: Westminster John Knox, 1984.

———. "The Story-Shaped Church: Critical Exegesis and Theological Interpretation." In *Scriptural Authority and Narrative Interpretation*, ed. Garrett Green, 161–78. Philadelphia: Fortress Press, 1987.

———. "The Unity We Seek: Setting the Agenda for Ecumenism." *Christian Century* 122, no. 16 (August 9, 2005): 28–31.

Littell, Franklin H. *The Anabaptist View of the Church*. Boston: Starr King, 1952.

Lively, Kit. "Baptist Leaders in Texas Criticize Southwestern Seminary." *Chronicle of Higher Education* (June 6, 1997). Accessed November 22, 2014. http://chronicle.com/article/Baptist-Leaders-in-Texas/75426/.

Loewen, Howard John. *One Lord, One Church, One Hope, and One God: Mennonite Confessions of Faith in North America. An Introduction*. Elkhart, Ind.: Institute of Mennonite Studies, 1985.

Lohmeyer, Ernst. "Vom urchristlichen Abendmahl (III)." *Theologische Rundschau* n.s. 9 (1937): 273–312.

Lolley, W. Randall, Eileen R. Campbell-Reed, Pope A. Duncan, Pete Hill, and Nancy A. Thurmond, eds. *Findings: A Report of the Special Study Commission to Study the Question: "Should the Cooperative Baptist Fellowship Become a Separate Convention?"* Atlanta: Cooperative Baptist Fellowship, 1996.

Longenecker, Richard N. *Galatians*. Word Biblical Commentary, vol. 41. Dallas, Tex.: Word Books, 1990.

Lorenzen, Thorwald. "Baptism and Church Membership: Some Baptist Positions and Their Ecumenical Implications." *Journal of Ecumenical Studies* 18, no. 4 (Fall 1981): 561–74.

Loya, Joseph A. and Julia Sheetz-Willard. "'On Being Christian Together': U.S. Faith and Order Commission Celebrates 50 Years—Oberlin College, July 19–23, 2007." *Journal of Ecumenical Studies* 42, no. 3 (Summer 2007): 463–68.

Lubac, Henri de. *Corpus Mysticum*: *L'Eucharistie et l'Église au Moyen-Âge*. 2nd ed. Paris: Aubier, 1949.

————. *Corpus Mysticum: The Eucharist and the Church in the Middle Ages*. Translated by Laurence Paul Hemming and Susan Frank Parsons. Notre Dame, Ind.: University of Notre Dame Press, 2006.

————. *Meditation sur l'Église*. 2nd ed. Paris: Aubier, 1953.

————. *The Splendour of the Church*. Translated by Michael Mason. Théologie, vol. 27. New York: Sheed & Ward, 1956.

Lumpkin, William L., ed. *Baptist Confessions of Faith*. Rev. ed. Valley Forge, Pa.: Judson Press, 1969.

————. *Baptist Confessions of Faith*. 2nd rev. ed. Revised by Bill J. Leonard. Valley Forge, Pa.: Judson Press, 2011.

Luther, Martin. "German Mass and Order of Service." In *Luther's Works*, ed. Jaroslav Pelikan, vol. 53, *Hymns and Liturgy*, 61–90. Philadelphia: Fortress Press, 1965.

Lutheran World Federation. "Action on the Legacy of Lutheran Persecution of 'Anabaptists'" (July 22, 2010). Accessed November 28, 2014. http://www.lwf-assembly.org/uploads/media/Mennonite_Statement-EN_03.pdf.

Lutheran World Federation and Anglican Communion. "Pullach Report" (1972). In *Growth in Agreement: Reports and Agreed Statements of Ecumenical Conversations on a World Level*, ed. Harding Meyer and Lukas Vischer, 14–32. Faith and Order Paper no. 108. New York: Paulist Press/Geneva: World Council of Churches, 1984.

Lutheran World Federation and Catholic Church. "The Gospel and the Church ('Malta Report')" (1972). In *Growth in Agreement: Reports and Agreed Statements of Ecumenical Conversations on a World Level*, ed. Harding Meyer and Lukas Vischer, 168–89. Faith and Order Paper no. 108. New York: Paulist Press/Geneva: World Council of Churches, 1984.

————. *Joint Declaration on the Doctrine of Justification*. Grand Rapids: William B. Eerdmans, 2000.

Lutheran World Federation and Mennonite World Conference. *Healing Memories: Reconciling in Christ. Report of the Lutheran–Mennonite International Study Commission*. Geneva: Lutheran World Federation and Strasbourg: Mennonite World Conference, 2010. Accessed November 28, 2014. http://www.lwf-assembly.org/uploads/media/Report_Lutheran-Mennonite_Study_Commission.pdf.

Lutheran World Information. "Lutheran–Mennonite Dialogue Moves Closer on Peace Issues, Future Cooperation" (September 17, 2014). Accessed November 28, 2014. http://www.lutheranworld.org/news/lutheran-mennonite-dialogue-moves-closer-peace-issues-future-cooperation.

Lutheran World Ministries and Bishops' Committee for Ecumenical and Interreligious Affairs. *The Common Statement on Justification by Faith from U.S. Lutheran–Roman Catholic Dialogue VII: A Fundamental Consensus on the Gospel*. Philadelphia: Board of Publications, Lutheran Church in America, 1985.

MacIntyre, Alasdair. *After Virtue: A Study in Moral Theory.* 2nd ed. Notre Dame, Ind.: University of Notre Dame Press, 1984.

Mahieu, Éric. "Introduction." In Yves Congar, *My Journal of the Council,* trans. Mary John Ronayne and Mary Cecily Boulding, ed. Denis Minns, v–xxxv. Collegeville, Minn.: Liturgical Press, 2012.

Malan, Gert J. "Does John 17:11b, 21–23 Refer to Church Unity?" *HTS Teologiese Studies/Theological Studies* 67, no. 1 (2011): 10 pages (doi: 10.4102/hts .v67i1.857). Accessed November 20, 2014. http://hts.org.za/index.php/HTS/ article/view/857.

Malone, Jonathan A. "Changed, Set Apart, and Equal: A Study of Ordination in the Baptist Context." Ph.D. diss., University of Dayton, 2011.

Mardaga, Hellen. "Reflection on the Meaning of John 17:21 for Ecumenical Dialogue." *Ecumenical Trends* 34, no. 10 (November 2005): 148–52.

Marshall, Bruce. *Trinity and Truth.* Cambridge: Cambridge University Press, 2000.

Martin, Dennis D. Review of *Evangelicals and Tradition: The Formative Influence of the Early Church,* by Daniel H. Williams. In *Pro Ecclesia* 18, no. 2 (Spring 2009): 216–19.

Massaux, Édouard. *Influence de l'Évangile de saint Matthieu sur la littérature chrétienne avant saint Irénée.* Louvain: Publications universitaires de Louvain, 1950.

———. *The Influence of the Gospel of Saint Matthew on Christian Literature before Saint Irenaeus.* Book 1, *The First Ecclesiastical Writers.* Translated by Norman J. Belval and Suzanne Hecht. Edited by Arthur J. Bellinzoni. New Gospel Studies, no. 5. Macon, Ga.: Mercer University Press, 1990.

Matera, Frank J. *New Testament Christology.* Louisville, Ky.: Westminster John Knox, 1999.

Mattingly, Terry. "A Baptist Minister's Eye-Opening Sabbatical." *San Angelo Standard-Times* (August 10, 2009). Accessed November 27, 2014. http://www .gosanangelo.com/news/2009/aug/10/terry-mattingly-baptist-ministers-eye -opening-sabb/.

Maurer, Christian. *Ignatius von Antiochien und das Johannesevangelium.* Abhandlungen zur Theologie des Alten und Neuen Testaments, no. 18. Zürich: Zwingli-Verlag, 1949.

McAfee, Tom, John Simons, David Music, Milburn Price, Stanley Roberts, and Mark Edwards, eds. *Celebrating Grace Hymnal.* Macon, Ga.: Celebrating Grace, 2010.

McLain, F. Michael. "Narrative Interpretation and the Problem of Double Agency." In *Divine Action: Studies Inspired by the Philosophical Theology of Austin Farrer,* ed. Brian Hebblethwaite and Edward Henderson, 143–72. Edinburgh: T&T Clark, 1990.

McClendon, James Wm., Jr. *Biography as Theology: How Life Stories Can Remake Today's Theology.* Rev. ed. Philadelphia: Trinity Press International, 1990.

———. *The Collected Works of James Wm. McClendon, Jr.* 2 vols. Edited by Ryan Andrew Newson and Andrew C. Wright. Waco, Tex.: Baylor University Press, 2014.

————. "The Radical Road One Baptist Took." *Mennonite Quarterly Review* 74 (2000): 503–10.

————. *Systematic Theology.* 3 vols. Waco, Tex.: Baylor University Press, 2012.

————. "What Is a Southern Baptist Ecumenism?" *Southwestern Journal of Theology* 10, no. 2 (1968): 73–78.

McClendon, James Wm., Jr., and John Howard Yoder. "Christian Unity in Ecumenical Perspective: A Response to David Wayne Layman." *Journal of Ecumenical Studies* 27, no. 3 (Summer 1990): 561–80.

McCormack, Bruce L. *Karl Barth's Critically Realistic Dialectical Theology: Its Genesis and Development 1909–1936.* Oxford: Oxford University Press, 1997.

McGoldrick, James Edward. *Baptist Successionism: A Crucial Question in Baptist History.* ATLA Monograph Series, no. 32. Metuchen, N.J.: Scarecrow Press, 1994.

Medley, Mark S. "Catholics, Baptists, and the Normativity of Tradition." *Perspectives in Religious Studies* 28, no. 2 (Summer 2001): 119–29.

Melanchthon, Philipp. "De Appellatione Ecclesiac Catholicae." In *Philippi Melanthonis Opera quae supersunt omnia,* ed. Karl Gottlieb Bretschneider and Heinrich Ernst Bindseil, 24:397–99. Corpus Reformatorum, vol. 24. Halis Saxonum, 1834–1860.

Mennonite World Conference. "Mennonite World Conference Response to the Lutheran World Federation Action on the Legacy of Lutheran Persecution of Anabaptists" (July 22, 2010). Accessed November 28, 2014. https://www.mwc-cmm.org/joomla/images/files/DialogueFiles/MWC _Response_to_LWF.pdf.

Meyer, Harding. "Die Prägung einer Formel: Ursprung und Intention." In *Einheit—Aber Wie? Zur Tragfähigkeit der ökumenischen Formel vom "Differenzierten Konsens,"* ed. Harald Wagner, 36–58. Quaestiones Disputatae, ed. Peter Hünermann and Thomas Söding, vol. 184. Freiburg: Herder, 2000.

————. *That All May Be One: Perceptions and Models of Ecumenicity.* Translated by William G. Rusch. Grand Rapids: William B. Eerdmans, 1999.

Meyer, Harding, and Lukas Vischer, eds. *Growth in Agreement: Reports and Agreed Statements of Ecumenical Conversations on a World Level.* Faith and Order Paper no. 108. New York: Paulist Press/Geneva: World Council of Churches, 1984.

Migliore, Daniel L. *Faith Seeking Understanding: An Introduction to Christian Theology.* 2nd ed. Grand Rapids: William B. Eerdmans, 2004.

Migne J.-P., ed. *Patrologiae Cursus Completus: Series Graecae.* Paris: Garnier, 1857–1866.

————, ed. *Patrologiae Cursus Completus: Series Latina.* Paris: Garnier, 1844–1864.

Miller, Donald E. *Reinventing American Protestantism: Christianity in the New Millennium.* Berkeley: University of California Press, 1999.

Minear, Paul S. *Images of the Church in the New Testament.* Philadelphia: Westminster Press, 1960.

Moltmann, Jürgen. *A Broad Place: An Autobiography.* Translated by Margaret Kohl. Minneapolis: Fortress Press, 2008.

————. *The Church in the Power of the Spirit: A Contribution to Messianic Ecclesiology.* Translated by Margaret Kohl. New York: Harper & Row, 1977.

————. *The Coming of God: Christian Eschatology.* Translated by Margaret Kohl. Minneapolis: Fortress Press, 1996.

————. *The Crucified God: The Cross as the Foundation and Criticism of Christian Theology.* Translated by R. A. Wilson and John Bowden. New York: Harper & Row, 1974.

————. *Experiences in Theology: Ways and Forms of Christian Theology.* Translated by Margaret Kohl. Minneapolis: Fortress Press, 2000.

————. *God in Creation: A New Theology of Creation and the Spirit of God.* Translated by Margaret Kohl. San Francisco: Harper & Row, 1985.

————. *The Spirit of Life: A Universal Affirmation.* Translated by Margaret Kohl. Minneapolis: Fortress Press, 1992.

————. *Theology of Hope: On the Ground and Implications of a Christian Eschatology.* Translated by James W. Leitch. New York: Harper & Row, 1967.

————. *The Trinity and the Kingdom: The Doctrine of God.* Translated by Margaret Kohl. San Francisco: Harper & Row, 1981.

————. *The Way of Jesus Christ: Christology in Messianic Dimensions.* Translated by Margaret Kohl. San Francisco: HarperSanFrancisco, 1990.

Monck, Thomas, et al. "An Orthodox Creed." Transcribed by W. Madison Grace II. *Southwestern Journal of Theology* 48, no. 2 (Spring 2006): 133–82.

Moody, Dale. *Baptism: Foundation for Christian Unity.* Philadelphia: Westminster Press, 1967.

Morgan, David T. *The New Crusades, the New Holy Land: Conflict in the Southern Baptist Convention, 1969–1991.* Tuscaloosa: University of Alabama Press, 1996.

Mullins, E. Y. *The Axioms of Religion: A New Interpretation of the Baptist Faith.* Philadelphia: American Baptist Publication Society, 1908.

Murphy-O'Connor, J. "Divisions Are Necessary (1 Corinthians 11:19)." In *Celebrating Paul: Festschrift in Honor of Jerome Murphy-O'Connor, O.P., and Joseph A. Fitzmyer, S.J.*, ed. Peter Spitaler, 9–14. Catholic Biblical Quarterly Monograph Series, vol. 48. Washington, D.C.: Catholic Biblical Association of America, 2011.

Murray, Paul D., ed. *Receptive Ecumenism and the Call to Catholic Learning: Exploring a Way for Contemporary Ecumenism.* Oxford: Oxford University Press, 2008.

National Conference of Catholic Bishops. *Doctrinal Responsibilities: Approaches to Promoting Cooperation and Resolving Misunderstandings between Bishops and Theologians.* Washington, D.C.: United States Catholic Conference, 1989.

Newman, Elizabeth. "Are Local Baptist Churches Wholly Autonomous?" *Baptist News Global* (June 12, 2007). Accessed November 23, 2014. http://baptist news.com/archives/item/2582-opinion-are-local-baptist-churches-wholly -autonomous.

————. *Attending the Wounds on Christ's Body: Teresa's Scriptural Vision.* Eugene, Ore.: Cascade Books, 2012.

———. "The Lord's Supper: Might Baptists Accept a Theory of Real Presence?" In *Baptist Sacramentalism*, ed. Anthony R. Cross and Philip E. Thompson, 211–27. Studies in Baptist History and Thought, vol. 5. Carlisle, UK: Paternoster, 2003.

———. "Remembering How to Remember: Harmon's Subversive Orthodoxy." *Pro Ecclesia* 18, no. 4 (Fall 2009): 375–80.

Newman, John Henry. *An Essay on the Development of Christian Doctrine.* 5th ed. London: Longmans, Green, 1887.

———. "Remarks on Certain Passages in the Thirty-Nine Articles." *Tracts for the Times* 90. London: J. G. F. & J. Rivington, 1841.

Niehbuhr, H. Richard. *The Social Sources of Denominationalism.* New York: Henry Holt, 1929.

Northern Baptist Convention and Disciples of Christ. *Christian Worship: A Hymnal.* Edited by William P. Shelton and Luther Wesley Smith. St. Louis: Christian Board of Publication, Bethany Press, 1941.

O'Connell, Maureen H. "Towards a Baptist (and Roman Catholic) Catholicity." *Pro Ecclesia* 18, no. 4 (Fall 2009): 381–85.

Oden, Thomas C., ed. *The Ancient Christian Commentary on Scripture.* Downers Grove, Ill.: InterVarsity Press, 1998–2010.

———. *Agenda for Theology: Recovering Christian Roots.* San Francisco: Harper & Row, 1979.

———. *Classical Pastoral Care.* 4 vols. Grand Rapids: Baker Books, 1987–1994.

———. *Life in the Spirit: Systematic Theology, Volume Three.* San Francisco: Harper & Row, 1994.

———. *The Living God: Systematic Theology, Volume One.* San Francisco: Harper & Row, 1987.

———. *The Rebirth of Orthodoxy: Signs of New Life in Christianity.* New York: HarperCollins, 2003.

———. "Then and Now: The Recovery of Patristic Wisdom." *Christian Century* 107 (December 12, 1990): 1164–68.

———. *The Word of Life: Systematic Theology, Volume Two.* San Francisco: Harper & Row, 1992.

Old Catholic Church and Eastern Orthodox Churches. "Eschatology" (1987). In *Growth in Agreement II: Reports and Agreed Statements of Ecumenical Conversations on a World Level, 1982–1998*, ed. Jeffrey Gros, Harding Meyer, and William G. Rusch, 264–66. Faith and Order Paper no. 187. Geneva: WCC Publications/ Grand Rapids: William B. Eerdmans, 2000.

Origen. *Origen On First Principles.* Translated by G. W. Butterworth. Gloucester, Mass.: Peter Smith, 1973.

———. *Origène Traité des Principes.* Vol. 1. Edited by Henri Crouzel and Manlio Simonetti. Sources Chrétiennes, no. 252. Paris: Éditions du Cerf, 1978.

Pagels, Elaine H. *Adam, Eve, and the Serpent.* New York: Random House, 1988.

———. *Beyond Belief: The Secret Gospel of Thomas.* New York: Random House, 2003.

————. *The Gnostic Gospels.* New York: Random House, 1979.

Pannenberg, Wolfhart. *Systematic Theology.* 3 vols. Translated by Geoffrey W. Bromiley. Grand Rapids: William B. Eerdmans, 1991–1998.

Parker, G. Keith. *Baptists in Europe: History & Confessions of Faith.* Nashville: Broadman Press, 1982.

Parsons, Mikeal C. "Luke among Baptists." *Perspectives in Religious Studies* 33, no. 2 (Summer 2006): 137–54.

Payne, Ernest Alexander. "Baptists and the Ecumenical Movement." *Baptist Quarterly* 8, no. 6 (April 1960): 258–67.

————. *The Fellowship of Believers: Baptist Thought and Practice Yesterday and Today.* London: Carey Kingsgate Press, 1952.

Pelikan, Jaroslav. *The Christian Tradition: A History of the Development of Doctrine.* Vol. 1, *The Emergence of the Catholic Tradition (100–600).* Chicago: University of Chicago Press, 1971.

————. *Credo: Historical and Theological Guide to Creeds and Confessions of Faith in the Christian Tradition.* New Haven, Conn.: Yale University Press, 2003.

————. *The Vindication of Tradition.* New Haven, Conn.: Yale University Press, 1984.

Pelikan, Jaroslav, and Valerie Hotchkiss, eds. *Creeds and Confessions of Faith in the Christian Tradition.* 3 vols. New Haven, Conn.: Yale University Press, 2003.

Pius XII. *Divino Afflante Spiritu.* In *Acta Apostolicae Sedis* 35 (Rome, 1943): 297–326.

————. *Divino Afflante Spiritu.* In *Rome and the Study of Scripture: A Collection of Papal Enactments on the Study of Holy Scripture together with the Decisions of the Biblical Commission,* 5th ed., ed. Conrad J. Louis, 79–107. St. Meinrad, Ind.: Grail, 1953.

Pontifical Biblical Commission (Catholic Church). *The Interpretation of the Bible in the Church.* Washington, D.C.: United States Catholic Conference, 1993.

Pontifical Council for Promoting Christian Unity (Catholic Church). *Directory for the Application of the Principles and Norms of Ecumenism* (March 25, 1993). Accessed November 29, 2014. http://www.vatican.va/roman_curia/pontifical _councils/chrstuni/general-docs/rc_pc_chrstuni_doc_19930325_directory _en.html.

Pool, Jeff B. "Christ, Conscience, Canon, Community: Web of Authority in the Baptist Vision." *Perspectives in Religious Studies* 24, no. 4 (Winter 1997): 417–45.

Prosper of Aquitaine. "Official Pronouncements of the Apostolic See on Divine Grace and Free Will." In *Defense of St. Augustine,* translated by P. de Letter, 178–85. Ancient Christian Writers, no. 32. Westminster, Md.: Newman Press, 1963.

Prudentius. *Peristephanon.* In *Corpus Christianorum: Series Latina,* vol. 126, *Aurelii Prudentii Clementis Carmina,* ed. Maurice P. Cunningham, 251–389. Turnhout: Brepols, 1966.

————. *Peristephanon.* In *Patrologiae Cursus Completus: Series Latina,* ed. J.-P. Migne, 60:275–590. Paris: Garnier, 1844–1864.

―――. *The Poems of Prudentius.* Translated by M. Clement Eagan. Fathers of the Church, vol. 43. Washington, D.C.: The Catholic University of America Press, 1962.

Psalms and Hymns Trust. *Baptist Praise and Worship.* Oxford: Oxford University Press on behalf of the Psalms and Hymns Trust, 1991.

Pullman, Philip. *The Amber Spyglass: His Dark Materials, Book 3.* London: Scholastic, 2000.

―――. *Northern Lights: His Dark Materials, Book 1.* London: Scholastic, 1995.

―――. *The Subtle Knife: His Dark Materials, Book 2.* London: Scholastic, 1997.

Radano, John A. "Report on Dialogue with Baptist World Alliance." *L'Osservatore Romano: Weekly Edition in English* (March 20, 2002): 9.

Radner, Ephraim. *The End of the Church: A Pneumatology of Christian Division in the West.* Grand Rapids: William B. Eerdmans, 1998.

Rahner, Karl. *Theological Investigations.* Vol. 6, *Concerning Vatican Council II.* Translated by Karl-H. and Boniface Kruger. Baltimore: Helicon Press, 1969.

―――. *The Trinity.* Translated by Joseph Donceel. New York: Herder & Herder, 1970.

Rahner, Karl, and Herbert Vorgrimler. *Theological Dictionary.* Edited by Cornelius Ernst. Translated by Richard Strachan. New York: Herder & Herder, 1965.

Randall, Ian. "Pro-Existence not Co-Existence: The Baptist World Alliance in the 1980s." In *Baptists Together in Christ 1905–2005: A Hundred-Year History of the Baptist World Alliance,* ed. Richard V. Pierard, 194–234. Falls Church, Va.: Baptist World Alliance and Birmingham, Ala.: Samford University Press, 2005.

Randall, John F. "The Theme of Unity in John 17:20–23." *Ephemerides Theologicae Lovanienses* 41, no. 3 (July–October 1965): 373–94.

Rathke, Heinrich. *Ignatius von Antiochien und die Paulusbriefe.* Texte und Untersuchungen zur Geschichte der altchristlichen Literatur, no. 99. Berlin: Akademie-Verlag, 1967.

Ratzinger, Joseph. "Dogmatic Constitution on Divine Revelation: Chapter II, The Transmission of Divine Revelation." Translated by William Glen-Doepel. In *Commentary on the Documents of Vatican II,* ed. Herbert Vorgrimler, vol. 3, 181–98. New York: Herder & Herder, 1967–1969.

Rauschenbusch, Walter. *Why I Am a Baptist.* Philadelphia: Baptist Leader, 1958. Originally published as a series of articles in *Rochester Baptist Monthly* 20 (1905–1906).

Reno, Russell R. *In the Ruins of the Church: Sustaining Faith in an Age of Diminished Christianity.* Grand Rapids: Brazos Press, 2002.

―――. "Out of the Ruins." *First Things* 150 (February 2005): 11–16.

―――. "The Return of the Fathers." *First Things* 167 (November 2006): 15–20.

Reimer, A. James. "Trinitarian Orthodoxy, Constantinianism, and Theology from a Radical Protestant Perspective." In *Faith to Creed: Ecumenical Perspectives on the Affirmation of the Apostolic Faith in the Fourth Century. Papers of the Faith to Creed Consultation, Commission on Faith and Order, NCCCUSA, October 25–27,*

1989, Waltham, Massachusetts, ed. S. Mark Heim, 129–61. Grand Rapids: William B. Eerdmans, 1991.

Rippon, John. *A Selection of Hymns from the Best Authors: Intended to Be an Appendix to Dr. Watts's Psalms and Hymns.* London: Thomas Wilkins, 1787.

Roberts-Thomson, E. *With Hands Outstretched: Baptists and the Ecumenical Movement.* London: Marshall, Morgan & Scott, 1962.

Robinson, Robert Bruce. *Roman Catholic Exegesis since Divino Afflante Spiritu: Hermeneutical Implications.* Society of Biblical Literature Dissertation Series, vol. 111. Decatur, Ga.: Scholars Press, 1988.

Rösler, Klaus. "Italy: When Baptists Marry Catholics." *European Baptist Federation News* (July 7, 2009). Accessed December 12, 2014. http://ebf.org/italy-when -baptists-marry-catholics.

Ross, Melanie. "Dunking Doughnuts? Rethinking Free Church Baptismal Theology." *Pro Ecclesia* 14, no. 4 (Fall 2005): 433–46.

Rusch, William G. *Ecumenical Reception: Its Challenge and Opportunity.* Grand Rapids: William B. Eerdmans, 2007.

———. *Reception: An Ecumenical Opportunity.* Philadelphia: Fortress Press, 1988.

———. "The State and Future of the Ecumenical Movement." *Pro Ecclesia* 9, no. 1 (Winter 2000): 8–18.

———. "What Are the Factors Necessary for a Conference on Faith and Order in North America?—A Report on the Graymoor Consultation." *Ecumenical Trends* 35, no. 4 (April 2006): 5/53–6/54.

Rusch, William G., and Daniel F. Martensen, eds. *The Leuenberg Agreement and Lutheran–Reformed Relationships: Evaluations by North American and European Theologians.* Minneapolis: Augsburg, 1989.

Scalise, Charles J. Review of *Towards Baptist Catholicity: Essays on Tradition and the Baptist Vision,* by Steven R. Harmon. In *Perspectives in Religious Studies* 35, no. 4 (Winter 2008): 433–35.

Schaff, Philip, ed. *The Creeds of Christendom with a History and Critical Notes.* 3 vols. 6th ed. Revised by David S. Schaff. New York: Harper & Row, 1931; repr., Grand Rapids: Baker Book House, 1990.

Schmid, Heinrich. *The Doctrinal Theology of the Evangelical Lutheran Church.* 3rd rev. ed. Translated by Charles A. Hay and Henry E. Jacobs. Minneapolis: Augsburg, 1961.

———. *Die Dogmatik der Evangelisch-lutherischen Kirche, dargestellt und aus den Quellen belegt.* 7th ed. Gütersloh: C. Bertelsmann, 1893.

Schnackenburg, Rudolf. *The Gospel according to St. John.* Translated by Cecily Hastings, Francis McDonagh, David Smith, and Richard Foley. 3 vols. New York: Seabury Press, 1980–1982.

———. *Jesus in the Gospels: A Biblical Christology.* Translated by O. C. Dean, Jr. Louisville, Ky.: Westminster John Knox, 1995.

Schoedel, William R. *Ignatius of Antioch.* Hermeneia. Philadelphia: Fortress Press, 1985.

Schramm, Richard. "ABCUSA–Church of the Brethren Relationship Reaffirmed." *American Baptist News Service* (February 26, 2004). Accessed December 12, 2014. http://archive.wfn.org/2004/02/msg00214.html.

Shakespeare, John Howard, ed. *The Baptist World Congress, London, July 11–19, 1905: Authorised Record of Proceedings.* London: Baptist Union Publication Dept., 1905.

————. *The Churches at the Cross-Roads: A Study in Unity.* London: Williams & Norgate, 1918.

Shurden, Walter B. "The Cooperative Baptist Fellowship." In *The Baptist River: Essays on Many Tributaries of a Diverse Tradition,* ed. W. Glenn Jonas, Jr., 241–68. Macon, Ga.: Mercer University Press, 2006.

————. *Not an Easy Journey: Some Transitions in Baptist Life.* Macon, Ga.: Mercer University Press, 2005.

————. "A Solicited Letter to the Study Commission." In *Findings: A Report of the Special Study Commission to Study the Question: "Should the Cooperative Baptist Fellowship Become a Separate Convention?"* ed. W. Randall Lolley, Eileen R. Campbell-Reed, Pope A. Duncan, Pete Hill, and Nancy A. Thurmond, 123–27. Atlanta: Cooperative Baptist Fellowship, 1996.

————, ed. *The Struggle for the Soul of the SBC: Moderate Responses to the Fundamentalist Movement.* Macon, Ga.: Mercer University Press, 1993.

Sibinga, Joost Smit. "Ignatius and Matthew." *Novum Testamentum* 8, no. 2 (April 1966): 263–83.

Sidebottom, E. M. *The Christ of the Fourth Gospel in the Light of First-Century Thought.* London: SPCK, 1961.

Simpson J. A., and E. S. C. Weiner, eds. *The Oxford English Dictionary.* 2nd ed. Oxford: Clarendon Press, 1989.

Small, Joseph D. "Theology's Passive Voice." *Perspectives: A Journal of Reformed Thought* 20, no. 9 (October 2005). Accessed November 29, 2014. https://www.pcusa.org/site_media/media/uploads/theologyandworship/pdfs/passive voice.pdf.

————. "The Travail of Faith and Order." *Pro Ecclesia* 18, no. 3 (Summer 2009): 241–54.

Smyth, John. *The Works of John Smyth, Fellow of Christ's College, 1594–8.* 2 vols. Edited by William Thomas Whitley. Cambridge: Cambridge University Press, 1915.

Songulashvili, Malkhaz. *Evangelical Christian Baptists of Georgia: The History and Transformation of a Free Church Tradition.* Studies in World Christianity. Waco, Tex.: Baylor University Press, 2015.

The Southern Baptist Theological Seminary. "Garrett . . . Ecumenical Baptist." *The Tie* 39, no. 6 (September 1970): 5.

Strong, Augustus Hopkins. *Systematic Theology: A Compendium.* 3 vols. in 1. Valley Forge, Pa.: Judson Press, 1907.

Sutton, Jerry. *The Baptist Reformation: The Conservative Resurgence in the Southern Baptist Convention.* Nashville: Broadman & Holman, 2000.

Swatos, William. "Beyond Denominationalism? Community and Culture in American Religion." *Journal for the Scientific Study of Religion* 20 (September 1981): 217–27.

Tabbernee, William. "Alexander Campbell and the Apostolic Tradition." In *The Free Church and the Early Church: Bridging the Historical and Theological Divide*, ed. Daniel H. Williams, 163–80. Grand Rapids: William B. Eerdmans, 2002.

———. "Unfencing the Table: Creeds, Councils, Communion, and the Campbells." *Mid-Stream* 35, no. 6 (1966): 417–32.

Talbert, Charles H. "The Bible's Truth Is Relational." In *The Unfettered Word: Southern Baptists Confront the Authority-Inerrancy Question*, ed. Robison B. James, 39–46. Waco, Tex.: Word Books, 1987.

Tanner, Norman P., ed. *Decrees of the Ecumenical Councils*. Vol. 2, *Trent to Vatican II*. London: Sheed & Ward/Washington, D.C.: Georgetown University Press, 1990.

Tavard, George H. *The Pilgrim Church*. New York: Herder & Herder, 1967.

———. "Scripture and Tradition: Sources or Source?" *Journal of Ecumenical Studies* 1, no. 3 (Autumn 1964): 445–59.

Teraudkalns, Valdis. "Episcopacy in the Baptist Tradition." In *Recycling the Past or Researching History? Studies in Baptist Historiography and Myths*, ed. Philip E. Thompson and Anthony R. Cross, 279–93. Studies in Baptist History and Thought, vol. 11. Milton Keynes, UK: Paternoster, 2005.

Thompson, Philip E. "Re-envisioning Baptist Identity: Historical, Theological, and Liturgical Analysis." *Perspectives in Religious Studies* 27, no. 3 (Fall 2000): 287–302.

———. "Toward Baptist Ecclesiology in Pneumatological Perspective." Ph.D. diss., Emory University, 1995.

Thurian, Max, ed. *Churches Respond to "Baptism, Eucharist and Ministry."* 6 vols. Geneva: World Council of Churches, 1986–1988.

Tilley, Terrence W. *Inventing Catholic Tradition*. Maryknoll, N.Y.: Orbis Books, 2000.

Tjøhom, Ola. "Catholic Faith outside the Catholic Church: An Ecumenical Challenge." *Pro Ecclesia* 13, no. 3 (Summer 2004): 261–74.

Toom, Tarmo. "Baptists on Justification: Can We Join the Joint Declaration on the Doctrine of Justification?" *Pro Ecclesia* 13, no. 3 (Summer 2004): 289–306.

Tupper, E. Frank. "Biblicism, Exclusivism, Triumphalism: The Travail of Baptist Identity." *Perspectives in Religious Studies* 29, no. 4 (Winter 2002): 411–26.

Vatican Council II (Catholic Church). *Acta Synodalia Sacrosancti Concilii Vaticani II*. Vatican City: Typis Polyglottis Vaticanis, 1970–1983.

———. Decree on Ecumenism (*Unitatis Redintegratio*, November 21, 1964). Accessed March 18, 2015. http://www.vatican.va/archive/hist_councils/ii _vatican_council/documents/vat-ii_decree_19641121_unitatis-redintegratio _en.html.

Vincent of Lérins. *Commonitorium. Florilegium Patristicum.* Edited by G. Rauschen and P. B. Albers. Vol. 5, *Vincentii Lerinensis Commonitoria.* Edited by G. Rauschen. Bonn: P. Hanstein, 1906.

―――. *Commonitorium.* In *Patrologiae Cursus Completus: Series Latina,* ed. J.-P. Migne, 50:637–86. Paris: Garnier, 1844–1864.

―――. "A Commonitory for the Antiquity and Universality of the Catholic Faith against the Profane Novelties of All Heresies." Translated by C. A. Heurtley. In *Nicene and Post-Nicene Fathers: Second Series,* ed. Philip Schaff and Henry Wace, 11:147–49. A Select Library of the Christian Church. New York: Christian Literature, 1887–1894; repr., Peabody, Mass.: Hendrickson, 1994.

Vischer, Lukas. "The Convergence Texts on Baptism, Eucharist and Ministry: How Did They Take Shape? What Have They Achieved?" *Ecumenical Review* 54, no. 4 (October 2002): 431–54.

―――, ed. *Spirit of God, Spirit of Christ: Ecumenical Reflections on the Filioque Controversy.* Faith and Order Paper no. 103. Geneva: World Council of Churches, 1981.

Volf, Miroslav. *After Our Likeness: The Church as the Image of the Trinity.* Sacra Doctrina: Christian Theology for a Postmodern Age. Grand Rapids: William B. Eerdmans, 1998.

―――. "'The Trinity Is Our Social Program': The Doctrine of the Trinity and the Shape of Social Engagement." *Modern Theology* 14, no. 3 (July 1998): 403–23.

Wainwright, Geoffrey. "World Methodist Council and the Joint Declaration on the Doctrine of Justification." *Pro Ecclesia* 16, no. 1 (Winter 2007): 7–13.

Walton, Robert C. *The Gathered Community.* London: Carey Press, 1946.

Wan, William. "For China's Catholics, New Pope Brings Hope." *Washington Post* (February 24, 2013). Accessed December 4, 2014. http://www.washingtonpost.com/world/asia_pacific/for-chinas-catholics-new-pope-brings-hope/2013/02/24/15df5676–7c42–11e2–9a75–dab0201670da_story.html.

Ward, Benedicta, trans. and ed. *The Sayings of the Desert Fathers: The Alphabetical Collection.* Kalamazoo, Mich.: Cistercian, 1975.

Warfield, Benjamin Breckenridge. *The Significance of the Westminster Standards as a Creed: An Address Delivered before the Presbytery of New York, November 8, 1897, on the Occasion of the Celebration of the Two Hundred and Fiftieth Anniversary of the Completion of the Westminster Standards.* New York: Scribner, 1898.

Weaver, C. Douglas. *In Search of the New Testament Church: The Baptist Story.* Macon, Ga.: Mercer University Press, 2008.

Webber, Robert E. *Ancient-Future Faith: Rethinking Evangelicalism for a Postmodern World.* Grand Rapids: Baker Books, 1999.

―――. *Worship Old and New: A Biblical, Historical, and Practical Introduction.* Rev. ed. Grand Rapids: Zondervan, 1994.

Werner, Dietrich. "Magna Charta on Ecumenical Formation in Theological Education in the 21st Century—10 Key Convictions." *International Review of Mission* 98, no. 1 (2009): 161–70.

Westin, Gunnar. *The Free Church through the Ages.* Translated by Virgil Olson. Nashville: Broadman Press, 1954.

Wiborn, Karin. "Joint Future: On the Way to a Uniting Church." *Baptist World: A Magazine of the Baptist World Alliance* 59, no. 3 (July/September 2012): 23.

Wicks, Jared. "Not So Fully Church: The Pope's Message to Protestants—and Catholics." *Christian Century* 124, no. 17 (August 21, 2007): 9–11.

———. "Questions and Answers on the New Responses of the Congregation for the Doctrine of the Faith." *Ecumenical Trends* 36 (July/August 2007): 1–8.

———. "The Significance of the 'Ecclesial Communities' of the Reformation." *Ecumenical Trends* 30, no. 11 (December 2001): 170–73.

———, trans. and ed. "Six Texts by Prof. Joseph Ratzinger as *Peritus* before and during Vatican Council II." *Gregorianum* 89, no. 2 (2008): 233–311.

Wietz, Chris, dir. *The Golden Compass.* Los Angeles: New Line Cinema, 2007.

Wilken, Robert L. *Remembering the Christian Past.* Grand Rapids: William B. Eerdmans, 1995.

Williams, Daniel H. "The Disintegration of Catholicism into Diffuse Inclusivism." *Pro Ecclesia* 12, no. 4 (Fall 2003): 389–93.

———. *Evangelicals and Tradition: The Formative Influence of the Early Church.* Evangelical Ressourcement: Ancient Sources for the Church's Future, vol. 1. Grand Rapids: Baker Academic, 2005.

———, ed. *The Free Church and the Early Church: Bridging the Historical and Theological Divide.* Grand Rapids: William B. Eerdmans, 2002.

———. "The Patristic Tradition as Canon." *Perspectives in Religious Studies* 32, no. 4 (Winter 2005): 357–79.

———. *Retrieving the Tradition and Renewing Evangelicalism: A Primer for Suspicious Protestants.* Grand Rapids: William B. Eerdmans, 1999.

Williams, George Huntston. *The Radical Reformation.* Philadelphia: Westminster Press, 1962.

Wilson, Jonathan R. "Can Narrative Christology Be Orthodox?" *International Journal of Systematic Theology* 8, no. 4 (October 2006): 371–81.

———. *Living Faithfully in a Fragmented World: From "After Virtue" to a New Monasticism.* 2nd ed. New Monastic Library: Resources for Radical Discipleship, vol. 6. Eugene, Ore.: Cascade Books, 2010.

———. *Living Faithfully in a Fragmented World: Lessons for the Church from MacIntyre's "After Virtue."* Christian Mission and Modern Culture. Harrisburg, Pa.: Trinity Press International, 1997.

Wilson-Hartgrove, Jonathan. *New Monasticism: What It Has to Say to Today's Church.* Grand Rapids: Brazos Press, 2008.

Winslow, Edward. *Hypocrisie Unmasked: A true relation of the proceedings of the Governor and company of the Massachusetts against Samuel Gorton of Rhode Island.* 1646. Reprint, Providence, R.I.: Club for Colonial Reprints, 1916.

Wood, Susan K. "Participatory Knowledge of God in the Liturgy." In *Knowing the Triune God: The Work of the Spirit in the Practices of the Church*, ed. James J. Buckley and David S. Yeago, 95–118. Grand Rapids: William B. Eerdmans, 2001.

World Alliance of Reformed Churches and Classical Pentecostals. "Word and Spirit, Church and World: International Pentecostal–Reformed Dialogue, 1996–2000." In *Growth in Agreement III: International Dialogue Texts and Agreed Statements, 1998–2005*, ed. Jeffrey Gros, Thomas F. Best, and Lorelei F. Fuchs, 477–97. Faith and Order Paper no. 204. Geneva: WCC Publications/Grand Rapids: William B. Eerdmans, 2007.

World Alliance of Reformed Churches and Orthodox Churches. "Agreed Statement on the Holy Trinity" (1992). In *Growth in Agreement II: Reports and Agreed Statements of Ecumenical Conversations on a World Level, 1982–1998*, ed. Jeffrey Gros, Harding Meyer, and William G. Rusch, 280–84. Faith and Order Paper no. 187. Geneva: WCC Publications/Grand Rapids: William B. Eerdmans, 2000.

World Council of Churches. *Baptism, Eucharist and Ministry*. Faith and Order Paper no. 111. Geneva: World Council of Churches, 1982.

———. *Baptism, Eucharist and Ministry 1982–1990: Report of the Process and the Responses*. Faith and Order Paper no. 149. Geneva: World Council of Churches, 1990.

———. *The Church: Towards a Common Vision*. Faith and Order Paper no. 214. Geneva: World Council of Churches, 2013.

———. "International Dialogues in Dialogue: Context and Reception." Tenth Forum on Bilateral Dialogues, Dar es Salaam, Tanzania, March 8–14, 2012. Accessed December 14, 2014. http://www.oikoumene.org/en/folder/documents-pdf/TheDarEsSalaamReportMay2012.pdf.

———. *Louisville Consultation on Baptism*. Faith and Order Paper no. 97. Louisville, Ky.: The Southern Baptist Theological Seminary, 1980. Published as *Review and Expositor* 77, no. 1 (Winter 1980).

———. "Member Churches: Church Families: Baptist Churches." Accessed December 5, 2014. http://www.oikoumene.org/en/church-families/baptist-churches.

———. "Member Churches: Democratic Republic of Congo." Accessed December 13, 2014. http://www.oikoumene.org/en/member-churches/africa/democratic-republic-of-congo.

———. *The Nature and Mission of the Church: A Stage on the Way to a Common Statement*. Faith and Order Paper no. 198. Geneva: World Council of Churches, 2005.

———. *The New Delhi Report: The Third Assembly of the World Council of Churches, 1961*. New York: Association Press, 1962.

———. *One Baptism: Towards Mutual Recognition. A Study Text*. Faith and Order Paper no. 210. Geneva: World Council of Churches, 2011.

———. "Report of the Section on Unity." In *The New Delhi Report: The Third Assembly of the World Council of Churches, 1961*, 116–35. New York: Association Press, 1962.

———. *Report of the Theological Commission on Tradition and traditions*. Faith and Order Paper no. 40. Geneva: World Council of Churches, 1963.

————. "Theological and Historical Background of the WCC Basis." Accessed December 11, 2014. http://www.oikoumene.org/en/resources/documents/other/theological-and-historical-background-of-the-wcc-basis.

————. *The Third World Conference on Faith and Order, Lund 1952.* Edited by Oliver S. Tomkins. London: SCM Press, 1953.

World Methodist Council and Catholic Church. "Denver Report" (1971). In *Growth in Agreement: Reports and Agreed Statements of Ecumenical Conversations on a World Level,* ed. Harding Meyer and Lukas Vischer, 308–39. Faith and Order Paper no. 108. New York: Paulist Press/Geneva: World Council of Churches, 1984.

Wright, Nigel G. *Disavowing Constantine: Mission, Church and the Social Order in the Theologies of John Howard Yoder and Jürgen Moltmann.* Carlisle, UK: Paternoster, 2000.

————. *Free Church, Free State: The Positive Baptist Vision.* Milton Keynes, UK: Paternoster, 2005.

Wuthnow, Robert. *The Restructuring of American Religion.* Princeton, N.J.: Princeton University Press, 1988.

Yoder, John Howard. "Karl Barth: How His Mind Kept Changing." In *How Karl Barth Changed My Mind,* ed. Donald K. McKim, 166–71. Grand Rapids: William B. Eerdmans, 1986.

————. *The Royal Priesthood: Essays Ecclesiological and Ecumenical.* Edited by Michael G. Cartwright. Grand Rapids: William B. Eerdmans, 1994.

Yoder, William E. "The Unorthodox Baptist Bishop: How One Church Leader in Georgia Is Breaking the Long-Standing Divide between Protestants and Orthodox." *Christianity Today* 57, no. 5 (June 2013): 48–51.

Zabriskie, Alexander C. *Bishop Brent, Crusader for Christian Unity.* Philadelphia: Westminster Press, 1948.

Zizioulas, John D. *Being as Communion: Studies in Personhood and Church.* Contemporary Greek Theologians, no. 4. Crestwood, N.Y.: St. Vladimir's Seminary Press, 1985.

Credits

Earlier versions of some material that appears in this book were previously published and have been used in substantially revised and adapted form with permission from the publications/publishers: "Why Baptist Catholicity, and by What Authority?" *Pro Ecclesia* 18, no. 4 (Fall 2009): 386–92; "Scripture in the Life of the Baptist Churches: Openings for a Differentiated Catholic–Baptist Consensus on Sacred Scripture," *Pro Ecclesia* 18, no. 2 (Spring 2009): 187–215; "*Dei Verbum* §9 in Baptist Perspective," *Ecclesiology* 5, no. 3 (September 2009): 299–321; "Qualitative Catholicity in Ignatius of Antioch—and the New Testament: The Fallacies of a Restorationist Hermeneutic," *Perspectives in Religious Studies* 38, no. 1 (Spring 2011): 33–45; "The Ecumenical Dimensions of Baptist Denominational Identity," in *Denomination: Assessing an Ecclesiological Category*, ed. Paul M. Collins and Barry A. Ensign-George, 34–49 (Ecclesiological Investigations, vol. 11; London: T&T Clark, 2011); "How Baptists Receive the Gifts of Catholics and Other Christians," *Ecumenical Trends* 39, no. 6 (June 2010): 1/81–5/85; "The Nicene Faith and the Catholicity of the Church: Evangelical Retrieval and the Problem of Magisterium," in *Evangelicals and the Nicene Faith: Reclaiming the Apostolic Witness*, ed. Timothy F. George, 74–92 (Grand Rapids: Baker Academic, 2011); "Remembering the Ecclesial Future: Why the Church Needs Theology," in *Theology in the Service of the Church: Essays Presented to Fisher H. Humphreys*, ed. Timothy George and Eric F. Mason, 82–95 (Macon, Ga.: Mercer University Press, 2008); "Ecumenical Theology and/as Systematic Theology," *Ecumenical Trends* 38, no. 9 (October 2009): 6/134–9/137, 15/143; "Free Church Theology, the Pilgrim Church, and the Ecumenical Future," *Journal of Ecumenical Studies* 49, no. 3 (Summer 2014): 420–42; "James Wm. McClendon, Jr.'s Narrative Theology in Ecumenical/Ecclesiological Perspective," *Pacific*

Journal of Baptist Research 9, no. 2 (November 2014): 1–10; "Baptists, Praying for Unity, and the Eschatology of Ecumenism," in *A Century of Prayer for Christian Unity*, ed. Catherine E. Clifford and James F. Puglisi, 115–26 and 140–44 (Grand Rapids: William B. Eerdmans, 2009).

Scripture Index

Author and Editor Index

Subject Index